SIMPSON

IMPRINT IN HUMANITIES

The humanities endowment
by Sharon Hanley Simpson and
Barclay Simpson honors
MURIEL CARTER HANLEY
whose intellect and sensitivity
have enriched the many lives
that she has touched.

The publisher gratefully acknowledges the generous support of the Simpson Humanities Endowment Fund of the University of California Press Foundation.

The Curious Humanist

The Curious Humanist

Siegfried Kracauer in America

JOHANNES VON MOLTKE

University of California Press

University of California Press, one of the most distinguished university presses in the United States, enriches lives around the world by advancing scholarship in the humanities, social sciences, and natural sciences. Its activities are supported by the UC Press Foundation and by philanthropic contributions from individuals and institutions. For more information, visit www.ucpress.edu.

University of California Press
Oakland, California

© 2016 by The Regents of the University of California

Library of Congress Cataloging-in-Publication Data

Names: von Moltke, Johannes, 1966- author.
Title: The curious humanist : Siegfried Kracauer in America / Johannes von Moltke.
Description: Oakland, California : University of California Press, [2016] | Includes bibliographical references and index.
Identifiers: LCCN 2016008379 | ISBN 9780520290938 (cloth : alk. paper) | ISBN 9780520290945 (pbk.) | ISBN 9780520964853 (ebook)
Subjects: LCSH: Kracauer, Siegfried, 1889–1966—Criticism and interpretation. | Film critics—Germany—Biography. | Motion pictures—Political aspects. | Motion pictures—History. | Motion pictures—Germany—History.
Classification: LCC PT2621.R135 Z94 2016 | DDC 834/.912—dc23
LC record available at http://lccn.loc.gov/2016008379

25 24 23 22 21 20 19 18 17 16
10 9 8 7 6 5 4 3 2 1

Contents

Acknowledgments		vii
	INTRODUCTION: SIEGFRIED KRACAUER AND THE POLITICS OF FILM THEORY	1
1.	METROPOLITAN CONTACT ZONES: KRACAUER IN NEW YORK	26
2.	TOTALITARIAN PROPAGANDA	44
3.	NAZI CINEMA	63
4.	FREEDOM FROM FEAR?	79
5.	FROM HITLER TO *CALIGARI*: SPACES OF WEIMAR CINEMA	93
6.	AUTHORITARIAN, TOTALITARIAN	109
7.	REFRAMING *CALIGARI*: THE POLITICS OF CINEMA	132
8.	*THEORY OF FILM* AND THE SUBJECT OF EXPERIENCE	148
9.	THE CURIOUS HUMANIST	169
10.	*HISTORY* AND HUMANIST SUBJECTIVITY	186
	EPILOGUE: SIEGFRIED KRACAUER AND THE EMERGENCE OF FILM STUDIES	200
	Notes	221
	Bibliography	283
	Index	303

Acknowledgments

Shortly before leaving Germany in 1933, Siegfried Kracauer published a volume of essays on the situation of white collar workers in the late Weimar Republic. Brilliantly written, the book offers a compelling glimpse into culture and society on the eve of Hitler's rise to power—but it also encapsulates something of Kracauer's method as a cultural critic and theorist. It is here that he proposes the notion of reality as *Konstruktion*—a construct that can never be captured in mere reportage but finds its most appropriate image in "the mosaic that is assembled from single observations on the basis of comprehension of their meaning."

Looking back at the years I have spent working on this book, I am drawn to this image of the mosaic as a composite of innumerable fragments that gradually allowed the overall picture of Kracauer's American years, his evolving understanding of the medium of film, and his curious humanism to come into view. However, far from consisting only of my own "single observations," this mosaic has been assembled from countless pieces proffered by others along the way as well, and I am glad to be able to acknowledge these contributions now.

The first pieces came into view in the classroom, when I offered a graduate seminar on Kracauer at the University of Michigan. I remain indebted to the wonderful students in that seminar and subsequent classes, for their enthusiasm and their willingness to engage with these materials from their many different disciplinary perspectives. It was one of these students, Kristy Rawson, who first prompted me to start assembling the pieces for the present book. Her paper on the articles Kracauer published in various American journals during the 1940s and '50s, stemming in part from her interests and background in American culture, clearly indicated that there remained a larger story to tell about the last quarter century of Kracauer's life, which he spent working and writing in New York. Together, Kristy I began to assemble Kracauer's American writings, which we published with University of California Press in 2012. That anthology served as the material basis for the present volume, which in this sense is an extension of our initial research.

That research has since taken me farther into various archives on both sides of the Atlantic than I had initially anticipated. This was without a doubt the most exciting and invigorating aspect of the work on *The Curious Humanist*, and I have countless archivists and staff members to thank for their patient assistance in retrieving ever more facets of the overall mosaic. Aside from the German Literary Archive at Marbach, which houses Kracauer's estate and without which this book would not exist, these include: the MoMA Film Study Center, the Rockefeller Archive Foundation, the National Archives at Kansas City, the Center for Jewish History, the Schlesinger Library at Harvard University, the Sterling Memorial Library at Yale University, the New York Public Library, New York University Archives, the Akademie der Künste in Berlin, and the Theodor W. Adorno Archive in Frankfurt, where Henri Lonitz kindly permitted me to peruse Adorno's annotated copies of Kracauer's books and manuscripts.

My work at these institutions would not have been half as productive but for Nathanial Brennan's unfailingly generous pointers. Nate knows many of these archives better than anyone else I know, and I continue to cherish every opportunity to trade notes with him on new leads and unexpected finds. On the other side of the Atlantic, Inge Belke served as my principal guide through the vast trove of Kracauer's papers in Marbach. Her detailed knowledge, her deep engagement with Kracauer's life and work, and the precision of her own research have been an inspiration for the writing of this book, and I treasure her friendship.

My thanks also, once again, to Rick Rentschler for his careful reading of the manuscript, always helpful suggestions, and indefatigable support at countless junctures over the years. To Tony Kaes for his comments on the manuscript and for sharing his work on the archival materials at Princeton University Press. To Noah Isenberg for reading the manuscript from the shared perspective of someone interested in the German émigré experience. To Anna Parkinson for helpful publishing advice and for advocating that Lili make an appearance in the images. And a great big thanks, in particular, to Dana Polan and Erica Carter for engaging so carefully with the book at a manuscript workshop in Ann Arbor: I hope they will discover in the following pages the traces of their incisive and enormously helpful comments.

I have presented parts of this manuscript on numerous occasions at different institutions, and I am extremely grateful for those opportunities as well as the intellectual impulses each visit provided. In particular, I would like to thank Hermann Kappelhoff and Bernhard Groß at the Freie Universität Berlin; Ulrike Weckel and, again, Bernhard Groß at the Ruhr-Universität Bochum; the organizers of the "Where Is Frankfurt Now?" conference at the Goethe Universität in Frankfurt; Barbara Thériault and Till van Rahden at the Université de Montreal; James Chandler and the Franke Institute for the Humanities at the University of Chicago; Ulrike Ramming and Elke Uhl at the Universität Stuttgart; Meike Werner and Helmut Walser-Smith at Vanderbilt University; Marcia Landy and Vladimir Padunov at the University of Pittsburgh; Sara Hall, David Rodowick, and the entire Chicago Film Seminar; Andreas Huyssen and the editors of *New German Critique*, who organized the stimulating symposium "Transatlantic Theory Transfer"; and my colleagues at Critical M.A.S.S. The memorable conference "Looking After Kracauer" that Gerd Gemünden organized at Dartmouth College provided an early impetus for the project. Gerd's role in shaping this book only gathered force over the years as we collaborated on an anthology of essays from the conference *(Culture in the Anteroom)* and continued the conversation on countless occasions, whether at cafés in Berlin or on the front porch of the Norwich Inn. I look forward to continuing these conversations even now that the book is complete.

I am particularly grateful to three people who generously shared their memories of Kracauer with me. Eileen Bowser and Helga Jauß-Meyer both welcomed me into their homes for memorable afternoons reminiscing about Kracauer's idiosyncrasies in New York and in Konstanz, respectively, over tea, coffee, and *Kuchen;* and Guy Stern, while recalling his conversations with Kracauer in New York about the publishing landscape in the Weimar Republic, implanted in my mind the image of Kracauer sitting in a café in Marseille, a typewriter on the chair across from him, typing up notes for his planned theory of film as Europe was closing, and fascism closing in, behind him.

I am fortunate to work among an incredibly smart, supportive, interdisciplinary faculty at Michigan, and I owe an enormous debt of gratitude to my colleagues in German Studies and Screen Arts and Cultures for engaging with my work over the years. During that time, several chairs in both units have lent their support: I thank Scott Spector, Helmut Puff, Caryl Flinn, and Markus Nornes, and I look forward to opportunities for repaying the favor. While occupying the chair's office in Screen Arts and Cultures, Markus went the extra step of leaving me the key to his beautiful office at the end of the hall in Asian Languages and Cultures, which became an invaluable refuge for the completion of this book. Other colleagues at Michigan whose input and interest in this project have sustained it over the years include Richard Abel, Fred Amrine, Kerstin Barndt, Giorgio Bertellini, Kathleen Canning, Hu Cohen, Lisa Disch, Geoff Eley, Caryl Flinn, Andreas Gailus, Phil Hallman, Julia Hell, Dan Herbert, Peter McIsaac, Sheila Murphy, Helmut Puff, Matthew Solomon, Scott Spector, Silke Weineck, and Damon Young.

Parts of this manuscript build on materials that I have previously published elsewhere: chapter 1 draws on the introduction that Kristy and I wrote for *Siegfried Kracauer's American Writings*; chapter 3 incorporates sections from a text originally written in German for *WerkstattGeschichte*; and chapter 8 builds on arguments I first developed in my contribution to *Culture in the Anteroom*. For institutional and financial support of my research and writing of *The Curious Humanist*, I would like to thank the Alexander von Humboldt Foundation for a generous fellowship, as well as Gertrud Koch and Hermann Kappelhoff at the Freie Universität Berlin; the Rockefeller Archive Foundation for a research grant to consult their archives; and the University of Michigan, where Associate Professor Support Funds, a Michigan Humanities Award, and a sabbatical leave were instrumental in allowing me to complete the manuscript. My thanks also to Mary Francis for her support over many years, and of this book in particular. She has been an extraordinary editor at the University of California Press, and I am delighted to now call her my colleague at Michigan. I also owe a debt of gratitude to Anne Canright, who edited my prose with a light touch and an eye for detail, and who reminded me time and again of the power of paragraph breaks. Mary Hennessy compiled the index.

If, from these many sources and contributions, the book has managed to assemble a coherent overall picture of Kracauer's American years and the importance of his work, it is only because of those closest to me—whether in Ann Arbor, Princeton, Utrecht, Vermont, or Berlin—who have furnished the mosaic's final, indispensable tesserae. Cliff Simms read what I considered a full draft of the manuscript until his comments showed me that it wasn't, challenging me to expand and unfold some of its basic concepts. Dorothea von Moltke asked just the right questions at the right times, including some that prompted me to turn my fascination with the politics of Kracauer's film theory into a book in the first place. Since then, my children have patiently accompanied its writing and endured the occasional absences it required: Lena, who was only half her current age when incessant talk about "Krac" first made her crack up, and Joris, whose budding interests in political theory and intellectual history now add fuel to my own. Kerstin, with whom I continue to construct the many-faceted mosaic of our lives together, has helped to assemble and reassemble the pieces (not only) for this book in more ways than I can count. For each and every little piece, and for keeping the big picture in perspective, I love and thank her.

Introduction

Siegfried Kracauer and the Politics of Film Theory

The émigré thinker should not pretend to begin a new life but should draw the consequences from his past life, from his entire experience, including the European catastrophe and the difficulties in the new country.

THEODOR W. ADORNO, 1945[1]

On April 15, 1941, the small steamship *Nyassa* left Lisbon on the same trans-Atlantic passage it had made in previous months. For this particular voyage, however, the comparatively small ship was retrofitted with two large dormitories in cargo holds forward and aft. On its last trip in December, the *Nyassa* had carried 451 passengers at full capacity. This time around, it accommodated a total of 816 refugees desperate to leave Europe. Upon their arrival in New York after a ten-day voyage, passengers described the traveling conditions as "abominable" and reported clashes among travelers with frayed nerves. But as they disembarked, a profound sense of relief must have prevailed: most of the refugees could count themselves fortunate for having secured a ticket in the face of extortion from speculators in Portugal, and for having escaped Europe as it became engulfed by the Fascist flood: under these circumstances, "every ship that left Europe ... was an ark [and] Mount Ararat was America."[2]

Among those leaving the ship in New York on that day were Siegfried Kracauer, the eminent German cultural critic, and his wife, Lili, *née* Ehrenreich. The couple undoubtedly shared the feelings of relief. Indeed, in future years they would mark April 25 as a "private holiday" and an occasion to recall the more pleasant aspects of the trans-Atlantic passage.[3] In an article published a year after their arrival, Kracauer explicitly reflected on "the marvelous first meeting with life in America as we entered New York harbor."[4] And yet the couple had anticipated the moment of arrival with great trepidation. After a long period in French exile; many anxious months spent securing affidavits, visas, money, and boat tickets; and the loss of their friend Walter Benjamin on the last leg of the arduous transit from Paris to Lisbon via Marseille and northern Spain, the Kracauers had reason to despair of their situation. On the eve of their embarkation on the *Nyassa*,

1. War refugees line the rails of the Portuguese ship *Nyassa* as it docks in New York with 816 passengers from Lisbon, April 25, 1941. (AP Photo/John Lindsay)

Kracauer wrote to his friend Theodor W. Adorno: "It is awful to arrive as we will—after eight years of an existence that does not deserve the name. I have grown older, also within myself. [. . .] I will arrive a poor man, poorer than I have ever been." Entreating Adorno and other émigré friends from the Frankfurt Institute for Social Research to help him gain a foothold in America, Kracauer desperately formulated the urgency and finality of his situation: "Now comes the last station, the last chance, which I must not gamble away, lest everything be lost."[5]

At the time he embarked on the *Nyassa*, Siegfried Kracauer was already over fifty years old. When he had been forced to flee for Paris in 1933, he had been at the height of his career as one of Germany's most influential cultural critics. He had published a book on sociology, a highly praised novel, and a fascinating study of contemporary middle-class culture.[6] As the Frankfurt-based film critic for the *Frankfurter Zeitung* and then, beginning in 1930, as the cultural editor for the paper's Berlin bureau, Kracauer had been at the epicenter of Weimar intellectual culture. Not only did he have an outlet for his own prolific cultural reporting and his influential essays, to whose regular composition he devoted himself "with the same love as to my novel,"[7] but he also enjoyed a privileged position as reviewer and gatekeeper for the published work of others. In this role, Kracauer had a hand in the publishing careers of novelists and essayists such as Joseph Roth, Thomas Mann, and Anna Seghers, of philosophers such as Edmund Husserl and Karl Mannheim, and of his friends Adorno and Benjamin. Kracauer had been aware of his influence and enjoyed his position. Even if his correspondence occasionally reveals a degree of envy for the security and recognition some of his friends had managed to find within the academy, he took satisfaction in his journalistic work. Far more than an almost daily chronicle of cultural events in the interwar Germany (though it was that, too), his journalism amounted to a form of trenchant cultural critique on a par with the philosophical interventions of his friends and colleagues. By the early 1930s Kracauer could happily claim that "taken together [my newspaper essays] produce a rather nice destructive effect."[8] As later anthologies of these essays such as *The Mass Ornament* and *Straßen in Berlin und anderswo* amply confirm,[9] he had found his voice as one of the leading intellectuals in the Weimar Republic.

For the exile, none of this confidence remained. While he was able to continue working briefly for the *Frankfurter Zeitung* in Paris and later secured occasional work as the French film correspondent for two Swiss newspapers, Kracauer's hurried flight from Berlin after the Reichstag fire in February 1933 left him adrift. He had become unmoored from the publishing world that had been his anchor in Germany—and which he himself had helped to anchor in turn. During the eight years in France, Kracauer was continually beset by material worries that affected his own and his wife's health. He managed to complete a second novel, *Georg*, begun during his years in Berlin, but he was unable to secure a publisher in exile; and while his work on a "social biography" of Jacques Offenbach was rewarded not only by publication but also by translations into multiple languages, these did not bring financial stability.

From at least 1937 on, Kracauer actively sought to establish connections to America in the hope of securing affidavits and a stable income. However, negotiations with Horkheimer's Institute for Social Research failed to lead anywhere; although the Institute offered supportive letters, relations were tense—particularly after a disastrous series of exchanges about a manuscript on propaganda that Kracauer had prepared for the Institute's *Zeitschrift für Sozialforschung*. Then, having been apprised of the possibility of affiliation with the Museum of Modern Art's newly established film library, Kracauer made a point of writing not one but three glowing reviews of MoMA's Paris exhibit "Trois siècles d'art aux États-Unis," and of its film program in particular.[10] On this occasion, he apparently also encountered the film library's curator, Iris Barry, for the first time. Whatever hopes he had for a collaboration with MoMA, they did not pan out for several years, during which the Kracauers were repeatedly interned in refugee camps and ultimately forced to flee the advancing German occupation to Marseille, and thence to Lisbon.

Having secured passage out of Europe at the last minute, Kracauer would spend the rest of his life in the United States.[11] It is today well known that during the quarter century following his arrival on board the crowded steamship, he eventually managed to grasp his self-proclaimed "last chance" by publishing two of the most important books on film of the postwar era. To an American public unaware of Kracauer's prolific publications prior to 1933, these two monographs established him as a leading theorist of cinema. *From Caligari to Hitler: A Psychological History of German Film* (Oxford University Press, 1947) modeled a form of criticism that read national cinema for its underlying sociopolitical meanings; and *Theory of Film: The Redemption of Physical Reality* (Princeton University Press, 1960) offered a sustained argument about film as a medium whose specific affinities with reality endow it with the power to "redeem" the material world.[12] Upon its release, Paul Rotha recognized *From Caligari to Hitler* as "a book which must at once be placed alongside the half-dozen most important works on the cinema"; together with *Theory of Film*, it remains a touchstone in film studies curricula even today.[13]

EXILE AND THE LIMITS OF EXTERRITORIALITY

> The stranger is being discussed here, not in the sense often touched upon in the past, as the wanderer who comes today and goes tomorrow, but rather as the person who comes today and stays tomorrow.
>
> GEORG SIMMEL, "The Stranger"

Apart from a handful of accounts of Kracauer's work on the *Caligari* book in the recently established MoMA film library, the often taxing path that led from the author's arrival in New York Harbor to these landmark publications remains relatively unknown.[14] Once he arrived in New York, thanks in particular to the tireless help of his friend Leo Löwenthal at the Institute for Social Research and of the art historian Meyer Schapiro, who had taken an interest in his work from afar, Kracauer sought to establish himself on the

2. Author portrait of Siegfried Kracauer, 1950s. (Deutsches Literaturarchiv Marbach)

American scene. Like his sojourn in France, the years that followed were marked by ongoing financial worries. Once in New York, Kracauer devoted his time to a string of grant applications, time-consuming consulting jobs, and various attempts to find permanent employment while continuing work on his monographs. With somewhat reluctant support from MoMA and only intermittent, unpredictable foundation support for the completion of book-length manuscripts, he often reverted to journalistic formats such as reviews and essays. But he could no longer do so from a relatively secure position as cultural arbiter, as during his years at the *Frankfurter Zeitung*. In New York, he encountered an entirely new publishing landscape. He had to learn English and find his bearings as occasional contributor and sometimes even as supplicant for contracted reviews. It is a testament to Kracauer's expertise and tenacity that he did manage to do so within months of his arrival, when he published his first film review in the *Nation*.[15]

Scholarship on Kracauer has tended to posit a break in Kracauer's thinking after he was forced into exile, finding the cultural sensitivity and dialectical richness of essays such as "The Mass Ornament" or the nuanced voice of *The Salaried Masses* before 1933 to be replaced by the heavier diction of the American reports and monographs.[16] Adorno lamented that his friend had given up too much of himself by switching from his sharp, original German prose style to English.[17] Even as well-meaning a critic as Miriam Hansen commented on the heavy-handedness of Kracauer's style in *Theory of Film*, whose "grandfatherly and assimilationist diction" she implicitly traces to the exile's overcompensation for his abiding sense of displacement.[18]

In keeping with this classic figure of the intellectual in exile, we have inherited a largely anecdotal account of Kracauer as a solitary figure cut off from the social and intellectual life of the city in which he spent the last quarter century of his life. Unfamiliar with the breadth of Kracauer's writings and activities during the 1940s and '50s, readers of *From Caligari to Hitler* in particular like to imagine him ensconced in the film library of the Museum of Modern Art, where he allegedly surrounded himself with piles of books, as if to stave off communication with others. From scattered evidence and from anecdotes told and retold in New York until they found their permanent place in the secondary literature, we have acquired an image of Kracauer as the émigré scholar toiling away at MoMA and otherwise out of touch with his Manhattan surroundings.[19] Kracauer's "problem," the critic Peter Harcourt noted in *Cinema Journal* two years after his death, was that he did not interact with his cultural context. Unlike his contemporary André Bazin, whom we easily locate in the Paris film scene of the 1940s and '50s, Kracauer "gives us the sense more of a man alone," a position that Harcourt finds both noble and "a little sad."[20] Some years later, Dudley Andrew would seize on this portrait of the critic as a lone intellectual in his influential overview *The Major Film Theories*, where he describes Kracauer as "the kind of man who decided after forty years of viewing film that he ought to work out and write down his ideas about the medium; so he went straight to a library and locked himself in. There, reading widely, thinking endlessly, and working always alone, always cut off from the buzz of film talk and film production, he slowly and painstakingly gave birth to his theory."[21] Andrew concedes this portrait to be "imaginary" (for one thing, it melds the story of *Caligari* with that of the later *Theory of Film*), and he has since revised his assessment; but in doing so, he has rightly noted that the reception of Kracauer was "doubly cursed" both by the unflattering comparison with Bazin and by the turn against realism with the advent of semiotics, structuralism, and "*screen* theory" in the 1970s.[22]

Even discounting the vagaries of reception history, Kracauer shared the fate of many émigrés attempting to gain a foothold in their new country, where lasting employment was difficult to come by and linguistic barriers were compounded by anti-immigrant and often patently antisemitic sentiment.[23] Like his travails in France, these were undoubtedly harrowing experiences. Yet it bears noting that, even in Kracauer's own assessment, they dovetail with a long-standing valorization of exile and alienation as the grounds for critical subjectivity. Accordingly, tropes of exile figure strongly in all of his writings, even predating his flight from Germany in 1933. One needn't read far into Kracauer's work to encounter the recurring motifs of shelterlessness *(Obdachlosigkeit)* and "exterritoriality." Like other Weimar intellectuals, Kracauer drew the former notion *The Theory of the Novel* by Georg Lukács, whose account of modernity clearly resonated with Kracauer's own during the early 1920s. Miriam Hansen labeled those accounts "lapsarian" for the way they repeat the motif of a fall from plenitude, leaving the modern subject ideologically shelterless *(geistig obdachlos)*.[24] Exposed on the "ruins of ancient beliefs," it is left to wander a post-lapsarian world, charting "highways through the void."[25]

This figure of the marginalized, wandering, and deracinated subject runs through the entire arc of Kracauer's writings. It forms the object of his essays and books in the early 1920s, and then returns around the end of that decade in slightly different forms. We find it in his well-known essays on "Those Who Wait" and on the salaried masses, as well as in his 1928 novel *Ginster*. The motif of the displaced subject guides his description of Jacques Offenbach in nineteenth-century Paris; it is reprised in crucial passages of *From Caligari to Hitler* and in essays on Hollywood during the

1940s. And the same trope continues to define his view in *Theory of Film* of the postwar present as an age of abstraction that leaves "man in our society . . . ideologically shelterless."²⁶

Kracauer considered the issue of exterritoriality significant enough to use the term as a label for a folder of correspondence with Adorno, to whom he also wrote at one point of his own "deep-seated need to live exterritorially." Twenty years into his émigré existence in Manhattan, he noted that "New York suits me, for it facilitates this exterritoriality."²⁷ But the notion far exceeds self-descriptions of this kind in Kracauer's work—or rather, it mediates there between autobiography and his theories of film and history. Thus, when Kracauer draws on the notion of exile as an epistemological figure designed to describe the conditions for the production of historical knowledge, the term's autobiographical dimension in the posthumously published *History: The Last Things before the Last* is unmistakable. Invoking his own previous work in *Theory of Film* and returning to a favorite passage from Proust, Kracauer likens the role of the historian to that of a photographer: a distanced observer, alienated from his surroundings, he produces objective records of (albeit subjective) excursions—whether into the realm of physical reality (as in film and photography) or into the realm of history. These reflections prompt Kracauer to articulate an epistemology of exile. Historical knowledge, Kracauer argues, is best constructed in "the near-vacuum of extra-territoriality": only in a "state of self-effacement, or homelessness," he asserts, can the scholar fully grasp the object of study.²⁸

These and similar claims in Kracauer's writings call up a long-standing discourse on exile that glorifies precisely the "freedom" of the migrant, making his or her "splendid isolation" and intellectual detachment the precondition for insight and critique, if not greatness. The notion of distance or alienation as enabling the production of knowledge (let alone art) has long informed histories and theories of exile. It is encapsulated most famously, perhaps, in Erich Auerbach's claim that *Mimesis* owed its existence to his ostensible isolation and lack of adequate library resources as he was writing the book in Istanbul.²⁹ Exilic subjectivity, which Kracauer himself once described as an "unlocalizable" position that "perambulates without a fixed abode," becomes productive in such accounts.³⁰ The intellectual in exile becomes a metaphor for the intellectual-as-exile, emphasizing the detachment that intellectual labor requires and exilic existence mandates.

The importance of such concepts for Kracauer's work is undeniable, and it has been recognized widely by his readers.³¹ Kracauer's biographers have seized on this motif to describe him as a nomadic, exilic thinker and an "author of exterritoriality."³² Martin Jay, who along with Hansen arguably did more than anyone to introduce Kracauer to a broader English-language audience, drew directly on the author's anxious insistence on his "chronological anonymity" when he first sketched his "extraterritorial life" a decade after his death.[33] And Enzo Traverso summed up his comparatively early and remarkably nuanced monograph on Kracauer with an image of the "nomadic intellectual tossed among different continents and cultures," unable to attach to anything but his own *Heimatlosigkeit*. Calling even Kracauer's language deterritorialized, Traverso notes that "if there is a thread to his nomadic existence, it is certainly what he called his 'exterritoriality.'" For Traverso, the term is not to be taken lightly—it describes, rather, a deep deracination that leaves Kracauer adrift, unable to put down roots either in Weimar modernity or in his stations of exile. Instead, Kracauer made himself "at home in his exterritoriality," cutting himself off both from Germany and from an American culture "that was not his and which he did not attempt to understand even as it was undergoing a period of profound renewal."[34]

Where the premises of exile and nomadism yield such apodictic conclusions, we do well not to adopt wholesale the figure of exterritoriality for our analysis of the thinker who employs it. We should guard, in particular, against all too ready clichés that reduce the experience of exile to absolute difference, deracination, or decontextualization, no matter how intellectually productive these may become. Might not exile, no matter how terrible, result neither in a wholesale loss of identity nor in assimilation and self-denial, but have the capacity to produce hybrid, fluid subjectivities as well? In revisiting Kracauer's American years, then, I neither subscribe to the notion of an exilic epistemology nor do I adopt the romanticizing view that would altogether conflate the figures of the intellectual and the exile. Against the celebratory and utopian accounts of exile as fecund intellectual detachment, but also against the view of exile as utter alienation, assimilation, or erasure, we should keep in mind the situatedness of exile, the way it is enmeshed in discursive networks, material culture, and the protocols of the everyday. Hamid Naficy is right to insist in this vein that "exile discourse thrives on detail, specificity, and locality. There is a there there in exile."[35]

This recognition underwrites a number of recent studies on exile, and it has led critics to reevaluate long-held notions of exilic alienation and productivity in cases ranging from Auerbach's conception of *Mimesis* in Istanbul to the role of America for Hannah Arendt, and from Theodor Adorno's American experience and to the broader case of the Frankfurt School in exile.[36] All of these studies critique a "general lack of consideration of the historical, geographic, and social milieu[x]" in which figures like Adorno, Auerbach, or the *Institut für Sozialforschung* found themselves during the 1940s;[37] they also demonstrate how renewed attention to the materiality of exile can reshape our understanding even (and precisely) of those thinkers who have helped to elevate the "splendid isolation" of exile, the "freedom of the migrant," into a trope of intellectual detachment, authenticity, and cultivation.[38]

The exile's "near-vacuum of exterritoriality," the "Teutonic cocoon" in which the Frankfurt School ostensibly enveloped itself during its New York years[39]—these are historical fictions, useful for certain epistemologies and narratives about exile theory and cultural difference, but not for the purposes of this book. However complicated and idiosyncratic Kracauer may have been, anecdotes about the isolation of this *"Einzelgänger"* or "lone wolf" misconstrue his work in the United States as cut off from all social interaction, film culture, and intellectual discourse.[40] The (re-)reading of Kracauer's American writings that I undertake in the following pages requires us to revise the emphasis on exterritoriality and exile and to insist that, for all the metropolitan anonymity it could afford, New York City is hardly reducible to an imaginary "no man's land of exterritoriality," as one of Kracauer's biographers has it.[41] Rather, it was a thriving hub of intellectual activity.

MANHATTAN TRANSFER

However exterritorial Kracauer may have felt his own existence to be, he spent his American years networking, collaborating, and publishing, generating a steady output of writings for journals and newspapers even as he kept his focus on the major monographs. As he put it in a letter to the cameraman Eugen Schüfftan in 1948, just a few months after the publication of *From Caligari to Hitler:* "I am writing articles, establishing contacts and watching out for something big to come."[42] Making a point of honing his proficiency in the language of his new country (the Kracauers were both naturalized in September 1946), he began publishing almost exclusively in English within half a year of arriving in New York.[43] Over the course of the following decades, he would go on to pen contributions to the key cultural publications of the day, among them established journals such as the *New Republic*, the *Nation*, and *Harper's;* nascent film periodicals such as *Films in Review, Film Culture*, and *Cinemages;* as well as *Partisan Review* and *Commentary*, the flagship journals of the New York Intellectuals during their heyday in the 1940s and early 1950s.[44] Together with the now classic monographs on film history and theory, these publications make up

Kracauer's American writings. In the chapters that follow, I will read these writings closely, with an ear for the historical debates out of which they arose and an eye for the intellectual landscapes they helped to shape.

In proposing to locate Kracauer and his American writings in this sense in the postwar New York scene, I do not wish to convey the impression that either he or his work stood at the center of ongoing debates. A middle-aged émigré marked by the traumatic experience of French exile and suffering from a lifelong speech impediment, Kracauer undoubtedly moved through various New York intellectual circles on tangential trajectories. Nevertheless, the contact zones he traversed and the networks he forged were, I believe, significant in ways that have not been apparent, either to commentators on Kracauer or to the disciplinary histories of film studies and film theory. In order to retrieve that significance, then, we must revise the ways in which we think of Kracauer's exile, of his marginality. We should ask instead what kinds of roots Kracauer put down in Manhattan, and what their significance might be for his thinking about film, politics, and culture during his American years. *The Curious Humanist*, thus, represents an attempt to rectify our received image of Kracauer's lonely exterritoriality by restoring the contexts in which Kracauer moved, thought, wrote, and published during the last twenty-five years of his life.

To refer to Kracauer's "American writings" is of course to claim that these texts somehow constitute a discrete subset of his overall work. It is also to suggest, however, that it matters where these texts were written: America does not represent simply a period in Kracauer's life (the last); rather, it is a "station," as he puts it—a culture, a political environment, and a city that left their mark on the émigré critic. America is the country of Hollywood, familiar to the émigré from many afternoons and evenings spent in Berlin movie palaces long before the Manhattan skyline comes into view for those aboard the *Nyassa*. Once he arrives in New York, that image changes in tangible ways that the film critic will in fact chart in an early essay from the 1940s. Titled "Why France Liked Our Films," that article signals the émigré's effort at identification, even in its choice of possessive pronoun, as I elaborate in more detail in the following chapter. As New York transforms for the "inveterate moviegoer" from a film set into a concrete grid of long avenues and his own, lived experience of "the hundreds of cross-town streets that end in the empty sky," so, too, does the city become a hub of networks, encounters, and exchanges.[45] To speak of Kracauer's American writings, in other words, means to locate him in Manhattan. Here, the Frankfurt Institut für Sozialforschung had resettled in 1934; here a coterie of young socialist intellectuals sought to remake

American cultural discourse through proliferating "little magazines" such as *Partisan Review, Commentary,* and *Dissent.* New York was where Kracauer took up work at the Museum of Modern Art immediately after arriving in 1941; where he watched movies in screening rooms and boisterous movie houses filled with German fifth columnists; and where his film and cultural criticism evolved alongside a set of ongoing conversations with and among his fellow intellectuals.

Manhattan was a site of cultural and intellectual exchange, and in this sense it was full of two-way streets. *To* this exchange Kracauer brought his experience as a German cultural and film critic, elaborating his film theory in implicit dialogue with his Frankfurt friends, now also in the United States. *From* this exchange he took new perspectives on Hollywood and on film as a propaganda medium, but also on his own past, which he literally re-viewed as he screened German films from the 1920s at MoMA. As a consequence, he also acquired new perspectives on the relation between film and politics, on the pitfalls and promises of liberalism and democracy, and on intellectual traditions of enlightenment and humanism. Charting the traffic in these ideas through Kracauer's writings, I see Manhattan as condensing a set of intellectual transfers between Frankfurt and New York, Europe and America, and among interlocutors who include the members of the Institut für Sozialforschung, the era's New York Intellectuals, and other recent émigrés, from Hans Speier and Ernst Kris at the New School, to Paul Lazarsfeld at Princeton and Columbia, to Hannah Arendt, Kracauer's fellow New Yorker on the Upper West Side.

Not all of these dialogues were conducted in person, or even explicitly conceived as direct exchanges. To a degree, then, some of the conversations I stage in this book (such as the one between Kracauer and Arendt) must be considered to be counterfactual: given the spatial proximity of the interlocutors as well as their shared interests in culture and politics, these could have—indeed should have—taken place (whether at cocktail parties, in living rooms, or in the pages of the "little magazines" and fledgling film journals of the day), but often they did not. In this sense, to construct them in this book is to chart missed encounters and paths not taken; but it is also to pinpoint the central, shared concerns that never animated just one individual critic, whether Kracauer or anyone else writing at the time. These included, above all, the concern with Nazism and the Holocaust in Germany, from which Kracauer had barely escaped—in other words, the "German Question" with which, Arendt held, "a generation of intellectuals had been forced to live for the better part of its adult life: *What had happened? Why did it happen? How could it have happened?*"[46] The same question that led

Arendt to search for the origins of totalitarianism lay behind Kracauer's work at MoMA, which sought to answer it by reviewing the films of the Weimar era. It was also the question that occupied social scientists studying "wartime communications" and developing the tools of what would soon become the discipline of communication studies. In New York, many of these studies were coordinated through the Humanities Division of the Rockefeller Foundation, which supplied the funding and whose associate director became something of a mentor for Kracauer even after his own grant had run out. In Washington, D.C., similar questions became the focus of secret reports written for the U.S. government by Frankfurt School members Franz Neumann, Otto Kirchheimer, and Herbert Marcuse.[47]

Other studies dealt with the consequences of fascism, the Holocaust, World War II and the threat of nuclear annihilation that it had unleashed. Commentators picked up on a widespread climate of fear, which was stoked not only by cold war armament and rhetoric, but also by the lingering aftereffects of antisemitism and the perception that American democracy, which had been rattled by depression and war, was perhaps less resilient than it appeared. The Studies in Prejudice project that members of the Frankfurt School undertook jointly with the American Jewish Committee during the 1940s demonstrated a persistent potential for fascism down to the very structure of individual personalities. The authors of the study were far less sanguine about the resilience of anything that might be called a liberal or democratic character, and Kracauer would have concurred: in articles on postwar Hollywood, he decried the shallowness of ostensibly liberal fare—"those movies with a message," as he called them.[48] By contrast, he found in "Hollywood's Terror Films" evidence of a widespread paralysis and ideological fatigue that might lend itself all too easily to the resurgence of prejudice analyzed in Löwenthal's *Prophets of Deceit* or in the landmark study *The Authoritarian Personality*, co-authored by Theodor Adorno.[49]

America, then, as Kracauer encountered it in New York (and he never ventured far beyond the city, except to vacation up the Hudson or perhaps in southern Vermont), was a highly politicized space. Emerging gradually out of the Depression under Roosevelt's New Deal, the United States entered World War II six months after Kracauer's arrival and after intense debates about isolationism and intervention that had split intellectuals in New York as elsewhere.[50] Subsequently, Jewish immigration and the Holocaust forced the discussion of homegrown antisemitism, and the Cold War put pressure on received notions of democracy and liberalism; while these had been tested already in the response to the Great Depression, McCarthyite anticommunism stretched them almost to the breaking point.

After August 1945 at the latest, the threat of nuclear war hovered over any political discussion, drawing into question basic notions of humanity and the future of the planet.

Kracauer, like many others, considered these politics to be inseparable from the cultural and aesthetic forms through which they became legible. For the New York Intellectuals, the privileged forms included mainly literary modernism and the arts of the avant-garde; for Kracauer, by contrast, film was the true linchpin.[51] Either way, culture was deemed politically central. Kracauer arrived in Manhattan in a period when it was no longer possible, in Lionel Trilling's words, "to think of politics except as the politics of culture."[52] With the stratification of culture into high, middlebrow, and mass culture, contributors to wartime and postwar debates, like Trilling and many of the writers for *Partisan Review*, for example, were interested not only in the changing functions of literature in this culture, but also in the place of film in that schema: its pretensions to art as well as its ideological place, its trivial and ornamental manifestations *and* its power to record, reveal, and redeem physical reality. In the political climate of the day, the stakes were perceived to be high: discussions about film, literature, and the arts were never just that but always also discussions at "the dark and bloody crossroads where literature and politics meet," about social and political values in the polarized, Cold War world that had emerged from the fight against fascism.[53]

THE POLITICS OF FILM (THEORY)

By situating Kracauer's American writings—and the two film books in particular—in the intellectual, cultural, and political contexts sketched here and to be fleshed out later, I aim to restore a historical dimension to some well-worn classics and to reinstate Kracauer as an active participant in the intellectual debates of his time. But in historicizing Kracauer's American writings in this way, my goal is finally to retrieve a political dimension of his film theory and criticism long after his mid-1920s brush with Marxism. This dimension, which I define in terms of Kracauer's lifelong commitment to an idiosyncratic and provocative notion of humanism, has everything to do with the liberal era out of which it emerges—including the assault by fascism, Nazism, Stalinism, and McCarthyism with which not only intellectuals in the United States had to grapple during the last quarter century of Kracauer's life.

While I consider these issues to have broad relevance for our ostensibly posthumanist present, for the ways in which we think of politics, debate the impact of technology and material culture, or write about history in the anthropocene, here I derive these issues from a reinterrogation of "classical" film theory that has been gaining traction for some time now. In the history of film studies as well as in the media studies present, Kracauer figures as a representative of this classical tradition alongside authors as different from one another as Béla Balázs, Rudolf Arnheim, Jean Epstein, Sergei Eisenstein, and André Bazin. Labeling his theory "classical" can make Kracauer's books—and the other theorists grouped under the term, for that matter—appear quaint and dated, safely contained in an earlier era that so-called contemporary film theory helped us supersede.

According to the progressivist assumptions underlying such thinking, *From Caligari to Hitler* and *Theory of Film* can now appear to students as labored contributions to an earlier set of debates at best, and as pedantic, theoretical aberrations at worst.[54] As an introductory survey on film theory describes it, *Theory of Film* became the "whipping boy" of 1970s film theory and its anti-veristic rage.[55] Even so, it remains a staple of film theory reading lists, routinely assigned together with Bazin as representing the realist tradition of classical film theory. Having still possessed enough theoretical energy during the 1960s and '70s to raise the hackles of political critics and (post)structuralist theorists, however, its half-life soon diminished. Respectfully referenced as it acquired patina on its academic pedestal, Kracauer's work became harmless—an example of what the Swiss author Max Frisch once called "the resounding ineffectiveness of a classic."[56]

We tend to think of the 1960s as the decade during which film (and other) theory became politicized and film studies became institutionalized. In this view, which Dana Polan describes as the flawed, "heroic" narrative of film studies' rise, the *politique des auteurs* yielded to a politics of the cinema anchored in social movements, ideology critique, and the rise of the New Left, which lent political legitimacy to its pursuits.[57] This narrative eclipses not only the earlier history of film pedagogy that Polan has charted, but also the history of classical film theory. In the "heroic" version of film studies' rise out of the 1960s, classical film theory quickly comes under fire, liable to be dismissed—at times quite explicitly—in a broadly oedipal gesture. While the political critics did maintain allegiance to the radical lineage of "classical" theorists like Eisenstein and to the energies of the avant-garde, they had little patience for either the formalist or the realist tendencies that, according to Andrew, dominated the field prior to the advent of structuralism and psychoanalysis.[58] One of the most remarkable jibes undoubtedly came in a well-known editorial statement of the *Cahiers du cinéma* on "Cinema/Ideology/Criticism." Here the editors collectively dismiss the realm that the forefathers, whether Bazin or Kracauer, theorized as the domain proper of the cinema—i.e., some idea of reality—as precisely the veil that needed to be pierced, the ideological curtain to be removed from the underlying, material state of affairs: "Seen in this light, the classic theory of cinema that the camera is an impartial instrument which grasps, or rather is impregnated by, the world in its 'concrete reality' is an eminently reactionary one. What the camera in fact registers is the vague, unformulated, untheorized, unthought-out world of the dominant ideology."[59]

This statement has the advantage of clarity, for unlike many of our received notions about classical film theory, it allows for the possibility that the latter implied a politics, albeit an "eminently reactionary" one. More common is the notion that contributors such as Balázs, Arnheim, Kracauer, and Bazin may have worked out some theories of medium-specificity and so advanced our understanding of formal and ontological issues in cinema, but that there was no connection between what they were investigating and any sense of the political. This view of classical film theory is not only apolitical, but ahistorical as well. On a biographical level, it overlooks important details such as Balázs's experience in the short-lived government of Béla Kun, the sharp and often ironic political tone of Arnheim's early film reviews, Siegfried Kracauer's emergent understanding of the social task of the film critic, and Bazin's deep engagement in the French resistance and in postwar efforts at worker's education, among other things. Of course, the apparent absence of politics may itself be interpreted as political—as the effect of emigration, or of Stalinism in the case of Eisenstein, the McCarthy era in the case of Arnheim or Kracauer. As Eric Rentschler notes in a fascinating reappraisal of Arnheim's early film criticism, the traces of its strong socio-political engagement were erased in the transition to the Cold War. "Might the McCarthy era," Rentschler asks, "and its suspicion towards progressive sensibilities, especially those of a Jewish emigrant from Germany with a leftist past, have played a role in Arnheim's decision to make the very considerable cuts" to *Film als Kunst* for its 1955 English translation?[60]

Such questions are important, to be sure, but the answers depend on how we frame the political. The kind of ideology critique bequeathed to us by the 1960s casts a glaring light on the progressive potential of Chaplin or the New Wave and on the reactionary politics of a John Ford, but perhaps it has also desensitized us to notions of the political that may be operative at other levels of representation or theory. What we need instead is to recover a sense of the politics of classical film theory itself—which is to say: we should reconstruct the historical and political questions to which theorists like Kracauer and Bazin considered "realism"—and, as I argue toward the end of this book, "humanism"—to be the answer. The politics of Kracauer's late film theory, I want to suggest, have become buried precisely to the degree that we have come to accept Kracauer as a canonical author of "classical film theory." We should unearth those politics.

This is what a historicizing approach such as I advocate here can enable. For it allows us to trace not only a degree of political instrumentalization that characterizes some of Kracauer's work, but also a more diffuse but no less effective film theoretical discourse on the politics of the aesthetic. Rentschler may be right to state that "given the difficult tenor of the Cold War epoch, Kracauer made certain that all traces of his former political convictions vanished from his work"[61]—but this assertion only holds to the degree that we clearly identify Kracauer's "former" convictions as Marxist and in need of suppression given the political climate of the McCarthy era. A different picture emerges if we locate the politics of Kracauer's writing not (or not exclusively) in the ideology critique of essays such as "The Little Shopgirls Go to the Movies" or of *The Salaried Masses* (and even here, Kracauer's subtle irony tends to undercut any straightforward unmasking of gender and class as ideological constructs), but in his lifelong interest in determining the relationship between material reality and what he ultimately terms "the humane"—in other words, in notions of humanist subjectivity and experience that Kracauer promulgates whether he is writing novels or criticism, theorizing about film or about history.[62] In this view, even a book like *Theory of Film* can hardly be considered "apolitical," as if, along with lingering Marxist identifications, it abandoned any attempt to think progressively about the politics of the aesthetic. While the book indisputably strikes a Cold War cord in some of its humanist credos, it should be read also as an attempt to rescue liberal humanism from itself by reinvesting it with notions of experience and dethroning the autonomous subject in favor of materiality and alterity.

As I hope to show in the chapters that follow, and in keeping with the spirit of Kracauer's own cultural critique, this book's historicizing approach is by no means intended to relativize Kracauer's insights by referring them to circumstantial and constantly changing historical conditions; nor is it designed to hive those insights off from the present by situating them definitively in a bygone past. Kracauer's critical theory of the cinema may have been historically specific, such that his American writings (like his previous work during the Weimar Republic and in French exile) do require historicization; but as critical theory, it also resists its temporal emplotment. For Kracauer, as for Benjamin before him, "actuality requires standing at once within and *against* one's time."[63] In keeping with the ethic of punctuality and untimeliness inscribed in the very concept of critical theory, the kind of historicization advocated here involves "both close attunement to the times and aggressive violation of their self-conception."[64] Kracauer's liberal humanist film theory and criticism, while demonstrably attuned to a contemporary critique of totalitarianism, was untimely in its wager on the power of experience and a curious humanism even in the mass medium of film. As such, it remains provocatively untimely *and* punctual in our neoliberal and ostensibly posthumanist present.[65]

Kracauer, I ultimately want to suggest, remained attentive throughout his American career to the representation of politics: it was in New York that he formulated his notion of film as a medium that helps to "disclose" a "secret history" of psychological dispositions behind the Weimar Republic's "overt history of economic shifts, social exigencies and political machinations."[66] And *Theory of Film* culminates explicitly in an argument about the restoration of the capacity for experience in an ostensibly postideological world. The theory of realism that he develops, as we will see, in response to the loss of experience and the totalitarian representation of politics he had analyzed during the 1940s amounts, in turn, to a politics of representation and subjectivity: a rethinking of the political fallout from war, terror, and totalitarianism in terms of aesthetic forms and the specific "affinities" of film as a photographic medium. *Theory of Film* does carry political convictions, whether previously held or not, concerning the fate of subjectivity, experience, humanism, and liberalism. We should not downplay the stakes of these convictions. They were formulated, after all, by a theorist who began his American career by charting the devolution of Weimar democracy toward Hitler in the medium of film, and who studied how film could both be wound into the coils of Nazi propaganda and unwound into limp assertions of liberal doxa by Hollywood. Against these bleak views of his favored medium, how could he find cinematic realism to hold out any hope, let alone the promise of "redemption," in *Theory of Film?* The answer, I suggest, lies in a deeply held conviction of the utopian potential of film. Even as he theorizes its illiberal manifestations, Kracauer holds on to the notion that this same medium might bring the politics of representation into equilibrium with the representation of politics—that the cinema might yet rekindle, in subjects who had been "liquefied" by propaganda, war, and terror, the capacity for human experience. This, I argue, is the politics of Kracauer's American writings.

Although my primary interest is conceptual rather than biographical, the book's chapters chart a roughly chronological path from Kracauer's

American debut with a review of Disney's *Dumbo* in 1941 to the publication of his *summa*, the *Theory of Film*, in 1960 and his posthumous work on historiography. This allows me to trace an arc from his early attempts at gaining his intellectual bearings in the United States, through a middle phase devoted to the analysis of cinema as an illiberal medium, to the elaboration of a film theory that seeks to rehabilitate the medium's utopian potential in terms of a revised enlightenment humanism. To recover the relevant contexts and references for this development of Kracauer's work, I construct a number of historical scenarios that ground the more abstract movement of film-theoretical motifs and ideas in concrete circuits of interaction and exchange. Although some of these scenarios admittedly involve a certain degree of imagination to fully uncover their relevance to Kracauer's writings, they are by and large archivally based. Relying on records that range from immigration documents to surviving notes and correspondence, from institutional memos to scattered autobiographical references in Kracauer's published writings, and from marginalia in books and manuscripts to anecdotal accounts by people who knew Kracauer, these scenarios help us to flesh out and revise the image of a monkish theorist working alone in a library behind a wall of books.

Having already begun here to chart the circumstances of Kracauer's arrival in New York on the *Nyassa*, I follow Kracauer in chapter 1 from New York Harbor into the city, so to speak, in order to map some of the contact zones in which the immigrant encountered his host country. This is a matter of historical research as much as of reading his earliest American texts. From his essays of the early 1940s, including the brief *Dumbo* review and the above-mentioned "Why France Liked Our Films," to increasingly bleak views of Disney and Hollywood around mid-decade, I reconstruct Kracauer's own assessment of the American scene in dialogue with the intellectual contexts out of which his thinking developed. These contexts include, first, the continuing, if fraught, contacts with the Frankfurt School in exile; second, the role for Kracauer of the New York Intellectuals and their little magazines; and third, what can only be described as the nonencounter with Hannah Arendt.

The last consequently figures in my own narrative as a particularly imaginary scenario, based on a single documented meeting. While Kracauer's and Arendt's lives and work in exile can be said to have run parallel in numerous and striking ways, they appear never to have intersected after meeting in Paris just once in 1939. If I nonetheless describe these parallels as significant, it is because the works that result from these stories of exile are mutually illuminating, whether in terms of their shared historiographical stakes or in terms of their distinct analyses of totalitarianism's origins. At the same time, while the failure of Kracauer and Arendt to connect or even acknowledge each other's work is an admittedly extreme case, it serves as a reminder that the various descriptions of Kracauer as an *Einzelgänger* in New York are not wrong: they are merely one-sided. As such, they have prestructured the reception of his American writings as idiosyncratic works *sui generis*, a tendency that *The Curious Humanist* seeks to undo by placing them in dialogue with important conversations of the time.

Against this backdrop, I consider Kracauer's main projects of the 1940s (with roots, in one instance, in an article for the *Zeitschrift für Sozialforschung* written during his French exile in the late 1930s). Each of these projects focuses in its own way on the relation between cinema and politics: on the use of the medium for propaganda, on its function as a repository of dispositions and mentalities that enabled the rise of Nazism, and on the politics of "terror" in a cycle of Hollywood productions from the 1940s that we now think of as films noirs. In each of these cases, Kracauer turns to film to diagnose a failure of liberalism, whose consequences he traces not simply in the subject matter of totalitarian propaganda or pretotalitarian cinema, but also in the cinema's aesthetic forms and their modulation of subjectivity. In keeping with contemporary arguments—whether by members of the Frankfurt School, by the New York Intellectuals, or by Arendt—Kracauer ultimately considers the subject of illiberal cinema to be defined by the lack, even the impossibility, of experience.

I develop this argument across several chapters. Chapter 2 focuses first on Kracauer's work on "totalitarian propaganda," which he developed on the margins of the Rockefeller Foundation's "Communications Group." To reconstruct the contours of this work, I revisit a heated trans-Atlantic exchange that Kracauer had with the leading members of the Institute for Social Research while still in Paris, and I trace its echoes as he tried to find his bearings in Manhattan. Drawing on an ill-fated manuscript that he had completed during the latter years of his French exile, Kracauer began elaborating his analysis of Nazi propaganda films and newsreels within weeks of his arrival in New York. For this purpose, he viewed films at local "Nazi theaters" in the Yorkville neighborhood as well as in the screening rooms of the Museum of Modern Art film library, and coordinated his efforts with the work of other émigré scholars such as Speier and Kris at the New School. He discussed his findings with important interlocutors such as John Marshall at the Rockefeller Foundation and the Columbia University art historian Meyer Schapiro. Kracauer's propaganda analysis, in other words, emerges atop a grid of paths that he traced across Manhattan Island, setting out from his midtown apartment to the film library at MoMA a few blocks away, but also to the theater full of Nazi sympathizers in the German neighborhood on the Upper East Side, to the Rockefeller Foundation on Fifth Avenue, and to the offices of his collaborators at the New School downtown. Out of these networked urban contexts, I argue, grew several papers and publications in which Kracauer began to outline the central concepts and concerns of the work on Weimar cinema that would culminate in *From Caligari to Hitler*: concerns with the relation between cinema and politics, distinctions between authoritarian and democratic forms of communication, an emergent theory of realism (albeit *ex negativo*), and the modulation of subjectivity at the movies. Although Kracauer developed these concepts out of work on outright propaganda, I argue that they have a bearing on Nazi cinema more generally, and on the projective logic of many of its blockbuster entertainment features in particular. Chapter 3 offers a reading of the 1941 film *Heimkehr* as a case study to illustrate this claim.

But Kracauer's underlying concerns about the cinematic trends went well beyond the context of totalitarian countries. Indeed, they carried over from Nazi cinema, Nazi propaganda, and the pro-Nazi audiences at the Yorkville cinema to the American scene at large, which Kracauer analyzed by way of the American screen. As his writings, notes, and correspondence reveal, Kracauer remained even in exile an "inveterate moviegoer" (as he puts it in *Theory of Film*), in tune with contemporary developments in cinema. Viewing the latest releases by Alfred Hitchcock, Robert Siodmak, and Fritz Lang, but also by the likes of Preston Sturges and Leo McCarey, Kracauer sensed that Nazi propaganda's investment in instilling and maintaining fear among its German audiences resonated, during the 1940s, with a sense of threat that permeated American culture and politics as well. From Hollywood, whose dark thrillers (only later identified as films noirs) Kracauer would analyze as "terror films" in an important 1946 article, to the landmark speeches of President Roosevelt, the themes of terror, fear, risk, and threat became pervasive. As I detail in chapter 5, they dominated the pages of *Commentary*, informed the annals of political science, fueled research projects on fascist agitators, and undergirded the steadily growing knowledge of the Holocaust, carpet bombing, and nuclear warfare. Though it was undoubtedly worse for the exile, the sense of fear (soon to be instrumentalized in the Cold War) was a defining aspect of the American experience during the midcentury "age of the crisis of man";[67] in some analyses—including Kracauer's own and in keeping with the earlier writings on propaganda—fear was a fact that threatened the very fabric of experience and the coherence of the subject, with grave political consequences for notions of participatory democracy.

This is the context in which we must situate the genesis of Kracauer's best-known and least appreciated book, *From Caligari to Hitler,* to which I devote the following three chapters. Published in 1947, the study was Kracauer's entry ticket to the United States in the sense that it brought him broader recognition than he had previously achieved through his articles and networking activities during the 1940s. Like the propaganda analysis, he composed the book during these years under the aegis of the recently inaugurated film library at the Museum of Modern Art. Arguing for a reconsideration of the ostensibly teleological and nationally specific approach for which *Caligari* has often been critiqued, chapter 5 draws out the echoes between Kracauer's assessment of Weimar cinema and his response to Hollywood's cycle of "terror films." Maintaining the focus on the contemporary American scene, chapter 6 then pursues influential intellectual contexts for the conceptualization of *Caligari* that have remained comparatively unacknowledged to date: even as Kracauer was reconsidering the films that he had originally reviewed during the interwar years in Germany in order to understand Hitler's rise to power, a number of prominent fellow exiles were similarly engaged in addressing "the German Question"—whether as sociologists and philosophers associated with the Frankfurt School or with the U.S. Office of War Information (Franz Neumann, Herbert Marcuse, Leo Löwenthal, Theodor W. Adorno), or as political theorists in dialogue with the New York Intellectuals (Hannah Arendt). As I argue in this chapter, we need to historicize *From Caligari to Hitler* by situating it within the discourse among nervous liberals about the "Authoritarian Personality" and the "Origins of Totalitarianism."[68] In the process, Kracauer's book—occasionally dismissed by later critics as a reductive or "essentializing" sociology of film—becomes newly legible as a seminal intervention in the debates on totalitarianism, liberalism, mass culture, and democratic representation.

Kracauer's specific contribution to these debates, I argue, consists in his turn to film as a medium of cultural expression. As I demonstrate in a close rereading of *Caligari* in chapter 7, Kracauer invests this medium with the promise of political transformation even in its bleakest manifestations. Read alongside contemporary accounts of totalitarianism and its threats, *From Caligari to Hitler* stands out for the way in which it combines an explicit discourse about cinema's function as an illiberal medium in authoritarian/totalitarian structures with an implicit utopian account of cinema's democratizing, humanist promise. *Caligari*'s conundrum revolves around the émigré's pressing question of why the Weimar Republic was no more able to actualize that promise than was Hollywood in the age of anxious postwar liberalism and the "crisis of man."

Kracauer's clear-eyed assessment of the twentieth century's threat to democracy, if not to humanity as a whole, did not dampen his hopes for cinema's ability to rekindle the dormant promise he had found even in his bleakest analyses. That promise, I argue in the final three chapters of this book, lies for Kracauer in cinematic realism, experience, and spectatorship—terms that are bound up in the broadly humanistic outlook that he formulates in his theoretical *summa*, the *Theory of Film*, and in the posthumous *History: The Last Things before the Last*. It is a curious humanism, to be sure, located midway between the "bleak liberalism" of contemporaries such as Adorno or Lionel Trilling and the liberal humanism of the Cold War years.[69] Kracauer's distinctive voice emerges from these contexts if we listen carefully for his attempts to divest the liberal's triumphalist faith in human universals of its central belief in the autonomous human subject. His investment in what he calls "the humane" curiously centers on a muted subject that, having lost the capacity for experience in the terrors unleashed by the totalitarian regimes, tentatively regains that capacity in the act of spectatorship—whether in the cinema or in the face of history.

Chapter 8 introduces this aspect of Kracauer's thinking by reading *Theory of Film* as an answer to the questions *Caligari* had raised. Where the latter had linked Weimar cinema to the loss of experience, thereby taking up an abiding motif of both the Frankfurt School's critical theory of modernity and Hannah Arendt's analysis of totalitarianism, *Theory of Film* reimagines the cinema precisely as the place where experience might regain a foothold. The centrality of this notion to Kracauer's thinking, already recognized in various ways by Miriam Hansen, is amplified, I suggest, if we place it in dialogue with Robert Warshow's theorization of film and popular culture as sites of "immediate experience."[70] A key player among the New York Intellectuals of the time, Warshow also read and commented on Kracauer's evolving drafts for *Theory of Film*. Accordingly, I situate the latter not only in the orbit of the Frankfurt School or of Classical Film Theory, but also within the animated debates about mass culture and "midcult" swirling around New York's little magazines at the time. By restoring the notion of experience to its central place in the elaboration of *Theory of Film*, and by placing that notion in dialogue with its theorization and use by Benjamin, Adorno, and Warshow, I challenge the critiques of "naive realism" that have been leveled at the book from within film studies, as well as the charge of postideological, universalizing humanism that Kracauer has incurred through some blandly affirmative formulations in the book.

Chapter 9 continues this argument to suggest that Kracauer finds in the experiential dimensions of film and spectatorship the political resources for an antitotalitarian subjectivity. While this project indisputably bears the mark of the Cold War humanist moment out of which it emerged—a moment emblematized most lastingly, perhaps, in Edward Steichen's 1955 blockbuster exhibit *The Family of Man* at MoMA—I argue that Kracauer's avowedly humanist politics should not be conflated with the facile universalism of that show. Rather, the political investment of Kracauer's film theory should be sought in his central concern with film spectatorship as an alienated, contracted form of subjectivity through which to apprehend the world. Viewed in its historical and biographical contexts as well as against the backdrop of Steichen's show (which Kracauer undoubtedly saw in its original form at the same museum at which he was pursuing his film work), *Theory of Film* emerges as a complex political project after the recent memory of dictatorship and before the explicit politicization of film theory in the decade following its publication.

Chapter 10 then follows the development of Kracauer's curious humanism through his final, posthumously published reflections on the writing of history. Arguably the central and normative category of *History: The Last Things before the Last* is the notion of "the humane." Alongside the explicit borrowings from *Theory of Film*, *History* continues to explore a fragile humanist subjectivity that finds its best expression even here in scopic scenarios: whether in the cinema or in the open field of historical inquiry, Kracauer's humanist subject is a subject of the look, a spectator.

An epilogue, finally, resumes the disciplinary perspective on Kracauer as a film theorist, locating the specificity of his contributions to film studies by situating him with respect to the fledgling professional organization, the Society of Cinematologists. Recent scholarship has begun to reflect in a sustained way on the historical origins of film studies and the institutional pathways that led to the formation of the discipline in the late 1950s and early 1960s. As I argue throughout the book, these are years that have profoundly shaped American intellectual history, but they are also foundational for cinema studies, as Peter Decherney, Saverio Giovacchini, Haden Guest, Dana Polan, Lee Grieveson, and Haidee Wasson, among others, have shown.[71] The key institutions here were not only universities and colleges, but also film clubs, film journals, and—again—the film library at the Museum of Modern Art, surely the epicenter of film education and scholarship in multiple ways after its founding in 1935. Surrounded by books in the library, but also always in implicit dialogue with Frankfurt friends, American scholars, foundation officers, and the left-liberal Intellectuals in

New York, Siegfried Kracauer published some of his most influential works during this period. Viewed in relation to the early work of the Society of Cinematologists, which counted Kracauer as a charter member, these writings gain further contours for their specific contribution to the field. At a time when film studies was still searching for its own institutional identity, Kracauer's writings were crucial signposts to orient the newly emerging discipline in the direction of a theoretically reflexive, humanist form of inquiry. As such, I conclude, both Kracauer and film studies remain relevant today, even as the field and its objects of study continue to transform and expand into media studies for a digital age.

1. Metropolitan Contact Zones
Kracauer in New York

> The newcomer establishes himself in America, and soon his contacts with the customs of this country are too intimate to permit dispassioned reflections about American Life.
> SIEGFRIED KRACAUER, "Why France Liked Our Films" (1941)

DISNEY'S "SHATTERED UNIVERSE"

In November 1941, barely six months after disembarking from the *Nyassa*, Siegfried Kracauer published his first piece of film criticism in English. To those who know him only as the author of *From Caligari to Hitler* and *Theory of Film* (but surely not to anyone familiar with his promiscuous, almost daily criticism for the *Frankfurter Zeitung* during the 1920s), it may come as a surprise to learn that Kracauer's American debut in the pages of the *Nation* took aim at Walt Disney's *Dumbo*, released two weeks prior to publication of the review.[1] How might this piece of Americana, a film about a flying elephant which Kracauer described as a "charming picture filled with marvelously conceived episodes," fit with the weighty concerns of the film theorist? Indeed, how does a discussion of animation square with Kracauer's better-known works on cinema as a symptom of Weimar Germany's failure, and on the relation between film and reality?

As we shall see, Kracauer would eventually take an interest precisely in the symptomatic function of Disney's films. And even in this discussion of *Dumbo*, he zooms in on the nature of the film medium and the question of realism. Attentive to detail, with a flair for implicit theorizing along the way, the review is reminiscent of some of Kracauer's best Weimar criticism *and* points forward to his later work.[2] He begins and ends the text with an appreciation of the various "happy inventions" in the film (such as Dumbo's drunken reverie of pink elephants), which he attributes to Disney's infallible "artistic instincts." But the review's underlying tone is deeply critical of Disney's turn, after the recent *Fantasia* (1940), to classical narrative and realistic motivation. Introducing a term that would come to figure centrally in his *Theory of Film* two decades later, Kracauer faults the director of

Dumbo for clinging to "camera reality" and for "imitat[ing] the technique of the realistic film." Animation, in contrast, comes into its own when—much like the earlier slapstick comedies of silent cinema—it "spurns traditional notions of reality and creates [its] own laws for the elements of our visible world." In other words, Kracauer grounds his critical assessment of *Dumbo* in a normative distinction between animation and realism.

Disney himself had set the standards for what the animated film could do in his earlier shorts such as *Plane Crazy* (1928) and *The Skeleton Dance* (1929). From such films, Kracauer extrapolates the notion that animation "tends toward the dissolution rather than the reinforcement of conventional reality, and its function is not to draw a reality which can better be photographed." Miriam Hansen notes a similar investment in animation's "anti-empirical exuberance" in the writings of Walter Benjamin;[3] but *Dumbo*, rather than simply using "the power of the cartoonist's pen" to assert the ability of an elephant to fly, resorts to conventional, narrative motivation by introducing a magical feather that allows its protagonist to take to the air. In other words, it thus supplies a reason, where animation as a cultural form has the power to dislodge everything from social conventions (to which, according to Kracauer, "Disney's feature films submit too readily") to instrumental reason itself. Kracauer's critical stance on *Dumbo* notwithstanding, in other words, his review offers a fundamentally positive evaluation of animation as a mass-cultural form, aligning his diagnosis with Benjamin's analysis of Mickey Mouse as a "dynamic figure of *disruption*."[4] In this reading—for which Kracauer also finds isolated instances in certain sequences of *Dumbo*—animation, like slapstick, can generate therapeutic laughter, harboring emancipatory and utopian potentials.

When Kracauer returns to Disney in an article published five years later, his assessment has undergone a fundamental shift—but then, so has the world. In a 1946 article published in *Commentary* under the title "Hollywood's Terror Films: Do They Reflect an American State of Mind?" Kracauer makes brief reference to Disney's most recent film, *The Three Caballeros* (1944/45), produced under the auspices of the Good Neighbor Policy. The film mixes animation, photography, and live action in a series of loosely connected musical numbers, strung together as a fantastic travelogue across South America. Featuring Donald Duck, some stereotyped cartoon characters who represent Mexico and Brazil, and a number of popular Latin American stars, the episodes culminate in a hallucinogenic explosion of movement and color that recalls *Dumbo*'s champagne-induced delirium in the "Pink Elephants on Parade" segment. In *Theory of Film*, Kracauer will eventually come to defend the looseness of episodic narrative construction, but in the immediate postwar moment, he has little patience for the way *The Three Caballeros* strings together its ever more discombobulated numbers. In the context of an argument about how the conspicuous tendencies toward sadism, violence, and the morbid in Hollywood films reflect the pervasive sense of "inner disintegration," Kracauer now reads Disney as "particularly sensitive to contemporary undercurrents of feeling": rather than utopian, Kracauer here considers Disney's cartoons symptomatic of a national state of mind, if not of the emerging global Cold War constellation more broadly.[5] Disney's sadistic universe now appears to Kracauer as a defense against utopia, an inscription of the global threat of extinction that undercuts the power of the subject to imagine the world to be different. Drawing on a related assessment that his collaborator and friend Barbara Deming had recently published in *Partisan Review*,[6] Kracauer contends that *The Three Caballeros* "shows us a universe torn to pieces as though it had been hit by a cluster of atomic bombs. That shattered universe is symptomatic of the way we feel about the world now around us. [. . .] Amid the debris of such a universe dark impulses are sure to find freer play."[7]

This is no longer the language of antiempirical exuberance, but recalls instead the "medicinal bath" of fun ("Fun ist ein Stahlbad") for which Disney's sadistic universe stands in Adorno and Horkheimer's contemporaneous *Dialectics of Enlightenment*.[8] In the 1930s, Benjamin had still harbored a critical enthusiasm for the way film "exploded this prison-world with the dynamite of the split second," claiming that this allowed us now to "set off calmly on journeys of adventure among its far-flung debris."[9] Barely a decade later, the debris has become real and radioactive, producing urban ruinscapes of previously unimaginable dimensions. The same aspects that Benjamin and Kracauer had valorized before the catastrophe have now lost their utopian potential for the preemptive diffusion of tension through collective laughter and for the "disruption" of the historical process.[10] They have become instead indices for history's catastrophic turn, which leaves "a wholly enlightened world radiant with triumphant calamity."[11] As such, films like Disney's retain their diagnostic, and even prognostic, value—but the temporal horizon against which one might situate Disney's animation, if not the medium of film as such, has shifted diametrically. Whereas Kracauer had previously perceived the cinema to project glimpses of a reconciled future, however tenuous and dimly perceived, any such opening is now foreclosed. In the shadow of war and the Cold War, Kracauer is disillusioned in his own intellectual project of demonstrating the potential of film to generate transformative moments, whether through realism, animation, or laughter. With a rising emphasis on security and the transition to a perpetual state of war during the 1940s, laughter itself ends up "suggest[ing] a conformist attitude," as Kracauer puts it in a 1950 article on Preston Sturges.[12] Its utopian dimension has been replaced by the immanence of the cultural symptoms one might detect at the movies.

In this respect, Kracauer's analysis of Hollywood in 1950 coincides with his similarly bleak view of Weimar cinema, which he had worked out in *From Caligari to Hitler* in the intervening years since the early *Dumbo* review. As I show in subsequent chapters, this overlap is explicit and hardly coincidental, as both assessments—of Hollywood and of Weimar—are born out of the same anxious postwar moment. They reflect an ongoing effort to understand totalitarianism both as a historical reality in Germany and as a present threat to liberal democracy in the United States. As Mark Greif describes this moment in his philosophical history of midcentury America, this moment saw the emergence of a broad and urgent discourse on the "crisis of man."[13] Kracauer often drew quite explicitly on this discourse; and he joined it implicitly, not only in the shared concern with the changing relation between the human and the technological (in this case, the technology of media such as the cinema), but also in his ongoing concern with the ways cinema both constructs and constrains human subjectivity. While I argue that Kracauer never fully gave up on the utopian kernel that he had discerned in cinema ever since he began writing about it in the early 1920s,[14] during the 1940s he clearly considered that kernel to have been thrown into crisis by the cinema's susceptibility to antidemocratic, authoritarian, conformist, and commercial pressures.

Like the utopian readings of cinema and laughter, this view of film as an illiberal medium had been a motif in Kracauer's film criticism since his beginnings as a writer for the *Frankfurter Zeitung*. It had taken on increasing urgency in the mid-1920s, when he took up the study of Marx and Marxism and eventually went head to head with the powerful Ufa studios in his role as the Weimar Republic's preeminent left-liberal film critic, now stationed in Berlin. Although neither the materialist vocabulary nor the subtly ironic tone of his analyses of white collar culture from the early 1930s would translate in any audible way into his far more straight-laced American prose, the critical stance of the 1940s was unmistakable and of a piece with Kracauer's earlier work: cinema, called on to imagine better worlds, had patently failed to realize the political hopes Kracauer had staked in it. From *The Cabinet of Dr. Caligari* to Hitler, and from *The Three Caballeros* to Truman and Eisenhower, films squandered their utopian energies by catering to antidemocratic trends and "dark impulses." Cinema had become symptomatic of the midcentury crisis of man.

And yet this view, expressed forcefully in *From Caligari to Hitler* and in essays on Hollywood for *Commentary, Harper's,* and *Films in Review,* was only one side of a dialectic that bound together cinema's failings with its persistent promises.[15] For throughout these years, Kracauer continued to elaborate his ideas about cinema as a phenomenological medium of experience and as the site for encounters with what it might mean to be human even in the face of the crisis diagnosed everywhere by the "fundamental anthropology" that Greif describes. When Kracauer finally completed the long-gestating book on film aesthetics that he had originally projected in French exile, and which he published as *Theory of Film* in 1960, it was ultimately the trust in cinema's powers that prevailed. Though couched in the language of experience rather than utopia, and of physical reality rather than social materialism, the final elaboration of Kracauer's film theory resumed motifs that would appear to have lain dormant during the 1940s. *Theory of Film* again valorizes the power of slapstick, of movement, of spectatorship, and of cinema's ability to render the world's image, indeed to "redeem" it. Even as the book rehearses the critique of Disney for the realism Kracauer had already found problematic in *Dumbo, Theory of Film*'s epilogue mounts Kracauer's most sustained defense of cinematic realism as a way forward out of the "ruins of ancient beliefs."[16]

Kracauer's American writings, then, confront us with a number of profound continuities and shifts—both with respect to his earlier, Weimar-era writings and with regard to the trajectory that leads from the review of *Dumbo* to the epilogue of *Theory of Film*. There are several ways of accounting for, and locating, the shifts: We could trace them on an aesthetic level by pointing either to an often-noted change in Disney's films from utopian to "artless" and from inspired creation to taylorized production, or to the endgame of the classical Hollywood studio system and the emergence of a new cinematic idiom in Italian Neorealism. Alternately, we could trace Kracauer's "epistemological shift" on the biographical level to a theoretical change of heart as he adapts to his new surroundings during the war years and, in particular, changes his understanding of Hollywood.[17] In yet another vein, we could trace Kracauer's various shifts in emphasis to the historical moment, seeking their causes in the impact of Hitler, the Holocaust, Hiroshima, and in the aftermath of war, during which Kracauer was writing. Or finally, we could see Kracauer's shifting positions as the movement of a larger dialectic, which ties the critique of mass culture to its redemption, much in the way Kracauer himself earlier worked through the reifying aspects of photography or the mass ornament in order to locate a utopian potential precisely in their alienating effects.[18] Each of these explanatory frameworks—aesthetic, biographical, historical, and dialectical—plays into Kracauer's shifting assessment of Disney and the function of laughter in the cinema, which I have glossed here as a first example for Kracauer's evolving critical positions upon his arrival in the United States. A second piece, published only half a year after the review of *Dumbo*, helps to elucidate further aspects of this evolution.

"NO LONGER A EUROPEAN OBSERVER": FROM PARIS TO NEW YORK

Although forced to live in penury for long stretches, Kracauer managed to keep up his cinema-going habits during the years of his French exile in Paris, where he remained a keen observer of the film scene. Writing principally for Swiss newspapers, he reviewed the work of René Clair, Jean Vigo, Jean Renoir, and Julien Duvivier, among others, and reported on general trends. In a 1939 overview entitled "Bemerkungen zum französischen Film" (Notes on French film), he took issue with some recent developments in French cinema—among them a preponderance of dialogue, a glut of "epic" films, and a failure to make good use of the medium by conjuring "the effect to be garnered from the small, the inconspicuous."[19]

Again, these are critical motifs that anticipate the full elaboration of film's affinities for the small, the overlooked, and the inconspicuous in *Theory of Film*. But these motifs were modulated by the transition to life in the United States, which left explicit traces in an article Kracauer published in the *National Board of Review Magazine* in May 1942 titled "Why France Liked Our Films."[20] The magazine supplied a brief biographical note at the head of the article, which located Kracauer's authority to write such a piece in the author's history of exile, noting that Kracauer "left Germany in 1933, and lived in France till a year ago when he escaped to America." But far more than Kracauer's French connection, I want to suggest, it is the pronoun in the first person that animates the article:[21] the author of "Why France Liked Our Films" is speaking as a member of a group, as an American to Americans about "our" cultural export. While this might seem an overreading of the title (which, after all, could have been supplied by the journal's editors rather than by Kracauer himself), it turns out to be the punch line of the entire article, which self-consciously works through the shift from a European perspective to an American one.

The essay opens with a question: "What would an intelligent European observer learn about American life from American films?" Confidently assuming the mantle of the expert at the outset, Kracauer announces that he will be "operating in the field of rather personal impressions." But he soon takes his subjective voice back in favor of "incontestable facts"—namely, that American films have exerted an inexorable pull on the intellectual elite in Europe, and in France in particular. In order to answer the question posed in the title, Kracauer first paints a picture of French cinema; it is the picture of a gaping void that American films helped to fill.

French cinema, Kracauer argues, has typically produced noncinematic films—films lacking movement, overburdened with dialogue, and out of touch with the cinema's specific ability to reveal material detail and to render the minutiae of everyday life. He finds that French films routinely neglect "the material details—all those objects and gestures that are so important on the screen and which only the camera is able to detect and endow with significance." Moreover, he faults the French for the "absolute predominance of the dialogue" on their screens.[22] Especially with the advent of the "talkies," French filmmakers had abandoned cinema's essential affinity for "showing hitherto unseen phenomena."

If this critique reads like a preview of coming attractions in *Theory of Film*, Kracauer's comments on the characteristic disposition of "the French soul," on the "paralysis" of French society, and on the stasis of its expression in films with "nothing but atmosphere" strikingly presage his diagnosis of middle-class paralysis in Weimar cinema in *From Caligari to Hitler*. We know from Miriam Hansen's work that Kracauer had been considering the central issues of *Theory of Film* already during his French exile, where he had taken extensive notes on the project and engaged in conversations about it with Walter Benjamin.[23] However, "Why France Liked Our Films" not only puts the theory of realism into dialogue with the theorization of national cinema in *From Caligari to Hitler* (with which *Theory of Film* is often mistakenly considered to be incompatible), but also begins to sketch out a new position from which to undertake that project—after the tragedy of Benjamin's suicide, after the harrowing escape from France, and from the still-uncertain existence in New York. In this regard, not only does the brief essay read as a compendium of Kracauer's thinking from the late 1930s (even the "little shopgirls" of his well-known series of essays from the *Frankfurter Zeitung* make an appearance here) through his final project, *History*; it also provides a concise map to Kracauer's own positioning as an intellectual in exile.

After having reviewed the French cinema—much as he would later study Weimar films at MoMA—as native informant and "intelligent European observer," Kracauer shifts the discussion to the American scene. Hollywood figures in this essay as a positive to the French negative. As we have seen, this assessment will shift substantially over his first decade in New York, but here we still encounter a series of strong oppositions: where France had wallowed in stasis, "Hollywood pictures appeared as the manifestation of movement and life"; where France failed to heed the details of the visible world, the action in American films "answers the demands of the film camera in that it extends over the whole material dimension and precisely includes that sector of reality which can be called camera reality." Kracauer finds evidence for these claims in the Western ("where else but in the Western do real horses gallop over real plains?"), in the physicality of slapstick comedy, in the "palpable" realism of Main Street, even in star vehicles such as *Stella Dallas*, and in generic fare from gangster, to boxing, to reporter and detective films. As it proceeds, Kracauer's argument becomes an ode to Hollywood, a tribute so full of unadorned praise that no reader could fail to see why France would have liked these films. For a cinema-starved nation, these were productions too realistic, too authentic, too visually compelling to pass up.

Kracauer does not end here; in a final set of twists and reversals characteristic of many of his best essays from both the Weimar era and the New York years, he once more reframes the inquiry and asks what it would mean to test these (imputed) French impressions of American cinema, and the latter's triumphant realism in particular, against the reality of life in America. At this point, the personal perspective that Kracauer had abandoned at the article's opening reasserts itself in striking ways. In the context of a learned argument about national cinemas and recent film history, we suddenly find Kracauer reliving his own arrival in the United States and elevating the exile's trajectory—much as he would later do on a more philosophical plane in *History*—to a privileged phenomenological standpoint. For there is "only one short moment," Kracauer claims, "in which the European observer can judge the validity of the image of American life he had received in European theatres: the moment of his arrival in this country . . . the marvelous first meeting with life in America." Recollecting "that decisive moment" in his own life merely a year prior to the publication of this article, Kracauer notes—now again in the first person plural: "As we entered New York harbor, the strange feeling of having already seen all this began to grow upon me." The urban landscape of New York, the detectives and immigration officials who board the ship, all appear to Kracauer as old acquaintances; to the self-described "passionate movie-goer" fresh off the boat, the entire scene becomes cinematic, akin to a dream: "Either he had been suddenly transplanted onto the screen or the screen itself had come into three-dimensional existence."

Significantly, this oneiric perspective, which provides the refugee with an epistemological perspective from which to judge—or better: recognize—the fundamental realism of Hollywood, remains fleeting. Kracauer ends his article by noting the way in which the immigrant's acclimatization shifts the perspective again and begins to reveal aspects of American reality that the cinema had failed to capture. As an example, he notes that filmic representations of New York "neither take notice of Broadway in the morning, nor do they picture the hundreds of cross-town streets that end in the empty sky."[24] To careful readers of Kracauer's work, this is not merely a question of adding nuance to stock footage of New York, but again an early formulation of film's affinities with the fortuitous and the endless, and of the medium's link to experience that Kracauer will elaborate in *Theory of Film*. To be sure, Kracauer will shift his evaluation of Hollywood in favor of Italian Neorealism over the years; but this shift, which we can trace through his essays from the 1940s all the way to the final shape of *Theory of Film*, will henceforth take place on new ground.

"Why France Liked Our Films" charts the map to that ground. Having begun the article as a European observer authorized to speak of France's film culture by virtue of the eight years he had spent in exile there; having then taken up the position of the refugee, whose flash of insight into American culture was condensed in "that decisive moment—the marvelous first meeting with life in American culture," Kracauer ends the article by adopting the first-person plural of his title—by writing as an American, so to speak. Noting new details of American life that become apparent to the immigrant only after a "slow process of personal adjustment," Kracauer concludes with the acknowledgment that "it is no longer a European observer who is making these observations."

"Why France Liked Our Films" provides a finely etched starting point for Kracauer's trajectory during his years in America. The essay itself sets up the investigation of what it meant for Kracauer to write as a self-identified immigrant who virtually stopped publishing in German after barely half a year in his new host country, who took on American citizenship at the first opportunity, and who, by the end of his life, felt distant from, and at times repulsed by, his home country.[25] If not (yet) an American, however, then who *is* making these observations? "Why France Liked Our Films" maps out a trans-Atlantic subjectivity, doubly anchored in his European and his American experience, as I detail below. By virtue of his prior qualifications and his ongoing connections with fellow émigrés at the relocated Institut für Sozialforschung, Kracauer still maintains his Frankfurt roots, to be sure. I will have occasion throughout this book to return to the role these roots played in Kracauer's work, as evidenced by his lifelong correspondence with figures like Adorno and Löwenthal and by several attempts, albeit abortive, at working together—whether on publications for the *Zeitschrift* or on a "test film" for the Studies in Prejudice project.

Clearly, then, Kracauer's Frankfurt roots did not wither in New York. At the same time, however, Kracauer's intellectual identity also shifted once he opened up to his new surroundings. He did so much sooner after his arrival than the Horkheimer circle, which remained cocooned for half a decade. But by the 1940s, with the United States at war with Germany, the émigrés—Kracauer and his fellow Frankfurters alike—found themselves in the open, so to speak: a number of them had joined the war effort by accepting research positions with the State Department, and all of them took part in ongoing conversations and debates about the totalitarian enemy, antisemitism, culture and politics. In those debates, earlier positions were substantively and methodologically transformed by the encounter with the American scene. For Kracauer, this encounter centered less on Hollywood (which he already knew from German and French screens, but which curiously he never visited in person) than on New York and on the contacts he made there after his arrival. By virtue of his new physical location and of his subsequent associations, we must also locate Kracauer among the American intelligentsia at midcentury, who would become known as the New York Intellectuals.

"A LOOSE-KNIT TRIBE": KRACAUER AND THE NEW YORK INTELLECTUALS

> Having managed to get [to America], he was in fact surprisingly successful.
>
> THEODOR W. ADORNO, "The Curious Realist: On Siegfried Kracauer" (1964)

The New York in which Kracauer arrived was a remarkable metropolitan landscape. Not only did the city itself fascinate the writer of "urban miniatures" and the inveterate moviegoer who found the film images in his mind superimposed by the reality of the city's avenues at daybreak and the cross streets running from the Hudson to the East River.[26] As Kracauer would soon realize, though, the city was also home to a heady community of intellectuals who set the tone for some of the most important debates and edited the most significant journals of the time. Unlike his fellow émigré Hannah Arendt, who like Kracauer had spent eight years in French exile before also arriving in New York in 1941, Kracauer never became a recognized member of that group; and yet there is much to be learned about his work, as well as about both New York and Frankfurt intellectual culture, if we take at face value what exile, geography, and personal inclination combined to make of Kracauer: a New York Intellectual.

Largely composed of secular, second-generation Jewish immigrants, the New York Intellectuals came of age during the 1930s. Mostly born and raised in New York working-class families with strong union ties, these young men started out as committed socialists who participated in the organizations, the institutions, and the debates of the American left. Whether autodidacts like Philip Rahv, accomplished young academics like Meyer Schapiro, Lionel Trilling, and Sidney Hook, or eager City College students like Irving Howe, Nathan Glazer, Daniel Bell, and Irving Kristol, they all soon combined their political allegiances with a fervent cultural commitment to the aesthetic avant-garde. The resulting intellectual profile, amalgamated from heritage, habitus, and a voracious appetite for learning, set the members apart from their surroundings, yielding a group that itself felt "proudly" homeless in the United States.[27] As Irving Howe would later put it in a phrase that resonates strikingly with Kracauer's "extraterritoriality," the New York Intellectuals grew up "*willing* a new life, [driven by] our tacit wish to transform deracination from a plight into a program."[28]

And yet the "sense of apartness" that Howe considered formative for the group's members was coupled, in David Denby's terms, with "an amazed and delighted discovery of the American turf"—a discovery of America's "classic texts, its real and mythic landscapes, the vitality of its cities and popular arts."[29] The story of the New York Intellectuals is in this sense itself one of Americanization, albeit of a slightly earlier date than Kracauer's—and it seems only natural that the recent exile would have sensed and cultivated some affinities with the "loose and unacknowledged tribe" (Howe) that included, among others, Philip Rahv, William Phillips, Clement Greenberg, Dwight Macdonald, Elliot Cohen, Robert Warshow, and Howe himself.[30] Though his name is rarely mentioned alongside these critics, Kracauer published in the journals favored (if not founded) by the New York Intellectuals, such as the *Nation,* the *New Republic, Partisan Review,* and *Commentary;* moreover, from his earliest years in the United States, Kracauer's work elicited response and generated discourse within these magazines and a variety of loosely related venues, including *Politics, Labor Action,* and the *New Leader.* In ways no less significant for not always being immediately apparent, then, Kracauer contributed to the central debates that defined the New York Intellectuals as a group.

A number of these critics ardently admired Kracauer's writings. Dwight Macdonald considered his September 1943 essay on the Nazi newsreel to constitute "the best writing on films to appear in a long time," and when Clement Greenberg invited Kracauer to contribute to *Commentary* a few years later, he had similar praise for his work.[31] Indeed, Kracauer's reputation as an astute and original film critic had preceded his arrival in New York. Besides Löwenthal, Kracauer owed his entry into the United States in large part to Meyer Schapiro, an important member of the group and, according to Howe, its "recognized scholar [and] inspiring moral force."[32] As early as 1937, Schapiro had discovered that Kracauer shared some of the sensibilities and interests that drove the New York Intellectuals—their concern with the fate of socialism, their interest in the links between economy and culture, their nervous attention to popular culture.[33] He certainly shared their bookish erudition, and we might even say their sense of style. Like many of the New York Intellectuals, Kracauer brought to bear in his writings the skills of a journalist, albeit one steeped in literary culture and with two novels to his name. And although we might grant Adorno's lament that, perhaps as a result of writing only in English, Kracauer became comparatively "ascetic with regard to his own verbal art" in America,[34] it is difficult to imagine that the consummate stylist ever lost his love for the carefully turned phrase, his delight in the witty formulation, or his appreciation for the dialectical significance of form.[35]

Like any discerning reader at the time, Kracauer would have found plenty of occasions to appreciate the stylistic brilliance and critical acuity of the essays, reviews, and debates that filled the little magazines of the day. As numerous commentators have pointed out, the New York Intellectuals were defined by the journals they edited as much as by the cultural or political theories they held. Indeed, it was the function of the little magazines, as Lionel Trilling put it in his introduction to the first *Partisan Reader*, to "organize a new union between our political ideas and our imagination."[36] The ways in which these journals established certain stylistic, intellectual, and political standards of discourse conveyed upon them the function of central institutions for a group that largely imagined itself as outside all institutions.[37] To be published in *Partisan Review*, remembers one writer, "was acclamation, [it] conferred a special ideological status on the accepted."[38]

It is not my aim here to reconstruct in full historical detail what constituted the "special ideological status" of the New York Intellectual of the 1940s, already the object of a substantial body of scholarship.[39] But we may note how, bound up with the weighty matter of presentation and form, several overarching concerns of the New Yorkers intersect with Kracauer's abiding interests: their interest in totalitarianism and popular culture, in avant-garde and kitsch; their attempts to understand the specificity of the American experience in relation to European letters, but also to forge an intellectual culture that extended beyond the national; their shifting assessment of the promises and failures of liberal democracy; and their insistence on the inherently political nature of culture.

In labeling Kracauer a New York Intellectual in his own right, I do not mean to imply that he moved easily among the established circles at *Partisan Review* or *Commentary*, or that his voice was recognized in any way as belonging among that group at the time. My claim is, rather, that the intellectual scene in New York constituted one of the key contexts in which we need to situate Kracauer's work if we wish to grasp both its genesis and its relevance. This sort of contextualization can and did involve personal contacts and exchanges, as between Kracauer and Greenberg or Warshow; but it involves also intertextual exchanges and what I might call counterfactual conversations. How else to describe the significant non-encounter between Kracauer and Hannah Arendt, another émigré to join the New York Intellectual scene, albeit far more visibly? At several points in the following chapters, then, I pursue the potential conversation that could—and, I argue, should—be staged between Kracauer and Hannah Arendt. Like him, she had written the social biography of a significant Jewish figure of the nineteenth century before finding a safe haven in New York.[40] There, like Kracauer, she spent the 1940s working on the Origins of Totalitarianism, which she located in nineteenth-century antisemitism, imperialism, and twentieth-century atomization, and which Kracauer extrapolated from the films of the Weimar period. It appears that their paths failed to cross in Manhattan in any way that might have left an archival trace. And yet there can be no doubt that Kracauer and Arendt were aware of each other's work in the pages of *Commentary, Partisan Review,* and the German-language newspaper of the Jewish émigrés, *Aufbau*. Given the importance of this counterfactual exchange, let me conclude my initial contextualization of Kracauer's American writings by tracing his relationship with Arendt, his compatriot among the New York Intellectuals, as a series of missed encounters.

NON-ENCOUNTERS: SIEGFRIED KRACAUER AND HANNAH ARENDT

It begins with an invitation in French exile in Paris. On Friday, November 24, 1939, Arendt addressed a brief note to "chère Madame et Monsieur," thanking Lili and Siegfried Kracauer for sharing a piece of good news and

3. Note from Hannah Arendt to Siegfried and Lili Kracauer, November 24, 1939. (Deutsches Literaturarchiv Marbach, courtesy Georges Borchardt, Inc.)

asking them to come visit the following Tuesday. The note is signed "bien cordialement à vous, Hannah Arendt."[41]

But here the archival trail already ends. We do not know whether the Kracauers were able to take Arendt up on her invitation, nor do we know what the "bonne nouvelle" might have been—a bit of information about a common acquaintance back in Germany, or in the exile community in Paris, where this note was written? A tip about how to navigate the bureaucracy involved in securing a coveted visa for emigration to the United States? A publishing opportunity? Perhaps even more significantly, we have no way of knowing what would have prompted the Kracauers to share any news with Arendt in the first place: Had they been put in touch with one another by a mutual friend, maybe even by Walter Benjamin? Had the Kracauers relayed the "bonne nouvelle" on behalf of someone else? Arendt hopes to see them *again* ("j'aimerais beaucoup vous revoir bientôt"): when and where had they met before? Did their paths cross in the Weimar Republic, when Arendt spent a year in Kracauer's hometown of Frankfurt and both subsequently moved to Berlin in the early 1930s? Was there a connection through the *Frankfurter Zeitung,* for which Kracauer worked first as a film critic and then as director of the *feuilleton* where Arendt would publish an occasional article?

If the short note triggers questions about the conditions for its existence and its prehistory, the absence of any further traces of meetings or exchanges between Kracauer and Arendt is even more tantalizing.[42] This is hardly for a lack of available documentation: both authors' lives and work left manifold traces in published correspondence and well-organized archival materials, not to mention their respective publications. But apart from the 1935 note, we have no record, published or otherwise, that any of the seemingly close connections, geographical proximities, or encounters by proxy ever led to renewed exchanges between Kracauer and Arendt themselves. Neither mentions the other by name in their correspondence. Kracauer merits no entry in the *Denktagebuch* Arendt kept in New York, nor does his name appear in the address book she carefully maintained from the early 1950s on.[43]

And yet Arendt's and Kracauer's well-documented biographies exhibit a stunning set of parallels—so many, in fact, that it is at times difficult to believe they did not intersect again after that Tuesday afternoon in Paris (assuming the Kracauers took Arendt up on her invitation at the time). Though they were separated in age by sixteen years, Siegfried Kracauer's and Hannah Arendt's lives in exile converge to an almost uncanny degree. Taken for themselves, these biographical convergences have no argumentative value, of course. But they do have a cumulative effect, if only for the way in which they might shape our thinking about this particular constellation of exile culture in New York around midcentury.

Having both lived in Frankfurt and Berlin in the years leading up to Hitler, Kracauer and Arendt promptly fled Germany for Paris upon the Nazis' seizure of power in early 1933. Arendt was twenty-six years old at the time, still married to her first husband, Günther Stern; Kracauer was already over forty, and French exile would test him more severely than the younger woman. But the émigré circles were clearly intimate enough for them to be aware of one another—a sense of shared fate that could only have increased with the political pressures on the German exiles after the invasion of France in 1940. Within these circles, Kracauer and Arendt would trace similar paths. Like many others—among them their mutual friend Walter Benjamin, a cousin of Stern's—both Kracauer and Arendt would find their way to Marseille in 1940, where they must have stood in the same lines to obtain coveted visas. Unlike Benjamin, they were further able to secure the transit across Spain to Lisbon, whence they sailed for the United States in the spring of 1941. Though we have no evidence to prove it, I find it particularly difficult to imagine that they would have failed to cross paths in their daily routines in Lisbon, during the anxious, months-long wait for trans-Atlantic passage.

The Kracauers were the first to leave this last remaining European outpost. They disembarked in New York barely a month before Arendt followed with her second husband, Heinrich Blücher. She was now thirty-four, and Kracauer had recently turned fifty; both would opt to remain in the United States for the rest of their lives, taking up residence within a few blocks of one another on Manhattan's Upper West Side. They soon acquired American citizenship and would publish their best-known works in their second country of exile. Upon their arrival in New York Harbor, and with the help of Jewish aid organizations, they immediately set out to build new lives for themselves, working harder than many of their fellow émigrés, it appears, to master the English language and begin publishing in the journals of their day. Attuned as they were to the publishing culture in New York, they presumably read each other's reviews and articles on politics, film, and culture in successive issues of *Partisan Review* and *Commentary*. Although they never published in the same issue, they were at one point apparently slated to do so: Arendt and Kracauer had both been invited to contribute to a "symposium" in *Commentary* of essays responding to the editor Elliot Cohen's 1947 article "Jewish Culture in America." Both sent in their responses and reviewed the galleys, though only Arendt's piece was ultimately published.[44]

The *Commentary* symposium unwittingly encapsulates the larger story of two intellectual biographies that appear to have converged numerous times to the point of touching without ever really intersecting. Of course, we might chalk up these apparently missed opportunities to differences of opinion, of approach, of subject matter, even to differences of temperament. Unlike Arendt, who assembled around herself a veritable "tribe" of interlocutors and moved quite easily among the New York Intellectuals (at least, until the publication of her essays on the Eichmann trial in the *New Yorker*), Kracauer—whom Rudolf Arnheim would later remember as "no less inclined to meet people, but . . . self-centered"—appears to have been somewhat shy and reticent in public, something of a pedant, and rather narcissistic in matters relating to his work.[45] Other differences would have been theoretical, methodological, conceptual: Kracauer's materialism and his particular brand of phenomenological thinking (what he liked to call "rag picking" and "construction in the material"), but especially his interest in film and mass culture, take him along rather different paths of discovery than Arendt's recourse to Aristotle, Kant, and the experience of the Greek polis. Finally, there may have been real antipathies—if not directly personal, then by association. For all we know, the warm tone of Arendt's 1935 note to the Kracauers owed to the duress of their shared circumstances and there was no real fondness on either side. To the degree that he was in her sights in New York at all, and although ironically he himself had a more than rocky relationship with the Institut für Sozialforschung, Kracauer may well have been tainted for Arendt by association with that "group of bastards" *(Schweinebande)* to whom Arendt had taken a disliking as early as the 1930s in Frankfurt (Adorno had been involved in the rejection of her first husband's habilitation thesis).[46] In the 1940s, when she found the Frankfurt School in exile to have mishandled Benjamin's legacy, Arendt became incensed at the "Hornochsen" (blockheads) Adorno and Horkheimer, ultimately accusing them (in a letter to Karl Jaspers) of betraying their Jewish heritage.[47] Though Kracauer's name is never mentioned, he may have fallen under the same verdict.

And yet, as Lars Rensmann and Samir Gandesha have recently and convincingly argued, there are a number of reasons why we should not let the real and profound animosity between Adorno and Arendt blind us to the many fruitful areas of convergence and overlap in their writings—the "intriguing shared motives, theoretical undercurrents, and implications of their work, which are grounded in common concerns for politically transformative human solidarity, difference, spontaneity, and plurality."[48] The same, I would argue, holds true for the ostensible disconnect between

Arendt and Kracauer. Given the number of close, missed, or virtual encounters between Arendt and Kracauer, we may be justified in bending what appear to be merely parallel intellectual biographies toward a posthumous exchange, in which their writings now converge and illuminate one another.

In staging this and other encounters—whether counterfactual or archivally verifiable, editorial or intertextual—the following chapters propose to ground Kracauer's writings on film in their American context, from the review of *Dumbo* and his musings on Hollywood during the early 1940s through the fully elaborated *Theory of Film* and the posthumous *History*. In doing so, I hope not only to reinvigorate discussion of some ostensibly ossified classics of film theory or of the generally overlooked work on history, but also to show how Kracauer might be thought of as amid, rather than extraterritorial to, the New York scene.

Incontrovertibly on the margins of movements such as the Frankfurt School or the New York Intellectuals, Kracauer was nonetheless able to forge compelling insights into the cultural phenomena of his day from what we might call a transnational perspective. The transfer between languages, between discourses, and between media and politics that he accomplished during his years in Manhattan combined his deep affinities with Critical Theory (and the critical theorists he had befriended and mentored) with a commitment to grasping his American surroundings—a success that even Horkheimer, with whom Kracauer maintained cordial relations at best, implicitly acknowledged. In response to one of Kracauer's first American publications, Horkheimer, in a 1943 letter to Kracauer, wrote that the latter's approach and style "withstands the transfer into English much better than Teddie's or my own way of expression."[49] At stake even in such an offhand remark is what the Germans might call *Theorietransfer*—or, in Edward Said's looser but influential parlance, the way theory travels.[50] Although the link between Frankfurt and New York was never fully articulated, there are, I submit, compelling points of convergence that allow us to rethink the relationship between the New York and the Frankfurt Intellectuals not simply in terms of missed opportunities but also as an occasion for developing the theoretical sightlines that emerge if we place these two influential schools of thought, usually associated with separate sides of the Atlantic, within the unifying perspective offered by Kracauer's American writings. This is the perspective of the chapters that follow.

2. Totalitarian Propaganda

AT THE MOVIES IN YORKVILLE

> The Nazis know how to arrange the propaganda content in a compelling way, and also they excel in persuasive cinematic devices.
>
> SIEGFRIED KRACAUER, "The Conquest of Europe on the Screen: The Nazi Newsreel 1939–40"

On Wednesday, May 7, 1941, only a few weeks after the Kracauers arrived in New York, the 96th Street Theater on Manhattan's Upper East Side premiered a recently imported film titled *Sieg im Westen* (Victory in the West). Produced by the German *Wehrmacht*, it had passed the U.S. censors as a newsreel. This classification was quickly disputed, however, by the Anti-Nazi League, which pointed out that some scenes were posed, that the film used dubbed music, and that it lasted almost a full two hours. Most importantly, it had a coherent narrative:[1] in a long historical arc that reaches back as far as the Thirty Years War (1618–48), we follow the story of the German nation, beleaguered by foreign powers and finally "raped" by the Versailles Treaty after World War I. As the voice-over puts it early on, "This film proclaims the fight of the German people that has been called many times over the centuries to defend its borders and its living space *[Lebensraum]*." From bucolic scenes of a peaceful Germany, *Sieg im Westen* then develops a narrative of German victimization and self-defense, culminating in the film's central subject: the invasion of the Low Countries and France in 1940 under the infallible leadership of the glorious *Führer*.

News of its avowed propagandistic intentions had preceded the film's arrival in the United States. *Sieg im Westen* had been circulating in other countries in an apparent effort to convince viewers of the inevitability of

4. Flyer for U.S. premiere of *Sieg im Westen* at 96th Street Theater in Yorkville, New York, May 7, 1941. (German Collection, The Museum of Modern Art Department of Film Special Collections, New York)

Axis might; its screening in the U.S. was similarly understood as an effort to dissuade interventionist voices and bully the country into staying on the sidelines of the *Wehrmacht*'s advances.[2] Even before its screening, the film had consequently drawn the protest of groups such as the Friends of Democracy, the German-American Congress for Democracy, and the Anti-Nazi League.[3] On the day of its U.S. premiere, members of these groups picketed the film, but they deterred few from entering: *Sieg im Westen*, advertised by the theater as "the greatest [film] that you've ever seen here," showed multiple times daily to full houses. Composed largely of ethnic Germans in a neighborhood that was home to the notorious German American Bund under Fritz Kuhn, the appreciative audiences cheered Hitler at every appearance. When the film concluded with images of the victorious *Führer* ambulating through the cathedral of Notre Dame in the conquered French capital, the crowds sang along to the patriotic, anti-French anthem "Die Wacht am Rhein."[4]

It is difficult to imagine Kracauer, the film critic and refugee from fascism fresh off the boat, crossing the picket lines and joining the vociferous, pro-German crowds inside the "Nazi cinema" on 96th Street.[5] And yet Kracauer visited the Yorkville theater no fewer than six times to see and study the film.[6] Sitting in the audience, he presumably took ever more detailed notes on the film's construction—its use of music and commentary, of editing and dramaturgical devices, its portrayal of the common soldier and the increasingly elusive *Führer*.[7] These notes as well as the viewing experience itself formed the basis for Kracauer's first longer piece of writing in English, a pamphlet entitled "Propaganda and the Nazi War Film." The brochure circulated in various mimeographed drafts during the early 1940s but only appeared publicly in 1947, when Kracauer included it as an appendix to *From Caligari to Hitler*.[8] There, it reads as a relatively detached, sober piece of formal film criticism. Elaborating a method of "structural analysis," Kracauer carefully details the strategies not only of *Sieg im Westen* but also of an earlier film about the Polish campaign, *Feuertaufe* (Baptism by Fire, 1940), and various Nazi newsreels. He systematically parses these films' editing, narration, and soundtrack, their recurring motifs as well as their telltale omissions, to show how they produce the totalitarian polity. But the circumstances of the brochure's conception and production suggest that more was at stake. Involving repeat visits to an urban theater in his new hometown and multiple encounters with the kind of Germans he had desperately sought to escape, "Propaganda and the Nazi War Film" is also a document of Kracauer's attempt to write himself into contemporary discourses on wartime communication (he explicitly hoped that the pamphlet would contribute to psychological warfare and proudly noted its reception in government circles in Washington). Moreover, Kracauer's visits to the 96th Street Theater show the resulting brochure also to be a piece of situated *cinema* analysis: a cultural ethnography, and an attempt to gain his intellectual bearings in a bewildering new world.

That world extended from the Yorkville theater on the Upper East Side of Manhattan, to the Museum of Modern Art in midtown where Kracauer composed his analysis, to the New School downtown. Of these locations, the theater was at once the most ephemeral and the most virulent. It endowed Kracauer's analysis with the authority of an experience that was doubtlessly painful—the proverbial "splinter in the eye" that Adorno considered "the best magnifying glass."[9] The MoMA film library, in contrast, became a base of operations from which to reflect on these and other experiences in the city. Its curator, Iris Barry, had helped Kracauer secure a grant from the Rockefeller Foundation that allowed him to serve, in Barry's words, as "a kind of theorist in the work which the Film Library is now contracting to undertake for government agencies."[10] Prior to the study of Weimar cinema that would occupy Kracauer for the following half decade, that work involved the analysis of German propaganda material as well as the viewing, description, and analysis of films to be considered for preservation on behalf of the Library of Congress.

But it was the third location, the New School downtown, that provided the immediate intellectual context for Kracauer's propaganda work. Here, two other recent émigrés had recently initiated a project on "totalitarian communication."[11] Focusing on radio broadcasts, Hans Speier and Ernst Kris had established a research group to analyze the language of German propaganda. Like Kracauer's work, the project was funded by the Rockefeller Foundation, whose director of humanities, the indefatigable John Marshall, put Kracauer in touch with Speier and Kris. Both the "totalitarian communication" project and Kracauer's work at MoMA formed part of a larger effort, spearheaded by the "Communications Group" at the Rockefeller Foundation, to study wartime mass communications, both by the Nazis and by Americans and the Allies.[12]

Many of the names of that group's prominent members can also be found in the archive of Kracauer's correspondence during those years. These contacts subsequently served as stepping stones for his further employment, research, and other activities in New York. Among them were not only Marshall himself, but also towering figures of American social sciences and communications research such as the political scientist Harold Lasswell; Paul Lazarsfeld, the Viennese émigré who headed the Columbia

Office of Radio Research (later Bureau of Applied Social Research), for which Kracauer and members of the Frankfurt School would eventually work as well; Hadley Cantril, the director of the Public Opinion Research Project at Princeton, who in the mid-1940s encouraged Kracauer to translate his work on cinema into the American context by working on Hollywood, and who subsequently hired Kracauer to work on a UNESCO project later published under the title "National Types as Hollywood Presents them"; and Charles Siepmann, communications analyst for the BBC, whose work Kracauer read carefully and who would review *Theory of Film* for the *Public Opinion Quarterly* in turn.[13] These contacts, in other words, placed Kracauer at the center of American debates on democracy, public opinion, totalitarianism, and propaganda.

As soon as he had taken up work at the film library, Kracauer's first job was "to develop methods by which the analysis of the German film output can be related to other types of German communication."[14] Originally described by Barry as "a study of wartime communication through film,"[15] Kracauer's work joined other Rockefeller-funded projects engaged in "process research"—a term coined by Lasswell for a series of intermedial, basic investigations aimed at establishing ways of mapping, analyzing, and interpreting propaganda, public opinion, and communication. At Marshall's request that he focus on this type of methodological research,[16] Kracauer would contribute his model for the "structural analysis" of Nazi newsreels. Eventually, though, his work would branch off, in keeping with the sponsorship by the Humanities Division of the Rockefeller Foundation, in a more interpretive and less quantitative direction, whereas the work in other affiliated projects would constitute the founding moment of communications research as a (largely quantitative and empirical) social science. As such, a number of these projects would subsequently be critiqued by some of the more prominent scholars involved, even if temporarily: Adorno's well-known misgivings about empirical social research—and specifically what came to be known as "administrative research"[17]—after his experiences with the Princeton Radio Research Project are perhaps only the most famous of these. Kracauer, too, would later argue the limitations of quantitative procedures in communications research; we will explore the implications of that move for Kracauer's contribution to the development of film studies in this book's epilogue.[18]

Regardless of how these divisions played out in the subsequent history of disciplinary formations, it appears characteristic of the historical moment that distinctions between quantitative and qualitative methods, and between the social sciences and the humanities, were not yet sharply drawn. Thus, the Frankfurt School could find ways of yoking its brand of critical theory to the kind of empirical research being done under Lazarsfeld, even though ultimately these two approaches diverged;[19] and Kracauer's theoretical work could still align with Speier and Kris's quantitative tabulations of, for example, "non-military sentences" as a percentage of all sentences in German radio broadcasts on different military campaigns.[20] Despite their emerging methodological differences, such projects, it was sensed, contributed to a common goal of understanding cultural and mass communication in the age of totalitarianism.

At the heart of the intense debates about these studies and their object (alternately "propaganda" or "communications") were consequently questions of media, public opinion, and democracy. The "Communications Group" weighed the American response to Nazi propaganda against fears of overreaching by directing and controlling public opinion in ways that would themselves be perceived as fascist or authoritarian.[21] Inevitably, in other words, communications research on propaganda was bound up with assumptions and debates concerning democracy: its characteristic forms of (and constraints upon) knowledge and communication, the use and abuse of public opinion, the ability of "the people" to speak back to its representatives. In searching for ways to counter the apparent successes of totalitarian propaganda, the options considered ranged from trust in rational discourse, to the privileging of "expert" over public opinion, to the adoption of authoritarian structures even by democratic government. As Peter Decherney's work has shown, such debates were inscribed deeply into the institutional, historical, and political contexts in which Kracauer took up work at MoMA.[22]

Although issues of political theory do not become explicit in Kracauer's propaganda writings, they certainly inform his theorization of how Nazi propaganda turns the promise of cinema to illiberal ends. Not only because it bookends *From Caligari to Hitler*, then, but also because it constitutes an important stepping stone in the development of Kracauer's thinking about the relation between film and politics from his newly acquired American vantage point, his propaganda analysis deserves a closer look. For as we shall see, the ideas Kracauer begins working out in his encounter with Nazi propaganda—some of which draw directly on his earlier Weimar essays and his study of totalitarian propaganda a few years earlier in France—retain a significant hold on his thinking. Their influence would become manifest both in the monograph on Weimar cinema that he was conceptualizing and writing at the film library during these same years and in his assessment of Hollywood after the end of World War II.[23] In other words, the propaganda studies in which Kracauer engaged immediately upon his arrival in New York prepared the ground, in important ways, for what we consider today Kracauer's main contributions to film theory.

Contrary to Decherney's claim that "it is difficult to extrapolate a general theory from Kracauer's detailed work" in "Propaganda and the Nazi War Film,"[24] that study—particularly when viewed in the broader context of both contemporary communications research and the subsequent evolution of Kracauer's thinking—evinces a manifest concern with the relationship between aesthetics and politics, between "film devices" and "the Swastika world," between "screen dramaturgy" and the tenuous promise of a liberal democratic order.[25] In his pamphlet, Kracauer explicitly advances a *method* of structural analysis that amounted, in the estimation of Marshall, to a "valid grammar of the film, with some regard to what might properly be called film rhetoric."[26] Erwin Panofsky indeed hailed "Propaganda and the Nazi War Film" as an "important general contribution on the structure of the 'documentary film.'"[27] More significantly, however, Kracauer appears to work in this essay from several guiding *theoretical* assumptions concerning both film's affinities to realism and its ability to modulate political subjectivities. At times only implied in "Propaganda and the Nazi War Film," these assumptions gain even clearer contours if we trace them not only forward into the work on *From Caligari to Hitler* and *Theory of Film*, but also back to Kracauer's earlier studies on propaganda from 1937. Contextualizing his first steps as an émigré scholar by locating Kracauer in the web of research and discourse on communications, propaganda, and totalitarianism, then, this chapter seeks to lay the groundwork for thinking of the American Kracauer as "a kind of theorist" of cinema, totalitarianism, and liberal democracy.

TOTALITARIAN PROPAGANDA: INSTRUMENTAL REALISM AND THE LIQUEFIED SUBJECT

Though written over half a decade prior to the book in which it would appear as an appendix in 1947, "Propaganda and the Nazi War Film" sounds a number of motifs that will be familiar to the reader who has just reached the concluding pages of *From Caligari to Hitler*. We find Kracauer analyzing German propaganda for what it tells us about German predispositions, and mapping the aesthetics of propaganda films—their characteristic editing techniques and camera angles, their narrative structures and "polyphonic" handling of sound and image—onto the totalitarian political system from which they derive. In other words, and in keeping with the

5. Original brochure of Kracauer's study on Nazi propaganda, 1942. (Siegfried Kracauer Papers, The Museum of Modern Art Department of Film Special Collections, New York)

impulse that fueled other research on "wartime communications" as well, Kracauer reads German propaganda symptomatically, using it to elucidate something about the nature of the enemy.[28] To do so, Kracauer first distinguishes between the voice-over commentary, the image, and accompanying music and sound effects as three different "channels" of cinematic communication. Attending to the ways these channels are alternately synchronized and opposed to one another, he parses recurring motifs in Nazi film propaganda and compares them to both Soviet revolutionary epics and German left-wing montage aesthetics. At the same time, he inquires into the symptomatic omissions of antisemitism and of the Nazis' own war casualties. Much of what he discovers in this way seems familiar enough today, and the elaborate "structural analysis" that he wishes to model appears overwrought, since it tends to produce insights that would be apparent without this methodological apparatus. What is interesting about Kracauer's analysis, therefore, is not so much that he shows how Nazi propaganda glorifies Hitler, how it arranges mass ornaments, how it sings the "Song of Songs of the German soldier," or how it exploits stark contrasts of light and darkness, white and black, dynamism and decay.[29] These insights are all incontrovertibly true, but they have the slightly impressionistic quality of surface observations strung together without much underlying logic or immediately obvious, generalizable consequences. In this sense, Decherney is certainly correct to claim that "Propaganda and the Nazi War Film" does not seem to offer a discernible theoretical framework.

And yet, as I have suggested, Kracauer's investigations evince a coherent, albeit implicit theoretical interest. The text's underlying sense of purpose becomes evident if we attend carefully to its central concern with the question of realism. Nazi propaganda, for Kracauer, constitutes an elaborate defense against reality; the Nazi film screen functions as a smoke screen that severs signs from their referents, reality from representation—and the viewing subject from its faculties for conscious reason and deliberation. Asserting that "the whole totalitarian system depended upon its ability to transfigure all reality,"[30] Kracauer defines Nazi propaganda in terms of its antirealist tendencies. This would hardly be surprising if it were not for the fact that Kracauer also defines cinema in terms of its penchant for realism. The use of film for propaganda purposes, in other words, involves an ontological contradiction: the assertion of reality by the film medium *and* its obfuscation by propaganda.

To a certain extent, the Nazi war film resolves this contradiction by strategically selecting its subject matter, a strategy Kracauer traces with a critical eye for omissions. The essay outlines the various ways in which film propaganda pursues its transfigurative task through ellipses that dramatize certain events and omit others ("a great deal of reality and enemy resistance disappears in the 'pockets' of the commentary").[31] But the tension between propagandistic fabrication and the cinema's reproduction of reality does not thereby disappear. Because of its claim to totality, Kracauer writes elsewhere, fascist propaganda "increasingly becomes caught up in antinomies and is consequently forced to shed ever more of its content and reveal ever more nakedly the will to power from which it derives."[32] Rather than resolve themselves, the antinomies of totalitarian propaganda assert themselves all the more powerfully in terms of its effects and in its instrumental approach to the medium of film.

Joseph Goebbels's respect for Eisenstein's *Battleship Potemkin* is well known. As he told a group of film journalists shortly after the Nazis seized power in 1933, *Battleship Potemkin* "is fabulously made, it is film art without parallel. [. . .] Whoever is not firm in terms of a world view could become a Bolshevist because of this film."[33] It only seems appropriate, then, that Nazi propaganda appears under Kracauer's gaze to engage in a kind of reverse engineering of Soviet cinema, from which Nazi propaganda borrows the epic structure and the emphasis on the collective but whose social realism it vehemently eschews. The formal hallmarks of this approach include, among others, a breathless pacing that refuses to allow spectators to come to their senses; a contrapuntal use of sound and image; and a "magic geography" of maps that show black enemy territory shrinking as if in fear of the advancing front lines of a brightly colored, expanding Germany. Captured by cameras that are "always panning, rising and diving," the image maintains a dynamic momentum that barely lets up.[34] What unites these various "film devices," as Kracauer calls them, is their collusion in obfuscating reality. Although Kracauer holds the medium of film to gravitate almost inevitably toward the rendering of profilmic reality, in the Nazi films under examination there remains no reality independent of its propagandistic construction. Its aim is precisely to erase any sense of "a reality based upon the acknowledgment of individual values."[35]

Instead, whatever reality the newsreels' documentary footage transports is turned into a means for propagandistic ends. Whereas he notes the emphasis on realism and documentation in official accounts and press reviews of campaign films like *Victory in the West*, Kracauer emphasizes repeatedly the *instrumentalization* of this appeal to reality by propaganda. Though the images may be unstaged, the editing upends their documentary value: style trumps ontology. The propaganda films, writes Kracauer, "are not concerned with portraying reality, but subordinate its insertion, and the method of its insertion, to their inherent propaganda purposes. These purposes constitute the very reality of the Nazi films."[36] Realism, an ineradicable dimension of even the most tendentious newsreel and indeed of the medium itself, becomes subordinate to the "reality" of the "totalitarian panoramas" Kracauer analyzes—which is to say: to the construction of political myths, historical half-truths, and "pseudo-realities" through the arrangement of its material.[37] Realism, the evidence of the indexical image, consequently becomes a propaganda tool—a strategic device designed to lower the spectator's defenses and make of her/him a pliable subject of totalitarian indoctrination. Thus, while the documentary material that led the American censors to classify and pass *Sieg im Westen* as a newsreel "bolster[ed] the impression that, through unfaked newsreel material, reality itself was moving across the screen," the propagandistic arrangement of this material "nipped in the bud any real meaning" that the documentary footage might convey.

Even as it embraces documentary forms such as the newsreel or the extended format of *Feuertaufe* or *Sieg im Westen*, Nazi propaganda bends them to inimical ends, substituting a second-order "pseudo-reality" for the reality effect that the documentary image portends. In so doing, it does not simply pass of fiction for reality, lies for truths. Nor does it invent and stage events ex nihilo to construct propagandistic scenarios from whole cloth. Rather than simply negate the relationship between cinema and any preexisting reality independent of its propagandistic construction, Nazi propaganda co-opts even the traces of that reality and integrates them into the totalitarian system. Film becomes a particularly powerful tool for instating the pseudoreality that is the ultimate object of fascist propaganda. An elaborate "screen dramaturgy" ensures that the medium's inherent realism, which Kracauer would subsequently theorize as the camera's affinity for the unstaged, the fortuitous, and the flow of life, is subordinated entirely to totalitarian ends. In Nazi Germany, "reality was put to work faking itself."[38]

The measured, occasionally even dry tone with which Kracauer analyzes Nazi film propaganda, let alone the schema of structural analysis that concludes "Propaganda and the Nazi War Film," betrays little of his encounter with *Sieg im Westen* and its audiences in the 96th Street Theater—except to note the way in which "people around me were noticeably amused and refreshed" by the interpolation of scenes from the soldiers' everyday life amid the barrage of maps, heavy artillery, and advancing armies.[39] Although it amounts to hardly more than a sideways glance at his neighbors in the theater, the palpable sense of reprieve that Kracauer observes speaks to his overall assessment of the film's relentless attack on the senses. In this context, the short interlude during which the soldiers take a break from their seemingly unstoppable march toward France becomes significant for his understanding of how the film shapes its message, the "sumptuous orchestration" of its "screen dramaturgy."[40] For the moment of amusement is but a brief respite with which propaganda baits the viewer. The inserted "camping idylls" may offer relief, Kracauer argues, but they do not permit release. Instead, "like spearheads, they drive wedges into the defense lines of the self, and owing to the retrogression they provoke, totalitarian propaganda conquers important unconscious positions."[41] The theater audience is treated to unstaged scenes only to make the staging of the film's message more palatable; allowed to take pleasure in the soldiers' everyday antics, the spectator will submit more readily to the film's politics.

Such a reading is symptomatic in the precise Freudian sense that Nazi propaganda's defense against reality indexes an underlying fear—namely, that it might fail in its totalizing and totalitarian aims: what if spectators begin to fill in the ellipses and "become aware of the void around [them]."[42] Kracauer detects this "secret fear" in the excessive nature of Nazi propaganda.[43] The onslaught of moving tanks, planes, and battalions seems to betray an implicit sense that "if, on the screen or in life, the dynamic power of that propaganda had slackened only for one single moment, the whole system might have vanished in a trice."[44] But far more importantly for our purposes, Kracauer appears to find the cause for this fear on the part of the Nazis in the very medium of film itself. It is as if the cinema, and particularly the "refractory" quality of the cinematic image, mounted an inherent resistance against its (ab)use by the Nazis.[45]

Already during the months leading up to his departure from France, Kracauer had taken extensive notes on a book on film aesthetics, in which he emphasized repeatedly the constitutive link between film and material reality: unlike theater, he noted there, "film brings into play the *whole world*," favoring endlessness over construction, and chance over necessity.[46] These are all traits that Kracauer will not fully and explicitly theorize as cinema's realist "affinities" until much later in the *Theory of Film* of 1960. There, he values precisely the realism of scenes such as the "campaign idylls" in which soldiers douse each other with water: in their seeming lack of motivation, such scenes appear to the author of the later book as manifestations of the "crude material life dear to the instantaneous camera."[47] The inclusion of this same crude materiality functions differently in the context of propaganda, where, Kracauer argues, it becomes instrumentalized.

It remains one of the unresolved contradictions of Kracauer's American work that in his early propaganda studies he does not trust the spectator to ferret out the unmotivated detail, the cinematic excess, or the humanity of the resting soldiers that might contradict their depiction as willing participants in a westward-moving war machine. As we shall see, Kracauer eventually regains that trust in the spectator, even as he substantially revises his sense of what kind of subjectivity might be at play in the cinema. During the early 1940s, however, and in the context of research on the totalitarian attack on the very notion of a human subject, the figure of the resistant, recalcitrant, let alone emancipated spectator remains impossibly remote.

And yet, I want to insist, there remains in Kracauer's thinking about the cinema an orientation toward the medium's inherent realism that provides a theoretical compass for charting even its most egregious abuses by the Nazis. Having begun working out his notions of "camera reality" in Marseille, Kracauer continued to weigh the question of cinematic realism as he analyzed Nazi propaganda during the year following his arrival in New York—and we can detect this notion of cinema as a realist medium at work behind the bleak assessment of manipulative images and duped spectators. For Kracauer remains convinced that, when it comes to cinema, "reality cannot be prevented from breaking through its delusive images"[48]—a claim that he backs up in at least two different ways in "Propaganda and the Nazi War Film."

The first of these comes, *ex negativo*, with the widespread recognition that Nazi propaganda (in this regard no different from many other forms of government communications then and since) skirts the issue of death. Apart from "two dead horses of enemy nationality," the campaign films show a war without casualties.[49] And yet, as Kracauer well knew, and as André Bazin would likewise emphasize, the reality of death and the realist powers of the cinema were closely linked. Death, wrote Bazin, "is surely one of those rare events that justifies the term ... *cinematic specificity.*"[50] That specificity, for Kracauer as for Bazin, has to do with the way the cinematic image puts the spectator into a relation with the reality of physical existence, of temporality, and of life. In some thought-provoking entries in his "Marseille Notebooks" two years earlier, Kracauer had noted the centrality of death in this gambit—the "death's head" that always shadows cinema's affinities toward lived, material existence.[51] Nazi propaganda contravened this tendency, since "the sight of death, this most definitive of all real facts, might have shocked the spectator deeply enough to restore his independence of mind, and thus have destroyed the spell of Nazi propaganda."[52] In its avoidance of death, Nazi propaganda betrays an (unconscious?) awareness of the powers of cinematic realism that it strains to hold at bay.

The second reference to the power of cinema's inherent realism comes in the form of an anecdote that Kracauer draws from a *New York Times* article about a German bomber pilot who had been shot down over Leningrad. As reported by the Russian author Tikhonoff, the pilot was forced to bail out after he had released his payload from an altitude at which he was unable actually to see his target. "As he drifted down the city came to meet him. He landed on the roof of a high apartment house and was found gazing wonderingly down onto the moonlit city."[53] The pilot is taken downstairs past bustling apartments, and the disjunction between Leningrad as a military target, on the one hand, and as a living city, on the other, becomes apparent. In Kracauer's retelling, this report becomes an allegory of spectatorship. Brought down from the aerial views supplied by the camera and the maps of the propaganda films to a street-level view of "busy lives" that Kracauer considers essential to the realist medium of cinema, the spectator relaxes as the world of material reality "comes to meet him." Under his wondrous gaze, that world asserts itself independently of its construction by propaganda—which is precisely the situation the propagandist "fears" and to whose avoidance he dedicates his resources.

In keeping with the psychoanalytic bent of this discussion, one might say that the fear of reality on the part of Nazi propagandists becomes externalized and directed against the spectator as an object of aggression. Kracauer is quite literal on this account, even as his language is metaphorical: if propaganda constitutes a form of psychological warfare, the Nazis wage that war on German audiences, including fifth-columnist, German-friendly crowds such as those in whose company Kracauer watched *Victory in the West* in New York: the war films, he argues, "tried to conquer and occupy all important positions in the minds of their audiences, so as to make their souls work in the interest of Nazi Germany. They treated souls like prisoners of war; they endeavored to duplicate in the field of psychology Germany's achievements in Europe."[54] In a motif that we find repeatedly in Kracauer's writings from the war and early postwar years, spectatorship is closely associated with paralysis; under the impression of totalitarian propaganda, world war, and the incipient cold war, Kracauer imagines audiences only as dupes, powerless to resist the overwhelming audiovisual stimuli issuing from the screen. As we shall see, he is hardly alone in diagnosing the fear-induced assault on the subject, both under totalitarian regimes and on the American scene (where he finds symptomatic indications in Hollywood's "terror films" of the 1940s). More curious, however, is again the fact that Kracauer's own film theory all along had also harbored resources for valorizing spectatorial subjectivity. To be sure, as I detail below, he vehemently critiques the propagandistic undoing of the subject. But he will welcome a similar undoing by the realist powers of the medium in *Theory of Film*.

Film propaganda, in Kracauer's reading, thus becomes a picture puzzle in which film appears alternately as the promise of realistic representation and as the principal medium of defense against reality. In attempting to solve this puzzle, Kracauer simultaneously begins to work out the theory of film that had begun to occupy him during his final years in France, and on which he would spend the better part of his American years. As exemplars of Nazi propaganda, films like *Victory in the West* constitute a limit case on which Kracauer first tests some of his theoretical convictions about the medium itself. For this theory, two aspects of Nazi propaganda are central: first, as I have been outlining, the abiding concern with realism as both style and ontology; and second, the question of propaganda's political effects on viewing subjects—whether in a Yorkville theater, among strategically selected international audiences, or back in Germany. Both are inscribed in the totalitarian project that the Nazis pursue through these films—a project that Kracauer, anticipating Arendt's more famous analysis, describes as distinct from merely despotic rule. Whereas the latter may banish the idea of freedom and the image of reality, Nazi propaganda "aims at totality" in the sense that it completely destroys reality's image and annihilates the very memory of freedom.[55]

As Kracauer shows, this process can become downright dizzying by design, to the point where "no one is sure whether [propaganda] serves to change reality or reality is to be changed for the purposes of propaganda."[56] It is in the resulting confusion, rather than in any of the manifest content or even in the putative "message" of these films and newsreels, that we should seek the ultimate and radical effect of totalitarian propaganda. For Kracauer, propaganda does not so much impart political messages as alter the very fabric of subjectivity. In order to demonstrate this radical power of Nazi cinema, he takes us down a rabbit hole of propagandistic invocations and denials of social reality, best exemplified by Leni Riefenstahl's film of the 1935 Nazi party congress, which Kracauer rechristens *Triumph of a Nihilistic Will*.[57] In a formulation that predates by twenty years Susan Sontag's analysis of Riefenstahl's "fascinating fascism," Kracauer writes:

> Aspects open here as confusing as the series of reflected images in a mirror maze: from the real life of the people was built up a faked reality that was passed off as the genuine one; but this bastard reality, instead of being an end in itself, merely served as the set dressing for a film that was then to assume the character of an authentic documentary. *Triumph*

of the Will is undoubtedly the film of the Reich's Party Convention; however, the Convention itself had also been staged to produce *Triumph of the Will*, for the purpose of resurrecting the ecstasy of the people through it.[58]

In this reading, Riefenstahl's film, while undoubtedly unique, exemplifies the structural features of totalitarian propaganda more broadly. In analyzing these features, Kracauer was able to draw not only on the incipient theory of film developed in the "Marseille Notebooks," but also on his earlier work, also in French exile, on totalitarian propaganda.

"TOTALITARIAN PROPAGANDA"

In early 1937, the Frankfurt Institut für Sozialforschung (now based in New York) commissioned a contribution on fascist propaganda for its journal, the *Zeitschrift für Sozialforschung*. Kracauer supplied an initial exposé titled "Mass and Propaganda," which he proceeded to elaborate in Paris, where Benjamin was simultaneously conceptualizing his famous essay "The Artwork in the Age of Mechanical Reproducibility," also for the *Zeitschrift* (in his piece, Kracauer cites an as yet unpublished version of Benjamin's text, with which he also shares some crucial conclusions on the political dangers of aestheticization). He spent the better part of a year working on the project, which drew on his earlier writings on class and culture in Weimar as well as on careful study of primary propaganda materials and scholarly literature. And yet Kracauer's contribution to the *Zeitschrift* never materialized as such. Citing both substantive concerns and the manuscript's unwieldy length, the members of the Institute refused to publish the piece. In the hands of Kracauer's Frankfurt friends in New York, the text underwent such drastic cuts and revisions that Kracauer decided to withdraw it from publication.[59] Adorno, Kracauer claimed, had distorted the article beyond all editorial custom to the point of appropriating it for his own ends. As he wrote to Adorno in the bitter exchange over the article, which would lead to a palpable cooling of their correspondence: "in truth, you have not edited my manuscript but used it as the basis for a study of your own."[60] While this may have been true (the redacted manuscript has not survived), Adorno was doubtless also right in replying that Kracauer might have dealt more pragmatically with the issue. "I can't help myself," he wrote in response to Kracauer's withdrawal of the article, "but I believe that the publication would have been in your specific interests."[61] Given the perceived need among American intellectuals and politicians to understand the fascist threat, Kracauer's study would almost certainly have opened doors in the

United States. Accepting the Institute's editorial interventions, in other words, might have shortened the Kracauers' suffering in French exile, which was to last and intensify drastically over the course of three more years.

Today, Kracauer's book-length essay "Totalitarian Propaganda" still reads as a trenchant analysis of fascist ideology.[62] The text's insights into the "anaesthetization of the masses" through propaganda aesthetics, into the deformation of subjectivity through terror, into the symptomatic truth of propaganda, and into the systematic undermining of democratic values are crucial to the formulation of not only "Propaganda and the Nazi War Film" but also *From Caligari to Hitler* as a whole. What is more, the study communicates directly with influential analyses of totalitarianism by Horkheimer, Hannah Arendt, and Franz Neumann. Although Kracauer's contract with the Institute and his work on this text predate his arrival in New York, "Totalitarian Propaganda" would have palpable repercussions for the recent émigré once he settled in Manhattan and embarked on a series of analyses of what we might label "illiberal cinema"—from Nazi propaganda to the political failure of Weimar as diagnosed in *From Caligari to Hitler*, to Hollywood's "terror films" and its pseudoliberal "movies with a message."[63]

"Totalitarian Propaganda" outlines the relation between propaganda, totalitarianism, and subjectivity in ways that resonate directly with the pamphlet that he authored half a decade later in New York. Drawing on primary sources from Italy and Germany, and in dialogue with the work of Horkheimer, Benjamin, and the Italian scholar and politician Ignazio Silone, this text represents Kracauer's most extensive and in-depth discussion of fascist propaganda. Even if Adorno apparently did not think so, the study at times skews heavily toward the Frankfurt School's brand of ideology critique, arguably betraying the circumstances under which it was commissioned.[64] At the same time, and although the book-length essay contains curiously few references to cinema (while *Sieg im Westen* and *Feuertaufe* had not yet been produced, it also seems that Kracauer had not yet seen Riefenstahl's film at the time, and encountered it first at MoMA, where Iris Barry had secured a copy), it provides a blueprint and an important, if unacknowledged, reference point for the analysis Kracauer undertook once he arrived in New York.

In particular, "Totalitarian Propaganda" develops a theory of propaganda's impact on the very structure of subjectivity. It is a materialist theory in that it concerns itself centrally and repeatedly with questions of ideology, capitalism, material interests, and class—building on Kracauer's own studies of the salaried masses in *Die Angestellten* and anticipating the centrality of the middle class for *From Caligari to Hitler*. And yet, in keeping with his own cultural critique of the 1920s, as well as with the basic tenets of the Frankfurt School, Kracauer also insists on the semiautonomy of culture and on the significance of what, in "The Mass Ornament," he had called "surface-level expressions." Though arguably "superstructural" in the vulgar Marxist sense, these surface expressions not only "provide unmediated access to the fundamental substance of the state of things";[65] they also have the same material power as ideology to affect the very core of subjectivity. It is no coincidence, then, that Kracauer's carefully researched manuscript reads as a disquisition on fascist ideology as much as a treatise on totalitarian propaganda. He is interested in the forms in which fascism appears, and in their effects. Kracauer advocates reading the surface-level expressions of propaganda, for only "the nature of the mask [might yield] the traits of the monster that dons it."[66]

To read this mask, Kracauer explores the various strategies of fascist propaganda, which range from the forms of aestheticization that Benjamin was working out in his artwork essay to outright terror, and from equivocation to mimicry.[67] Kracauer is concerned particularly with tracing the effects of such strategies at the "psycho-physical" level—in other words, in the construction of totalitarian subjectivity. In this regard, as I shall detail in subsequent chapters, he not only joins the ongoing projects of members of the Frankfurt School (some of which he references explicitly), but also anticipates the major studies of totalitarianism to come out of New York during the following decade, both by the Institut für Sozialforschung (Studies in Prejudice) and by Hannah Arendt.[68]

While it is ultimately terror that undoes the subject of propaganda in the most profound ways (to be traced below), forms of mimicry and equivocation that Kracauer identifies as characteristic of Nazi propaganda similarly play out in the realm of subjectivity. For totalitarian propaganda, according to Kracauer, does not simply produce the lie; it blurs the very distinction from truth. The "mission" of propaganda, as Kracauer already describes it in the 1936 manuscript, is "to generate an oscillation of lie and truth that makes it impossible to distinguish between the two, so as to induce in the recipient of propaganda the same confusion that befalls visitors of a mirror maze *[Spiegelkabinett]*."[69] Like Riefenstahl's film, which he will later analyze along similar lines, totalitarian propaganda puts the subject into a state of persistent vertigo *(Schwindelgefühl)*. This may result from the endless doubling of illusion and reality in *Triumph of the Will;* from propagandistic "mirror reflexes," which consist in the projection of traits of the national self onto the alien other (or, as Adorno puts it in his reformulation of Kracauer's prose, the fact that "propaganda declares of others that of which it is itself guilty");[70] from unpredictable but recurrent oscillations between truth and lie, "between fear and hope, pleasure and loss, hatred and love;"[71] or from the fear induced by totalitarian terror. This fear, Kracauer explains, "has a specific meaning in the framework of totalitarian propaganda. The hydraulic pressure under which it puts people is designed to liquefy the very structures *[Zusammenhänge]* that are considered to be most firm. [. . .] Chronic fear deracinates, unhinges the entire psycho-physical organization."[72] Caught in the unpredictable and oscillating snarls of propaganda, the subject of totalitarian rule is fearful, unhinged, liquefied.[73]

It is important to recall that Kracauer's 1937 analysis of totalitarian propaganda predates his careful study of the newsreel and is largely silent on film. Its analysis of propaganda's assault on the structure of subjectivity certainly resonates strongly with the ways one imagines Kracauer may have felt undone by audience reactions in the Yorkville theater, but it is somewhat less obvious how Nazi war films and newsreels "unhinge the entire psycho-physical organization" through their aesthetic, textual structures. In Kracauer's analysis, such structures appear manipulative, to be sure; but there is a clear sense in which the barrage of maps and advancing armies and the judicious use of voice-over seem almost persuasive to Kracauer, particularly when compared to the superabundance of commentary in American newsreels.[74] This is not to take issue with the underlying tenets of his propaganda analysis, but to suggest that this analysis develops its full force elsewhere. In order to take the measure of Kracauer's understanding of totalitarian propaganda, I suggest, we must turn to the most prominent fiction films flickering across German screens during the very same months in which Kracauer was elaborating his understanding of totalitarian propaganda in France and the United States. To do so, let us return to the movies on the other side of the Atlantic in the late summer of 1941.

3. Nazi Cinema

RETROGRAPHIC SELF-REVELATIONS: *HEIMKEHR*

What should be chalked up to oneself appears elsewhere instead.

SIEGFRIED KRACAUER, "Totalitäre Propaganda"[1]

In a busy small town, a marquee beckons audiences with a large star poster and the Fox weekly newsreel. Among the spectators pressing into the theater are the young cinema addict *(Kinoratte)* Marie and her fiancé, Fritz, accompanied by a neighbor from their hometown who has just been called up for military service. The theater is packed. Smoke and chatter fill the auditorium until the newsreel grabs the spectators' attention with images of swimsuit-clad women in an American beauty contest. Carl, the neighbor, smiles and tells Marie how attractive he finds the spectacle, but an angry spectator in the next row reprimands him sharply for talking. Now a military parade flashes on screen and the audience applauds. When the parade concludes with the national anthem, everyone stands to sing along—except for Marie, Fritz, and Carl, who get up but remain silent. This draws the ire of those around them; the crowd angrily demands that they join the singing. When the three refuse, a brawl ensues. The police are on hand but do not intervene. For Fritz, who is beaten by the irate crowd, the evening at the movies proves fatal. Having failed in their efforts to secure medical help for him, Marie and Carl are eventually forced to flee the city in their horse-drawn carriage with Fritz's corpse as their cargo.

This episode occurs about halfway through the 1941 German feature film *Heimkehr* (Homecoming/Return), directed by Gustav Ucicky. The sequence clearly signals the central role of cinema as a space of national(ist) discipline, and it might be seen as an illustration of Nazi cinema's role in creating and enforcing a German *Volksgemeinschaft*—were it not for the fact that

Heimkehr appears to reverse all the national signifiers. For Marie, Fritz, and Carl turn out to be the only Germans in this theater. Like the military that appears on screen, the nationalist majority here is Polish. The Germans, in turn, are the victims of murderous, rioting Poles and an inactive police force. The action takes place in 1939, but instead of the Germans preparing to invade Poland, it is the Polish army that gears up for war in the village streets outside the movie theater. Cinema is featured in the film as a nationalist medium of consent and coercion, but at the expense of the Germans.

Heimkehr hit German theaters in August 1941—roughly three years after the "Reichskristallnacht," during which the police had watched the anti-Jewish riots without intervening; two years after the Germans had unleashed World War II by invading Poland; and approximately a year after the Berlin premiere of *Baptism by Fire,* the propaganda film of the Polish campaign that Kracauer had encountered in New York earlier that same summer, and which he was analyzing along with *Victory in the West* as *Heimkehr* had its gala premieres in Berlin and Vienna. Once it began its run, the self-reflexive *Heimkehr* would have unspooled on German screens as part of the regular evening program, including the weekly newsreel. The latter would have elicited enthusiastic responses not for Polish but for German military triumphs (as becomes explicit in *Die große Liebe,* which premiered a year after *Heimkehr* and at one point features the star Zarah Leander as part of the audience taking in a wartime newsreel).

Heimkehr multiplies medial, national, and ethnic signifiers in a maze of semiotic mirrors. An anti-Polish propaganda film, it does not simply denigrate the Poles by showing them to be degenerate, debased, and simply different; it also casts them in many ways as *similar* to German society, its cultural practices and its national-socialist terror. The film takes this mirroring of the Nazi self in the Polish other to a confounding extreme: in ways that remain to be shown, *Heimkehr* depicts the lawless persecution and murder of German minorities in Poland in iconic images that belong to the history of the Holocaust—in other words, it mobilizes a visual archive of perpetration for the depiction of German victimization. This, I wish to suggest, is the kind of inversion that Kracauer had in mind when he described totalitarian propaganda as offering "Selbstenthüllungen in Spiegelschrift," or retrographic self-revelations.[2] Such inversions, indeed, are central to the project of Nazi cinema well beyond the propaganda materials Kracauer was analyzing. Though they play a central role in classical instances of Nazi propaganda such as Riefenstahl's films, Fritz Hippler's *Der ewige Jude* (The Eternal Jew, 1940), or Hanns Springer's *Ewiger Wald* (Eternal Forest, 1936), the full range of ideological motifs that he details in

"Totalitarian Propaganda" arguably pervade the Nazi feature film to at least the same degree.

Kracauer would view many of these films (apparently from a collection of captured prints) on behalf of the Museum of Modern Art and in close coordination with Frank Capra's Army Morale films unit during the summer of 1942.[3] Some of those films provide him with the opportunity to comment on the workings of Nazi ideology—its ability to obfuscate real social contradictions behind notions of the *Volk* and the *Volksgemeinschaft*, its heroization of death in *Hitlerjunge Quex* (*Hitler Youth Quex*, 1933, dir. Hans Steinhoff), or its regime of terror, for which Kracauer finds a referent in the pre-Nazi *Danton* (1931, dir. Hans Behrendt).[4] If I choose to focus here not on any of the films Kracauer discusses (he also viewed propaganda classics such as *S.A. Mann Brand* [1933, dir. Franz Seitz] and *Friesennot* [1935, dir. Peter Hagen]) but on *Heimkehr*—which presumably he did not see—it is because I find the latter to encapsulate these motifs in almost crystalline form: *Heimkehr*, I submit, is an ideal type of the admixture of entertainment and propaganda under the Nazis, on a par with the more frequently studied marquee productions such as *Quex* or *Jud Süß* (1940, dir. Veit Harlan). The film is full of confounding equivocations, which seem to operate on a psychoanalytic logic of projection, condensation, and displacement and which are by no means treated reflexively in the film; and yet, the film is unmistakably cognizant of its operations on some profound level, generating rather precisely the kind of "mirror maze" that Kracauer found to induce vertiginous effects in the viewing subject. His analysis helps to unpack the seemingly contradictory encounter of history and aesthetics, politics and textuality, in the film.

Heimkehr was one of only five films to receive the designation "Film der Nation" between 1933 and 1945.[5] It was a prestige production of Nazi cinema: launched by Goebbels himself in December of 1939, it spared no costs, consuming a full 40 percent of the production company's annual budget. Given the considerable star power involved, wages presumably accounted for the lion's share of the costs. Paula Wessely led the list, receiving top billing alongside her equally famous husband, Attila Hörbiger. Director Ucicky, who had worked with both of his main stars before, also teamed up again with the scriptwriter Gerhard Menzel, with whom he had already landed political and box office hits such as *Flüchtlinge* in 1933; together, they had also helmed two of the three most successful productions of 1940—the third being Harlan's *Jud Süß*.

According to the script, the film takes place in a small village in Volhynia, a Polish area that had been under Russian control until 1919. Today,

Volhynia is part of the Ukraine, but in the wake of the German invasion of 1939, and under the terms of a secret addendum to the Hitler-Stalin pact, it had fallen to the Soviet Union. By the time of the film's premiere, however, Germany had already launched the attack on the Soviet Union and advanced toward the east; when audiences first got to see the Polish military mobilizing for war outside the municipal cinema in the film, the area had in fact been occupied by the Germans. That said, the film itself was not shot in this geopolitically charged locale: location shooting for the village scenes took place in the German-occupied Polish town of Chorzele, whereas the municipality of Lutsk, where the trio goes to the movies, was elaborately staged in the Wien-Film studios back home.[6]

After premiering at the Venice film festival in August 1941, the film was first shown in Vienna and then had its German premiere in the fall of 1941, one of sixty-seven feature films that sold 892 million tickets in over seven thousand movie theaters in Germany during that year. Like the scene at the movie described above, such figures serve as a reminder of the role of cinema as the Third Reich's principal medium of propaganda and entertainment, rivaled only by the ubiquitous *Volksempfänger* (people's receiver) radio. But *Heimkehr* stood out. Praised by the streamlined press as a "great document of our times," the completed film was predictably deemed "politically and artistically particularly valuable" *(staatspolitisch und künstlerisch besonders wertvoll)*.[7] Goebbels counted individual sequences among "the best ... ever recorded for film."[8]

What was all the hype about? After the opening credits, two title cards superimposed over an image of furrows in a plowed field promise "the story of a handful of German people whose ancestors emigrated to the East many, many decades ago, since the homeland had no space for them." And yet the film that follows is concerned neither with the emigration to Poland, where the story takes place, nor with the ostensible lack of living space *(Lebensraum)*, but, as suggested by the title, with resettlement back to the "Reich." The experiences of these returnees, the title concludes, "stand for those of hundreds of thousands who shared the same fate."

The theme of returning to the homeland had already been popular in much earlier Nazi films such as Menzel and Ucicky's own *Flüchtlinge* or Luis Trenker's *Der verlorene Sohn* (1934). *Heimkehr*, however, uses this theme only as a pretext for its actual political agenda. For its fictional representation of how the so-called *Wolhyniendeutsche*, a German minority in eastern Poland, were mistreated by the Poles serves as a filmic justification after the fact for the German invasion of Poland in 1939. In addition, the film may have been designed to counter any public misgivings over the actual resettlement of ethnic Germans from Volhynia in late 1939 and early 1940.⁹

Heimkehr centers on a small ensemble of characters grouped around the strong and resolute Marie (Paula Wessely), who becomes both the incarnation of, and the spokesperson for, the German minority. The film shows their struggle to carve out a living, generate a sense of community, educate their children, and care for their sick in the face of growing harassment and persecution by the Poles. *Heimkehr* not only dramatizes various attacks on Germans but also shows how the Polish authorities tolerate a state of lawlessness.

The first extended sequence stages the expropriation of a German school by the Poles. The German minority is forced to watch as Polish boys and young men toss books and furniture (among them a blackboard showing the number of inhabitants and the population density of "Großdeutschland") into a bonfire. Marie attempts to intervene with the Polish mayor, but is no more successful here than in her appeal to the next higher authority in Lutsk. Brief cutaways to the Polish foreign minister Józef Beck show him expressing his regrets, shrugging his shoulders, and explaining that there is nothing he can do. After Fritz's dramatic death (which incidentally dispatches one of the major stars and the lead's romantic love interest only halfway through the film), Carl is apprehended and imprisoned on charges of having provoked the riot, despite his clearly being an intended victim. Further blows to the Germans follow: the Poles expropriate the "Deutsches Haus" without explanation or compensation; the German doctor is waylaid, shot, and blinded by Poles; and finally the upright Martha Launhardt is stoned to death by a Polish mob.

The taut series of dramatic events that occur between the lynching of Fritz at the cinema and of Martha by the local mob ends on a historic date: on August 31, 1939, the German community gathers around a *Volksempfänger* to listen to Hitler's speech on the eve of war between Germany and Poland. Like the cinema, the radio functions here as a medium of phatic communion, not only among the listeners in the village but also between them and the radio community in the "homeland."¹⁰ But this only increases the dramatic impact of the peripety when Polish police burst into the room and break up the peaceful gathering around the radio. Invoking a previously decreed limitation on the freedom of assembly, they arrest the Germans, herd them onto flatbed trucks, cover them with netting, and transport the entire group to a prison. Here, the Germans pass the night jammed together without food or room to move. Dimly lit long shots alternate with carefully illuminated close-ups of anguished faces to generate the sense of a *Schicksalsgemeinschaft* (community of fate) put to the test.

At this point, Marie emerges clearly as the luminous heroine of the film. With an impassioned paean to the values of *Heimat*, she rekindles her compatriots' hope, eventually leading them in a harmonious *Heimatlied*.[11] Despite this show of bravery and resolve, the Germans' fate appears sealed when the Poles move them into a basement room the next morning and soldiers open fire from machine guns inserted through small openings near the ceiling. But at this very moment, the German *Wehrmacht* comes to the (last-minute) rescue, first with planes and shortly thereafter with tanks that rumble into town and assure the liberation of the prisoners. The final sequence shows them on the westward trek toward the German Heimat, where an enormous image of the *Führer* awaits them as they cross the border "heim ins Reich" (home into the realm).

Goebbels could hardly contain his pathos in responding to the film, which he deemed "devastating and gripping"; some scenes, he opined, were "truly heart-rending *[auflösend]*."[12] One need not share the propaganda minister's enthusiasm to concede that *Heimkehr* is undoubtedly a well-made film: it is carefully scripted to bring conflicts to a head at dramatic moments; various ultimatums and other deadlines contribute to the forward momentum and the rhythm of the narration, which is underscored by the expressive music and the remarkably active, mobile camera. As a high-profile propaganda production, *Heimkehr* pulls all the stops and plays its audience in all registers.[13] By the same token, it helps to exemplify precisely the dizzying effects that Kracauer considered to be at the heart of totalitarian propaganda. In order to reconstruct the force of his argument in detail, it pays to attend to the historical and political equivocations that structure the film.

At first blush, as I have suggested, *Heimkehr* appears to narrate the resettlement of ethnic German minorities from the conquered Polish territories. The film's propagandistic intention in this regard is to narrativize and legitimate recent historical events. When Goebbels commissioned a film on the fate of the *Wolhyniendeutsche* in December 1939, Germany had already annexed Austria and the Sudetenland in the previous year and recently launched World War II with the invasion of Poland on September 1, 1939. The film is clearly designed to legitimate this act after the fact by depicting the atrocities committed by Poles against Germans.[14] Analogous to the German war propaganda and Hitler's infamous pronouncement of September 1 that "as of today we are returning fire," *Heimkehr* casts the war of aggression as an act of legitimate defense.

So much for the manifest political function of *Heimkehr*. However, by the time the film premiered at the Venice Biennial one and a half years later, the *Wehrmacht* had already advanced into the Soviet Union (where, among other things, it had now conquered Volhynia from the Soviets). With the help of the death squads, or *Einsatzgruppen,* of the Security Police and the *Sicherheitsdienst,* the Nazis had long since unleashed a rather different set of resettlements and acts of terror: broad swaths of the conquered Polish territories, now designated as the "Generalgouvernement," were Germanized by either murdering the resident Poles or herding them together in villages from which the Jewish population had previously been transported to ghettos and concentration camps. Whereas the film casts its story as one of German victimization under anti-German laws, the historical situation turns out to consist of a complex mix of ethnic populations in a largely lawless realm. By the time *Heimkehr* was completed and had its various high-profile premieres, the Germans were practicing the same forms of ethnic cleansing here as in the rest of the *Reich.* The national and ethnic reversals that we noted in the sequence at the movies in Lutsk, in other words, begin to proliferate: they define the film's treatment of the entire geopolitical situation at the time.

Just as importantly, however, we can trace these reversals at the aesthetic level as well. The dramatic structure of the film, its iconographic references, its intermedial allusions, and even its musical accompaniment all conspire to produce the dizzying forms of mirroring that Kracauer describes as typical of totalitarian propaganda. Attending to these various aesthetic dimensions of the film, we soon discover another ideological layer of this construct: beneath the legitimation of the invasion of Poland, there is a hidden and deeply contradictory but parallel discourse on the contemporary persecution of the Jews by Germans.

To unearth this discourse, we need only look more closely at the ways in which the German minority is mistreated in the film. The forced evacuation of the school at the beginning, for example, involves not only the destruction of furniture and the sadistic treatment of a caged bird (which a Pole tosses into the fire), but also a small-scale book burning. While Germans had engaged in this practice on a mass scale upon Hitler's seizure of power in 1933, the Germans in the film are depicted as law-abiding, pacifist citizens who suffer their fate seeking not revenge but only legal recourse: self-proclaimed "good angel" that she is, Marie implores her fiancé, Fritz, to check his manly impulses for revenge and his conviction that "violence can only be broken by violence."

In the film, the Germans have no rights and the Poles refuse to grant them their way of life. Early on, one of the Germans doubts whether "there are still any rights for us in Poland," and another rails against the practice of expropriation: "A state should not take the liberty of seizing other people's property," for after all even Poland has laws—"laws for the protection of minorities." It bears repeating that these sentences are uttered in a film screened in Germany in 1941, where the state for years already had routinely "taken the liberty" of seizing Jewish property and systematically disregarded, if not outright undid, any legal protection of minorities. From today's point of view, we can only speculate how contemporary viewers would have dealt with such quasi-schizophrenic contradictions—whether they would have perceived them as such in the first place, or whether the film was not designed, according to Kracauer's hypothesis on totalitarian propaganda, as "a probe, by which it reassures itself that the masses have been rendered fully submissive. In this way one calls a sleeper's name in order to confirm how fast he is asleep."[15]

Could spectators even have derived a sense of legitimization for acts of injustice from the fictional depiction of unjustly treated Germans? The film appears to harbor a knowledge of German crimes, which it displaces onto the Poles, so that one is tempted to infer a form of disavowal on the part of the audience: I know, but I don't know. By the same token, it confirms the validity of Kracauer's analytical terminology, which locates the particular cynicism of totalitarian propaganda in mirror reflexes and the undoing of logical oppositions between fact and fiction, truth and lie. "Instead of avoiding contradiction, [propaganda] exhibits it unthinkingly," he notes; truth becomes "totally reversed by attributing to the enemy precisely those deeds and machinations that are one's own."[16]

In *Heimkehr*, those machinations are not limited to expropriation and book burnings, but include public attacks such as the one that blinds Dr. Thomas or the murder of Carl by the mob at the movies—a murder that, like the others in the film, goes unprosecuted and unpunished. The lynching of Martha Launhardt, finally, underlines the pogromlike character of anti-German violence in the film: a shirtless Polish man tears off Martha's blouse; even though she is still able to evade his grip, he has managed to rip off her necklace as well. When he holds it up for the jeering bystanders to see, the camera lingers on the swastika pendant. This is followed, as I described above, by the prohibition on assembly and on radio listening, by the forced transport of Germans on flatbed trucks and the mass internment in the dark prison. Back at the cinema, an enraged Polish audience member had called for "exterminating *[ausrotten]* the German pigs"; but the *Wehrmacht* prevents this Polish "final solution" to the German problem at the last minute as a *deus ex machina:* in another liberty that the film takes with historical events, it is the Germans, not the Soviets, who force the Poles to flee the city.

It is difficult not to see in this catalogue of abuses visited in the film on the German minority precisely the kind of "mirror maze" that Kracauer finds characteristic of totalitarian propaganda—and its tendency to generate "retrographic self-revelations" in particular. For if we ask what forms of injustice Germans visited on Poles and Jews at the very moment at which they premiered a film depicting the heinous mistreatment of Germans by Poles, the parallels are rather staggering. As we know from historical research, the Polish campaign quickly led to the systematic expropriation of Jewish and Polish property after an initial phase of looting and confiscation. Expropriated farms and estates were later given to the resettled ethnic Germans from the Eastern regions. In two massive campaigns during the fall of 1939 and spring of 1940, the *Einsatzgruppen* had murdered more than fifty thousand Poles; another twenty thousand were transported to concentration camps, among them the camp at Auschwitz, which originally had been established specifically for this purpose.[17] These contexts are relevant for the production context of *Heimkehr*, because even during the shooting phase in early 1940 and around the very locations to which the team had traveled from Vienna, the *Einsatzgruppen* were carrying out the planned mass murder of Poles and Jews. Whereas the spectators in the cinema were to celebrate the westward trek of ethnic Germans "heim ins Reich" at the film's apotheosis, mass deportations in the opposite direction had long begun; indeed, the production team apparently crossed paths on its trip to the Polish location with a train full of concentration camp inmates.[18]

Historical events in occupied Poland hold up an inverted mirror to their representation in the film—but so does the persecution of Jews in Germany itself, which appears to have provided the foil for the film's fashioning of Polish atrocities. A month before the Berlin premiere of *Heimkehr*, Hermann Göring had charged Heydrich with devising a "comprehensive solution to the Jewish question." But Jews had already been subject to curfews since September 1939, and they had been forbidden from owning radios. Only weeks before the first spectators filled the showings of *Heimkehr* on Kurfürstendamm in Berlin, Nazi authorities had introduced the yellow star as compulsory identifier of Jews in public. This is not to mention the systematic erosion of legality and justice in the Third Reich.

It would be wrong to dismiss these and other parallels between the actions suffered by Germans in the film and those perpetrated by Germans in reality as mere coincidence. But how, then, are we to understand the filmmakers' recourse to images of Nazi atrocities? And how do we evaluate the film's explicit moral appeal to values that Germany had long since dispatched—including those of justice, the law, peacefulness, and empathy?

How should we imagine the contemporary reception of a monologue by Dr. Thomas, who toward the end of the film declares that "it should be forbidden to lie in your bed as long as someone else freezes to death outside in the street; forbidden to pat your stomach and burp contentedly, 'Gosh, I'm full,' when at the same hour, the same minute, the same second, hundreds of thousands of other humans moan in the agony of starvation, if they are still capable." How, in other words, should we understand such a moment in which contemporary reality appears to pierce the manifest propaganda content, even if only as an irritating, paradoxical symptom?

For Kracauer, propaganda becomes totalitarian to the degree that it manages not to hide but to make irrelevant such glaring contradictions. In the process, the integrity of the subject erodes. This has to do not only with the hydraulic pressure exerted by widespread terror, but also with the erosion of the distinction between self and other in a hall of mirrors. In Nazi cinema, the very notion of the "other" becomes permeable in the sense imagined by Kracauer: it is constituted as a projection, an inverse mirror image of the self. Whether we think of the Poles in *Heimkehr* or the Jew in *Jud Süß*, of the Puerto Ricans of *La Habanera* (1937, dir. Detlev Sierck) or the English who wage war on the Boers in *Ohm Krüger* (1941, dir. Hans Steinhoff), we can discern a distinct pattern of using the other to project traits that the self considers loathsome and pursues with heightened aggression against the other. As Kracauer puts it, "What should be chalked up to oneself appears elsewhere instead."[19]

Thus, the swarthy, authoritarian Puerto Rican Don Pedro may exert a temporary, fatal attraction on Zarah Leander's Astrée in Sierck's film, but *La Habanera* introduces a Nordic scientist as a foil to critique Pedro's tight-fisted, anti-American regime. In the film, the Caribbean island of Puerto Rico figures both as the racialized, tropical other, to be colonized, civilized, and democratized by the Western scientists, *and* as the projection of the isolated, authoritarian state that is Germany in 1937.[20] *Ohm Krüger* similarly deploys the British Empire in a double role as both oppressor of the Boer minority in South Africa *and* the mirror image of the German State of 1941. The film legitimates war against the English precisely by projecting onto them the decision to wage total war. Two years after the invasion of Poland, a year after marching into Paris, a few months after unleashing the Battle of Britain, and on the eve of the assault on the Soviet Union, *Ohm Krüger* depicts the British as the aggressor: halfway through, a British admiral outlines the need to put an end to sentimental talk of humanity *(Humanitätsduselei)* by burning farms, separating families, and forming concentration camps, making no distinction between military and civilians. What these films share with *Heimkehr*, in other words, is an imaginary projection of German victimization in order to legitimate an imperialist agenda.[21]

Need it be added that the inversions analyzed here share the logic of antisemitism? In the history of Nazi cinema, that logic is exemplified by the central aesthetic device in another state-sponsored film from 1941: the dissolve in Veit Harlan's *Jud Süß*. At the beginning of the film, a close-up of Württemberg's coat of arms dissolves into a similarly shaped sign with Hebrew lettering; subsequently, we dissolve from the protagonist as a bearded Frankfurt Jew with sidelocks to the clean-shaven Süss Oppenheimer on his way to Stuttgart. These and other dissolves merely exhibit the similarity between the ostensibly different images that they connect. Critics have seized upon this conspicuous device to pinpoint the visual logic of anti-Semitism in the film. Linda Schulte-Sasse sees in this construction of the Jew as other "the constitutive social fantasy of Nazism," but notes that "it is as if the film were revealing its projections onto the 'Jew' to be nothing but projections."[22] Eric Rentschler phrases a similar observation regarding the instability of projection in terms of the doppelgänger motif, noting that "the Nazis constituted a double, a self that they could acknowledge only in the form of a reverse image. The frightening reality intimated by *Jew Süss* is that under his masks the Semite is an Aryan."[23]

As if the dissolves in *Jud Süß* did not make the point clearly enough, Goebbels spells out the logic of antisemitism in a contemporary article published in *Das Reich*, one of his most perfidious diatribes. Under the title "Mimicry," he develops an invective against the Jewish ability to adapt, a trope familiar from canonical antisemitic literature and films such as *Der ewige Jude* or *Jud Süß*. But before long, the text begins unraveling: when Goebbels blames Jewish chutzpa for the claim that "not the murderer is guilty any longer, but the one who was murdered," we have arrived at the center of the hall of mirrors: an antisemitic text that imputes to the victims of persecution not only guilt, but also the ideology that underpins the inversion of guilt and innocence, aggression and victimization. Indeed, as if both aware of and oblivious to his own brazen logic, Goebbels goes on to note the inevitable undoing of this ideology at the hands of the ideologue. Thus, when he claims that the Jews, as manipulators of meanings and appearances, "begin to stumble" *(sich verhaspeln)* and "suddenly betray themselves" at the height of their rage, he might as well be describing the raging logic of his own text. Fittingly, this logorrhea culminates in the doubled exclamation that "it's the Jews' fault" ("Die Juden sind schuld! Die Juden sind schuld!"), thus enacting the gesture of blaming the victims, which he had initially laid at the feet of the Jews.[24]

For Adorno and Horkheimer, such projections are endemic to the dialectic of enlightenment: "There is no anti-Semite who does not feel an instinctive urge to ape what he takes to be Jewishness."[25] Goebbels is hardly an exception, developing in "Mimicry" precisely the ideological operation that Adorno and Horkheimer analyzed as "false projection" and "mimesis of mimesis" at the limits of enlightenment. "False projection," they write, "makes its surroundings resemble itself. [. . . It] displaces the volatile inward into the outer world."[26] As Kracauer likewise suggests, and as these few examples were meant to show, Nazi propaganda films involve false projection in this same sense. In films like *Heimkehr*, impulses that are not acknowledged by the nation and yet have been enacted by it (such as total war or ethnic persecution) are attributed to the national other: the country to be, or already, invaded.

This is precisely the claim that Kracauer had developed some years earlier in his broader discussion of totalitarian propaganda—which is to say: in the article that Adorno and Horkheimer had critiqued and rewritten beyond repair. As we saw in the preceding chapter, Kracauer argued that Nazi propaganda unwittingly revealed the self in a series of "mirror reflexes," thereby rendering legible the underlying visual repertoire, its politics and ethics, in inverted letters, or *Spiegelschrift*. *The Dialectic of Enlightenment* would pick up precisely this theoretical motif, arguing that "in the image of the Jew that the Nazis erect before the world, they express their own essence."[27] As Kracauer claimed and *Heimkehr* amply confirms, Nazi propaganda in this sense becomes an echo chamber in which various national and ethnic signifiers project and ricochet in profoundly disorienting fashion. The effects, however, were real, and terrifying by design. Having expelled and projected the aggressive traits of the self onto the other in the cinema and in accordance with the logic of antisemitism Nazi politics either reincorporated it through invasion—or annihilated it.

TOTALITARIANISM AND DEMOCRACY: BEYOND THE BINARY

Kracauer's analyses of Nazi propaganda earned him both interest and praise in Washington; indeed, he was for a time hopeful that his work would lead to gainful employment in the State Department.[28] John Marshall considered it a form of "genuine esthetic criticism . . . which is based on careful study and analysis." As such, he found it to be aligned closely with the Rockefeller's funding priorities, since it provided a "good example of the strictly humanistic outcomes of this kind of study."[29]

Closer to home, "Propaganda and the Nazi War Film" also garnered criticism from a politically astute, well-meaning friend. The art historian Meyer Schapiro, who had taken an interest in Kracauer's work after a mutual acquaintance brought the book on Jacques Offenbach to his attention in 1937, had done as much as anyone else to bring the couple to New York. When, within a year of his arrival, Kracauer completed his study on Nazi propaganda, Schapiro promptly wrote to congratulate his friend on his achievement. He admired Kracauer's facility with the English language as well as his analyses, of Riefenstahl's film in particular. But he also had "some political criticisms to make" of Kracauer's pamphlet. Anticipating later critiques of *From Caligari to Hitler*, Schapiro took issue with the author's tendency to posit an essential national character. From his own materialist standpoint, too, he questioned the primacy of culture over politics in Kracauer's approach to film.[30] What irked Schapiro most, though, was the dichotomous treatment of totalitarianism and democracy. Indeed, he went so far as to accuse Kracauer of having himself fallen under the spell of propaganda, albeit of the anti-totalitarian kind.

Specifically, Schapiro faulted the pamphlet for its all-too-neat equation of fascism with the emotional appeal of propaganda, and democracy with the ostensibly rational treatment of information. Did not democracy, too, rely heavily on "pseudo-reality" and propaganda, whereas notions of unbiased information were largely ideological constructs? In fact, did not American democratic culture produce the same kinds of spectacle, if not of the same magnitude, as the Nazis had put on at the Nuremberg party rallies? Accordingly, Schapiro opined, "almost everything you say about pseudo-reality and propaganda vs. information seems to me to describe a fully developed or extreme case of situations which we see clearly enough already in our own society."[31] In Schapiro's critical view, the American case was not as far removed from the Nazi menace as Kracauer wished it to appear; liberal democracy was hardly insulated from the totalitarian tendencies found in the propaganda films. As Hans Speier, one of the directors of the "Totalitarian Communications" project at the New School with which Kracauer was loosely affiliated, had put it succinctly in the inaugural issue of *Social Research*, "There is propaganda not only in dictatorships but also in democracies."[32]

Upon receiving Schapiro's letter (while on vacation in upstate New York), Kracauer acknowledged receipt and thanked his friend for his detailed engagement with his text. Unfortunately, we have no record of Kracauer's further response, which presumably evolved in subsequent personal conversations between the two men on his return to the city. During these conversations, Kracauer may well have referred back to his earlier work on propaganda, which he had defended against Adorno's massive editorial interventions by stressing precisely the point on which Schapiro was now most keen. As Kracauer put it in the tense correspondence with Adorno over the matter, the latter's reworking mischaracterized "fascism as a completed thing that can be confidently categorized. You identify it with counterrevolution from the start, place its interests in binary opposition to those of the majority, and omit the ambiguity of its relation to capitalism."[33] In other words, Kracauer here takes exactly the materialist position that Schapiro is looking for (and which one would have expected Adorno and the editors at the *Zeitschrift für Sozialforschung* also to adopt).

Although the conversation between Schapiro and Kracauer remains an object of speculation, we can trace some of Kracauer's reactions to Schapiro's critique in subsequent writings.[34] Not only does *From Caligari to Hitler* reference the latter's work, but in the revised version of "Propaganda and the Nazi War Film" that was later included in the book, we no longer find talk of "the natural inclination of Germans for thinking in anti-rational mythological terms." Instead, Kracauer only refers more circumspectly to a "traditional German penchant" in this regard.[35] And in the preface to the book, Kracauer explicitly distances himself from national essentialisms when he avers that "to speak of the peculiar mentality of a nation by no means implies the concept of a fixed national character." There, Kracauer also defends his methodological commitment to culture and "psychological tendencies" over the more traditional materialist categories of class and ideology, since "notwithstanding their derivative character, psychological tendencies often assume independent life, and ... become themselves essential springs of historical evolution."[36]

Nonetheless, Schapiro's principal critique concerning the dichotomy of propaganda and information, terror and liberalism, raises a larger point regarding Kracauer's work on German film during the 1940s—if not contemporary communications research on propaganda more generally: How sharply could one distinguish between education and propaganda, truth and deception, even in liberal societies?[37] To what degree was propaganda research such as Kracauer's concerned with national specificity, and how might it resonate in, or even translate to, the American context in which it evolved? What, indeed, were the politics of the critique of totalitarianism? For according to Schapiro, by portraying Nazism as radically different from liberal democracy, Kracauer undercut the possibility of recognizing totalitarian tendencies within democratic regimes—a crucial task for any progressive form of critique.

And yet Schapiro's implicit claim that totalitarianism and democracy differed only in degree, not in kind, arguably overstates the case in the other direction. As Kracauer wrote in a letter to Paul Lazarsfeld after the exchange with Schapiro, he was "quite willing to agree upon the fact that also democracies include much sham reality of the kind of the Nuremberg Party Congress" and that fascism had no monopoly on "stage-managing" mass communication.[38] Clearly still in response to Schapiro's critique that fascist propaganda was simply the "fully developed" version of tendencies incipient in democracies as well, Kracauer continued: "There is nevertheless a decisive difference between the sham reality here and there—a difference connected with the law that the steady increase of quantities leads, of necessity, to qualitative changes." The essential difference, he held, was that "whereas the democracies utilize to a certain extent staged effects, the maintenance of the Nazi system depends upon their exploitation. It is possible to imagine a democracy renouncing any such effects; the Nazi realm could not exist without these maneuvers of totalitarian propaganda." Asserting a difference in kind between totalitarianism and democracy, Kracauer concluded that Schapiro's more radical assertion of continuities leveled important distinctions that obtain between different modes of political spectacle, propaganda, and indeed, political regimes.

To put the matter differently, we might think of the political stakes that Schapiro's critique raises in terms of the different conceptions of totalitarianism by Hannah Arendt on the one hand, and the Frankfurt School on the other. Whereas Arendt always insisted on the incommensurability of totalitarianism, whose radically new character challenged even received categories of historical and political understanding,[39] the Frankfurt School tended to view totalitarian governments as outcroppings of "progress," as the all-but-predictable outcome of the entwinement of myth and reason analyzed in *Dialectic of Enlightenment*. Where did Kracauer's work fall in this spectrum? And what, consequently, were the politics of his film criticism and theory?

Like the other issues raised by Schapiro, these are questions to which Kracauer's two major film books can be expected to respond. Emerging from the early work on Nazi propaganda that it incorporates as an appendix, *From Caligari to Hitler*, in particular, does not simply chronicle the history of Weimar cinema but resonates with the political debates of the 1940s as well. For Kracauer undoubtedly framed his arguments in political terms—after all, as I have already mentioned, he thought of them as a contribution to psychological warfare and thus deliberately sought out and welcomed the political instrumentalization of his studies for government purposes. Like many of his fellow émigrés, he was explicitly interested in seeing his work taken up at the UN or in Washington, where, he claims, some of his early analyses of propaganda were indeed "well received";

arguably, they were even operationalized in the production of the Capra unit's Army Morale films.[40] In keeping with this sense of the political use-value of his research, Kracauer writes in the preface to *Caligari*, dated May 1946: "I have reason to believe that the use made here of films as a medium of research can profitably be extended to studies of current mass behavior in the United States and elsewhere. I also believe that studies of this kind may help in the planning of films—not to mention other media of communication—which will effectively implement the cultural aims of the United Nations."[41] In this sense, *From Caligari to Hitler* belongs to the corpus of political contributions that one contemporary reviewer labeled "win-the-peace-books":[42] as Kracauer put it in a preliminary report on the *Caligari* project, "[the book's] methods of approach to the core of a people's life may prove particularly interesting after the war when contacts will be resumed."[43]

Before that book was published, however, Kracauer penned an article for *Commentary* that seizes on some of the motifs he had developed in his analysis of Nazi propaganda—particularly the relation between terror and subjectivity that occupied him throughout the war years. While the article, titled "Hollywood's Terror Films," thus continues the investigations prompted by Kracauer's propaganda research, it shifts these to a new terrain, which will be the focus of the following chapter. As if in answer to Schapiro's misgivings about the binary distribution of terror and reason in totalitarian versus liberal politics, Kracauer now investigates the question of terror not in Nazi Germany but at the epicenter of American culture. Hollywood, too, could exemplify the illiberal power of cinema.

4. Freedom from Fear?

HOLLYWOOD'S TERROR FILMS

If you watch closely enough, you will find horror lurking behind the idyll.

SIEGFRIED KRACAUER, *Theory of Film*

When the influential journal *Commentary* was founded under the auspices of the American Jewish Committee in 1945, its principal editor, Elliot Cohen, described it as an act of faith—"faith in the intellect, in the visions of visionary men, in the still, small voices of poets, and thinkers, and sages." *Commentary*, he wrote in the editorial statement for the first issue, would "bring to bear upon our problems the resources of science, philosophy, religion, and the arts, by seeking out authentic voices and giving them open-house in which to be heard."[1]

This was a full-throated declaration of faith in Jewish traditions even in the face of the still-emerging facts of the Holocaust, of the atom bombs that had been unleashed only three months earlier, and of a general, deep postwar "unease of breathing air almost visibly clotted with fantastic utopias or unimaginable cataclysms."[2] But it was also a pragmatic faith in the editors' abilities to seek out and recruit those "authentic voices," to find the visionaries, poets, thinkers, and sages who would contribute to the fledgling journal.[3] In fact, in an era of intense competition for writers and contributors to the burgeoning field of "little magazines," especially in New York, faith alone would not fill the pages. Cohen ended his editorial statement on the image of himself and his fellow editors—among them Clement Greenberg and Nathan Glazer, soon to be joined by Robert Warshow—as well-diggers rolling up their sleeves. "And in the sweat of our brows, we dig."[4]

By the time the first issue hit the news stands, the group had dug up an impressive array of authors, described retrospectively by Glazer as an "odd mix" of Jewish and non-Jewish authors associated with other journals (most importantly with *Partisan Review*), German-Jewish émigrés, Ivy League professors, "and a varied group of left freelance writers."[5] Featuring the likes of George Orwell, Harold Rosenberg, Franz Rosenzweig, and others, *Commentary*'s roster of authors, as well as its editorial commitment to speak to both a Jewish and a general audience,[6] would turn the project into one of the most influential journals in a crowded field of publications—but not without further "digging" by the editors. And so, within four months of *Commentary*'s launch, Clement Greenberg reached out to another German-Jewish émigré. In a letter of March 27, 1946, Greenberg wrote in his function as associate editor to one "Dr. Kracauer" to inquire whether he might write "an article for this magazine on the Jew as portrayed in the movies." Noting that the editors were familiar with his writing, he assured Kracauer that they "very much desire[d] to have [him] contribute to *Commentary*" and invited him to offer alternatives if the subject suggested by the editors did not appeal to him.[7]

Although Kracauer was hard at work on the *Caligari* book at the time, he still depended on freelance work to supplement his own and his wife's limited income. Accordingly, he took up the invitation from the well-paying journal and submitted a manuscript titled "Freedom from Fear: An Analysis of Popular Film Trends."[8] The ensuing editorial process made for a somewhat rocky start, but this exchange initiated a relationship with *Commentary* and with its editors that would last for years to come—resulting in further publications and a lasting intellectual friendship with Robert Warshow, in particular.[9]

When Kracauer's article appeared in the August issue, it had been retitled "Hollywood's Terror Films." Although the author did not approve of the change, the new title did have the advantage of naming at the outset the principal "popular film trend" that the piece would analyze. It was a recent trend, and Kracauer considered it disturbing. In his view, Hollywood was ringing in the postwar era by continuing, if not increasing, its wartime habit of depicting sadism and spreading fear. With its relatively short cycle of anti-Nazi films, launched by Warner Brothers' *Confessions of a Nazi Spy* (dir. Anatole Litvak) in 1939, Hollywood had joined the fight against Hitler by depicting "a reign of terror ranging from Gestapo tortures to ever-impending threats, from shining parades to silent agonies, all of it bathed in the oppressive atmosphere of Nazi-conquered Europe."[10]

But what had been justified during the war years, when the turn to violence was motivated by the need adequately to depict the Nazi enemy, now took on a different set of meanings altogether. In recent films such as *Shadow of a Doubt* (1943), *Dark Corner* (1946), and *The Spiral Staircase* (1946), that same oppressive atmosphere had come home to roost, with criminals settling in plain American towns, breeding insecurity and springing murderous traps. In these films, Kracauer averred, "the weird insecurity of life in German-occupied countries is shifted to the American scene."[11]

What was troubling, then, was not so much these films' generic interest in horror—"thrillers," after all, were "a venerable type of film"—but the particular modulations of sadism and fear that they expressed. Kracauer considered the recent wave of "terror films" to go beyond the conventions of the genre, whether anti-Nazi or thriller, which had previously stipulated clearly identifiable villains and patently fictional scenarios; instead, those scenarios had now become everyday, and the villain was no longer clearly indistinguishable from everyman: "evil no longer marks and defines a person's face or manner."[12] The titular terror had become pervasive.

The essay is thus full of formulations that convey the perceived permeation of postwar existence by feelings of panic, fear, horror, and dread. In Hollywood's terror films, Kracauer wrote, "everyday life breeds anguish and destruction," and "panic ... saturates the whole world."[13] Inanimate objects take on threatening dimensions; *Spiral Staircase* mixes movie houses and murder scenes, while the *mise-en-scène* of bars and pawn shops turns *Dark Corner's* lower Manhattan into a dark and duplicitous urban space. As the boundary between the thriller's generic settings and the "American scene" erodes, so does that between films and their social context. Reading the films symptomatically, Kracauer finds "sadistic energies at large in our society," where an "all pervasive fear ... threatens the psychic integrity of the average person."[13]

To more recent cinephiles and film scholars, these descriptions of Hollywood's signature films from the mid-1940s will have the familiar ring of descriptions of film noir. Though the term had not yet been coined, Kracauer's short piece already assembled all of the principal narrative, thematic, and stylistic aspects that subsequent critics have traced in this genre: the significance of its dark settings; excessive, unmotivated violence; the role of sadism—and the central motif of fear and "terror." In addition, Kracauer's essay invites us to reconsider the historical specificity of the films he discusses. In particular, spatial considerations play a central role, as Kracauer imbues aspects of set design and *mise-en-scène* with psychosocial content.[14]

Space in these films is opaque, "chance arrangements of inanimate objects are made conspicuous, somber backgrounds assert themselves." Repeatedly, *mise-en-scène* appears to conspire against the protagonists. Trying to understand who exactly is framing him for what, the private investigator in *Dark Corner* moves about a lower Manhattan that looks like a "region of anarchy and distress, [. . .] a realm in which dumb objects loom monstrously high and become signal posts or stumbling blocks, enemies or allies."[15] Nor is this depiction of space limited to noir: it is in this same essay that Kracauer reads the flimsy construction (if not complete lack) of spatiotemporal unity in Disney's *Three Caballeros* (see chapter 1) as indexing a "universe torn to pieces as though it had been hit by a cluster of atomic bombs."[16] In these spatial references, the "terror" of the title translates into the postwar and post-Hiroshima moment in which Kracauer is writing.

At the same time, Kracauer discovers in contemporary noir the familiar signs of Weimar cinema. Working out the argument of what will soon become *From Caligari to Hitler*, he appears to overlay the history of German film—from which scores of directors, writers, and technicians had immigrated to Hollywood—onto Hollywood. Consequently, we find the spaces of Weimar cinema asserting themselves as yet another spatial layer in "Hollywood's Terror Films": Kracauer explicitly compares the representation of Third Avenue in *Dark Corner* and *Lost Weekend* to "shots of street life [. . .] prominent in German films of the pre-Hitler Weimar Republic period that described the tragedies of instinct-possessed beings."[17] This palimpsest of spaces culled from Hollywood and Weimar, imbued with meanings that range from pretotalitarian to postatomic, becomes labyrinthine in its own right: it is difficult to discern whether Kracauer is proceeding chronologically here, or whether, as I suggest in the next chapter, he entered Weimar through film noir, reading the prewar origins of totalitarianism through its postwar consequences.

Accordingly, beyond the spatial sensitivities that Edward Dimendberg rightly attributes to Kracauer,[18] this text also develops a significant temporal dimension, indicating its precise historical locus. Elaborating a labyrinthine notion of space, "Hollywood's Terror Films" describes a time out of joint. While the fear and violence that characterize these films in Kracauer's view had their rightful, politically and aesthetically motivated place in the anti-Nazi film of the war years, they now appear to him unmoored and unmotivated—persisting as an atavism, an apparently nonsynchronous feature out of step with any sense of postwar normalization. We get a picture of temporal and political suspension—a zero hour that Hannah Arendt describes elsewhere as the "abyss of empty space and time"[19] between the "no longer" of the recent war experience and the "not yet" of any recognizable postwar order. In political terms, it is an uncertain time between the recently vanquished threat of Nazism abroad and a potential rise of fascist tendencies in the United States. Kracauer's 1946 piece for *Commentary* registers this suspension of time, using cinema to describe a postwar present that is neither fully closed off from the past nor ready to confront implications of that past in order to rebuild. This is a present, in other words, that is neither stable in its direction nor open to the future in any clearly discernible way. Though not devoted to the question of temporality per se, "Hollywood's Terror Films" takes aim at the peculiar historical limbo crystallized, for Kracauer, in the disintegrating universe of *The Three Caballeros*, where—just as in film noir—"dark impulses are sure to find freer play."

FREEDOM FROM FEAR: TERROR AND THE LOSS OF EXPERIENCE

> Chronic fear deracinates.
>
> SIEGFRIED KRACAUER, "Totalitäre Propaganda"

In a reference to Roosevelt's 1941 State of the Union address, which subsequently became known as the "Four Freedoms" speech, Kracauer had originally entitled his *Commentary* article "Freedom from Fear." In the speech before Congress, Roosevelt listed four freedoms central to his vision of the American democratic polity.[20] The first two were the positive freedoms ("freedoms to") of speech and religion—principles grounded in a discourse of universal human rights. In outlining the second two freedoms, by contrast, Roosevelt was clearly, if implicitly, responding to the more specific and recent experience of depression and war: emphasizing the importance of "freedom from want" and "freedom from fear," he articulated the widespread sense that both want and fear posed threats to democracy every bit as serious as the undermining of free speech or the freedom of religion.

Looking forward "to a world founded upon [these] four essential freedoms," Roosevelt's speech all but acknowledged the persistence of these threats in the present. Whereas the wartime economy and the policies promulgated under the New Deal would eventually alleviate the most acute effects of the depression, the sense of fear remained enduring and pervasive, leading E. B. White to declare, in the middle of what Arendt called "the long Roosevelt administration":[21] "I live in an age of fear."[22] We have seen variants of this affect play out in the form of "terror" in Kracauer's investigation of Hollywood, and, as I argue in the next chapter, the same sense of paralysis structures his contemporaneous study of Weimar cinema. Both his increasingly somber view of Hollywood and his bleak view of German cinema before Hitler, I now want to suggest, must be viewed in the context of a broader discourse during the 1940s on the relation between terror and politics, fear and subjectivity, culture and democracy.

To be sure, Kracauer was virtually alone in his turn to cinema as a medium in which to register, critique, and ultimately work through these issues. But while this makes his voice unique, he also joined a chorus of others investigating authoritarianism, political paralysis, and above all the lingering sense of fear, through social research, political science, and critical theory. In this sense, Kracauer belonged to a group that Ira Katznelson has recently described as "particularly attentive" in the way it "watched and evaluated how the New Deal took up custody for liberal democracy."[23] That group included Kracauer's Frankfurt friends, who were involved, during the 1940s, in a major series of "studies in prejudice" designed to identify antidemocratic tendencies and unmask fascist agitators as "prophets of deceit."[24] Prominently, the group also included Hannah Arendt, who was working out the arguments for her later *Origins of Totalitarianism* in essays she was publishing in the same journals—*Partisan Review* and *Commentary*—in which Kracauer's writings on film appeared during the 1940s. And it included the broader coterie of New York Intellectuals identified with those journals, who likewise were seeking to articulate the postwar predicament in terms of the relation between cultural hopes and anxieties, between the threats to democracy and its resilience.

Though formulated in various ways, depending on the disciplinary background of a given contributor and on the more or less scholarly character of different publication venues, these attempts of intellectuals to make sense of their time often amounted to a critique of terror and fear, as well as an examination of their effects on politics and on political subjects. Contributions ranged from sweeping assessments of the general atmosphere of fear all the way to diagnoses of the very structure of personality and individual (in)capacity for action ("paralysis"). In Mark Greif's compelling account, this was an "age of the crisis of man."[25] The debates, at once maieutic and urgent, that shaped this age took aim at the area where politics, culture, and the personal meet, shuttling back and forth between seemingly irreducible individual affect, representation, and the civic life of democracy. Whether discussing the "crisis of the individual" in a series of journal articles, investigating the origins of totalitarianism, or studying forms of antisemitic prejudice, scholars and public intellectuals from Arendt to Löwenthal and from Adorno to Lasswell were seeking to contribute, like Kracauer, to understanding the political consequences of "Hitler's ascent and ascendancy";[26] their analyses coincided in an urgent interest in how the persistent threat of terror undid and rewired basic human responses—and by extension the very foundations of democratic subjectivity.[27] Whether writing as public intellectuals in the little magazines or as scholars affiliated with the Institute for Social Research and the American Jewish Committee, these authors shared Kracauer's pressing concern for democracy as a problem of representation and for the place of the human subject in the machinations of political orders.

Although the sources of this concern would appear to have lain overseas, in the rise of fascist movements and governments and in the resulting war that the United States joined both in Europe and in the Pacific, the sense that antidemocratic tendencies might gain a foothold in the United States had emerged soon after Mussolini's rise to power in the early 1920s. In Mussolini's wake, dictatorship gained a distinctive, if ultimately passing, appeal in America.[28] This American "romance" of the dictator found cultural expression in everything from the apparently unproblematic branding of a new car model as "The Dictator" to a film such as *Gabriel over the White House* (1933, dir. Gregory La Cava), which imagines a passive Herbert Hoover–like president made over into a Roosevelt-like activist by a car accident. Apparently imbued with a sense of God-given duty (he had been visited in his coma by the titular angel), a completely transformed president assumes and expands executive powers to right the social wrongs plaguing his nation. At the climax of the film—which is full of references to contemporary concerns about crime, unemployment, and the 1932 "Bonus March" of WWI veterans on Washington, D.C.—the president defends his decision to suspend Congress if necessary. Accused by a Congressman of imposing dictatorship, that quintessential "other" of democracy, the fictional president fires back: "If what I've planned to do in the name of the people makes me a dictator, then it is a dictatorship based on Jefferson's definition of democracy: a government for the greatest good of the greatest number."

The American romance of dictatorship was ultimately short-lived, but the fears on which it had fed grew throughout the Depression era and took on specific political form after the entry of the United States into World War II in the wake of Pearl Harbor. Already in July 1940, a poll showed that almost three out of four Americans believed the Nazis had already begun to organize a fifth column in the United States. Activities of the Bund and screenings of *Victory in the West* in major cities during the summer of 1941 only reinforced this sense of infiltration, as did the pervasive presence of right-wing orators who emulated Nazi leaders in an attempt to sway public opinion. These figures, among whom Fritz Kuhn and Father Coughlin were merely the most visible, had been the object of explicitly anti-Nazi films such as *Confessions of a Nazi Spy*, whose lingering effects Kracauer would later trace in "Hollywood's Terror Films."[29]

The perceived threat that fascism might take root in the United States outlasted the war; nor did that threat disappear with the advent of the Cold War, even if the McCarthy era coined the dubious notion of "premature antifascism" to brand as communist those who had taken that threat too seriously too soon. As attention began to shift from Nazism and Italian Fascism to totalitarianism as an overarching concept that also included Stalinist socialism, numerous studies appeared to confirm the latency of fascism in American society. Fusing empirical social research with psychoanalytic approaches, these studies tended to focus on personality structures, the correlation of different forms of prejudice, and the links between personality and ideology.[30] The conclusions tended to be dire. Weighing recurring and patterned forms of prejudice against less pronounced "democratic patterns," investigators warned of the continuing threat that protofascist mentalities held for the liberal order. As a reviewer of several such studies concluded, "American culture, by creating personalities that need race prejudice to maintain their psychic balance, has created an enormous potential for fascism."[31]

A number of theses studies were commissioned by the American Jewish Committee, which partnered with Horkheimer's Institute for Social Research on the major initiative to study prejudice across various domains—from antisemitism in imperial Germany to empirical investigations of the "authoritarian personality" in the contemporary United States. As I discuss in the following chapter, the latter study, which was coauthored by Adorno, constitutes an important intertext to Kracauer's *From Caligari to Hitler*. But another book from the "Studies in Prejudice" series, an investigation of fascist fear-mongering published in 1949 as *Prophets of Deceit*, is of immediate relevance here too. The book, coauthored by Leo Löwenthal and Norbert Guterman, was designed to offer "diagnostic insight into [a] latent threat against democracy."[32] Without exaggerating the role of demagogy in the early postwar years, it bespeaks the enduring sense of threat emanating from the "agitators" (as the study calls them) who had captivated audiences before and during World War II.

These orators played, Max Horkheimer suggested in terms he might as well have lifted out of *From Caligari to Hitler*, "upon psychological predispositions" that were socially created but latent, amenable to psychoanalytical decoding.[33] Taking their cue from Horkheimer, Löwenthal and Guterman consequently studied agitation as a "surface manifestation of deeper social and psychological currents." They showed how the agitators exploited a pervasive sense of social malaise, painting a hostile world in which atomized individuals could only be saved from life-threatening conspiracy by the "Great Little Man" as which the agitator liked to portray himself. Reading "agitational themes" the way Kracauer read both Hollywood and Weimar cinema around the same time, Löwenthal and Guterman claimed that these themes "directly reflect the audience's predispositions"; in order to decipher the "psychological Morse Code" in which the diatribes were delivered, one had to look like a psychoanalyst for their latent social meanings.[34]

In light of interventions such as Löwenthal and Guterman's, but also given the American romance of the dictator and the public presence of such figures as Kuhn and Coughlin, the title of Nobel laureate Sinclair Lewis's 1935 novel *It Can't Happen Here* was easily deciphered by contemporaries as the ironic warning as which it was intended. The resistance that book met in Hollywood only deepened its author's sense that "democracy is certainly on the defensive."[35] Nervous liberals, to adopt Brett Gary's useful phrase, reacted by revising their trust in the people (now reconceptualized as dangerous "masses") and advocating an "expert-centered national security liberalism."[36] Even before the American entry into war, the prominent political scientist Harold Lasswell, to offer but one example, had pondered the "possibility that we are moving toward a world of 'garrison states,'" in which the dominance of the businessman, expert in bargaining, would be replaced by the supremacy of the soldier, expert in violence. This state was new, not because of the dominance of the military, but because of the novel alliance between military, violence, and technology. Describing his construct as "frankly imaginative," Lasswell nonetheless insisted on its relevance as a heuristic for gauging current and future realities. In particular, he noted that the rise of what he called "modern violence"—whether in the form of military aggression or totalitarian terror—led to a pervasive "socialization of danger" and the universalization of fear.[37]

Formulated by Lasswell in the terms of political science, these tendencies clearly occupied contemporary observers and public intellectuals at large. Nowhere were they sensed to be more pressing, perhaps, than in the circles of New York intellectuals concerned with positioning themselves and their understanding of culture and political subjectivity in relation to fascism, Stalinism, and liberal democracy. We find the New York Intellectuals debating these issues, for example, in a series of articles that *Commentary* devoted to "the crisis of the individual." Taking as their point of departure the profound violation of human and civil rights and the utter dehumanization of millions in the Holocaust, the editors voiced their suspicion that this development was "more than a temporary by-product of war." Beginning in late 1945, a few months before Greenberg contacted Kracauer, and over the course of the year that followed, commentators were invited to "treat the problem, not in hortatory fashion or noble abstractions—neither to preach nor to scold—but to analyze, appraise, and give us fact and judgment, and if possible guidance and new objectives."[38]

In the editors' brief, terror was implicitly totalitarian—but commentators tended to trace both its roots and its effects across the ostensible divides between fascism and democracy, socialism and liberalism. By and large, the tone of the contributions was declensionist and conservative, a lament over lost values and traditions dating back to the eighteenth century or—in the hands of contributing *Commentary* editor Sidney Hook—an anticommunist affirmation of liberal pragmatism.[39] Some, however, laid the reasons for the contemporary situation at the doorstep of liberalism itself. Thus, the prominent philosopher John Dewey noted the intrinsic tendency of industrial capitalism to reduce "the mass of human beings . . . to a state of insecurity and fear" through ever accelerating spirals of depression.[40] And Hannah Arendt traced the current crisis back to imperialism, turning to Hobbes as "the only first-rank philosopher who ever stated the hidden principles implicit in bourgeois attitudes." As she would later work out more fully in *The Origins of Totalitarianism*, the decline of the nation-state was linked to the terror of the classless mob and the essentially egalitarian threat "that each man can kill his fellow-man," which hovered just beneath the surface of the liberal order.[41]

Dewey and Arendt shared the critical diagnosis of a profound and unsettling sense of fear with the more conservative contributors to the series. Running beneath the political differences, in other words, was the common motif of disorientation, uncertainty, and dread that Paul Valéry had articulated already in the interwar period. Pitting hope against fear, he found the latter to have won out in ways that resonated for the contributors to the series in the mid-1940s: "We fear the future, not without reason. We hope vaguely, we dread precisely; our fears are infinitely more precise than our hopes."[42] But it was Leo Löwenthal, Kracauer's Frankfurt friend and a member of the Institut für Sozialforschung, who spelled out the historical dimensions of terror with the greatest specificity and force.

In his contribution to the *Commentary* series, Löwenthal described the effect of terror as the "atomization of man"—a diagnosis that he derived from his analysis of fascism, but which (in keeping with the work of other Frankfurt School authors such as Franz Neumann and Otto Kirchheimer) he considered "deeply rooted in the trends of modern civilization, and especially in the pattern of modern economy."[43] Viewed in the perspective of the camps and the Holocaust, the "crisis of the individual" was nothing short of the "breakdown of personality," most evident in the loss of victims' capacities for fantasy, imagination, and memory. In terms that would become consequential for Kracauer's analysis of the relation between cinema and experience, Löwenthal analyzed the effect of these transformations as the collapse of experience, which transformed the human being "from an individual, whose essence is continuity of experience and memory, into a unit of atomized reactions." Terror, in other words, undid human subjectivity. Without the capacity for experience, one could no longer speak of the individual; personality had shrunken to a "cluster of . . . reflexes" conditioned by expected, avoided, or materialized shocks. Consequently, there was no longer any sociality to speak of—under conditions of terror, humans lose their sense of responsibility toward others and revert to a state of nature, to raw material, or to "surplus" to be annihilated.[44]

This analysis of fascist terror and its impact anticipates rather precisely Hannah Arendt's more famous account of totalitarianism. But like Arendt, who finds the origins of this phenomenon to predate the Holocaust (in the rise of nineteenth-century antisemitism and imperialism), Löwenthal traces totalitarian terror not simply to fascism as the radical other of democracy, but to "certain cultural tendencies emerging from the crisis of the liberal era."[45] In other words, while Löwenthal undeniably derived his definition of terror from its actual implementation by the Nazis, seeing it as the very essence of totalitarianism, he tracked its effects to the ground of homegrown fears. In particular, Löwenthal identified a pervasive sense of shelterlessness that derived from a nonsynchronous "tradition of individualism" in the age of "modern collectivism." Bereft of genuine experience, modern man "feels alone, deprived of the material and moral heritage which was the basis of his existence in liberal society."[46]

Drawing on another famous speech by Roosevelt, Ira Katznelson titles his recent, thought-provoking reassessment of the history of the New Deal *Fear Itself*. In keeping with the image presented above, Katznelson describes that era as pervaded by an "ambit of permanent fear," which "provided a context and served as a motivation for thought and action both for America's leaders and ordinary citizens."[47] In keeping with Gary's analysis of the nervous liberals' reactions to this situation, Katznelson describes how government policy was formulated as a response to the perceived need to "restore a higher degree of coherence and certainty."[48] Although his analysis focuses mainly on the level of policy, Katznelson helps to outline the significant changes that fear wrought at the level of subjectivity. For as he describes it, an overwhelming sense of contingency rendered decision-making unmanageable, thus challenging citizens' ability to participate meaningfully in democratic politics. Caught in a broader "atmosphere of unremitting uncertainty about liberal democracy's capacity and fate,"[49] people perceived threats and risks as fundamentally unmeasurable, exceeding the subject's capacity to assess and act on them. In this regard, Katznelson's analysis resonates with notions of the "risk society" developed for a broader, less historically specific understanding of modern social structures. Framed by world wars, carpet bombing, and nuclear bombs, the New Deal, then, would appear as an emblematic historical instance of this broader concept.[50] What we might describe as a historical "emotional regime" of fear put pressure on liberal values, if not on the construction of subjectivity itself.[51]

Like his propaganda analysis, which had sounded the motif of fear in emphasizing propaganda's impact on the "psycho-physical structure" of the individual and the liquefication of the subject, Kracauer's writings on Hollywood belong to this moment. His "terror films" would have resonated in their historical and intellectual contexts not only with the potent, if diffuse, political affect of fear, but with specific ideological concerns that he ultimately spells out in the essay. Thus, he reads Hollywood's turn to terror not as fascist per se, but as the index of an "emotional preparedness." That preparation, moreover, consisted precisely in the kind of widespread fear that others as well had diagnosed as a sign of the age, and that prepared the ground for the "agitators and rabble rousers" whom Löwenthal and Guterman studied in *Prophets of Deceit*.

This fear, Kracauer concluded, "springs from a crucial dilemma," which he couched in terms of the nascent Cold War's polarities. Critical of the "system of free enterprise" that ensnarls its subjects, Kracauer could no more abide "the totalitarian potentialities inherent in any system of planned economy." But like the contributors to the *Commentary* series who had deduced the "crisis of the individual" from the liberal order itself (rather than simply pointing to the totally "other" totalitarian enemy, as Schapiro had accused Kracauer of doing), he considered the paralyzing nature of fear to be homegrown, endemic to liberalism in its *laissez-faire* variants. In this reading, it is not Nazism or Stalinism, but democracy itself that, "based upon individual freedom, seems economically out of joint;" consequently, Kracauer avers, the liberal order resorts—in its films as much as in its policies—"to makeshifts and breed[s] nightmarish dreams of fascist pseudo-solutions worse than the ills they are intended to cure."[52]

The sadistic and nightmarish scenarios of what we now call film noir, in other words, unsettle the ostensibly liberal democratic order from which they emanate. Kracauer here points to the constitutive tension between freedom and equality that other commentators at the time would similarly attempt to map in the emerging Cold War coordinates of liberal democracy on the one hand and totalitarianism on the other.[53] Consequently, the political order is under siege just as much from within as from the global tensions without. Hollywood's films index an uncanny liberalism, and in the disjointed time of the mid-1940s, democracy itself hangs in the balance. The discovery of totalitarian tendencies in postwar American films, then, begins to answer Schapiro's concerns about the dichotomies of Kracauer's propaganda analysis: where "terror" becomes a category of analysis to be applied to American culture, as in "Hollywood's Terror Films," the ostensibly clear distinction between democracy and its totalitarian other also begins to erode.

Hollywood, in other words, is the symptom of a political impasse, which its recent output allows Kracauer to diagnose in turn. But what is perhaps even more striking than this symptomatic criticism (which, in the hands of other commentators, will morph all too easily into the anticommunism of subsequent years), is the rather more principled argument about cinema's affinity for the horrific—and its relative weakness in formulating an effective antidote. We will reencounter the association of films with terror, which Kracauer had already been thinking about during his years in France, toward the end of *Theory of Film*, where the topic receives a somewhat different treatment than in "Hollywood's Terror Films." In this essay, however, the apparently strong link between film and horror correlates with a comparatively weak link between film and democracy. In the films under discussion, Kracauer finds the characteristic terror balanced by nothing other than the dramaturgical magic wrought by psychoanalysis or the "ministrations of the [Catholic] Church." Postwar Hollywood cinema appears to favor terror as an attraction, whereas any characters engaged in combatting its effects merely pay lip service to a liberal, democratic politics rather than putting that politics into practice through lived ethics and action. As Kracauer notes in a searching article on the "vaguely liberal" wave of other postwar films such as *Boomerang, The Best Years of Our Lives,* and *Gentleman's Agreement,* "All these fighters for democracy are talkers rather than doers." There is, Kracauer notes in a memorable formulation, "a surfeit of eloquence in these films," which are all "a shade too wordy."[54]

Other films appear only to exacerbate the issue, even where they are designed to champion democracy and the American way of life. In Kracauer's mid-decade assessment of Hollywood, little of his earlier faith in "our films" remains. America as promise for the previously "Americanized" European exile has been replaced, not by a sober, realistic treatment of urban streetscapes, as Kracauer had hoped at the conclusion of "Why France

Liked Our Films." Rather, articles like "Those Movies with a Message" and "Hollywood's Terror Films" point up Hollywood's retreat from the problem of representing, let alone engaging, democracy; the most unabashedly propagandistic contributions to the war effort—Kracauer cites Capra's *Why We Fight* series—still "walk on eggs the moment they approach the positive aspects of that which they defend." The army morale films can offer nothing but "strangely evasive scenes from life under democracy that betray indecision rather than confidence, lip service instead of action."[55] If Hollywood is any guide—and for Kracauer it most emphatically is—then the central conundrum of the immediate postwar era is at once aesthetic and political: beset by fear, democracy, we might say, lacks representation.

This, I now wish to suggest, is precisely the central political and aesthetic problem that Kracauer tackles in *From Caligari to Hitler*, a book that consequently becomes legible not simply as a treatise on the failed democratic experiment that was the Weimar Republic, but also as a reflection on the world as it presents itself to Kracauer from his wartime and postwar vantage point in Manhattan. *From Caligari to Hitler* is best understood, in other words, if we reverse its teleology and inquire into the path that leads from the historical reality of fascism, fear, and the "crisis of the individual" to the reappraisal of Weimar cinema—that is, from Hitler to *Caligari*.

5. From Hitler to *Caligari*
Spaces of Weimar Cinema

> To view old films also means to inspect one's own past. As a rule, this revision brings to light unexpected results.
> SIEGFRIED KRACAUER, "Wiedersehen mit alten Filmen" (1938)

Conceived from the start as a history of German cinema, *From Caligari to Hitler* is devoted to the years between 1918 and 1933. The book covers this period chronologically to mount its now famous argument about the Weimar Republic, its films, and their political implications. From its beginnings onward, that argument holds, Weimar cinema reflects the Germans' mental dispositions, the authoritarian fixations that led to the rise of Hitler—if it didn't in fact help prepare that rise, as the title suggests: more than just chronology, *From Caligari to Hitler* strongly implies causality.[1]

These are bold claims that have undoubtedly contributed to the book's success: they are readily summarized and they invite debate.[2] By the same token, the book's strong thesis has lent itself to easy critiques. Detached from the films and the history on which it is based, the claim that cinema mirrors national dispositions that lead inevitably to fascism has been dismissed as essentialist, reflectionist, and overly teleological—if not as altogether too German: "If one shared [Kracauer's] belief in national souls," wrote the reviewer for the *New York Times*, "one might call his own method profoundly Teutonic. His love of darkly evocative historical utterances is positively Spenglerian." And in an indictment of the émigré author's perspective he adds, "*From Caligari to Hitler* looks very much like a refugee's revenge."[3]

At issue in the reference both to Spengler's narrative of decline and to Kracauer's ostensibly compromised objectivity as an exile is the book's status as history. In this view its relentless focus on Hitler as the *telos* of Weimar cinema constructs an all-too linear narrative with the benefit of hindsight. In a 1949 book review, Kracauer had applauded the author of *The Dragon in the Forest*—a recently published, semiautobiographical novel by a fellow émigré about a boy growing up in pre-Hitler Germany—for capturing "something as evasive as the mental climate of those years" and for resisting the temptation to "play the prophet in retrospect."[4] And yet, invested in nothing if not capturing the "mental climate" of the Weimar years, *From Caligari to Hitler* has struck subsequent critics as yielding to that same temptation. Its readings of interwar films amount, in Gertrud Koch's terms, to "an apocalyptic prophecy *a posteriori*."[5] Or, to adopt Thomas Elsaesser's formulation, they were conjured "in the blinding light of hindsight," which lent the book a peculiar Freudian temporality of *Nachträglichkeit* (afterwardness): Hitler, its endpoint, becomes an event "in search of its cause, whose consequence it could claim to be."[6]

It is difficult to imagine that such crucial historiographic and methodological questions simply escaped Kracauer during the conceptualization and writing of *From Caligari to Hitler*. He had engaged already during the 1920s in careful considerations of historiographical method in essays and book reviews, and he would again take up these considerations in a sustained way—albeit without referencing his own work on *Caligari*—in his posthumously published reflections on historiography.[7] There, he would elaborate in great detail upon the techniques by which historians construct the unity of a period, marshal evidence, and uncover causality after the fact; he would worry specifically about all forms of top-down history that superimpose extrinsic historical ideas or present interests on the minutiae that make up the material archive; and he would distinguish between a positive, carefully mobilized, "revealing hindsight" and "the kind of hindsight which falsifies historical reality by reading alien meanings into it."[8]

But what is history if not the attempt to make sense of the past after the fact and on the basis of hindsight—whether blinding, as Elsaesser suggests, or revealing, as Kracauer allows? Hannah Arendt, who, like Kracauer in *From Caligari to Hitler*, spent the better part of the 1940s attempting to understand the origins of totalitarianism, would go on to reflect explicitly on the temporality involved in interpreting the cataclysmic events of the decade. In "Understanding and Politics," originally published in *Partisan Review*, Arendt insisted precisely on the retrojective logic required to grasp developments that become legible only at their culmination—whether in the figure of Hitler, in Nazi rule, or in the system of terror epitomized by the camps and the Holocaust. As she put it, "The understanding of political and historical matters, since they are so profoundly and fundamentally human, has something in common with the understanding of people: who somebody essentially is, we know only after he is dead."[9] This assertion, to be sure, carries forward Hegel's image of the owl of Minerva taking flight only at dusk. But for Arendt, the object of that phrase was no longer the advent of philosophy: it was instead the urgent need to find answers to the "German Question."[10]

For Arendt, the answers to the question of what had happened, why, and how could not be deduced from a study of the past as linear chronology. Like Benjamin, her one-time brother-in-law, chess partner, and friend in French exile, Arendt conceives history as a meaningful category only if constructed as a prehistory of the present—Benjamin's *Jetztzeit*, in which the past flashes into illumination and manifests as an event. This moment, which Benjamin explicitly describes as a moment of danger, is for Arendt (who now writes after the Holocaust) the irrevocable rupture of civilization in the mid–twentieth century. The camps are the sign, totalitarianism is the name that she gives this event. In view of this cataclysm, she argues that the past "comes into being only with the event itself. Only when something irrevocable has happened can we even try to trace its history backward. The event illuminates its own past; it can never be deduced from it."[11]

Arendt's notion of historical understanding has profound consequences for the conceptualization of historical *origins*—the titular object of her book on totalitarianism. If the past becomes legible only in light of the transformative, culminating event, then the past origins of that event similarly come into view only *ex post facto*. "What the illuminating event reveals is a beginning in the past which had hitherto been hidden; to the eye of the historian, the illuminating event cannot but appear as an end of this newly discovered beginning."[12] The implications of Arendt's somewhat counterintuitive claim that an event "can never be deduced" from the past (which could be mistaken for the claim that we can never learn from history) become clear if we take seriously the idea that an event can "illuminate" history. Again, the echoes of Benjamin—a mutual friend of Arendt's and Kracauer's—are strong (it was, after all, Arendt who gave the title *Illuminations* to the first English-language collection of Benjamin's essays, which included his influential theses on the philosophy of history). Like a searchlight, the advent of totalitarianism brings into view a constellation that otherwise would have remained invisible and that could therefore not be considered an origin, or a beginning, other than retroactively.

It is in this sense that antisemitism and imperialism constitute "origins" of totalitarianism for Arendt. And it is in a related sense, I wish to suggest, that we must read the ostensible teleology that leads from Wiene's 1919 *The Cabinet of Dr. Caligari* to Hitler: the latter could not be deduced from the former; but illuminated by the advent of Hitler, by the event of National Socialism, the cataclysm of a world war, and the revelations about the

Holocaust, Wiene's film—indeed, the medium of cinema as such—becomes legible as an important origin, a "newly discovered beginning."[13] By the light of the movies, Kracauer reconstructs the "secret history involving the inner dispositions of the German people." And it is in a deliberately retrospective gesture that "the disclosure of these dispositions through the medium of the German screen may help in the understanding of Hitler's ascent and ascendancy."[14]

Hardly a "refugee's revenge," in other words, *From Caligari to Hitler* is the result of specific historiographic choices that subsequent critics have alternately hailed as a path-breaking genealogy of the present or dismissed as so many distortions of the past under the pressures of exile.[15] Leonardo Quaresima has claimed that *From Caligari to Hitler* generally, and its "anticipationist" line of interpretation in particular, "can and must be historically contextualized";[16] but to do so means more than to demonstrate in which ways the book may have been "hampered by the special conditions in which it was written" or how exile "distorted" its argument.[17] Rather, the book demands to be read in this perspective not simply as the psychological history of German film, as its subtitle designates it, but also as a book of and about the same postwar American present that concerns Kracauer in "Hollywood's Terror Films"—a present in which cinema appears allied with an illiberal politics of representation and with the loss of experience. In such a historicizing view, we need not adjudicate between views of Kracauer's book as either a timeless model or a circumstantial, and therefore inconsequential, study. Rather than either defending its claims wholesale or claiming that the book's truths are buried beneath so many "distortions," we should ask in what ways these distortions, if they did exist, became productive. For just as Kracauer would later elaborate on the historian's epistemological vantage point as the "son of two times,"[18] so does the author of this "psychological history of the German film" clearly inhabit both his Weimar past and the New York present that I have begun to map in the previous chapters.

In a letter to Erwin Panofsky during the very late stages of work on *Caligari*, Kracauer described himself as "a doctor who is performing an autopsy and at the same time doing a cross-section of a piece of his own past, which is now completely dead."[19] The image is a strange one, the metaphor mixed: as Dr. Kracauer autopsies Weimar cinema, what does it mean for a "piece of his own past" to be on the operating table? How can the living analyst claim that a piece of him is "completely dead"? To be sure, the implicit sense of this past as an amputated, phantom limb defines the experience of the refugee—not just in Kracauer's case; as Anton Kaes would have it, Kracauer's work in the film library is that of a trauma victim bound to rehearse and repeat the past.[20] But the cross-section of the (former) self is also a vivisection: the confrontation with Weimar cinema is also a confrontation with the "illuminating events" of the war and of the postwar moment in which it occurs—an analysis not only of a "completely dead" past, but also of the analyst's present. As Kracauer had reminded himself in his Marseille notebooks, one should always "factor in how [an] interpretation is conditioned by its time."[21] *From Caligari to Hitler* in turn demands to be read in this double register: both as a book of film history and as the document of a lived historical conjuncture, an émigré's wartime and postwar experience geographically located in midtown Manhattan. Only then will the book's central gamble with film, history, and politics become fully apparent. As I intend to show, it is precisely the question of democratic representation that animates Kracauer's investigations of Weimar cinema during the same period in which he is working on totalitarian propaganda and "Hollywood's Terror Films."[22]

Often maligned or simply disregarded even by otherwise well-meaning critics, *From Caligari to Hitler*, as Quaresima rightly insists, "deserves to be reread."[23] In taking up this project over the following chapters, I first reconstruct the book's argument in terms of an underlying spatial imagination that it shares with the article on Hollywood's "terror films." To further probe the politics of that argument, I then contextualize the book with reference to other émigrés' treatment of the "German Question" (chapter 6). On this basis, I subsequently revisit some of the critiques of Kracauer's history of Weimar cinema before finally reading the book once more against the grain, so to speak, to pinpoint its implicit theorization of a different configuration of film and politics than the one that led from *The Cabinet of Dr. Caligari* to National Socialism (chapter 7). Placed in the context of both his own ongoing projects and contemporary attempts to come to grips with the origins of totalitarianism and the ramifications of authoritarianism alike, *From Caligari to Hitler* can and should be reread as part of a larger project involved in working out the utopian promise of film in and against its illiberal manifestations.

LABYRINTHS, DETOURS, VISCOUS SPACE: THE SPATIAL IMAGINATION OF WEIMAR CINEMA

Written by a trained architect, *From Caligari to Hitler*—like the contemporaneous "Hollywood's Terror Films"—advances its argument in spatial terms. Not only does Kracauer note the "conspicuous role of architecture"

6. *New York Times* advertisement for *From Caligari to Hitler,* April 27, 1947.

in Weimar cinema; he also employs spatial categories as tropes through which to read that cinema and its meanings. In the introduction, which draws on notes he had apparently made for his book on film aesthetics (which would later become *Theory of Film*), Kracauer emphasizes the cinema's ability to shape and to set in motion a spatial world—a form of "spatial conquest" that Erwin Panofsky had famously described as the medium's characteristic "dynamization of space."[24] Film is an exquisite spatial medium to Kracauer not simply because it represents space, but because, as Panofsky had argued, in the cinema "space itself moves, changing, turning, dissolving, and recrystallizing."[25] In an argument that he will flesh out and modulate in the later theory book, Kracauer derives from this spatiality of the movies the properties of film: its "mission in ferreting out minutiae," its ability to "capture ... mass displays, casual configurations of human bodies and inanimate objects, and an endless succession of unobtrusive phenomena."[26] Cinematic space, according to Kracauer, becomes a "hieroglyph" in which to read everything from the "casual configurations" of the social world to "psychological dispositions," as well as a collective mentality. Films like *The Cabinet of Dr. Caligari*, Kracauer notes, hieroglyphically "expressed the structure of the soul in terms of space."[27]

Recall how in "Why France Liked Our Films" Kracauer celebrated Hollywood's characteristic "sense of realism" not for the way it treated the stories (many of which, Kracauer noted, "turned out to be a blank"), but for its "backgrounds": the palpable main streets, the bustle of Manhattan, the "real horses [that] gallop over real plains" in the western. The latter genre, Kracauer had noted was "representative of the swiftness of action," which "answers the demands of the film camera in that it extends over the whole material dimension and precisely includes that sector of reality which can be called camera reality."[28] This ode to the cinema, which Kracauer reprises in the 1946 introduction to *From Caligari to Hitler*, centers on its considerable power as a realist medium through which spectators relate to and move in space. Though they may be glued to their seats, Panofsky argues, "aesthetically, [they are] in permanent motion," able to explore vicariously a world that becomes magnified by its mediation on screen.[29]

Borrowing from a long tradition of theorizing about this spatial power of the medium, Kracauer is here invoking a trope that had fascinated the critic Jules Romains some thirty years earlier. Romains had anticipated many of the motifs that would occupy film theorists over the coming century—central among them the curious sense of mobility—when he wrote "The Crowd at the Cinematograph" in 1911: while the spectators' "bodies slumber and their muscles relax and slacken in the depths of their seats, they pursue burglars across the rooftops, cheer the passing of a king from the East, or march into a wide plain with bayonets or bugles."[30] In keeping with the palpable excitement that emanates from Romains's identificatory prose, Kracauer still thrills to the cinema's peculiar aesthetics of movement and space in the introduction to *From Caligari to Hitler*.

And yet, in his book Kracauer essentially maintains that Weimar cinema fell short of this inherent potential of the medium. In this sense, as I will argue more fully later on, *From Caligari to Hitler* is devoted to mapping a utopia of cinema only *ex negativo*—by showing time and again how it failed to realize a medial promise. To a certain degree, we could map this lack generically: where Romains revels in chase scenes, large-scale pageantry, and the open plains of the western, Weimar cinema is associated to this day with the power of studio-bound *mise-en-scène*, or what Kracauer labels "studio constructivism." From the painted sets of expressionist cinema through the *Kammerspielfilm* ("chamber drama" film), from the "long procession of 100 per cent studio-made films"[31] after *Caligari* to the staged numbers of the musicals in the late Weimar Republic, and even in the crowd-studded spectaculars from Lubitsch to Lang, the wizardry of the Babelsberg studios predominates, and it inflects Kracauer's spatial argument.[32] To him, even the documentary footage of Walter Ruttmann's *Berlin, Symphony of a Great City* fails to connect to the profilmic reality it ostensibly captures, as its "innumerable streets ... resemble the studio-built thoroughfare of Grune's *The Street* in yielding an impression of chaos."[33] Time and again, instead of the thrill of urban chase scenes or the uninhibited movement across wide-open plains, we find in *From Caligari to Hitler* descriptions of an arrested mobility and of static, strictly delimited spaces.

Reading set design as hieroglyphics, Kracauer describes the architecture of Weimar film as labyrinthine, an "ornamental system" that "expand[s] through space" in a film like *The Cabinet of Dr. Caligari* and contracts into the minimal sets of the *Kammerspielfilm*. Space consequently figures in Kracauer's book as a constraint; even where plotwise a film travels to exotic locales, as in Joe May's *Das indische Grabmal*, its production design and shooting location tether the project to provinciality, rendering it "a prisoner's daydream." That dream's language is nationally specific, and Kracauer immediately provides its translation: "The prison was of course the mutilated and blockaded fatherland; at least, this was the way most Germans felt about it. What they called their world mission had been thwarted, and now all exits seemed barred."[34]

Labyrinths abound. An expressionist classic such as Lang's *Der müde Tod* (Destiny, 1921) features the recurrent image of an impenetrable wall that "runs parallel with the screen so that no vanishing lines allow an estimate of the wall's extent."[35] Far from a neutral medium, space becomes in these films a dense, almost viscous environment: as if to parody the spatial trope of the cinematic chase scene, a pair of lovers in the Chinese episode of Lang's film is pursued literally at an elephantine pace. In Arthur Gerlach's *Vanina* (1922), which features a climactic but thwarted attempt to escape from a dungeon, Asta Nielsen and her lover are forced to negotiate similarly labyrinthine terrain: "Instead of giving the impression of speed," Kracauer writes, "this sequence shows the couple walking endlessly through endless corridors. It is an escape in slow motion." As a result, cinema's powers to "spatialize time and dynamize space" appear reversed: "The terrorized fugitives experience one moment as an eternity, and limited space as space beyond any limits."[36] Weimar cinema becomes legible in Kracauer's retrospective view as a prison-house where Germans had locked themselves in and thrown away the keys.

Accordingly, the dichotomy between the cinema's inherent promise of spatial dynamization and Kracauer's diagnosis of stasis and constraint maps onto a second pair of spatial terms that structure Kracauer's account even more prominently: the distinction between outside and inside. This is not merely a matter of the preponderance of *Kammerspiel* interiors over views of the city, let alone the countryside. Rather, the inside/outside dichotomy governs the very logic of Kracauer's analysis, where it serves to characterize both profilmic space and its national as well as psychological implications. The emphasis on the "studio constructivism" of expressionist cinema becomes legible as a form of retreat—a stunted development of the postwar subject that replaces outward movement toward maturity with the solipsistic interiority of "the soul." In a characteristic formulation that brings together film production and ethnopsychology, the German "withdrawal into the studio was part of the general retreat into a shell."[37]

From its expressionist beginnings through the elaborate staging of Ufa spectaculars such as *Metropolis* to both the realist fare and the escapist musicals of the crisis years, Weimar cinema is characterized by its unique *mise-en-scène*, its emphasis on lighting and set design. Far from working only from plot summaries, as critics have occasionally contended, Kracauer reflects on the centrality of staging and space for films as diverse as Lubitsch's historical productions and Lang's spy thrillers and science fiction. This attention to spatiality seeps from the era's film sets into the architectonics of *From Caligari to Hitler* itself. If we were to think of the book in spatial terms, it too would be full of dead ends, blind corridors, nested spaces, and thwarted vistas. As opposed to cinema's inherent promise, its reality in

Germany during the 1920s appears to Kracauer as closed off against that promise. Consequently, the dominant tropes of his analysis correspond closely to the prison-house of "studio constructivism" that Kracauer diagnoses in Weimar cinema. The book's protagonist, the middle-class German soul, appears immobilized as if under a hypnotic spell. Mentally shelterless, it responds to the "shock of freedom" only by retreating into a shell and falling into a "widespread inner paralysis."[38] The "stabilized period" after the end of inflation and in the wake of the Dawes Plan offers no room for maneuver but only "frozen ground."[39] The paths Kracauer follows through the spaces of Weimar cinema point inward, with "mythic compactness" and no way out.[40] For all its oft-indicted linear teleology, its one-way street from 1919 to 1933, the book is dominated by a centripetal imagination. It features circles, spirals, vortices, and whirlpools as recurring motifs; we get lost in long corridors, retreat from streets into parlors, withdraw from the outside world into that of the soul.[41]

This spatial argument provides the framework in which the aesthetic and political norms underpinning Kracauer's history of German film, and indeed his broader theoretical pursuits, are inscribed. Though these norms are by no means realized in Weimar cinema (on the contrary), they undergird the architectonics of Kracauer's argument, which, as we have seen in previous chapters, is anchored in a realist aesthetic and a political commitment to the notion of participatory liberal democracy. In his 1947 book, Kracauer equates the retreat into closed spaces both with an antirealist tendency and with an inability or reluctance to enter the political realm. Apart from the "timid heresies" and "brief reveilles" of the late Weimar Republic, the cinema's tendency toward "introversion" is tantamount to a refusal of realism, the political consequences of which Kracauer works out over the course of the book.[42]

Even the "new realism" of the stabilized period—i.e., the infusion of *Neue Sachlichkeit* into film style and narrative—marks for Kracauer a "state of paralysis."[43] Borrowing the term "studio constructivism" from Paul Rotha to describe the "curious air of completeness, of finality, that surrounds each product of the German studios," Kracauer spells out the normative implications of his aesthetic argument: "Organizational completeness can be achieved only if the material to be organized does not object to it. [. . .] Since reality is essentially incalculable and therefore demands to be observed rather than commanded, realism on the screen and total organization exclude each other. Through their 'studio constructivism' no less than their lighting the German films revealed that they dealt with unreal events displayed in a sphere basically controllable."[44] Kracauer's language indexes his political evaluation of such aesthetic choices, which amount to a form of total domination and control that tolerates no dissent; the subjection of semiotic materials by the cinema's impersonal agency evokes the submission of docile subjects to totalitarian rule.

And yet, prominent in this assessment of expressionist *mise-en-scène* are also countervailing realist norms of observation, incalculable chance, and ambiguity—terms that will become fully explicit only in Kracauer's much later *Theory of Film*. Like the brief reference to cinema's utopian potential in the introduction, however, passages such as the above-cited indictment of "studio constructivism" index an underlying theoretical groundwork where the two film books are linked. For they suggest that realist norms underpin Kracauer's American writings from the analysis of propaganda (which, we recall, was devoted to showing up the "sham reality" of totalitarian representations) through the theoretical *summa* of 1960. The latter is the object of the chapters that follow, but we might note here already that, in sharing the theoretical and political premises of the later work, *From Caligari to Hitler* in a sense formulates the central questions to which *Theory of Film* offers the answers: questions concerning the link between cinematic realism, experience, and politics.

As Kracauer's spatial reading makes clear, these issues remain fundamentally unreconciled during the Weimar years. The failure of Weimar cinema's protagonists to escape the confines of their studio-built labyrinths not only undercuts the medium's capacity for realism but also mirrors the German citizens' "escape from freedom" (Fromm) into reassuring authoritarian structures.[45] In this sense, *From Caligari to Hitler* equates an encroaching fascism with enclosure; a democratic order, by contrast, would require space in which to move, to gain experience and formulate independent judgments, to interact. In Kracauer's reading, Weimar cinema appears to foreclose on this possibility just as it fails to realize the medium's realist potential. Unable to imagine an alternative to tyranny other than spiraling chaos, the cinema—like Weimar politics—proves all but incapable of sketching even the outlines of a participatory, liberal political order. Hence Kracauer's pithy conclusion that the "potentialities of liberalism seem, temporarily, exhausted."[46] To the German subject as refracted in the spatial designs of Weimar cinema, democracy appears merely as an "odious confusion."[47]

To the degree that the spatial binaries of stasis and mobility, and of hermetic and open, centripetal and centrifugal space, undergird similarly stark alternatives of realism and expressionism, authoritarianism and democracy, we appear to have come full circle from the earlier work on propaganda that bookends *From Caligari to Hitler*, and which Schapiro had roundly critiqued.⁴⁸ Schapiro's principal complaint, it will be recalled, concerned the conceptual firewall that Kracauer had seemingly erected between Nazi propaganda and democratic "information," between totalitarian "sham reality" and democratic "realism." This political critique implied both that Kracauer overstated the case against Weimar and that he adopted an unexamined norm of liberal democracy, the latter presumably owing to the recent émigré's uncritical acceptance of his new homeland.

But a closer look reveals that both extremes of this nationally overdetermined binary are attenuated in Kracauer's writings. Beyond the seeming reduction of aesthetic and political alternatives to an either/or of expressionism and realism, totalitarianism and democracy, we find more dialectically nuanced positions. Kracauer detects the promise of cinema, its ability to reconnect spectators with the world, even as he chronicles its pretotalitarian doldrums. And he certainly remained attuned to the shortcomings of liberal democracy in the Hollywood output that Kracauer had greeted so enthusiastically in "Why France Liked Our Films." As he turns his attention to Hollywood's terror films even while working on *From Caligari to Hitler*, the picture darkens. Weimar and Hollywood enter into a curious superimposition.

In *From Caligari to Hitler*'s attention to space, we can detect the architectonics of a book devoted to a closed historical era and a social class that looks inward rather than out. However, as I have suggested, we should read the book keeping in mind the historical contexts in which it was written. Against the backdrop of Kracauer's work on Hollywood discussed in the previous chapter, we can see in *Caligari* the reflections of the more contemporary and proximate developments that had occupied him during the 1940s. In a reversal of film historical models of influence, according to which the expressionist leanings of German émigré directors and technicians gave rise to the *mise-en-scène* of film noir, we might say that *Caligari*'s labyrinthine spaces mirror the dimly lit streets and blind alleyways of noir. Those dark corners, in which battered heroes lose their bearings, seem to provide a template for Kracauer's assessment of Weimar cinema. The kindred, labyrinthine logic of noir space and narration is legible even in the films' titles, such as Edgar Ulmer's emblematic *Detour* or Henry Hathaway's *The Dark Corner*. The particular spatiality of film noir resurfaces in the very language of *From Caligari to Hitler*.

More than just a spatial congruence, the noir cycle also provides a prominent narrative template through which to consider Kracauer's autoptic work. Now-classic films such as Billy Wilder's *Double Indemnity* (1944), Michael Curtiz's *Mildred Pierce* (1945), Robert Siodmak's *The Killers* (1946), and Jacques Tourneur's *Out of the Past* (1947) all famously foreground the narrative trope of the flashback. Not coincidentally, these are titles that have come to define film noir as a cycle whose traumatized male leads often find themselves framed. As hapless as they are hardboiled, private investigators and small-time criminals end up caught in dark worlds and murky pasts that they cannot elucidate. In Kracauer's analysis, as we have seen, the middle-class "German soul" of Weimar cinema is similarly entrapped. Casting a backward glance from the 1940s to the 1920s, and from New York to the Germany he left behind, Kracauer offers a prolonged flashback—a trope readily familiar not only from Weimar cinema (where it does appear with some frequency) but also from any number of films that Kracauer might have watched in New York cinemas during these years.

In this sense, the noir cycle frames *Caligari*'s account of Weimar cinema, which maps the urban space of contemporary American films onto the guiding tropes of Kracauer's investigation. Thomas Elsaesser has argued that Kracauer cuts Weimar films to the measure of classical Hollywood narration and underreports the characteristic stylization, indirection, ambiguity, and excess of Weimar cinema. Kracauer, he claims, often brushes over "the very resistance that makes these films different from realist-illusionist (that is to say, classical Hollywood) narratives."[49] But what are we to make of the fact that the noir narratives to which Kracauer seems to have assimilated the films from the Weimar Republic are themselves resistant to the "realist-illusionist" model—that they are characterized by those very tropes that Elsaesser finds missing from Kracauer's account? Writing about 1940s Hollywood, Dana Polan has emphasized precisely this dimension of noir—its inherent contradictions, its ambiguities and excesses—which he reads as signs of a breakdown of both narrative and the studio system.[50] A classic like *Detour*, Polan points out, becomes "nothing so much as a vast bad-joke version of the classic narrative," whose transparency and self-confidence as a cultural form enter into a profound crisis during the 1940s.[51]

It is this crisis that Kracauer inhabits when writing about the symptomatic failures of Weimar democracy as seen through its films. *From Caligari to Hitler*, consequently, becomes legible as the projection of the writer's American present onto his German past—a conceptual overlay that reveals the contours of *both* eras.

This superimposition becomes virtually explicit in the 1946 *Commentary* article "Hollywood's Terror Films," which Kracauer wrote during his work on *Caligari*. That article's assessment of contemporary Hollywood appears to overlap so closely with the simultaneous work on the book as to occasionally render it all but indistinguishable.[52] As we saw in the last chapter, the picture that Kracauer paints of postwar Hollywood is one of a cinema adept at strong depictions of pervasive horror but unable to formulate adequate alternatives. The stereoscopic overlay with the *Caligari* book is striking. We have already noted the explicit reference in the 1946 article to the motif of the street in Weimar cinema, which figures so prominently in *From Caligari to Hitler;* but we can trace the echoes further still. As if conflating the two national cinematographies, or at least projecting the analysis of one onto the diagnosis of the other, Kracauer rehearses identical concepts, uses the same formulations, and discovers matching motifs. If postwar Hollywood spreads terror, so does *The Cabinet of Dr. Caligari* "spread an all-pervading atmosphere of horror"; if Wiene's expressionist masterpiece "overflow[ed] with sinister portents, acts of terror and outbursts of panic," so do Siodmak's and Wilder's postwar thrillers.[53] Whether in 1920s Germany or in the United States of the 1940s, we find the unsettling figure of the "murderer among us," whom Kracauer identifies equally in Fritz Lang's *M* (1931) and Alfred Hitchcock's *Shadow of a Doubt* (1943). Here as there we encounter the struggling (national) soul, cinema and society paralyzed by impossible alternatives. In postwar Hollywood, we recall, this takes the form of a "crucial dilemma" between capitalist "free enterprise" and totalitarian "planned economies." Topical though this Cold War reference may appear, the notion of an ideological "crucial dilemma" recurs in the title of a seminal chapter in *From Caligari to Hitler*. Here—drawing on his own 1922 essay "Those Who Wait"[54]—Kracauer outlines a widely perceived lack of spiritual shelter *(geistige Obdachlosigkeit)*; caught between the Scylla of tyranny and the Charybdis of "instinct-governed chaos," the "German soul" appears "mentally unprotected" and "in search of solid refuge." "Hollywood's Terror Films" goes a long way toward tempering the awkward national essentialism of this image by suggesting that the same diagnosis applies to the contemporary sociopolitical context in the United States.

The parallels could be multiplied further, as Kracauer himself recognized when he wrote in a letter to C. Wright Mills in 1945 that "there may be a few analogies between the situation in pre-Hitler German and the present American situation."[55] What makes these analogies significant, however, are the political conclusions that Kracauer draws. If postwar Hollywood seems unable to give voice to any substantive notion of a democratic politics, so does Weimar cinema consistently fall short of penetrating (let alone defending) "that odious confusion called democracy."[56] The central argumentative strand of the book, worked out most prominently in the chapter on *The Cabinet of Dr. Caligari*, revolves around the ubiquity of (expressionist) horror and the false dichotomy between tyranny and chaos. The book is designed, in other words, to demonstrate Weimar cinema's—and, by implication, German citizens'—inability to conceive of a substantive, political alternative to the false choice between orderly submission and anarchic disorder.

When, in a rare explicit reference to "today" in the body of his book, Kracauer explicitly cross-references this argument with the postwar present from which he is writing, the connection hinges on politics. Discussing the dearth of detectives in German cinema, he invokes the rationality of these figures as indices of enlightenment and individual freedom and reads their replacement by the figure of the tough "private eye" as a symptom of the weakening power of rationality—or what Max Horkheimer analyzed around the same time as the "eclipse of reason."[57] In keeping with his articles from the mid-1940s onward in which he traces the compromised liberalism of Hollywood, Kracauer further considers Weimar cinema to resemble postwar America in that it "walked on eggs" wherever it might have approached a positive formulation of liberal, nonauthoritarian politics. As he noted in an early draft of the introduction to *Caligari*, "The contemporaneous imagination [of Weimar Germany] identified freedom from tyranny not so much with the prospect of true freedom as with the dissolution of any society. There was, indeed, not a single German film which substantiated freedom so as to make it seem attractive."[58]

The shared analytic vocabulary employed to account for films from two rather different cinematic and political contexts might lead one to suspect the single-mindedness of the critic and to assume a certain rigidity of mind, not flexible enough to account for obvious distinctions.[59] In identifying *"geistige Obdachlosigkeit"* as both an interwar German and postwar American phenomenon, for example, was Kracauer subsuming the differences between the two sociopolitical contexts under some overarching concept of modernity? And was he simply subjecting both Weimar and the United States to the same critique of subjectivity that he had initiated in the 1920s with essays such as "Those Who Wait"?

This is possible, but we should also attend to the historical and political specificity of the dilemmas engulfing and transforming the modern subject. Whereas the 1920s critique still outlined a broadly "lapsarian" view of modernity, as Miriam Hansen has shown, Kracauer's critique of the 1920s from the point of view of the 1940s (and his concurrent critique of the 1940s) unfolds against the backdrop of cataclysmic events that color the narrative of *From Caligari to Hitler* and the assessment of Hollywood alike.[60] At stake is no longer the restitution of spiritual shelter, but the need to grasp the fatal turn of historical events—the need, in Hannah Arendt's terms, for *understanding*.⁶¹ And the subject that responds to these events can no longer be the one that waits in active passivity. Rather, the proliferating references to paralysis, lack of orientation, timidity, and fear in both *From Caligari to Hitler* and "Hollywood's Terror Films" index political subjectivity *as a problem* both for the pretotalitarian state and for the state of democracy in postwar America. To grasp the shared contours of the superimposed spaces of expressionism and Hollywood, Weimar Germany and the postwar United States, we will need to account not only for the narrative and stylistic echoes of Weimar cinema in film noir, but also for the shared impulse that animates the kind of symptomatic reading Kracauer pioneered: an impulse that is ultimately political and derives from a deep concern over the fate of the human subject, of democracy, culture, and representation—both in interwar Germany and in the United States. For this purpose, it is less useful to trace the continuities and discontinuities of Kracauer's critique of modernity than to further historicize his work in the political and intellectual contexts of the 1940s in which it was written.

6. Authoritarian, Totalitarian

> Instead of proving immune to Nazi indoctrination, the bulk of Germans adjusted themselves to totalitarian rule with a readiness that could not be merely the outcome of propaganda and terror.
> SIEGFRIED KRACAUER, *From Caligari to Hitler*

ESCAPE FROM FREEDOM

From Kracauer's correspondence with Datus Smith, his publisher at Princeton University Press, it appears that he had intended to begin *From Caligari to Hitler*—then still titled, provisionally, *A History of German Cinema*—by asking: "How did Hitler become possible?" Although he consented readily to remove this "ominous question," from the first line of the book at least, he insisted that "I cannot prevent the book from answering, among other things, this question."[1] The final version of the introduction, correspondingly, ends by vindicating his proposed psychological approach as a way to fill in some of the "striking gaps in our knowledge of German history from World War I to Hitler's ultimate triumph—the period covered in this book."[2] Behind the overt shifts chronicled by historians, economists, and political scientists, Kracauer contends, "runs a secret history involving the inner dispositions of the German people. The disclosure of these dispositions through the medium of the German screen may help in the understanding of Hitler's ascent and ascendancy."[3]

In view of such formulations, it is worth remembering, as I pointed out in the last chapter, that Kracauer deliberately sought out and welcomed the political instrumentalization of his studies for government purposes. In particular, his interpretation joined a number of influential "psycho-cultural" approaches to German reeducation that were being pioneered at the time by psychiatrists such as Richard Brickner and anthropologists such as Margaret Mead and Gregory Bateson, with whom Kracauer overlapped during his time at MoMA.[4] But in addition to its potential usefulness for denazification and reeducation in Germany, Kracauer's work, as I have been suggesting, also tapped into political contexts on this side of the Atlantic, where it joined the growing diagnostic literature on the factors that contributed to the rise of Hitler. Driven by the more or less explicit fear that "it *can* happen here," much of this literature grew out of the concerns of wartime communications studies that had provided the immediate context for Kracauer's earlier propaganda work (see chapter 5). In the introduction to *From Caligari to Hitler*, Kracauer explicitly cites Franz Neumann's influential *Behemoth*, which C. Wright Mills had hailed in the *Partisan Review* as a "definitive analysis of the German Reich."[5] However, Kracauer does not adopt Neumann's Weberian Marxism and his materialist analysis of Weimar's failure and Hitler's rise so much as he borrows from the psychosocial approach of the Frankfurt School as exemplified in the work of Erich Fromm. Fromm's *Escape from Freedom*, which Kracauer also cites, had appeared in 1941, the year Kracauer arrived in the United States.[6] Although Fromm had left the Institut für Sozialforschung by this point and disagreements with Horkheimer and Adorno over his critique of Freud would ensue,[7] his analysis of authoritarianism remained influential for the Frankfurt School. *From Caligari to Hitler* relies heavily on Fromm's analysis of authoritarian rule as an ontogenetic development gone awry. In other words, Kracauer finds enacted in the cinema the same drama of failed individuation that Fromm diagnoses as the root of fascism.

For Fromm, individuation is profoundly dialectical. The child's growing freedom as an individual, its emancipation from parental and familial ties, is inseparable from feelings of isolation, anxiety, and powerlessness. "Healthy" development, then, involves the sublation of this dialectic in a "spontaneous relationship to man and nature, a relationship that connects the individual with the world without eliminating his individuality." The two principal conduits toward such a healthy form of individuated social being and the corresponding "integration and strength of the total personality" are for Fromm (much as for Hannah Arendt after him, though she would have shunned the psychoanalytic underpinnings) love and productive work.[8] In the absence of such integrative measures, the fragile process of individuation all too easily resolves its inherent dialectic in regressive forms. Unable to reverse the process itself, the subject flees from an anxiety-producing sense of freedom, which it can only perceive as isolation, into submission.

Fromm's analysis encapsulates ontogenetically the development that Adorno and Horkheimer later formulate as the dialectic of enlightenment— the entwinement of myth and reason, subjugation and emancipation. Fromm calls this the "dialectic character of the process of growing freedom," according to which the subject becomes at once "more independent, self-reliant, and critical and ... more isolated, alone, and afraid."[9] Unlike Adorno and Horkheimer, Fromm harbors a belief in normative, healthy psychosocial development that could outrun this dialectic in principle. Empirically as well as psychoanalytically, however, he concedes this to be a fairly weak hope. For the subject all too easily turns away, or "escapes," from freedom and takes refuge in masochistic or sadistic forms of symbiosis.[10] This, then, is the basis of what Fromm, drawing on fascism's self-description as an authoritarian political system, calls the "authoritarian character." In this dynamic, he claims to locate "the personality structure which is the human basis of Fascism."[11] It describes a character dominated by admiration for, and submission to, as well as desire of authority. Often projected onto a "magic helper"—incarnated in this case by Hitler—these are libidinal attractions that significantly can find expression even in rebellion, though never in revolution.[12] For the authoritarian character "loves those conditions that limit human freedom, he loves being submitted to fate."[13]

Readers of *From Caligari to Hitler* will readily recognize in Kracauer's film analyses several of the motifs elaborated by Fromm—indeed, the former appear to be peopled by the very character types that Fromm sets forth: the rebel who ultimately submits to authority; the passive character who trusts in Fate; the masochistic lover who fails to act on better knowledge or reason; the recurrent figure of the policeman as Fromm's "magic helper" who, "with an imperious gesture . . . stops the waves and, like Moses leading the Jews across the Red Sea, pilots the child safely through the petrified traffic"; and a whole "procession of tyrants" who act out the authoritarian character's sadism.[14] Even Kracauer's chapter titles evoke Fromm's analysis, as they chronicle German cinema's devolution from the early "shock of freedom" to "mute chaos," and "from rebellion to submission."

Confronted with the prospect of freedom, like Fromm's subject, the "German mind" emanating from the country's films harbors "qualms about those deep-rooted dispositions which had supported the collapsed authoritative regime," but those qualms "constantly interfered with the desire to keep them alive."[15] Kracauer consequently traces authoritarian dispositions from imperial Germany and the *Kinoreformbewegung* of the early 1910s to the ornamental crowds who glorify authoritarian leaders in *Nibelungen* (1924, dir. Fritz Lang) and *Metropolis* (1927, dir. Fritz Lang). Entire cycles appear defined by their endorsement of such dispositions: the street films follow middle-class male protagonists on their nighttime escapades to "emphasize desertion of the home, but still in the interest of authoritarian behavior, [. . .] an escape that amounts to an antidemocratic, antirevolutionary rebellion";[16] youth films, in keeping with Fromm's analysis of the affirmative function of the rebel, "affirm fixation to authoritarian behavior precisely by stressing rebellion against it";[17] and the Fridericus films "advocate the resumption of authoritarian behavior, presupposing a mentality that would prefer even a tyrannical regime to chaos."[18] With *Fridericus Rex* (1922), indeed, the cinema becomes rather explicitly a site for resolving, by means of identification, the dialectic of individuation that Fromm had analyzed. Wishing both to adopt and to resist the "idealistic concept of the autonomous individual," viewers could "participate in the ruler's glory and thus drown the consciousness of [their] own submission to him."[19] Under Kracauer's lens, even a film like *The Last Laugh* becomes emblematic for the way in which it turns the protagonist's uniform into a quasi-religious icon of authority, allowing the film to advance, "however ironically, the authoritarian credo that the magical spell of authority protects society from decomposition."[20] The porter, like so many other figures in Weimar cinema, embodies the failure to replace authority by spontaneous individuality.

The examples could be multiplied—but so can the references: while clearly influential for Kracauer's thinking, Fromm's study was hardly the only one to investigate the structure of the authoritarian personality, let alone the origins of totalitarianism. If we wish to locate Kracauer's analysis of Weimar cinema in the intellectual context of the 1940s, two other studies stand out as far more influential. Although he could not have drawn on them at the time, since they were being developed simultaneously with his work on *Caligari* and only published afterwards, these studies were so closely aligned with Kracauer's work that he might as well have adopted their titles for his own book: for as we have already seen, *From Caligari to Hitler* relied heavily for its argument on the notion of "the authoritarian personality," the subject of a major, influential study co-authored by Adorno under the aegis of the American Jewish Committee and the Frankfurt School; at the same time, Kracauer's book was devoted to understanding the origins of totalitarianism, which Hannah Arendt was working out in a series of essays for *Partisan Review* and *Commentary* during the 1940s (the completed book appeared in 1951).

To draw these connections is not to suggest that these studies are in any way interchangeable, even if their titles may have been.[21] Clearly, they cover vastly different ground: Arendt traces the origins of totalitarianism to nineteenth-century antisemitism, the rise of imperialism, and the terror of the camps, whereas *The Authoritarian Personality* is devoted to analyzing character structures in postwar American society. Nor do they share the same methods and approaches: Arendt worked from history and archival sources and draws inspiration and argument from literary works, whereas the authors of *The Authoritarian Personality* engaged in empirical social research and adopted a psychoanalytic vocabulary that was largely anathema to Arendt. Moreover, it would not have occurred to the authors of either of these studies to turn to fiction films as sources for their arguments: this remains Kracauer's signal contribution to the debates at the time. Consequently, we may measure both the remarkable convergences and the limits of any comparison between his book and the above-mentioned studies by returning to two of the quintessential films on which Kracauer bases his narrative: Robert Wiene's *Cabinet of Dr. Caligari* and Fritz Lang's *Metropolis*. Here we can see how Kracauer looks back at Weimar through film to draw out the "potentially fascistic individual" that is the object of *The Authoritarian Personality*, and to trace the relation between atomization and "mass man" that Arendt considers in the lead-up to totalitarianism.

THE AUTHORITARIAN PERSONALITY OF DR. CALIGARI

> If a potentially fascistic individual exists, what, precisely, is he like? What goes to make up antidemocratic thought?
>
> THEODOR W. ADORNO et al., *The Authoritarian Personality*[22]

In keeping with its prominent place in the teleology of Kracauer's book, *The Cabinet of Dr. Caligari* remains the film that best exemplifies the authoritarian character—albeit with a twist, for in Kracauer's analysis, *Caligari* was framed. The frame narrative that bookends Robert Wiene's famous expressionist film sets up two hapless young men and a woman to look like fools, when by all rights Dr. Caligari should have been indicted for murder and the abuse of authority. This, in a nutshell, is Kracauer's argument in his influential analysis of the film, first published in *Partisan Review* in March 1947 before appearing as the fifth chapter in *From Caligari to Hitler* later that year.[23]

The central plot is well known to students of cinema: A mad scientist by the name of Caligari wreaks havoc in a small German town, where he dispatches his somnambulist medium, Cesare, to murder innocent victims. The first among these is young Alan, whose death leads his friend Francis to investigate while their mutual love interest, Jane, narrowly escapes and the police pursue false leads. The chase ends in an insane asylum, where Francis manages to prove that the director has taken on the identity of an eighteenth-century hypnotist, "becoming" the fabled Caligari in the process. The delusion unmasked, the director goes raving mad and ends up imprisoned, straitjacketed and shackled, in an expressionistically painted cell.

The moral of this "horror tale in the spirit of E.T.A. Hoffmann" is obvious to Kracauer, who interprets it allegorically. Pitting the youths' commitment to fact-finding, crime-solving, and enlightenment against the maniacal and tyrannical excesses of the murderous doctor, *The Cabinet of Dr. Caligari* appears to be nothing short of a "revolutionary story" that "stigmatize[s] the omnipotence of a state authority manifesting itself in universal conscription and declarations of war." Caligari personifies this omnipotence, standing "for an unlimited authority that idolizes power as such," whereas his medium, Cesare, represents "the common man who, under the pressure of compulsory military service, is drilled to kill and to be killed." The revelation of the asylum director's true identity at the end of the film seals its "revolutionary meaning": "reason overpowers unreasonable power, insane authority is symbolically abolished."[24]

Or so it might have appeared, had the film not turned the tables on Francis's antiauthoritarian ratiocination by introducing a frame story, which embeds the tale of Caligari as one long flashback. As Kracauer puts it, this narrative device transforms the original "account of real horrors [. . .] into a chimera concocted and narrated by the mentally deranged Francis." Reversing the terms of the embedded story, the frame shows the young generation—including Francis, Alan, Jane, and even Conrad Veidt's Cesare—to be insane; Werner Krauss's wise doctor, by contrast (whom Francis now *mistakes* for Caligari), becomes Fromm's "magic helper":[25] the reveal at the end of the film shows him watching over the other characters, working to cure their delusions. In Kracauer's interpretation, the political consequences of this decision were momentous. An ostensibly revolutionary story had been turned into a "conformist" plot that "glorified authority and convicted its antagonist of madness."[26]

The framing of the story, in other words, is central to Kracauer's interpretation of the film's meaning—but it also provides the model for his hermeneutic method, which constructs multiple, layered frames of reference around the film. To Kracauer, the "revolutionary story" of *The Cabinet of Dr. Caligari* is nested inside these frames as though in a series of Chinese boxes;[27] the task of interpretation, then, is to articulate the relations between these different layers of signification. We have already considered two of these: the first, allegorical frame defined the embedded story's characters in terms of postwar German politics; and the second, narrative frame reversed the terms of the first interpretation. Kracauer then posits a third frame, which, like the first, operates in terms of personification. Relying heavily on a personal account by Hans Janowitz, one of the screenwriters, he blames the director for having introduced the frame story and diluted the film's putatively radical politics.[28] As a result, the political allegory spills from the diegesis to the production context, since Kracauer implicitly equates Wiene with the omnipotent director of the asylum. The screenwriters, by contrast, are the story's hapless youths, left only to "rage against the framing story [which] perverted, if not reversed their intrinsic intentions."[29]

To this multiply layered set of narrative and interpretive frames, Kracauer's reading adds one more twist. For in the final analysis, it is neither Caligari/Wiene/the State nor Cesare/the screenwriters/the WWI conscript, but the mechanism of *the frame itself* that keys the allegorical meaning of the film. Containing the original story, the framing device indexes a different form of containment that Kracauer locates at the historical, psychosocial level—the outermost Chinese box, so to speak, and undoubtedly the most significant frame that he constructs around *Caligari*. Here, the plot device becomes the signifier for the inner dispositions of middle-class Germans during the early years of the Weimar Republic, which, as we have seen, Kracauer reads in terms of spatial containment: "by putting the original into a box," he argues, the final version of the film "faithfully mirrored the general retreat into a shell." Having taken apart, lined up, and then reassembled the nested boxes that together form the layered text of *The Cabinet of Dr. Caligari*, Kracauer concludes that the film emblematizes the Germans' tendency "to withdraw from a harsh outer world into the intangible realm of the soul."[30]

This, of course, is also Kracauer's argument in the book from which the earlier-published "Caligari" chapter was drawn. *From Caligari to Hitler* is in this sense but another frame around the interpretation of Wiene's film, with which it shares the central argument regarding the "inner dispositions of the German people."[31] And it turns out that in Kracauer's logic of nested signifiers, the innermost Chinese box—a small, fictional character—looks like the larger-than-life, historical figure that ultimately envelops it: bracketing the titular teleology as its origin and endpoint, Hitler and Caligari resemble each other in their role as tyrants lording over a people who gave up their autonomy in favor of authoritarian dispositions.[32]

Kracauer's analysis of these dispositions in Weimar cinema is clearly indebted, as I have shown, to Fromm's psychoanalytic account of (failed) individuation. But in the postwar context in which the book is written, it also communicates with another set of investigations devoted not to interwar Germany but to the contemporary United States: the Studies in Prejudice commissioned by the American Jewish Committee. Launched in 1944, the project was carried out by the AJC and the Institut für Sozialforschung in their newly established Department of Scientific Research jointly directed by Max Horkheimer and the psychologist Samuel Flowerman. Work on the project would continue well past the 1947 publication of *From Caligari to*

Hitler, yielding a number of volumes published in the late 1940s—including Guterman and Löwenthal's previously mentioned *Prophets of Deceit*. The most significant publication in terms of its scholarly impact as well as its role in defining the shifting shape of Critical Theory during Horkheimer's and Adorno's American years was undoubtedly *The Authoritarian Personality*. Based on studies carried out in California, that book appeared in 1950 with Adorno's name alphabetically atop the four coauthors listed on the title.[33]

As Anton Kaes has suggested, "the larger research initiative that explored the authoritarian mindset resonated with Kracauer's own ongoing project of exposing proto-fascist attitudes in Weimar Germany."[34] But how might we imagine this resonance, and what was the specific place for film in such research initiatives? The Studies in Prejudice reports were grounded, like Kracauer's analysis, in the assumption of a certain "mentality" and its cultural/ideological effectiveness for the life of a nation. *The Authoritarian Personality* derives variants of this mentality from patterns that express deep-lying trends in the individual personality. Various empirical experiments reported in that study establish these patterns cumulatively by cross-referencing different types of prejudice and showing the correlation between sociopolitical factors (as measured by the PEC or "political and economic conservatism" scale), racial attitudes (as measured by the E or "ethnocentrism" scale), and antisemitism, the central motivating concern of the AJC-sponsored study. Its signal contribution, however, turned out to be the formulation of yet another scale for evaluating prejudice: based on the correlation of all the other scales as well as previous studies (including *Prophets of Deceit*), the study's authors devised the "F-scale" to measure fascist tendencies.

Like Weimar cinema for Kracauer, the F-scale provided a composite set of traits (or, in Kracauer's language, "predispositions") that defined the "potentially fascistic individual." Alternately defined in the study in terms of "prefascist tendencies" or "antidemocratic potential,"[35] a "high scorer" on the F-scale had a character "whose structure is such as to render him particularly susceptible to anti-democratic propaganda."[36] It was the social scientist's task to decode these traits by translating an ensemble of political and psychological predispositions as well as a range of racial, social, and gender prejudices into varying degrees of potential for fascism. Kracauer, we might say, took the measure of Weimar cinema in comparable ways. Though working through the medium of cinema and in the historical context of pre-Hitler Germany, he was similarly concerned to catalogue those "'giveaways' of antidemocratic trends" that the authors of *The Authoritarian Personality* hoped to capture through experimental procedures.[37] Under Kracauer's gaze, a film like *Caligari* produces such giveaways at every narrative and stylistic level—from the investment of characters with absolute authority or complete submissiveness to the use of recurring visual motifs such as the fairground, circular movement, or even the iris that marked scene transitions; from the nested construction of the narrative to the expressionist treatment of set design and the use of light and shadow. All of these index what the social scientific study calls "personality" or character, and what Kracauer calls the mind or, in this case, the soul: "*Caligari* shows the 'soul at work.'"[38]

Reviewing the burgeoning scholarly literature on authoritarianism in the wake of *The Authoritarian Personality*, social scientists complained about what they perceived as the fuzziness of the study's categories, its "bewilderingly varied and uneven assortment of research procedures," as well as its failure to distinguish between the various levels at which authoritarianism may be located—from individual psychological dispositions to the structure of political systems.[39] While it is true that the studies conducted by participating researchers resulted in a sprawling volume (as Horkheimer famously quipped, the authors did not have time to write a shorter book), this multiplication of referential layers—from the personal to the political, from the social to the national—is precisely one of its strong claims: the experiments, the scales, and the interview material were designed, after all, to allow precisely such assertions about the ways certain traits that seemed innocent enough on one level could manifest on another as nefarious political tendencies—a claim that Kracauer extended, in turn, to the cinema. Here, seemingly inconsequential motifs or gestures such as that of a man laying his head in a woman's lap become legible, by virtue of their ceaseless repetition across numerous films, as signs or "hieroglyphs" of the same authoritarian character that *The Authoritarian Personality* sought to elicit through the F-scale.

In the context of this comparison it is noteworthy that the ostensibly eclectic procedures of the authoritarianism study were not limited to questionnaires and interviews, but in two prominent instances included visual materials as well. A particularly intriguing set of experiments involved the "thematic apperception test": subjects were shown a series of photographs selected for their semiotic indeterminacy—the authors refer to them as "ambiguous pictures."[40] Participants were then asked to tell stories that they saw played out in the photographs, and the experimenters in turn analyzed these narratives for what they revealed about the subject's "fantasied environment and fantasied way of dealing with that environment."[41] In their evaluation of responses, the study's authors distinguished not only

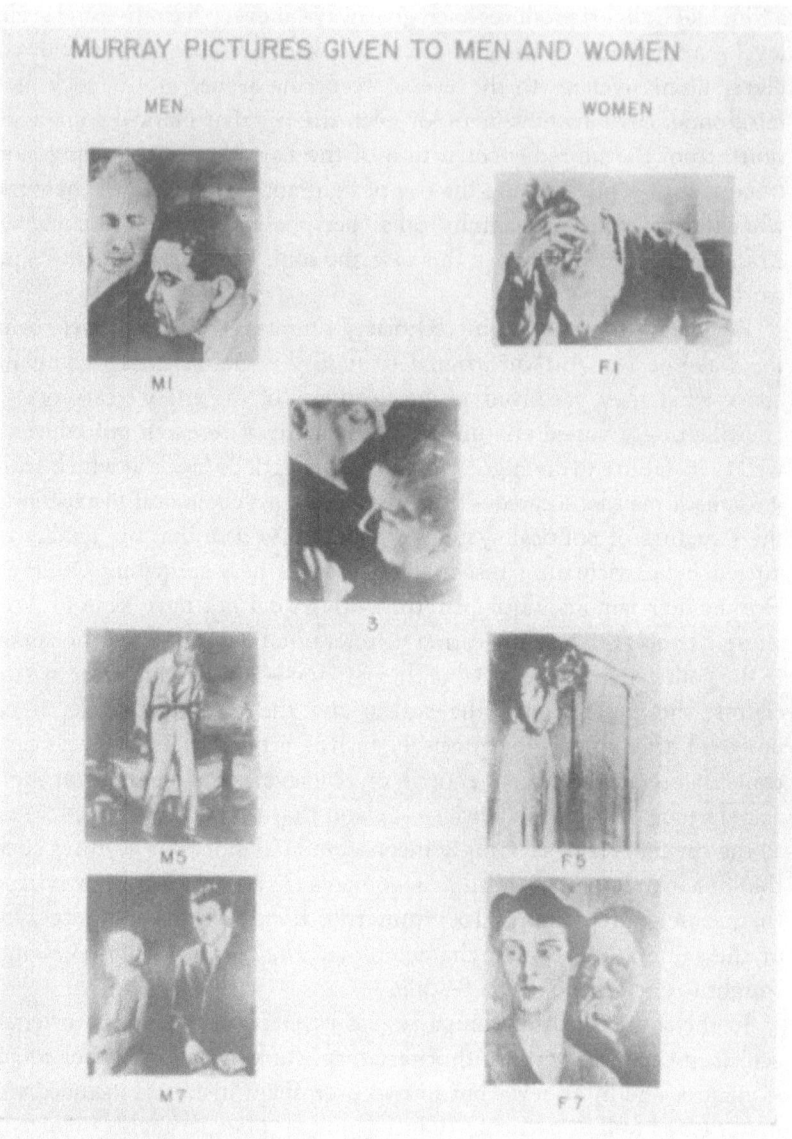

7. "Thematic Apperception Test" from *The Authoritarian Personality*, Theodor W. Adorno et al. (New York: Harper, 1950). Courtesy of AJC Archives and Records Center.

between low and high scorers, i.e. between potentially democratic and antidemocratic subjects, but interestingly also between men and women. Depending on whom the subjects identified with and how they inflected the image through their own narrative, the study then mapped different types of responses along various spectra of dominance and submissiveness, aggression and succor, etc. Although this is not the place to recapitulate in depth the results concerning different "scorers'" relation to father and mother figures, racial constellations, and various imagined scenarios, it seems significant that the authors assumed a correlation between images, their interpretation, and personality structures and that they held that these could be studied empirically.

Kracauer would hardly have shared the empiricist bent of the thematic apperception test; indeed, in a 1952 article for *Public Opinion Quarterly* he critiqued precisely the kind of "coding" involved in the evaluation of data such as this experiment yielded.[42] And yet, *From Caligari to Hitler* shares with *The Authoritarian Personality* the impulse to "read" images as indices of psychological dispositions—even if the empirical study analyzed the interpretation of images by subjects, whereas Kracauer interpreted their aesthetic function in the context of cinematic narratives. Those narratives do not "reflect" a nation's mentality any more than the images in the thematic apperception test could reveal the truth about a character; rather, in their different ways, these images encode gestures, spaces, and social relations ("casual configurations of human bodies and inanimate objects," as Kracauer puts it)[43] that demand to be read—and which both Kracauer and the authors of *The Authoritarian Personality* do read—as symptoms. The "thematic apperception test" finds its correlate in the way Kracauer submits recurring visual motifs of Weimar cinema to interpretation: the submissive male resting his head in the woman's lap, the policeman guiding the child through the maelstrom of the metropolis, the fascination with circles and spirals.

While this convergence on the role of the image as a repository of social gesture and a conduit to psychological predispositions is largely theoretical (and, in addition to the proximate context of the Studies in Prejudice, could be traced backward to the influence of Panofsky and the iconology of the Warburg School),[44] Kracauer's work intersected in quite practical ways with the Studies in Prejudice around another visual aspect of that sprawling project. At some point late during the war, the idea arose to expand the arsenal of testing procedures from interviews and questionnaires to include a test film.[45] Even as he continued to work on the *Caligari* book, Kracauer at this point joined several meetings of the Scientific Research Advisory

Council in New York and offered his services. Recruiting him for his film expertise, Horkheimer asked Kracauer to work on the film script, which he revised and annotated, making suggestions for testing antisemitic attitudes through film. Although the precise extent of his involvement remains unclear, Kracauer clearly worked on at least one version of the script (if he did not write that version himself); he corresponded with Horkheimer about the project, which listed him as an "outside collaborator"; and he attended the advisory council meetings as a guest alongside regulars such as Paul Lazarsfeld, Margaret Mead, and Robert K. Merton.[46] In its discussions, this group treated the test film as a laboratory situation from which to glean the presence or absence of prejudice, antisemitism, and authoritarianism. Kracauer may ultimately have felt uneasy about submitting the film medium to the protocols of social psychology; and yet, as his previously quoted self-description as a doctor dissecting the undead cadaver of the Weimar era suggests, he, too, took the attitude of a clinician: to Kracauer, Weimar was the laboratory where he could surgically extract the authoritarian personality from the era's films. From this perspective, the project reads as an extension of *From Caligari to Hitler* by means of communications research.

The test film, for which the Department of Scientific Research approached major Hollywood players such as Elia Kazan and Dore Schary, was never produced (though some have suggested that Schary borrowed liberally from the various treatments and planning discussions when he produced *Crossfire* for RKO in 1947). It was to have staged a dramatic scene in a crowded subway, which would have culminated in a woman getting pushed out of the moving car. Several characters would have been introduced in the run-up to this incident as possible perpetrators—a "tough guy," a club-footed man, and a character who in different versions of the film would be cast alternately as a Jew, an African American, a German, or an Englishman. During a blackout, passengers would have sought to assign blame for the accident in ways reminiscent of the political discussion at the end of Brecht's *Kuhle Wampe* (1931); then the lights were to have come back on—first in the film, where the woman turned out to be unharmed, and then in the theater, where audience members would have been asked to respond to a questionnaire. "You, too, have been eye-witnesses of the accident," the final title was to proclaim. "What is your opinion?"

As can be seen in the earliest plans for such a film, the specificity of visual communication was crucial. Horkheimer's sketch for a "Research Project on Anti-Semitism," published in 1941 in the Institute's journal *Studies in*

Philosophy and Social Science, first articulates the idea of a test film. Here we find the notion that a film might help detect forms of prejudice that remain hidden in interview situations. Operative behind this claim, as Gertrud Koch has shown, is not only the assumption that the image provides a less mediated conduit to affect the imaginary than does language, but also the sense that the movies confront viewers with powerfully configured stereotypes that have become reified as second nature.[47] What Koch formulates here in terms drawn from Adorno's and Horkheimer's contemporaneous work *The Dialectic of Enlightenment* could just as well describe Kracauer's working hypothesis in *From Caligari to Hitler:* films reflect the "unseen dynamics of human relations"; their "pictorial and narrative motifs" become legible to the analyst as "outward projections of inner urges."[48] This is by no means to suggest, as others have, that "the test film project was conceived according to the theoretical principles Kracauer was developing in *From Caligari to Hitler.*"[49] The typology and the experimental set-up derive quite obviously and explicitly from the Studies in Prejudice project rather than from Kracauer's work. But what become apparent at this brief intersection of the two projects are shared assumptions about the evidence of the image, or about the "visible hieroglyphs of the unseen dynamics of human relations."[50]

To the degree that it intersects in these ways with the various components of the sprawling Studies in Prejudice, *From Caligari to Hitler* is as much a book about the wartime and early-postwar American present as it is a history of German film. Not only were these studies kindred "investigations of character," as Noah Isenberg has pointed out;[51] but across their considerable differences of method and approach, they also shared assumptions about the functioning of ideology, about the powerful, subterranean currents that could link apparently innocuous motifs (a lack of introspection or anti-intellectualism in the *Authoritarian Personality;* a man laying his head in a woman's lap in *Caligari*) to an individual's or a nation's fascist tendencies. Both studies, in other words, were concerned with the symptomatology of fascism; both were grounded in a sense that fascism was a continuing threat to liberal democracy even after the end of the war.

The origins of that threat, however, lay in more than the structure of personality or the genesis of prejudice. In addition to the psychological dimension announced in the book's subtitle, *From Caligari to Hitler* explicitly sought to reconstruct antecedents to Hitler in sociopolitical categories that exceeded and subsumed the individual subject: in the forces of modernity, the masses, and the middle class. Nowhere did these forces crystallize more clearly for him than in Fritz Lang's *Metropolis.*

THE ORIGINS OF TOTALITARIANISM IN WEIMAR CINEMA

> ... The most essential political criterion for judging the events of our time: Will it lead to totalitarian rule or will it not?
>
> HANNAH ARENDT, "Social Science Techniques and the Study of Concentration Camps"

Few filmmakers feature as prominently in *From Caligari to Hitler* as Fritz Lang, and with good reason: Lang's oeuvre covers a particularly impressive breadth of popular blockbusters and modernist modes, his style ranging from the expressionism of *Destiny* (Der müde Tod, 1921) to the New Objectivity of *Spies* (1928), his contributions covering the genre spectrum from science fiction and fantastic thrillers like *Woman in the Moon* (1929) to the Mabuse type to *M*'s 1931 ripped-from-the-headlines story about serial murder. Lang's work, in other words, is representative of a broad cross-section of Weimar filmmaking.

Accordingly, a film like Lang's *Metropolis* occupies a paradigmatic place in *From Caligari to Hitler*—all the more so for being particularly amenable to the kind of symptomatic reading Kracauer promulgates in the book. *Metropolis* is the only film Kracauer discusses in detail in two separate chapters of the book—first, to illustrate the "grand-style manner" of films during the stabilization period and then again to exemplify what the films of this period "divulged ... after the manner of dreams."[52] *Metropolis*, he claims, was "more explicit than all others" in that "the paralyzed collective mind seemed to be talking with unusual clarity in its sleep."[53] Subsequent critics tend to agree. Although the film has meanwhile undergone numerous versions and accrued various meanings that would not have been available at the time, it still stands as a "psychogram or fever-chart of the 1920s," a Janus-faced look "back to the rebellion of a modernist avant-garde and forward to quiet submission under an authoritarian leader."[54]

Based on a potboiler plot by Thea von Harbou, Lang's film strikes Kracauer as particularly "rich in subterranean content that, like contraband, had crossed the borders of consciousness without being questioned."[55] On one level, Kracauer reads the film—like all of Weimar cinema—as a portent of things to come. For this purpose, he initially focuses on plot and character to describe the film's narrative of rebellion and submission. Instigated by the robot Maria, the uprising of the workers leads to a trite reconciliation that Kracauer adds to his list of abortive rebellions in Weimar cinema: like Alan's and Francis's investigations of the fraudulent Dr. Caligari, the workers' revolutionary spirit is reframed by *Metropolis* as a misguided protest, safely contained by the film's end. The trite message of mutual tolerance and cooperation among labor and capital that concludes the film leaves intact the authority that the workers set out to depose. The authoritarian father figure Fredersen may appear softened by the end, and the mad scientist Rotwang vanquished,[56] but for Kracauer they nonetheless join the "unholy procession" of Caligaris, Homunculi, and Mabuses who would transmogrify from screen characters into political actors at the end of the Weimar Republic.[57] In keeping with these personifications, Fredersen, the industrialist ruler of *Metropolis*, anticipates Joseph Goebbels. Both the fictional character and the propaganda minister appeal to "the heart" as a way of tightening their grip over the ruled.

But this seemingly plot-based approach only constitutes Kracauer's first pass at the film.[58] The force of his reading develops, rather, on a second, aesthetic level that we might call iconological or simply visual. Leonardo Quaresima has rightly noted that Kracauer's "iconological method" goes well beyond what readers might expect from its programmatic enunciations in the introduction.[59] Consequently, it is worth dwelling briefly on the way Kracauer develops his argument about *Metropolis* in the visual register. In *Metropolis*, he argues, two visual systems signify; the operative distinction is between the tightly controlled "ornamental" (or "decorative") scheme, on the one hand, and an implicit standard of realism, on the other, which would loosen the reins on visual patterning. The realist pole, however, is generally repressed by the "pictorial structure" of the film.[60] The fact that this is a *structuring* absence in a number of films that Kracauer analyzes, a repression rendered manifest within the visual logic of the films themselves (and not some external factor derived from retrospective teleology), allows him to speak of the films' politics, their symptomatic function as expressions of psychological dispositions. Again, this argumentation proceeds not simply on the level of plots and plot summaries: the operative terms here are entirely visual.

The conclusions, however, are sociopolitical. As in the case of *Caligari*, which showed the authoritarian "soul at work" in its expressionist design as much as through plot and character, *Metropolis* gives visual shape to politics. Again, Kracauer traces a contradiction between plot and image, between manifest and latent content. By the trite logic of Thea von Harbou's plot, Fredersen's son Freder mediates between capital and labor by uniting his father with the leader of the workers. The concluding image pictures this trio, which excludes both the mad scientist (who has just dropped to his death from the top of the cathedral) and the woman from the restitution of social order among men, thereby suppressing the overlapping threats of gender, technology, and Jewishness that had been raised during the film.[61]

The intergenerational male trio personifies the film's "motto": the heart (Freder) magically resolves the contradiction between hand (workers) and brains (capital).

But if this were true, Kracauer argues, the film would have to reflect the change visually as well. In particular, labor would no longer be the object of an "all-devouring decorative scheme" whose "ornamental patterns" have served to mark capital's omnipotence throughout the film: "Artist that he was, Lang could not possibly overlook the antagonism between the breakthrough of intrinsic human emotions and his ornamental patterns."[62] And yet the conclusion of the film is anchored by the symmetrical arrangement of the workers, a configuration for which Kracauer had famously coined the term "mass ornament" during the Weimar Republic: as they march toward the portal to the cathedral where the climactic reconciliation takes place, the workers appear in a perfectly arranged triangle at the bottom of the image, making an orderly entry into a symmetrically centered composition of the overall frame.

While it has been argued that in *Caligari* Kracauer undid much of what he had achieved in his Weimar essays, we can note that here, too, he discloses the rationality of the mass ornament. Although no longer willing to grant its ambivalent *legitimacy* after its fascist abuses, Kracauer nonetheless continues to assert the mass ornament's truth value. The "pictorial structure" of *Metropolis*, he writes, still harbors a "degree of reality [...] higher than that of artistic productions which cultivate outdated noble sentiments in obsolete forms." That reality consists precisely in the replacement of realism by ornamentalism, a move that abstracts from the real conditions of existence and thereby speaks the truth about the prevailing abstractness and the degree of alienation it implies. That is why this film, like all of Weimar cinema, becomes for Kracauer a privileged source for writing (psychological) history.[63]

When Kracauer published "The Mass Ornament" in two installments for the *Frankfurter Zeitung* in 1927, he may well have had *Metropolis* fresh on his mind as he described the ways in which Euclidean geometry shapes the mass and evacuates individuality in the rational design of the ornament: "It is only as a tiny piece of the mass that the individual can clamber up charts and can service machines without any friction."[64] Correspondingly, when the machines break down in *Metropolis*, the geometry of the ornament, if not the "pictorial structure" of the film as a whole, is on the verge of disintegrating. Rather than symmetrical shapes, the masses now assume the flowing character of the water that threatens to drown them—organic forms, in other words, that contradict the rationality of the mass ornament.⁶⁵ As the workers and their children enter the upper city, they seem to "flood" the streets, filling all available spaces among the abandoned cars like water overflowing a broken dam.

Though not a symmetrical ornament in the way Kracauer defines the term in 1927, the water motif becomes a signifying "ornamental pattern" in the film as well. It illustrates the threat of the crowd by aligning it with the natural force of a flowing river and the protofascist, misogynist trope of the dangerous "flood" that Klaus Theweleit analyzes in *Male Fantasies*.⁶⁶ That threat is then contained at the conclusion, when "the workers advance in the form of a wedge-shaped, strictly symmetrical procession which points towards the industrialist standing on the portal steps of the cathedral. The whole composition denotes that the industrialist acknowledges the heart for the purpose of manipulating it; that he does not give up his power, but will expand it over a realm not yet annexed—the realm of the collective soul."⁶⁷

The politics of this conclusion go beyond the restitution of order; they herald a new form of domination. Although the film ostensibly focuses on Freder's rebellion and grants him the final word in his role as the heart/mediator, the ornamental pattern effects an ideological substitution. Where the opening shift change put on display the workers' "mechanical," quasi-military discipline, the ending enacts what Kracauer calls "totalitarian discipline," in which the masses have repressed the need for rebellion, internalized the rigidity of the mass ornament, and acquiesced to "totalitarian authority."⁶⁸

With this assertion, Kracauer enters the territory of Hannah Arendt's contemporary investigations of totalitarianism, and not just terminologically. Rather, the two authors share an interest in understanding the specific relationship between modern masses and authoritarian rule that is at the heart of totalitarianism; and both seek to locate this relationship in a prehistory that leads, for Kracauer, from Caligari to Hitler, and for Arendt from nineteenth-century antisemitism to the camps.

For Arendt, too, totalitarianism involves not simply "mechanical" coercion but the production of mass consent toward a leader, which Kracauer detects in the "pictorial" register of *Metropolis*. Totalitarianism, Arendt writes, "is never content to rule by external means . . . ; thanks to its peculiar ideology and the role assigned to it in this apparatus of coercion, totalitarianism has discovered a means of dominating and terrorizing human beings from within. In this sense it eliminates the distance between the rulers and the ruled."⁶⁹ In place of this distance, Arendt intriguingly postulates a relationship of mutual representation between the *Führer* and the masses—precisely the kind of ornamental reciprocity that *Metropolis* produces on the visual level, where "the all-devouring decorative scheme ... marks the industrialist's claim to omnipotence."[70] The totalitarian leader, Arendt writes, "depends just as much on the 'will' of the masses he embodies as the masses depend on him. Without him they would lack external representation and remain an *amorphous horde*"—in other words, the kind of multitude that is raised as a specter in the middle but is symptomatically absent from the conclusion of Lang's film, one no longer contained within the "pictorial structure" of the geometric ornament.[71]

The dialectics of leader and masses form a central concern for both Kracauer and Arendt. Indeed, the section in *Origins of Totalitarianism* on totalitarianism proper begins with a chapter on "the masses," which Arendt calls agglomerations of people "not held together by a consciousness of common interest." In other words, they are not classes, and class consciousness, however dim, is replaced by "the psychology of European mass man."[72] In the masses that enable totalitarianism and that totalitarianism in turn produces, the very category of the individual implodes (a process that climaxes irreversibly in the camps). So does the capacity for experience.[73] In a formulation that reprises Löwenthal's diagnosis of the "Atomization of Man" and the debilitating effects of fear in his contribution to the *Commentary* "Crisis of the Individual" series, Arendt writes that totalitarian movements "are mass organizations of atomized, isolated individuals" who have succumbed to "essential homelessness."[74] This atomization, the creation of "mass man," is the basis for one of the central features Arendt attributes to totalitarian movements: a characteristic power to "organize the masses into a collective unit to back up their lies with impressive magnificence."[75] This assessment echoes Kracauer's earlier analysis of totalitarian propaganda. One thinks immediately, of course, of Riefenstahl's Nuremberg images—but given the retroactive logic that Arendt diagnoses here (producing the truth of the lie after the fact by producing the crowd), Kracauer's teleological readings seem less willful and more part of the very logic he, like Arendt, is tracing on the path to totalitarianism. No wonder Kracauer was reading crowd formations *backwards* in *From Caligari to Hitler*, from *Triumph of the Will* to Arnold Fanck's mountain films.[76]

But there is also a more substantive reading of the masses in Kracauer, which, like the motifs of the tyrant or of chaos (the false opposite of tyranny), are central to the argument of *From Caligari to Hitler*. The masses, Kracauer holds, "haunted the imagination" in the postwar period. They assumed their definitive form in films like *Metropolis*, as we have seen, but also in Ernst Lubitsch's historical pageants, from *Madame Dubarry* (1919) to *The Loves of Pharaoh* (1922) and *Deception* (Anna Boleyn, 1920). Masses turn in these films from historical forces endowed with a political will and revolutionary rationality into "dynamic units sweeping through large spaces"—patterns, arabesques, mass ornaments with a rationality of their own.[77] Lubitsch's ornamental arrangement of the masses, while connoted negatively in *From Caligari to Hitler*, is productive or "realist" as a pictorial index, regardless of his tendency to "dissolve history into psychology" in his plots. Rather, Lubitsch reveals the historical force of the mass as an agent of atomization. Significantly, this again happens at the level of the image. Describing Lubitsch as a puppeteer, Kracauer finds him to give "multitude, and in contrast, loneliness, a new force." In his crowd films, the mass often "decomposes" so as to reveal a single figure at its center who remains alone, in a void. "Thus the individual appeared as a forlorn creature in a world threatened by mass domination. Paralleling the stereotyped plot of all those pageants, this pictorial device treated the pathetic solitude of the individual with a sympathy which implied aversion to the plebeian mass and fear of its dangerous power."[78]

Lubitsch's handling of the masses, in other words, indexes the atomization of the individual as its dialectical pole. This motif is central, of course, not just to Lubitsch's films but to a far broader critique of modernity—one that Kracauer shares with any number of critics in the wake of Lukács, Simmel, and Weber.[79] Centering on figurations of the mass as "amorphous horde," as multitude, as mob—but also as the unrealized subject of democracy—this critique takes on a particular valence both in interwar Germany, where it anchors discussions of the country's first and ultimately failed attempt at democracy, and in the postwar United States, where it is hotly debated among "nervous liberals."

Although Kracauer and Arendt cover different intellectual, chronological, and geographical ground, it may be worth recalling that from their shared New York present they overlap in their mutual concern with the interwar years in Germany—what Arendt describes as the "general mood which pervades the pretotalitarian atmosphere,"[80] or, in Kracauer's terms, the period that led from Caligari to Hitler. Sketching a portrait of the "front generation," Arendt describes the pretotalitarian mood as one in which "all traditional values and propositions had evaporated"; this generation's "antihumanist, antiliberal, anti-individualist, and anticultural instincts," she argues, provide a fertile ground for totalitarian dispositions.[81] Kracauer deploys virtually the same vocabulary in his indictment of the "nihilism" emanating from films like *Danton* (1920, dir. Dimitri Buchowetzky) and

Madame Dubarry—films that psychologize the French revolution and "drain [it] of its significance." In keeping with his methodological emphasis on the way the films' historical subject matter signifies in the moment of their production, Kracauer reads them as symptoms of "strong antirevolutionary, if not antidemocratic, tendencies in postwar Germany."[82]

This historically specific notion of the ideological vacuum that leaves the individual unmoored and susceptible is one that Kracauer and Arendt share throughout their work. Introducing the "crucial dilemma" that he finds articulated in Weimar cinema—the false alternative between tyranny and chaos at the expense of any progressive, liberal, or democratic perspectives—Kracauer, too, casts his backward glance at the interwar years. "Whoever lived through those crucial years in Germany," he writes, "will remember the craving for a spiritual shelter which possessed the young, the intellectuals."[83]

And for those who do not remember, there is Kracauer's 1922 essay "Die Wartenden" (Those Who Wait). There, he paired a critique of modernity as the driving force of alienation, atomization, and relativization with a scathing indictment of various movements that had sprung into the breach. These amounted, in Kracauer's view, to false solutions—such as messianism, anthroposophy, the sectarianism of the George circle, religious renewal, or even Weberian skepticism. Only the attitude of "those who wait," for Kracauer, was sustainable—an attitude of "tense activity" and "hesitant openness" that is distinguished from mere indecision by its turn from metaphysics "into the world of *reality* and the domains it encompasses."[84]

Caligari reprises these motifs almost verbatim, though the vindication of waiting is now replaced, given the historical perspective, with a critique of indecision.[85] In addition to the various lines of escape he had critiqued in his earlier essay, Kracauer retrospectively sees a resultant "state of paralysis. Cynicism, resignation, disillusionment: these tendencies point to a mentality disinclined to commit itself in any direction."[86] The inability to decide and, more importantly, to act—to have and to maintain the courage of one's own convictions—Kracauer locates psychologically in middle-class dispositions. In keeping with the book's recurrent spatial motif of retreat, he locates these dispositions in the figure of the petit bourgeois male who ventures out, tentatively, only to return home again to the enclosure of the bourgeois interior as a psychological "shell." Although Kracauer treats this motif on various analytical levels—the retreat of film production into the studio, the retreat from realism, the retreat from politics—he locates its visualization in the cinema's recurrent image of the man laying his head in the woman's lap, as at the close of Karl Grune's *The Street*. For Kracauer, this image encodes the failure of an Oedipal process, the inability of the Weimar middle-class man to leave boyhood behind, to liberate himself from a masochistic "longing for submission" and dependency on the mother figure. In keeping with Fromm's and the Frankfurt School's analysis of the authoritarian character, as we have seen, this inability was tantamount to the failure to establish an autonomous subjectivity that might serve as the basis for mature political action. The inability to resolve the Oedipal complex, in other words, becomes for Kracauer a failure to formulate a democratic subject after the demise of the *Kaiserreich*.

What Kracauer sees on the visual level, Arendt carries forward in her political theory, which reformulates Kracauer's "general retreat into a shell"[87] as a misconstrual of the private realm as a safeguard against politics. For Arendt, the central figure here is the philistine, corralled by the most philistine member of the Nazi elite, Heinrich Himmler. The philistine, according to Arendt, "is the bourgeois isolated from his own class, the atomized individual who is produced by the breakdown of the bourgeois class itself."[88] The breakdown of clear class distinctions reprises the theorization of modernity as the dissolution of stable categories (Arendt's notion that "all traditional values and propositions had evaporated" after World War I).[89] Where classes had served to organize cultural belonging, the "atomized individual" now dissolves into the anonymous mass, ready to be mobilized by the likes of Himmler for the "greatest mass crimes ever committed in history."[90] As in Kracauer's psychological framework, such mobilization becomes possible because of the weak subjectivity of "mass man," who, "in the midst of the ruins of his world," clings to "nothing so much as his private security." But the retreat into the shell of privacy fails to reckon with the destruction of that very shell in totalitarianism's classless society: "Nothing proved easier to destroy," writes Arendt, "than the privacy and private morality of people who thought of nothing but safeguarding their private lives."[91]

Arendt and Kracauer share a critique of modernity and the political fungibility of "mass man," but this is also where we need to begin charting the specificities of their respective arguments by acknowledging their differences. For Arendt, as we have seen, locates the dangerous power of the "plebeian mass"—as well as of the "mob," from which she distinguishes the mass historically and theoretically—in its unmooring from class and in its resulting cooptation: no longer held together by common interests, the mass becomes so much clay for totalitarianism to mold. In contrast, Kracauer builds his retrospective argument about the "pretotalitarian" years between *Caligari* and Hitler around the psychology of the middle-class male;[92] the author of *Die Angestellten*, in other words, begins his analysis not from classless masses but from a class-based analysis, even if that class turns out to be held together by a particularly shaky form of pseudo–class consciousness.

Similarly, there are important distinctions to be drawn between the two authors' central notions of propaganda, dictatorship, and totalitarianism itself. Indeed, although it appears prominently in the discussion of *Metropolis,* totalitarianism per se is not a central analytical category for Kracauer. Far more important in anticipating the rise of Hitler is the figure of the *tyrant,* whom Arendt distinguishes sharply from the totalitarian leader. One of the central arguments that Arendt develops during the 1940s, after all, concerns the specificity of totalitarianism as distinct from earlier revolutions, dictatorships, and forms of tyranny. Unlike these forms of authoritarian rule, totalitarianism is defined by its increasing and endless use of terror even in the face of shrinking opposition (Arendt calls "total terror the essence of totalitarian government"), by the massive increase in innocent victims, and by the arbitrariness of terror.[93] The fundamental novelty of totalitarian systems in the twentieth century has a direct consequence for the political theorist, who must develop a corresponding new vocabulary, since "all our concepts and definitions [are] insufficient for an understanding of totalitarian phenomena [and] all our categories of thought and standards for judgment seem to explode in our hands the instant we try to apply them here."[94] This, indeed, is one of Arendt's fundamental claims: the unprecedented and unique nature of totalitarianism mandates the formulation of new analytical categories.

Now, we might say that the same assumption underwrites Kracauer's work on *From Caligari to Hitler* as well. Before the publication of that book, few critics had taken cinema seriously enough to consider it worthy of monographic attention, let alone of analytic protocols that tied the films of a nation to its politics, its history, its class habitus. Re-viewing Weimar cinema in Manhattan during the 1940s was not simply a matter of augmenting our knowledge of film history or even of helping us to "understand [...] Hitler's ascent and ascendancy";[95] it was, rather, Kracauer's response to the "German problem" and to the shortcomings of received economic, sociological, and political explanatory frameworks. In this situation, he turned to culture—and to cinema as mass culture in particular—literally for new ways of seeing the period that had led up to Hitler. As an analytical lens, he argued, the cinema could yield explanations that were not accessible "within the normal field of vision," explanations that tapped "a secret history involving the inner dispositions of the German people."[96]

This approach may seem well worn to us after a period in which *From Caligari to Hitler* stood as the "classic" text of a broadly accepted paradigm for studying "national cinemas." The wax and wane of theoretical predilections has cast a shadow on the practice of "symptomatic readings," and the paradigm of national cinema itself can now seem passé as we train our attention increasingly on the "transnational" functioning of film production, distribution, exhibition, and discourse. But we should remind ourselves that today's (or yesterday's) classics were conceived as interventions in pressing historical and conceptual impasses, which they reformulated in new and decisive ways. To read the origins of totalitarianism in the popular medium of cinema was, in the immediate postwar years, nothing short of a provocation.

7. Reframing *Caligari*
The Politics of Cinema

> What felicitous sources for an art, such a combination of infatuation with meaningless motion, thrilled senses and fairground smells!
>
> SIEGFRIED KRACAUER, letter to Erwin Panofsky on "Style and Medium in Motion Pictures," February 4, 1947

From Caligari to Hitler was published to mixed reviews. Early commentators recognized the novelty of Kracauer's method, making explicit note of his turn to film as an object for psychosocial analysis. The reviewer for *Commentary* held that "the most impressive aspect of Dr. Kracauer's book is his method. [. . .] Even more than the actual history itself, the method employed will be of great value to American students of the movies."[1] Iris Barry—who would know, given that she had sponsored Kracauer's research for the book at the MoMA film library—wrote in the *New Republic*, "This is the first time that a sober and protracted study of human behavior has been carried out by the light of the screen."[2] These responses index the perceived novelty of a book that took film seriously as a historical source. Not only was Kracauer "one of the first people ever to devote himself full-time to a scholarly study of Germany cinema," as Anton Kaes has pointed out;[3] he also formulated an approach to national cinema that linked aesthetic with political considerations, thereby moving film historiography out of its initial, positivist phase with its focus on securing prints and compiling filmographies.[4]

This new approach proved lastingly influential. In keeping with this emphasis on approach and method, *Time* spoke of Kracauer as a "psyche-interpreter" of the movies, wondering out loud what "an intense look at Hollywood films would tell the doctor about the U.S. mind and heart."[5] This reviewer and others like him, who complained about the fact that *From Caligari to Hitler* limited itself to the German national context,[6] might have found an answer in Kracauer's writings on Hollywood from the 1940s. Here, as we have seen, he brought to bear the methods he had developed in his study of Nazi propaganda and Weimar cinema. Although plans to write a follow-up volume "from Shirley Temple to Truman" never moved beyond the status of a running gag between Kracauer and Panofsky, others would take up Kracauer's methods in monographs on the American (and later the German) cinema.[7] In 1950, the psychologist couple Martha Wolfenstein and Nathan Leites published *Movies: A Psychological Study*, which appears to have overlapped in so many ways with both the promises and the shortcomings of Kracauer's own work that his rather critical review of the book in the *Public Opinion Quarterly* seems narcissistically to exaggerate the small differences;[8] he was far more encouraging of another project that his work helped to inspire, Barbara Deming's *Running Away from Myself: A Dream Portrait of America Drawn from the Films of the Forties*, which, though published only in 1969, was completed in 1950 and acknowledges its debt to Kracauer on the first page. Deming, a close friend of Kracauer's, was also instrumental in translating the method of *From Caligari to Hitler* into policy—if not for the United Nations, as Kracauer had hoped, then for a major film project at the Library of Congress. Here, collection criteria were devised explicitly with the thought in mind that future Kracauers would have the same resources for writing a national history through film as Kracauer himself had had at the MoMA film library.[9]

Kracauer's method, indeed, exerted an influence well beyond the United States. It shaped an entire generation of film critics, particularly in Germany, where authors writing for the influential *Filmkritik* would recall later that the book was permanently checked out from the university library by the journal's founding members.[10] A classic in film studies, *From Caligari to Hitler* has become an unspoken basis for critical and theoretical claims, especially about national cinemas. Writing in 1989 and without making explicit reference to Kracauer, Andrew Higson, one of the key scholars in these debates, defined the approach to national cinemas through a series of questions that had informed the conception of *Caligari* forty years earlier: "What are these films about? Do they share a common style or world view? What sort of projections of the national character do they offer? To what extent are they engaged in 'exploring, questioning and constructing a notion of nationhood in the films themselves and in the consciousness of the viewer'?"[11] As the paradigm of national cinemas has receded in theoretical importance with the rise of globalization and transnational frameworks, so has Kracauer's influence waned in terms of explicit or implicit reference.[12] But it still lives on in publishing programs that devote themselves unproblematically to national cinemas, as well as in the basic rhetorical "tool kit" of cinema studies and film journalism.[13]

In the political climate at the time of the book's publication, however, there was also a far rougher tone, and a number of contemporary readers were less generous in their assessments than those writing in *Time* or *Commentary* (let alone Barry, who had a vested interest in seeing *Caligari* warmly received). I already referred to Eric Bentley's put-down of *Caligari* in the *New York Times* as a "refugee's revenge," but arguably the harshest critique—especially in light of the political arguments we have been tracing in tandem with Adorno and Arendt—came from Dwight Macdonald. This was the same New York critic, it will be recalled, who had praised Kracauer's propaganda analysis as "some of the best writing on film" in the early 1940s. In his review for *Partisan Review*, which had only recently published the "Caligari" chapter in the February issue, Macdonald picks up on his earlier assessment but now uses it do damn Kracauer with faint praise. "As one might expect from the author's previous writings on films," he concedes, "there are many fine perceptions in this elaborate study." Macdonald goes on to critique the book severely, faulting it for not working comparatively; for carrying the psychoanalytic method too far and neglecting manifest meanings in favor of hidden ones; and for wrangling the evidence to fit the argument. *From Caligari to Hitler*, he claims, is "a 'thesis book' of the most crude and naive kind, using special pleading and farfetched interpretations to wrench the data into a simplistic pattern." Given Kracauer's investment in understanding the origins of totalitarianism in Weimar cinema, Macdonald's labeling of the book's method as "totalitarian" in its own right must have stung.[14]

If Macdonald placed Kracauer's ideology critique of the 1940s under ideological suspicion, however, he was outdone by his colleague Seymour Stern, who engaged in full-throated red-baiting. Writing in the anti-Stalinist, liberal magazine *The New Leader*, Stern accused Kracauer of "quoting extensively from official Communist sources" and of relying heavily on the opinions of the "official film critic of the American Communist Party," Harry Alan Potamkin. Stern consequently considered communism to color the "political theory of the book," which faulted Weimar for failing to generate and sustain a democratic spirit and democratic attitudes. "Unfortunately," Stern concludes, Kracauer "makes it unmistakably clear that what he really means is, in effect, Communist spirit and Communist attitudes."[15]

Such invective indexes the temperature of contemporary discourse in New York during the Cold War; it also may illustrate the considerable "moral temper" of an influential cultural critic like Macdonald, a member of the *Partisan Review* crowd and a self-described "expert mudslinger."[16] But critiques such as these, even where they patently overreach in their anticommunist zeal, also pinpoint a central concern that we have not yet

PARTISAN REVIEW

MARCH-APRIL, 1947

ARTHUR KOESTLER
    London Letter

JAMES BURNHAM
    Observations on Kafka

GRANVILLE HICKS
    The Future of Socialism

ISAAC ROSENFELD
    The Brigadier (a story)

WILLIAM BARRETT
    Dialogue on Anxiety

DELMORE SCHWARTZ
    The Good, the True, and the Beautiful

SIEGFRIED KRACAUER
    Caligari and Hitler

MARY McCARTHY
    George Kelly and American Comedy

JAMES JOHNSON SWEENEY
    An Interview with Henry Moore

2

60c

8. Cover of the March–April 1947 issue of *Partisan Review*, which included prepublication of the *Caligari* chapter from Kracauer's book. (Boston University Archives)

fully addressed: the politics of Kracauer's approach. In this respect, Stern is not wrong about Kracauer's leftist leanings;[17] but neither is he right to "attack the book as if there were something illegitimate about trying to throw some light on the German problem," as Robert Warshow points out in his rebuttal in the following issue of the *New Leader*.[18] The question, rather, is on what normative grounds Kracauer tackles this problem, both politically and aesthetically. What are the assumptions under which he relates film and politics, and what configuration of that relationship would enable us to imagine alternatives to authoritarianism and totalitarianism, whether in Weimar or beyond?

In this respect, among others, *From Caligari to Hitler* appears by some accounts to have become something of an embarrassment. *Caligari* barely deserves mention, for example, in Miriam Hansen's *Cinema and Experience*, surely the most important and comprehensive work on Kracauer to have appeared in recent years; and entire anthologies on Kracauer's prolific writings can afford to overlook what is arguably still the most widely recognized title in his oeuvre. As Leonardo Quaresima puts it in the introduction to the 2004 edition, critics today treat the book "as if it was considered hopelessly inadequate and feeble, the inference being that Kracauer's true originality and importance are to be sought elsewhere."[19] What appears to be missing from the book in particular is the dialectical sensitivity that characterized some of Kracauer's best writing from the Weimar years. The 1927 essay on photography, to take but one example, may have mounted a critique of the medium every bit as strident as the later critique of Weimar cinema—indicting photography for its ahistoricity, its lack of memory, its alliance with positivism and historicism, and its essentially affirmative character. *From Caligari to Hitler*, as we have seen, critiques Weimar cinema in similarly resolute fashion for its authoritarianism, its lack of political courage, and its affirmative character in the face of the growing threat of Nazism. But the photography essay, like others from the period, ultimately tests its own conclusions by asserting the truth value of photography and detecting in it a utopian kernel: photography, precisely by holding up a distorted mirror to society, becomes a medium through which to imagine a changed, reconciled world.

The same figure of thought recurs in "The Mass Ornament," also from 1927: by representing to society its own abstraction and complete rationalization, the mass ornament makes it possible also to imagine a reasonable *(vernünftig)* use of *ratio*. The political investment of these essays is never nostalgic, nor conservative: the way out of modernity's pernicious effects is forward, by pushing through its limitations until they reverse themselves.

As Kracauer puts it, "The process leads directly through the center of the mass ornament, not away from it." Hence the famous conclusions that capitalism "rationalizes not too much, but rather *too little*," and that photography permits the "reflection of the reality that has slipped away" from consciousness.[20] In its place, consciousness can then "establish the *provisional status* of all given configurations, and perhaps even ... awaken an inkling of the right order of the inventory of nature"—an order intimated in the works of Kafka and in the montage aesthetics of film, which put into play the disjointed pieces of an alienated world.[21]

Photography and film, mass culture and modernity, in other words, hold out a promise in Kracauer's essays from the 1920s. In a "go-for-broke game" that will either bankrupt society through complete alienation or harness a reflexive notion of alienation to the project of enlightenment, media such as photography and film occupy a decisive position. As distorting mirrors, they are the sites at which alienation can become reflexive, and where consciousness can confront the failure of rationalization to generate a social order governed by reason *(Vernunft)*. From the earliest essays on, then, Kracauer considers photographic media to harbor a considerable power of estrangement, by which they hold up a distorting mirror to society. Already in 1923, he identifies this power as central for film theory (or what he calls the "as yet unwritten metaphysics of film").[22] "Authentic cinema," he notes in his review of *Die närrische Wette des Lord Aldini* for the *Frankfurter Zeitung*, "is tasked with ironizing the illusoriness of our lives by exaggerating their unreality and thereby pointing toward true reality."[23] Like photography, which Kracauer describes as "a means of alienation," film can renew our perception and intimate different configurations of culture, politics, and society.[24]

Little of this utopian discourse appears to survive in *From Caligari to Hitler*. Why, one might wonder, could the authoritarianism of *The Cabinet of Dr. Caligari* not have been legible as an antidote, as the distorted mirror image that allows a potentially authoritarian social order to become reflexive and change course? Why did Kracauer consider the "surface approach" of *Berlin, Symphony of a Great City*, which forces "human beings ... into the sphere of the inanimate," merely empty formalism rather than an opportunity to grasp modernity's reifying tendencies?[25] Why did he no longer detect in the ambivalent play of revolt and submission, authority and madness, a go-for-broke game with authoritarianism? Why was "chaos" simply the opposite of tyranny and no longer ambivalent, as the chaotic "blizzard of photographs" had been during the Weimar Republic or as abstraction had been in "The Mass Ornament"?[26] And why did Kracauer not follow through on the analysis of mass ornaments in *Metropolis*—which he still reads in 1947, as we have seen, as indices of totalitarianism—by inquiring also into the dialectical promise of such dystopian images?

On one level, the answer to these questions is clear enough: such hopeful interpretations no longer had any place in a world in which the go-for-broke game with history had been definitively lost, resulting precisely in "the eradication of consciousness" that Kracauer had seen as the stakes involved in the bet on media and modernity. Failure to win this bet, he had contended, would result in reason reverting to myth; "the nature that [consciousness] failed to penetrate would sit down at the very table that consciousness had abandoned."[27] With the rise of Hitler, the war, and the Holocaust, precisely this had come to pass: the wager was lost. Working in New York alongside other commentators on the "German Question," on the authoritarian personality and the origins of totalitarianism, Kracauer added cinema to their archives and experimental data sets. In the atmosphere of continuing fear and the incipient cold war, he shared their bleak assessments of the prospects for liberalism and the project of enlightenment.

As a consequence, critical theorists were reluctant to spell out clear alternatives. We have already noted Kracauer's recurrent critique of Hollywood's inability to formulate a positive representation of the liberal democracy it ostensibly touted. The same might be said of large-scale social science projects such as *The Authoritarian Personality*, which seems unable to match the well-defined high scorer on the F-scale—the potentially fascist individual—with a similarly clear-contoured low scorer: far more difficult to identify a democratic personality than an authoritarian one, it appears.[28] The conclusion to the study similarly appears to "walk on eggshells," as Kracauer had put it in relation to Hollywood's liberal-minded films. After demonstrating in one experiment after another how susceptible their subjects were to authoritarianism, the authors assert simply "the potential, residing within the people, for moving in a different direction."[29]

The conclusion to Hannah Arendt's *Origins of Totalitarianism* is even more perfunctory in its baffling brevity. Added to the second edition of the book in 1958, it consists merely in the bold assertion, unfounded by anything in the analysis of the preceding five hundred pages, that "every end in history necessarily contains a new beginning." Citing Augustine, Arendt defines this possibility of beginning as "the supreme capacity of man; politically, it is identical with man's freedom."[30] This category is central to the further development of Arendt's thought, where it becomes theorized as "natality." But in *Origins of Totalitarianism*, it appears merely as an appendage.

From Caligari to Hitler, it would appear, offers no such hope, however perfunctory. Its final paragraphs merely reiterate the anticipationist argument and vividly describe the gloom spread by the proto-Hitlerian protagonists of Weimar cinema: "Personified daydreams of minds to whom freedom meant a fatal shock, and adolescence a permanent temptation, these figures filled the arena of Nazi Germany. Homunculus walked about in the flesh. Self-appointed Caligaris hypnotized innumerable Cesares into murder. Raving Mabuses committed fantastic crimes with impunity, and mad Ivans devised unheard-of tortures. [...] It was all as it had been on the screen. The dark premonitions of the final doom were also fulfilled."[31] Whereas the media essays of the 1920s had adopted the conditional mood at their conclusions to maintain the possibility of a future different from the rationalized present of modernity, *Caligari* ends in the past indicative: the wager was lost.

And yet, submerged in *From Caligari to Hitler*, I wish to suggest, we can also detect a discourse on the utopian potential of cinema that carries forward the constructivist readings of the 1920s. It is a muted discourse that will only become explicit in the *Theory of Film*, but for our present purposes it is worth noting that the later volume with its decidedly hopeful gesture toward the "redemption of physical reality" shares a common origin with *From Caligari to Hitler*. As I have previously pointed out, we can trace both books back to Kracauer's notes on film aesthetics from the late 1930s and early 1940s.[32] Those documents show an ongoing phenomenological commitment: an interest in cinema's capacity to record and reveal reality, and in its dispassionate, estranging, "non-anthropocentric" functions in particular. They also show an interest in linking aesthetic, social, cultural, and political considerations in ways that connect the approach of the Weimar essays to the groundwork for the two film books written in New York.[33]

Thus, in his three-page "Notes on the Planned History of the German Film" from 1942, Kracauer still speaks of Weimar cinema's ability to "portray [...] apparently familiar objects and make them seem new," whether by means of expressionism or of realism. The Germans, he claims in these notes, "widened the dominion of the cinema in two directions: they incorporated in it the terrific visions of a mind put out of joint, and at the same time introduced a truly cinematic realism." Many of *Caligari*'s dominant lines of inquiry are laid here: into the "symptomatic value" of German films, which he considers "particularly transparent"; into the ideological function of Weimar cinema to hide from the middle classes their material conditions of existence; and into the "waning substantiality of the German democracy."[34] But at the same time, the plan nuances these questions with a commitment to the minute, the overlooked, and to the same "inconspicuous surface-level expressions" that, according to "The Mass Ornament," would permit "unmediated access to the fundamental substance of the state of things."[35] Kracauer is fascinated here, as throughout his career, by the ability of the cinema to pull out background detail through a close-up, to magnify minutiae, or inversely to transform the human being who acts out his or her role in front of the camera into "an object among objects."[36]

In the "Notes," which served as a grant proposal for the Guggenheim Foundation, Kracauer lays out succinctly the importance of "little things" and their relationship to "history's moving forces" for the humanities at large. Characteristically, Kracauer develops this broad claim by way of a seemingly remote reference—in this case, to farming and engineering—as if to model the very practice he is advocating:

> Both the farmer and the engineer know something about the importance of seemingly unimportant details. Many small factors, they know, must work together to ripen the corn or to make a complicated machine function. Their experience teaches them to distrust the pretensions of pure ideas while at the same time they find in little things more than just little things. Such an outlook proves helpful, too, in the field of humanities, where any survey interested solely in the display of ideas runs the risk of missing the ideas' very significance. [. . .] To focus directly upon ideas is at any rate a sure means never to grasp them. But it may well happen that a close scrutiny of some minor event of the kind favored on the screen allows one secretly to watch history's moving forces in full action. Ideas manifest themselves rather in by-ways, in unobtrusive facts. And in examining these facts, it is often as though one looked through a narrow window at strange scenes that, outdoors, would be entirely invisible.[37]

This passage is richly evocative of many assumptions and motifs that guide Kracauer's thinking through its various phases from the early Weimar years through the posthumous book *History*. Thus, the brief methodological sketch hints at Kracauer's dialectical interest in "unobtrusive facts" *and* in "history's moving forces"; his phenomenological approach to the "many small factors [that] make a complicated machine function"; the emphasis on the epistemological power of vision, on "*watch[ing]* history's moving forces" on screen and finding a perspective—if not a medium (film)—from which to perceive the otherwise invisible. In that perspective, we might even find a resonance of the extraterritorial position that Kracauer liked to espouse. Like the exile he himself became after 1933, and like the historian whose ideal vantage point Kracauer would locate in an exilic "near vacuum of extra-territoriality,"[38] here we find the critic peering "through a narrow window at strange scenes" of which he is not part but that he is privileged to see—whereas those who populate those same scenes "outdoors" see nothing.[39]

In addition to these motifs, however, the cited passage also enacts a structural paradigm of Kracauer's thinking: his tendency to work through oppositions such as that between "little things" and "pure ideas" by keeping them in motion—"in a fluid state," as he would put it. How else to resolve the apparent oxymoron of "find[ing] in little things more than just little things" or "seeing what is invisible"?[40] This commitment to conceptual fluidity is in evidence from the early essay that sides with "those who wait," through the give-and-take between formative and realistic "tendencies" of photography, between cinema's powers to "record" and "reveal," all the way to the methodological reflections at the close of *History* regarding "top-down" and "bottom-up" modes of inquiry and the relationship between the general and the particular. It also plays a role in the ostensibly rigid interpretive framework of *Caligari*.[41]

To recover this conceptual fluidity, or what Miriam Hansen rightly describes as Kracauer's "rhetorical staging of ambivalence," we need only attend to the strongly developed figurative discourse that does double duty in *From Caligari to Hitler*.[42] On the one hand, Kracauer deploys metaphor, personification, and analogy to tie down the symptomatic meanings of individual motifs. The "Notes" speak in this vein of the "unhappy, homeless soul moving like a stranger through the world of normal reality." Likening films to the daydreams of society, *Caligari* offers countless similar analogies, according to which Dr. Caligari is like Hitler, bourgeois interiors mirror the middle-class soul, and "human ornaments denote ... the omnipotence of dictatorship."[43] Such linkages describe the reflectionist argument of the book. Precisely to the degree that this argument proceeds figuratively, however, it remains in flux even as it attempts to pin down meanings.

We might illustrate this fluidity by looking at Kracauer's deployment of water as a metaphor at a crucial juncture in *From Caligari to Hitler*. As Christoph Brecht has pointed out in a particularly astute reading of the book, Kracauer attempts to clinch his argument about the authoritarianism of the *Caligari* film by introducing the symbols of the river and the whirlpool: "While freedom resembles a river," he writes, "chaos resembles a whirlpool. Forgetful of self, one may plunge into chaos; one cannot move on it."[44] This rather willful attribution of symptomatic meanings is characteristic of the apparently self-assured coding of visual motifs in *From Caligari to Hitler*— but it also begs some obvious questions. As Brecht points out, "The image of the river symbolizes not only the path to freedom, but also the trajectory that leads 'from Caligari to Hitler.' And the whirlpool of chaos designates not only the incapacity for emancipation and self-determination, but also a non-determinist relationship to history, which recognizes even in catastrophe the possibility that things might have been otherwise."[45] In other words, whereas "chaos" figures in *Caligari* principally as the false alternative to tyranny, thus usurping the conceptual and semantic place of freedom and democracy as "correct" or logical alternatives,[46] metaphors of disorder also point toward a different politics of representation and cinema in the book.

To recover these instances, one needs to read *From Caligari to Hitler* against the grain of the political teleology it maps. In the terms laid out in the previous chapter, this would involve reading for ways out of the labyrinth, for moments that allow us to imagine cinema working in directions other than inward, for the promise of movement as against the emphasis on paralysis. We would have to attend to those instances where Kracauer imagines an opposite and countervailing force to the "centripetal" spatiality that I mapped earlier—moments when he considers a film like *The Joyless Street* to embark into an "open universe," compared to which "the world of *Variety* is rather an indoor affair."[47] Moments, in other words, when the blind alleyways and stunted trajectories open up the enclosed space of cinema and politics to new encounters with alterity. In the terms offered by Brecht, we would need to note how the overarching teleology that leads as if in a straight line from Caligari to Hitler is undermined by an allegorical strain that probes individual motifs and images beyond merely assigning them a place in the historical and political narrative.

Besides the equivocations around rivers and whirlpools, we might point in this vein to Kracauer's manifest fascination with the fairground—as yet another spatial figure of chaos, but also as both a site of origin and a metaphor for cinema. Intent to paint the fair as a vortex of chaos and an "enclave of anarchy in the sphere of entertainment," Kracauer, in the chapter on *The Cabinet of Dr. Caligari*, intriguingly describes precisely the "eternal attractiveness" of the fair:

> People of all classes and ages enjoy losing themselves in a wilderness of glaring colors and shrill sounds, which is populated with monsters and abounding in bodily sensations—from violent shocks to tastes of incredible sweetness. For adults it is a regression into childhood days, in which games and serious affairs are identical, real and imagined things mingle and anarchical desires aimlessly test infinite possibilities. By means of this regression the adult escapes a civilization which tends to overgrow and starve out the chaos of instincts—escapes it to restore that chaos upon which civilization nevertheless rests.

As if suddenly recognizing that his own description might be understood to valorize the carnivalesque space of the fair as a powerful moment of the civilizational process—one pole of its dialectics, and a corrective to its excesses—Kracauer reins in these meanings with the concluding sentence of the paragraph: "The fair is not freedom, but anarchy entailing chaos."[48] Once again, the willful attribution of signification strains against the manifest possibility for alternative readings. It is as if Kracauer had to stress that "the fair is not freedom" precisely because he knows it could be.[49]

By the same token, so could cinema. After all, Kracauer is clearly aware of the origins of cinema as fairground attraction, a point that he emphasized in his enthusiastic response to Panofsky's famous essay "Style and Medium in Motion Pictures," whose relevance to Kracauer's approach we already saw in chapter 6. Panofsky had sent Kracauer a newly published, revised and expanded version of his essay a few months before *From Caligari to Hitler* appeared in print, and Kracauer promptly responded with a letter on February 4, 1947. Here, in the context of an argument about the "affinity of the screen for materialistic thinking," he enthuses about the popular beginnings of the medium: "What felicitous sources for an art, such a combination of infatuation with meaningless motion, thrilled senses and fairground smells!"[50] This enthusiasm survives unabated in the figurative discourse of *From Caligari to Hitler*, where it resurfaces in a racially and erotically charged metaphor. Here, Kracauer describes the cinema of the "archaic" period predating the birth of Ufa and the Weimar Republic as a "young street arab." The attraction of this image to Kracauer becomes clear when he contrasts it with misguided attempts to nobilitate the new medium by assimilating it to literature (as in the *Autorenfilm*) or art (as in the *film d'art*). Throughout his career, Kracauer disdained any such attempts to yoke cinema to forms of culture and distinction that it was better suited to critique. Against the bourgeois designs of the *Kinoreformbewegung*, Kracauer vastly prefers the attraction of cinema as an "uneducated creature running wild among the lower strata of society." Kracauer's imagination of the "young street arab" is undoubtedly primitivist and orientalist, but through this "noble savage" as a figure of otherness he also projects a utopian image of cinema that establishes the "freedom of film from cultural ties and intellectual prejudices."[51]

This is a far cry from the reflectionist arguments that recur throughout the book, and it should prompt us to remain sensitive to Kracauer's enthusiasm for the possibilities of cinema even amidst the gloom he chronicles during its Weimar history. Boxed in by the book's teleological and reflectionist argumentation in the same way that Kracauer himself finds the revolutionary story of Caligari to be boxed in by the frame narrative, *From*

Caligari to Hitler formulates a utopia of cinema.[52] Though this utopia remains largely unrealized except for isolated instances (Ernö Metzner's "truly heretic" *Überfall* of 1929, for example), we can glean its possibility from certain moments, such as when Kracauer is moved by the "gesture of solidarity between two human wrecks" at the end of *Der letzte Mann* (The Last Laugh, 1924, dir. F.W. Murnau), right after he has dismissed the film for its message that "authority alone fuses the disparate social spheres into a whole."[53] In a similar epiphany, the still photographs in *Menschen am Sonntag* (People on Sunday, 1930, dir. Robert Siodmak et al.) suddenly "demonstrate how little substance is left to lower middle-class people."[54]

We can also sense the promise that Kracauer attaches to cinema in his assessment of Karl Grune's *Die Straße* (The Street, 1923), a film that clearly made a lasting impact from the time Kracauer witnessed its premiere in Frankfurt. Now, writing from New York, he assimilates it in a rather outrageous gesture to the Fridericus films by virtue of their shared concern with rebellion and submission. And yet the film's promise for a theory of cinema is still palpable in Kracauer's claim that here "a realism breaks through which has nothing in common with the cheap realism of conventional productions; it is a militant realism challenging the penchant for introspection."[55] Indeed, like his far more positive reviews of Grune's film from the 1920s (let alone his various "street essays" of the Weimar era), this assessment inflects his reading of cinematic streets generally in *From Caligari to Hitler:* they become legible as a dream image in Kracauer's readings, betraying discontent and opening the possibility of critique.

Or we could point to the ambivalent place of G.W. Pabst in Kracauer's account. Although Kracauer somewhat forcibly integrates Pabst's work into a narrative of missed opportunities, bland political neutrality, and melodramatic aberrations during the "stabilized period" of the Weimar Republic, his endorsement of Pabst's realism is unmistakable. Despite his melodramatic tendencies, Kracauer argues, Pabst manifests a "keen concern with given reality" and manages to "mobilize the camera to photograph the casual configurations of real life," thereby providing "insight into the symptoms of social morbidity" rather than simply reflecting or endorsing the latter.[56] Even an ostensibly "negligible" film such as *Abwege* (The Devious Path, 1928) "manages to evoke the impression that his characters are as they are because of the emptiness of the world they inhabit."[57] In other words, Pabst manages to critique rather than affirm the emptiness of an increasingly authoritarian order.

Finally, looking back at Kracauer's phenomenology of Weimar surfaces and ahead to *Theory of Film*'s intense concern with "physical reality," we might trace a submerged utopian discourse about the cinema in the way readings of various films in *From Caligari to Hitler* gravitate to the world of objects. Thus, even the most antirational "instinct-films" of Carl Mayer "pave the way for truly cinematic narration" by "conquering the domain of objects for the screen," in ways that the book's introduction had spelled out as normative.[58] There, Kracauer had noted how "the screen shows itself particularly concerned with the unobtrusive, the normally neglected," including "casual configurations of human bodies and inanimate objects."[59] If we follow this line of thinking through the individual readings of films by Mayer, Pabst, Lubitsch, Lang, or Metzner, we find that the object world figures in similar ways. Although there is undeniably a discourse on objects in *Caligari* that assimilates them to irrationality and authoritarianism,[60] the phenomenologist in Kracauer cannot help but convey his fascination with cinema's power to invest objects with the ability to speak, to transform our perception. In this vein, we find Kracauer drawing our attention to the way Mayer inherits slapstick conventions and "seizes upon the world of objects [...] in the interest of dramatic action."[61] *Der letzte Mann* develops a sort of magical power that "lures scores of [...] objects out of their seclusion"; and Pabst "features objects because they make up the kind of reality he wants to explore. In a decaying or transitional world, whose elements fall asunder, the objects rush out of their hiding-places and take on a life of their own."[62]

These examples may suffice to indicate that *From Caligari to Hitler* maintains an interest that Kracauer had adumbrated in his "Notes on the Planned History of German Film" but would not work out more fully until completing his "book on film aesthetics," as he referred to *Theory of Film* during the decades he spent working on it. That interest might be described in terms of phenomenology, realism, and humanism, but it also concerns a configuration of film and politics distinct from the one that had led, in Kracauer's estimation, to Hitler. Buried in *From Caligari to Hitler* is a politics of the aesthetic that Hermann Kappelhoff, in *The Politics and Poetics of Realism*, has linked to the far more recent work by Jacques Rancière:[63] the belief that cinema might redistribute the sensible in nonauthoritarian, nondivisive ways.[64] "What Kracauer was considering in the film archive at New York's MoMA, what he was rethinking once again in a language different from his native tongue, is the cinema as image space, in which social conditions become visible as the possibilities of living-in-society. [...] Kracauer's book gives us a view of cinema as part of the politics of aesthetics."[65]

In *From Caligari to Hitler*, this remains an unrealized project, which makes for the constitutive tension we have traced in the book, and in its figurative discourse in particular. We might now redescribe this as a tension between a work of criticism, designed to assess and evaluate cinema in its political context, and the impetus of an underlying theory, designed to elucidate the possibilities of cinema, its potential for an emancipatory politics. Crossing the political wires with the aesthetic, we could say that Kracauer stages a struggle between authoritarianism and realism or, conversely, between expressionism and democracy. In the political context of the time, he is unable to interpret that struggle in terms other than a losing battle for the latter terms. As a work of criticism, *From Caligari to Hitler* is devoted to demonstrating Weimar cinema's *failure* to promulgate an aesthetics that could adequately address the initial "shock of freedom" and transform it into politically efficacious visual terms. This is not to say that Weimar democracy failed because Weimar cinema was unable adequately to represent it; rather, what Kracauer demonstrates over and over in his book is that Weimar cinema never managed to render fully intuitable any forms of social and political organization that could transcend what he describes as "widespread inner paralysis." Judging by his analysis of Hollywood, this is a problem that the American cinema inherits in the postwar years—inner paralysis being merely another term for the perceived suspension of historical time after the war.

This is admittedly a rather bleak view—both of a *posthistoire* at which the historical dialectic has come to a standstill, and of the cinema as an artform that consistently fails to live up to the utopian energies that theory, including Kracauer's own, would ultimately attribute to it. In this sense, we seem to have arrived back at the analysis of the culture industry from the *Dialectic of Enlightenment*—closer, perhaps, to Frankfurt than to New York. But here we might note that for Kracauer, the place where historical time might gain traction again, so to speak, is *the same place* in which he had registered its suspension: the cinema. In its inherent affinities for the otherwise overlooked, in its phenomenological power to reveal "things normally unseen"—in other words, in its potential as a *realist* medium—Kracauer sees the promise of a true alternative to the authoritarianism he has traced through Weimar and into the postwar United States. In this sense, the "redemption of physical reality" that *Theory of Film* will now attribute to the medium is tantamount to its redemption from the false alternative between tyranny and chaos.

As he returns to his Marseille notebooks after working through *From Caligari to Hitler*, realism becomes the name for the emancipation from authoritarian fixations—whether of meanings, of personality structures, or of political regimes and their "sham reality." As I will show in the next chapter, the central mediating term between this notion of realism and its politics is experience—a capacity that, according to one of the central motifs of critical theory, is on the wane in postwar modernity. While this diagnosis will be familiar from classical texts such as Benjamin's "Storyteller" or Adorno's *Minima Moralia*, which equate experience with the anomie of modernity, with the numbing involvement in war, or with the rise of technological media, we may recall that it is also part and parcel of the diagnosis of authoritarianism that members of the Frankfurt School were working out during the postwar years in the United States. The authoritarian personality, the authors of that study claimed, was characterized among other things by "the inability to have experience."[66]

Cinematic realism, as Kracauer argues explicitly in the conclusion to *Theory of Film*, bears the promise of restoring precisely that ability, of rendering the world fully intuitable and thereby facilitating a political stance outside the false opposition between tyranny and chaos. Although it will take him well over another decade to work out fully these powers of the cinema in *Theory of Film*, he has detected such emancipatory moments all along in the cinema's fundamental phenomenological bent—whether in the carnivalesque pleasures of the fairground, in the "brief reveille" of realism during Weimar, in the animated films of Disney, or in the neorealist films coming from Italy after the war.[67] From the perspective established by *From Caligari to Hitler* in the context of postwar approaches to the German Question, we may read Kracauer's film theoretical *summa* as a response to the questions that those approaches had raised in turn. As the next chapter argues, it is a response formulated once again between "Frankfurt" and "New York," drawing centrally on Kracauer's experience—and on notions of experience formulated—on both sides of the Atlantic.

8. *Theory of Film* and the Subject of Experience

> A decisive theoretical work on film is of the greatest importance—and I mean this emphatically, not just in the habitual sociological sense: for it is here that we can register the deepest layers of a shift in experience that reaches all the way into perception.
> THEODOR W. ADORNO, letter to Siegfried Kracauer, October 17, 1950[1]

In the history of film theory, Siegfried Kracauer's *Theory of Film* occupies a no-man's land between the heady days of "classical film theory" with its investment in medium specificity and the legitimacy of cinema as an artform, on the one hand, and the subsequent phase of theorizing on the other. Long labeled "contemporary" but now largely thought of as the discourse of "political modernism," the latter phase moved away from classical concerns toward newfound interests in language, psychoanalysis, structuralism, and ideology.[2] But even for the former era, *Theory of Film* came belatedly—after Bazin had already launched film theorizing on its "realist" trajectory, and after the debate about film as art had run its course. To these lines of inquiry, Kracauer's late theory provided a "grand closing gesture" at best.[3] For the theorists who came after, by contrast—from the "young Turks" at *Cahiers du cinéma* to the more systematic approaches elaborated by Christian Metz in France and in the pages of the British journal *Screen*—Kracauer's realist theory became a "whipping boy" for outmoded approaches more generally (to cite one retrospective anthology of film theory).[4]

In this chapter and the next, my goal is to relocate Kracauer from that no-man's land and to situate the development of *Theory of Film* in New York, where the relation between film, mass culture, and experience also occupied some of the key contributors to the cultural debates of the postwar era. To grasp the politics and the continuing relevance of Kracauer's realist aesthetics, I propose, we must recall the multiple conversations that shaped the book—conversations that involved not only the Frankfurt friends but also the New York Intellectuals. Among these, the young critic Robert Warshow emerges as a crucial interlocutor, although Kracauer's book must also be situated in relation to the swirling debates on literature, film, and mass culture in the "little magazines" at the time.

As I will show, these conversations have a direct bearing on how we evaluate the role of experience as a crucial concept in Kracauer's thinking about film's promise. Although we had occasion in the last chapter to retrace that promise even in *From Caligari to Hitler*, it begins to take on more clearly defined contours as Kracauer formulates his theory over the course of the 1950s. What ultimately emerges from the critique of illiberal cinema that he elaborated over his first American decade, I will argue, is a renewed focus on cinema's potential as a medium of experience. As such, Kracauer conceives of cinema in a broadly humanist perspective. This, too, may describe the place of his work in the history of film theory, though we will have to account for the quirks of Kracauer's humanism in the context of a broadly liberal humanist conception of culture during the Cold War. Reconstructing the valences of experience in these overlapping contexts, moreover, will allow us to gauge the politics of Kracauer's film theory by relocating it within a trans-Atlantic perspective. Viewed from such a perspective, Kracauer's conclusions regarding the promise of film transcend the Cold War humanist moment out of which they were generated.

MASSCULT, MIDCULT, MOVIES: ROBERT WARSHOW AND THE IMMEDIATE EXPERIENCE

> We mean by abstract: really not thinking through experience. What is the subject of our thought? Experience! Nothing Else!
> HANNAH ARENDT, *The Recovery of the Public World*

To reread *Theory of Film* in a trans-Atlantic perspective is to reconsider who Kracauer's real and imagined interlocutors were for this project. Judging by the references in the published book, some of these were remote, to be sure—whether temporally, as in the numerous references to Béla Balázs or to literature on film from the Weimar era; or geographically, as in the similarly frequent references to French sources. Some of the latter certainly constitute traces of the Marseille notebooks, while others testify to Kracauer's up-to-date engagement with French discussions on cinema, including the budding movement of *filmologie*.[5] But other interlocutors were closer, as the surviving manuscripts reveal. A "tentative outline" records critical comments by not only Adorno and Rudolf Arnheim, who was teaching at Sarah Lawrence College in nearby Yonkers, but also a third reader who appears in the margins of the document: Robert Warshow, then editor of *Commentary* and a frequent contributor to *Partisan Review* and the *Nation*, where, as we have seen, Kracauer had also published.[6]

Warshow was a brilliant critic whose writings covered everything from contemporary Hollywood to Krazy Kat, from the middlebrow style of the *New Yorker* to the bland, noncommittal universalism that he detected both in the plays of Arthur Miller and in his "fossilized" liberal audience.[7] Despite his considerable contributions and his unique voice, Warshow died too young, perhaps, to be remembered as a major contributor to the debates of the times. But Thomas Jeffers nonetheless considers him in retrospect as "surely the archetypal *Commentary* writer"—by which he could have meant everything from his stylistic brilliance, to his wide range of cultural interests, to the occasionally virulent anti-Stalinism that colored both Warshow's attack on the Rosenbergs and his anti-anticommunism.[8] All these aspects of Warshow's brief publishing career are readily confirmed by the posthumous anthology of his writings, first published under the title *The Immediate Experience* in 1962.[9] To the degree that editing and publishing in journals such as *Commentary* or *Partisan Review* conferred membership status among the group, Warshow—a member of the editorial staff of both of these magazines—was a representative figure in the New York intellectual scene. But he also stood apart by virtue of his unique take on film and popular culture.

Numerous commentators have seen the New York Intellectuals' key contribution to cultural debates to have consisted in bridging European modernism and the avant-garde, on the one hand, and the politics of the anti-Stalinist American left on the other (until, that is, the New Yorkers' politics veered into neoconservative positions in response to the counterculture of the 1960s; it is anyone's guess how Warshow would have positioned himself in this seismic shift).[10] For most contributors at the time, this meant not only a rejection of dogmatic and ossified forms of socialist culture, or what Warshow indicted as Stalinist liberalism, but also a disdain for American popular culture, including Hollywood.[11] Besides the vexing issue of Stalinism (including the debates about anticommunism and anti-anticommunism),[12] few concerns animated the New York Intellectuals more during the 1940s and '50s than the distinction between high and low culture, between art that "stirs a free and rich passage of materials from dream to experience and from experience to dream" and mass culture that "tries to cage the unconscious."[13] As Andrew Ross has shown, the stakes of these debates were high, both culturally and politically. They reflect a moment at which intellectuals found themselves more centrally involved in the process of cultural legitimation than ever before; but that legitimation, Ross argues, is profoundly conditioned by the Cold War. In these debates, mass culture becomes an object of containment, a disease to be controlled. The same immunological discourse that governs anticommunist exhortations to contain the spread of "world communism" (itself a "malignant parasite," in George F. Kennan's words) also fuels the New York (and Frankfurt) Intellectuals' diatribes against mass culture.[14]

Clement Greenberg had launched the opening volley with his seminal 1939 article "Avant-Garde and Kitsch," which drew the line between the avant-garde that "moves" and academicist kitsch that "stands still."[15] Greenberg's brief but enormously influential piece, which notably took the question of aesthetic, social, and cultural experience as its starting point, considered the avant-garde "the only living culture that we now have." By contrast, kitsch—which for Greenberg included everything from popular, commercial art and literature to magazine covers, from Tin Pan Alley to Hollywood—was derivative and dead, a mechanically produced "ersatz culture" trading in "vicarious experience and faked sensations."[16] Nor was kitsch a prerogative of the industrialized West or of advanced capitalism; on the contrary, Greenberg's principal examples concerned the function of kitsch in Stalinist Russia and the fascist resentment of culture. The distinction between the avant-garde and kitsch was founded in an antitotalitarian politics and the "de-Marxisation of the American intelligentsia" in the wake of the Moscow trials and the Hitler-Stalin pact of the mid to late 1930s.[17]

From here it was a short step to Dwight Macdonald's indictment of mass culture as a "parasitic, cancerous growth," a standardized product to pacify the masses.[18] With their pronounced affinities for the avant-garde and modernism in the arts, the New York Intellectuals worried out loud about the convergence of high and mass culture, the way that the modernist forms of the Bauhaus, for example, "trickled down, in a debased form of course, into our furniture, cafeterias, movie theatres, electric toasters, office buildings, drug stores, and railroad trains."[19] In the eyes of critics like Greenberg, Macdonald, or Irving Howe, it was bad enough that "mass culture is not and can never be any good."[20] Worse still was the apparent blurring of cultural boundaries. In Macdonald's alarmist prose, the insipient "merger" between high and low yielded "a tepid, flaccid Middlebrow Culture that threatens to engulf everything in its spreading ooze." Along with radio and pulp magazines, he singled out the cinema for its "deadening and warping effect," a "culture-pattern" that had been "stamped deep into the modern personality."[21] When the New York Intellectuals did turn their attention to film, the assessments tended to be bleak, as, for example, in Macdonald's pair of influential articles for *Partisan Review* denouncing the paralysis of cinema under Stalinism in the Soviet Union.[22] This did not keep these critics from worrying, however, about the "growth of a vast middlebrow society" in their own country.[23]

Claiming a spurious universality, middlebrow culture did away with all sense of value and morality, but also with history and politics, as Warshow, too, would argue.[24] Like Kracauer, whom Leo Löwenthal would later remember as a "thorn in the side of middle-brow taste," the New York Intellectuals had little patience for the pretensions of late-capitalist consumer culture.[25] But these could also be dismissed too easily out of hand, rather than forming the object of careful, at times even empathetic, analysis, as did the culture of the salaried masses under Kracauer's scrutiny, or anything from cartooning to the western under Warshow's. Like the contemporaneous critique of the culture industry by Adorno and Horkheimer and like Löwenthal's sociological analyses of popular literature (both of which became important points of reference for critics such as Macdonald), the New York Intellectuals' theory of mass culture generally dismissed the popular—and especially the more pernicious middlebrow—as "imposed from above. It is fabricated by technicians hired by businessmen; its audiences are passive consumers, their participation limited to the choice between buying and not buying."[26]

For all their incisive rhetoric, these positions suffered from an intransigent highbrow stance, an inability to account for the material dismissed as middlebrow kitsch. As a result, critics like Greenberg or Macdonald remained unable to further develop theories in response to the changing historical functions of mass culture.[27] Like the more mandarin Frankfurt School theorists of the "culture industry," these critics could only engage with popular culture, including the movies, by self-consciously identifying with their "fellow highbrows" as an endangered species.[28] In keeping with the politico-aesthetic program of *Partisan Review*, they called for a revival of the spirit of the old avant-garde by "re-creat[ing] a cultural ... elite as a countermovement to both Masscult and Midcult" lest "this country go either fascist or communist."[29] As is evident from such pronouncements, these debates were always implicitly antitotalitarian. Much like the contributions by Adorno, Horkheimer, and Löwenthal that they invoked, they linked both mass and middlebrow culture to an antidemocratic, authoritarian character. Branded as protofascist where it was not openly critiqued as Stalinist, mass culture bred "adultized children and infantile adults" incapable of genuine (aesthetic) experience.[30]

But here, as on other issues, the New York Intellectuals spoke not with one voice. In fact, one is inclined to argue in retrospect that the lasting appeal of their writings resides in their agonistic character, their spirit of open, if occasionally overheated, debate. In these debates, Robert Warshow stood out not only by virtue of the "rigorous, laconic clarity" of his style (no less incisive but far gentler in its irony than Macdonald's),[31] but also for his resolute commitment to reading film as part of popular culture, and for taking the latter seriously when few others would. "Not 'only' a film critic, but rather a popular-culture man," Ernest Callenbach called Warshow in a review of the posthumously published *Immediate Experience*. Warshow pioneered a form of cultural criticism that "was willing to be serious about things most intellectuals think beneath them—and thus he got closer to the fabric of life than most of us."[32] Much like Kracauer, he could find in the works of popular culture both a utopian promise of immediacy and the perils of what Herbert Marcuse called "the affirmative character of culture."[33] He could delight in the "ZIP" and "POW" with which evil always triumphed in the *Krazy Kat* cartoons, in the sheer intensity of experience afforded by what he called "*Lumpen* culture," and even in the "sudden moments of power" in Soviet films that otherwise stirred his anger for their frivolous fetishization of technique.[34] In other words, Warshow was considerably less worried about the blurred boundaries between high and low culture than were some of his fellow New Yorkers. Emphasizing the "actual, immediate experience of seeing and responding to the movies as most of us see them and respond to them," Warshow advocated—and practiced—a phenomenology of popular culture that shares a number of features with Kracauer's work from the Weimar years through *Theory of Film*. Mass culture, Warshow ventured, was a central facet of contemporary existence, to be treated by the critic as "the screen through which we see reality and the mirror in which we see ourselves."[35] Like Kracauer, Warshow read the surface manifestations of cultural life for their social meanings. "In some way," Warshow admitted in a programmatic (under)statement, "I take all that nonsense seriously"—especially the "nonsense" that was cinema.[36]

For Kracauer, too, no object was too low or abject to be worthy of his attention: in numerous texts and through his posthumous *History*, he would reiterate his attention to "overlooked" modes of being and the interstices of culture as one of his central methodological tenets. To be sure, Kracauer brought the devotion to the movies with him to exile from his years as a film critic in Germany. But in his commitment to working out an experiential aesthetics of the cinema, he was closer, perhaps, to his New York contemporaries than to his friends from Frankfurt, who continued to champion the cause of an autonomous art. It seems significant in this respect that, like *From Caligari to Hitler*, *Theory of Film* at every turn argues decidedly against nobilitating film as a traditional artform, making a claim instead for film's power to revise the very notion of what constitutes the cultural category of art in the first place. Given the role of film as a mass medium, that category would include the popular by definition, a thesis explicitly ruled out in Adorno and Horkheimer's theorization of the culture industry.

Warshow's nuanced appraisals of popular culture, and of the movies in particular, were anchored in the notion of experience. As we shall see, this is a notion that Warshow theorizes less thoroughly, perhaps, than Kracauer, who owes a debt also to Critical Theory. Yet it is significant to note that this is where Warshow, like Kracauer, locates the specific cultural value of cinema as well as of his approach. The "fundamental *fact* of the movies," he contends after an explicit acknowledgment of his debt to Kracauer, is not only "a fact at once aesthetic and sociological, but also something more. This is the actual immediate experience of seeing and responding to the movies as most of us see them and respond to them."[37] As opposed to high-minded art criticism on the one hand and sociological generalizations on the other, Warshow advocates an approach to movies and popular culture that begins with the critic's own response, with the experience of reading, looking, or watching, and with the explicit "acknowledgment of [the critic's] own relation to the object he criticizes."[38]

Warshow practiced what he preached. Many of his reviews and articles have a disarmingly personal tone, out of which he then develops larger discussions: a contemplation of his father's corpse yields the portrait of a generation of leftist Russian Jewish immigrants in New York; an encounter with his son's love for comic books turns into a subtle discussion of censorship; and his sense of outrage at the anticommunism of Leo McCarey's *My Son John* remains palpably on the surface in his review of the film. Of Chaplin, whom "we have, apparently, loved," he asks whether our love was ever requited. And the force of a film like Rossellini's *Paisan*, he avers, lies "in certain images of danger, suffering, and death that remain in one's consciousness with the particularity of real experience."[39] Experience in the sense of "the way we really feel about our lives" is the touchstone of Warshow's investigations of popular culture and the movies.

Nobody would confuse Kracauer's film theory with Warshow's film criticism, but we may note here how both critics assume the constitutive role of subjective experience for a sensitive, phenomenologically oriented account of the medium. We still lack translations of Kracauer's witty and theoretically astute film reviews from the 1920s. From translations that do exist, however, English readers might recall the identificatory elements (not to be confused with narcissistic self-display)[40] in Kracauer's series of essays on the "little shopgirls" at the movies and on the salaried masses working hard to keep up appearances in the waning days of the Weimar Republic.

Now, it would be wrong to claim that the quirky, ironic tone of the alert city-dweller from the almost daily *feuilleton* pieces of the 1920s survives in a tome like *Theory of Film*. But even this book arguably is based in the sort of impactful, immediate experience that Warshow privileges.

An anecdotal recollection of Kracauer's first film experience and its lasting effect in the preface condenses the argument that he will make at the end of the book about the centrality of experience to our understanding of the medium. Recalling his encounter with film as a young boy, he writes: "What thrilled me so deeply was an ordinary suburban street, filled with lights and shadows which transfigured it. Several trees stood about, and there was in the foreground a puddle reflecting invisible house façades and a piece of the sky. Then a breeze moved the shadows, and the façades with the sky below began to waver."[41] That image—"the trembling upper world in the dirty puddle"—emblematizes the medium of film for Kracauer. As a medium of reflection it captures an unseen upper world, sets it in motion, transforms it through the "wavering" of the surface, and renders it accessible to experience. Kracauer recalls returning home from this "intoxicating" impression to "commit my experience to writing." The resultant treatise was to bear the title *Film as the Discoverer of the Marvels of Everyday Life*. Although it would take long years and multiple displacements in exile for this adolescent theory of film to materialize in New York, it seems but a short step from "discovery" to "redemption," and from "everyday life" to "physical reality." All of these notions—including redemption, which for Kracauer translates into the German *Errettung* (rescue) rather than the fully religious *Erlösung*—remain grounded in the evidentiary power of the spectator's experience. Consequently, when Kracauer broaches the subject of spectatorship in the book, when he approvingly cites the experience of a French "film addict" or recounts the "frightening experience" of "inveterate moviegoers" who may have found themselves at some point confronted with moving images unaccompanied by any sound whatsoever, the author's own subjectivity hovers just below the surface of his text.[42]

We will return below to the complex forms in which cinema and experience are articulated in Kracauer's work, but let us first trace how Warshow articulates his foundational commitment to experiential immediacy. From the shared premise that the critic ought to "acknowledge his own relation to the object he criticizes," Warshow develops a critique of contemporary culture and its effects on experience that, in a vocabulary slightly different from his own, we might label a critique of reification. Warshow's essays indict cultural practices, from publishing to the movies, for the obfuscation of authentic needs and the abstraction of human relations in received ideas, opinions, and ideologies that subjects mistake, in turn, for their own experience. By the same token, all of Warshow's essays implicitly call for forms of cultural practice and criticism that might rekindle genuine modes of "actual, immediate experience." In the popular figure of the gangster, for example, he could also diagnose a symptomatic obfuscation of experience, seeing that figure as "the 'no' to that great American 'yes' which is stamped so big over our official culture and yet has so little to do with the way we really feel about our lives."[43] Whether writing about what he rather glibly considered the Rosenbergs' shocking alienation from their own experience in prison ("almost nothing really belonged to them, not even their own experience") or about the way in which the *New Yorker* deals with experience, "not by trying to understand it but by prescribing the attitude to be adopted toward it," Warshow indicts middlebrow culture across the political spectrum for estranging midcentury Americans from their lived reality.[44]

In this respect, his critique overlaps with that of fellow New York Intellectuals such as Macdonald and Greenberg. However, Warshow is far less dismissive of the redemptive potential of Greenberg's kitsch or Macdonald's midcult. To be sure, Warshow shares the position that readers and viewers of popular culture merely receive preformulated ideas, sociological theories, or misguided pretensions to art, rather than gaining access to the real conditions of their existence. But Warshow sees this tendency only exacerbated by (film) critics who fail to see the experiential qualities of the movies behind readymade categories drawn from sociology or misplaced aesthetic formalism.

In his emphasis on experiential immediacy, Warshow joins a long tradition of both antitheoretical conservative and radically progressive political thinkers who have placed their faith in experience as a fundamental human capacity and form of interacting with the world. Martin Jay, who in *Songs of Experience* brilliantly chronicles the role of experience in Western thought from the Greeks to poststructuralism, has drawn attention to the shifting uses of this notion. But even as he acknowledges the poststructuralist critiques of the primacy of experience, he notes that over the centuries philosophers and critics have tended to "believe that something called 'experience' is a foundational term, able to provide an incorruptible immediacy that somehow avoids the mystifications of ideology or representation."[45] Warshow tapped into this notion of experience. Just as Susan Sontag would later famously argue "against interpretation," Warshow is at pains to restore a mode of reception and interaction with art and the world that does not overlay experience with innumerable hermeneutic layers. As Sontag puts it in her influential 1964 essay, "to interpret is to impoverish, to deplete the world—in order to set up a shadow world of meanings. [. . .] The world, our world, is depleted, impoverished enough. Away with all duplicates of it, until we again experience more immediately what we have."[46] Cinema, for Sontag, is "the most alive, the most exciting, the most important of all art forms" precisely because of its ability to outrun interpretation and break through to the immediacy of experience, to strike the viewer with the "beauty and visual sophistication of the images." Sontag's notion that "in good films, there is always a directness that entirely frees us from the itch to interpret" owes a clear debt to Warshow's essays from the previous decade.[47] By the same token, it anticipates the reception of Kracauer's *Theory of Film* among the so-called sensibilist film critics in Germany during the following decade.[48]

In privileging the notion of experience as an aesthetic and subjective category, Warshow sought to break through the false alternatives of aesthetic versus sociological criticism. Although he tended to place Kracauer in the latter camp, based on the arguments he had made in *From Caligari to Hitler*, Kracauer had in fact repeatedly formulated a similar call to "meld . . . the sociological and the aesthetic approach."[49] In a grant proposal to the Guggenheim Foundation, Warshow noted: "The sociological critic says to us, in effect: It is not *I* who goes to the movies; it is the audience. The aesthetic critic says: It is not the *movies* I go to see; it is art."[50] By contrast, the form of critique that Warshow advocated would begin with the centrality of *both* subject ("I") and object ("the movies") as they encounter one another in the medium of experience. This would be a liberating, utopian encounter in which subject and object become transparent to one another in the sense formulated, again, by Sontag some years later: transparence, she writes, "is the highest, most liberating value in art—and in criticism—today. Transparence means experiencing the luminousness of the thing in itself, of things being what they are."[51]

Unfortunately, Warshow's untimely death meant that the proposal to fashion—and theorize—a new form of film criticism remained just that: a grant proposal. From the posthumous anthology of his writings, however (for which the proposal now serves as a preface),[52] the contours of Warshow's approach are readily apparent—much as they would have been to a discerning reader of the "little magazines" at the time the essays were originally published. We should count Kracauer among those readers.

In those same magazines, he would have found other writers debating the role of experience as well in ways that define the New York Intellectuals' aesthetic politics. From the earliest days of their involvement with *Partisan Review*, William Phillips and Philip Rahv had promulgated a form of non-doctrinaire leftist literary criticism that emphasized the experiential dimension of literature as central to any evaluation of its realism or social relevance. Questions of sensibility of feeling, they held, were equally as important, if not more, as the social realism of a novel's subject matter, or the socialist realism of its form.[53] This tendency was only strengthened after the relaunch of the magazine with greater independence from the Communist John Reed Club that had served as its sponsor until Phillips and Rahv took over as editors in 1937.[54] In an article titled "The Cult of Experience in American Writing," Rahv further refined this notion, noting the failure of writers on the Left to "lift experience to the level of history" and thereby establish the central importance of experience as a mediating force between the individual and the collective, between subjectivity and the social.[55] At stake in these debates was consequently the ability to ground politics in a notion of experience that was at once aesthetic and social, that could bring European modernism and abstract expressionism into the purview of a progressive, anti-Stalinist stance. As Harvey Teres puts it in his thought-provoking, revisionist account of the New York Intellectuals, the *Partisan Review* crowd "wished to see politics transformed, so that it might give due emphasis to subjective experience, to the moral, spiritual, and cultural dimensions of political life, and to greater flexibility and experimentation with regard to a range of ideological issues."[56] In this sense, the notion of experience was central to the renewal of the left in the wake of Stalinist terror and the critique of totalitarianism. The New York Intellectuals envisioned "a politics that could address subjective experience, encourage diversity, accommodate spontaneity, and adjust to complexity and uncertainty."[57] What they could not abide, however, was the notion that subjective experience might be ideologically scripted—whether from the Stalinist left (as in the case of the Rosenbergs, according to Warshow) or in terms of a mainstream, middlebrow liberal humanism that subsumed the specificity of experience in overarching concepts of a common humanity. A case in point was the "insistent editorializing" of Edward Steichen's blockbuster 1955 MoMA exhibit *The Family of Man*, which we will consider in the next chapter.[58]

In the aesthetic politics of most New York Intellectuals, the emphatic notion of experience found its legitimate expression in high art: in the poetry of T.S. Elliot and the many authors featured regularly in the pages of *Partisan Review*, in the works of the abstract expressionists whom Clement Greenberg would champion, and in the canon of European modernism, from Kafka to Joyce, Brecht to Orwell. What few could envision, however, was that the movies could function as a medium of experience in anything but the perniciously middlebrow, universalizing mode of Steichen's *Life* aesthetics. To have outlined the ways in which one might take lowbrow culture and the movies seriously (without thereby either collapsing them with high art or celebrating them as some form of organically popular American folklore) was the signal accomplishment of Robert Warshow's short career within the group.

Warshow formulated his fundamental question at the close of an important essay for *Commentary* in 1947. Having surveyed the communist legacy of the 1930s that defined his cohort, as well as the pressures exerted on that legacy by both Stalinism in the Soviet Union and the rise of middlebrow culture in the United States, Warshow concluded by asking: "How shall we regain the use of our experience in the world of mass culture?"[59] Kracauer's *Theory of Film*, I propose, takes up this same question, modulated by two further contexts: On the one hand, his answer derives from his own earlier insights, in *From Caligari to Hitler* and the work on Nazi propaganda, into how the cinema could fall short of its utopian promise precisely by paralyzing the subject's very ability to have and access experience. On the other hand, this understanding of experience itself was inflected by Kracauer's long-standing engagement with the work of his friends Theodor Adorno and Walter Benjamin, and with their diagnosis of the waning of experience in modernity and under fascism. Taking up the thread of these debates as if in answer to Warshow's query, Kracauer formulates a theory of film as a medium of experience, and of realism as its style.

PAISAN: A PARADIGMATIC FILM

> The average spectator knows more about reality than is offered him in our movie houses. It should be the other way round.
>
> SIEGFRIED KRACAUER, "The Mirror Up to Nature"

Kracauer's work during the New York years communicates closely with Warshow's, whether through editorial comment or explicit reference. The two men had been in contact about various articles that Kracauer proposed to *Commentary*, and they even appear to have competed for space to write on film in the pages of *Partisan Review*.[60] As both their published and unpublished writings of the time indicate, the two men shared an intense interest in the cultural landscape of their day, which—again unlike their more unabashedly Europhile and avant-garde-minded colleagues—they found to be mapped most clearly in the movies. From Chaplin to Italian Neorealism, Kracauer and Warshow reviewed the same films and books on the cinema. Problems of realism and alienation figured centrally among these; but it is the fate of experience that, as we have seen, constituted the starting point for Warshow's work. It was also a recurring theme in Kracauer's essays from the 1940s, and in *Theory of Film* it emerges as the book's conceptual *telos*.

If, as I will argue, Kracauer's elaboration of the relationship between film and experience was ultimately more nuanced than Warshow's, this may have had to do partly with the more occasional style of the latter's articles compared to Kracauer's long-gestating, magisterial book on film aesthetics; and one can only wonder how the dialogue might have developed had Warshow lived to work out his proposed book for the Guggenheim grant and see the publication of *Theory of Film*. For all their differences, Warshow and Kracauer let themselves be guided by a profound cinephilia that helped them illuminate the utopian and redemptive qualities of the movies.[61] The two authors shared the diagnosis of the reification of experience—whether at the hands of ideology and opinion-mongering, as Warshow claimed, or, as we shall see in Kracauer's case, as the fallout of scientific progress and some more generalized notion of abstraction, behind which lingered the experience of the loss of experience under totalitarianism. Similarly, both critics harbored a belief that one could reconnect to this lost experience and gather up its shards within popular culture and at the movies. The route to this redemption, for Warshow as for Kracauer, was film, and realism in particular—whether in the form of the gangster film or the western with its open plains and its *parti pris* for the Davids over the Goliaths;[62] in the found story or the episode; or even in actors like Gary Cooper and Gregory Peck who "are in themselves, as material objects, 'realistic,' seeming to bear in their bodies and their faces mortality, limitation, the knowledge of good and evil."[63]

The convergence of Kracauer's and Warshow's critical sensibilities manifests even where the two authors disagree on a given film or filmmaker, as in the case of Rossellini's *Paisan*. Composed of six loosely connected episodes, this film about the gradual liberation of Italy by the Allied invasion in 1943–44 was widely recognized already at the time of its release in 1946 to constitute a significant milestone in the history of cinema. Most famous and influential was certainly André Bazin's appraisal of the film, along with Orson Welles's *Citizen Kane*, as one of "the two most significant events in [the] evolution in the history of cinema."[64] Praising Rossellini's "revolutionary humanism," Bazin treated *Paisan* as the paradigmatic film in the development of Italian Neorealism. From its approach to narrative (which Bazin likened to the short story as compared to the novel) to its cinematography and its "communicative generosity," the film inspired in Bazin both gushing praise and the kind of detailed observation and analysis out of which he generated his overarching realist theory of the cinema.

As "one of the greatest films ever made," *Paisan* was clearly a touchstone of similar import for Kracauer's thinking.[65] Warshow, however, who had read some of Kracauer's writing on the film, was less sanguine, faulting large parts of *Paisan* for an excess of sentimentality and for sidestepping questions of morality and politics. In its apparently noncommittal approach to postwar Italian reality, Warshow complained, *Paisan* made the death of a fascist equal the death of a partisan. Kracauer had similarly noted that in the detached, observational style of the film, the American liberators looked much like the German conquerors; but whereas this was for Kracauer a sign of Rossellini's salutary refusal to signpost ideologically "correct" readings, Warshow worried that thereby "moral and political differences [were] obscured."[66]

And yet it is precisely this indifference that both critics also prize. In contrast both to the politics of Soviet montage and to "those movies with a message" that liberal-minded Hollywood churned out during the late 1940s, Kracauer appreciated Rossellini's "thorough distrust of [. . .] 'messages.'"[67] Here was a director who "deliberately turn[ed] his back on ideas" and refused to reduce images to symbols or to inflate individual moments to universal generalities. Warshow, in turn, sounds even more like Kracauer than Kracauer himself in his enthusiasm for Rossellini's ability to convey the "visible fact[s] of experience" and "the particulars of [. . .] physical presence" without charging them with symbolic meaning or subsuming them under ideological concepts.[68] Like Bazin on the other side of the Atlantic, both Warshow and Kracauer draw out this specificity of Rossellini's aesthetic choices by opposing them to Hollywood strategies. Where American war films require good to triumph and the death of a fighting soldier to have meaning, Warshow submits, Rossellini refuses to overlay his images with universalizing messages. His "greatest virtue as an artist" is consequently the "feeling for particularity. In the best parts of *Paisan* it is always the man who dies, and no idea survives him unless it is the idea of death itself."[69] In this way, Rossellini's images pierce the skin of the film; they remain "in one's consciousness with the particularity of real experience."[70]

This is not to say that the two critics consider the film to be wholly without meaning, message, or moral. For Warshow, *Paisan* deals centrally with the inevitability of death and suffering; for Kracauer, the film shines in its insistence on human dignity. But this effect is not achieved, as in Hollywood's liberal-minded films of the same era, by fiat or by a "surfeit of eloquence." Rossellini conveys "articulate experience" by virtue of the fact that he shows more than he tells.[71] Like Bazin in Paris, then, the two critics in New York receive Rossellini's films as a breath of fresh air, attributing to *Paisan* a sort of aesthetic transparency that responds to their most deeply held notions of what cinema is and should be: a realist medium. Kracauer lauds the mingling of languages and use of long shots, and considers the street scenes "a model of artistic intelligence." And Warshow enthusiastically discusses the way characters, who in an important sense "remain strangers" to the spectator, are the more "*visibly* real" for being less clearly individualized.[72] To both critics, Rossellini's (neo)realism—his turn to the experiences of ordinary people and his "infatuation with reality," as Kracauer puts it in his unpublished review—exemplifies cinema's power to rekindle experience.[73]

Theorizing this power derives its urgency from the politics of the cinematic image that preceded the arrival of Rossellini, not only in the history of Italian cinema but also in Germany and Hollywood. As we saw in the previous chapters, Kracauer had found the promise of cinema to be buried under the "studio constructivism" of the Weimar years and in Hollywood's bungled response to totalitarianism and terror even after WWII, let alone in the propaganda productions during the war. The films from those years had appeared to him constricting, allowing no way out of their labyrinthine sets and emotional entanglements. But even as he was writing *From Caligari to Hitler* and "Hollywood's Terror Films," Rossellini had appeared to him to offer a way out of these structures. By the time he writes *Theory of Film*, he theorizes the director's paradigmatic status explicitly, invoking his example to emphasize the importance of unscripted acting, of endowing the physical environment with expressive power, of leaving the mix of different languages untranslated and unresolved. Again and again Kracauer returns to the film to exemplify other aspects of his theory as well: the ability of sound to elicit "psychophysical correspondences," i.e. to link the representation of physical reality to affect; the affinity of the episodic format as well as of the "diffuse and very cinematic" wartime setting for indeterminacy and endlessness; and the importance of unmotivated detail, "scenes and images, found in the world around the story proper," which Rossellini "single[s] out with unrivaled precision."[74]

What we begin to see here, in other words, are the contours of Kracauer's theory of cinematic realism. For Kracauer, Rossellini's films are paradigmatic not only for the way they take up war and fascism as subject, but aesthetically as well. Italian Neorealism for him points the way out of the labyrinth, enabling a reencounter with experience—a concept that for Kracauer as for Warshow becomes foundational for the renewal of humanist film criticism and theory.

THEORY OF FILM AND THE DIALECTICS OF EXPERIENCE

> The medium of his thought was experience.
> THEODOR W. ADORNO, "The Curious Realist"

We have already noted the centrality of Kracauer's early filmgoing experience for his later theoretical account, but the place of experience in *Theory of Film* extends far beyond the well-chosen anecdote. Kracauer assigns the concept a central role in his book, whose task is ultimately not to trace the photographic pedigree of film or to catalogue its "affinities," let alone to present a naively realist ontology of the medium. Rather, it is to offer a "philosophy of our times"[75] by elucidating the nature and role of "film experience" as part of a general aesthetics.[76] The specificity of film within that aesthetic philosophy, in turn, lies in its particular investment in experience. Truly "cinematic," according to this argument, are those films "which incorporate aspects of physical reality with a view to making us experience them."[77] It is this link to reality and experience rather than any artistic pretension that imparts aesthetic validity to film.

As I discuss in more detail below, Kracauer pits the concretion of film experience against a number of cultural phenomena and tendencies that make up "the intellectual landscape." These range from the loss of binding beliefs and a somewhat underspecified waning of ideological certainties to the growing role of instrumental reason, science, and what he calls "abstractness." As he puts it in one of the final sections of the book (titled "Experience and Its Material"), "the remedy for the kind of abstractness which befalls minds under the impact of science is experience—the experience of things in their concreteness."[78] Kracauer goes on to illustrate the importance of the concrete with a conspicuously localized example that he had already employed in chronicling his first impressions as an immigrant in "Why France Liked Our Films." Whereas the grid of Manhattan's streets is a well-known fact, he argues, "this fact becomes concrete only if we realize, for instance, that all the cross streets end in the nothingness of the blank sky."[79] For abstract knowledge to gain traction in a world increasingly dominated by scientific paradigms, Kracauer suggests, it needs to be grounded in concrete experience. *Theory of Film* is devoted to defining cinema as the medium through which such experience might be restored to modernity—"redeemed," as Kracauer puts it in the subtitle of the book.

The centrality of experience to Kracauer's film aesthetics has been recognized most clearly by Miriam Hansen, who argues that "what *Theory of Film* can offer us today is not a theory of film in general, but a theory of a particular type of film experience, and of cinema as the aesthetic matrix of a particular historical experience."[80] Hansen describes that experience in general terms of alienation, disintegration, and fragmentation, all of which inform Kracauer's thinking from the earliest essays and reviews through the late monographs on film and history.[81] But by the time he writes *Theory of Film*, this historical experience also includes the histories of terror, totalitarianism, and authoritarianism that had occupied him in his writings on cinema and propaganda during the 1940s. Rereading *Theory of Film* at the Manhattan crossroads that Kracauer invokes in its conclusion, in other words, requires specifying the kinds of historical experience that are most relevant to the book's argument about "film in our time" (as the epilogue is titled).

As I already noted in my discussion of those writings and the contexts in which they developed, one of the principal motifs here was precisely the *loss* of experience. We saw in the conclusion to the previous chapter, for example, that according to Adorno and his colleagues the authoritarian personality was characterized by the "inability to have experience"; coupled with this personality's acceptance only of what is like itself and the refusal to accept difference, this contributed centrally to identifying the "high scorer" on the F-scale—in other words, the "potentially fascistic individual."[82] Leo Löwenthal, who studied the speeches of fully constituted fascist individuals in *Prophets of Deceit*, had similarly linked the decomposition of individuality to the loss of experience under fascism. In his contribution to the *Commentary* series "The Crisis of the Individual," Löwenthal had laid the modern phenomenon of atomization at the doorstep of totalitarian terror and found its most devastating effect to consist in the "breakdown of the continuum of experience." Confronted with the unpredictability of totalitarian terror, the individual "does not know what he may experience; and what he has already experienced, is no longer important for his person or his future." This loss of experience reduced the human from an individual to "a unit of atomized reactions."[83] As we have also seen, the effects of this reduction outlasted fascism in a pervasive atmosphere of fear and in the sense of paralysis that Kracauer had traced in "Hollywood's Terror Films."[84]

Hannah Arendt had reached quite similar conclusions to Löwenthal's in *The Origins of Totalitarianism*. There she noted the tendency of totalitarian movements to so fanaticize their adherents that they "can be reached by neither experience nor argument," and not even torture or the fear of death could rise to the level of experience any longer.[85] In the final sections of the book, Arendt extends this line of argument from the members of the movement to the reign of ideology and terror and the "organized loneliness" of its subjects. Here, echoing Kracauer's analyses from his late French exile and just after his arrival in the United States, Arendt stresses repeatedly the destruction of experience operated by propaganda. Subject to the stringency of totalitarian ideology, propaganda applies a type of deductive reasoning "emancipated" from both reality and experience.[86] The result is remarkably similar to the psychophysical effects Kracauer had identified: under totalitarian propaganda, writes Arendt, "men lose the capacity of both experience and thought. The ideal subject of totalitarian rule is not the convinced Nazi or the convinced Communist, but people for whom the distinction between fact and fiction (i.e. the reality of experience) and the distinction between true and false (i.e. the standards of thought) no longer exist."[87] The loss of experience is a correlate of totalitarianism's utter dehumanization of the world.

These conclusions, which we have been tracing throughout the present book, form the crucial backdrop for Kracauer's turn to the notion of experience in his theory of film. Their importance is enhanced not only by the place of experience in the writings of the New York Intellectuals, and in the film and popular culture criticism of Warshow in particular, but also by the fact that Kracauer's closest friends from the Frankfurt years had been urgently concerned with the notion of experience throughout their careers. The diagnosis of a "withering of experience" constitutes one of the central premises of Critical Theory, from Walter Benjamin's lament on the decline of storytelling and his writings on Baudelaire and on the Work of Art, through Adorno's *Minima Moralia* and his late remarks on film as a form of subjective experience.[88] At stake in all these debates are the role of technological media and modernity, to be sure, but also the very notion of subjectivity after World War II and the Holocaust. Given the liquidation of subjective autonomy under terror and totalitarianism, and given the power of propaganda to entrap the subject in a hall of mirrors, was there any way to trust the evidentiary power of subjective experience, let alone its mediated construction in the cinema?

To investigate the role of experience in these debates is to inquire into its proper *place:* is it, as conservatives and pragmatists, thinkers from the French existentialists to Raymond Williams and up through the present resurgence of phenomenology, might claim, the guarantor of subjectivity and the wellspring of proper theorizing? Can experience still be allied, even in and through modern media, with Warshow's or Sontag's vaunted "immediacy"? Or is it, as Terry Eagleton posited in an attack on Williams, his erstwhile teacher, the "proper home of ideology," false consciousness, the very opposite of understanding?[89] Is experience an unquestionable property of the subject, whose authority it helps to ground, or is it only through experience that the subject is constituted in the first place?[90] Does it make sense to speak, as Walter Benjamin occasionally did, of experience without a subject, an absolute experience that "implies a point of indifference between subject and object, an equiprimordiality prior to their differentiation"?[91]

With Benjamin and Adorno to one side and Warshow to the other, I suggest, Kracauer would have felt acutely the pull of these competing claims and their weighty intellectual genealogies. *Theory of Film*, I submit, amalgamates these and lends them a unique inflection. Besides forming the *basso continuo* of *Theory of Film*, "the momentous issue of the significance of the film experience"[92] is raised explicitly in two prominent, linked passages of the book. Kracauer broaches the issue in the crucial chapter on the spectator, at the end of which he suspends the discussion; he then takes it up again in the previously mentioned section, "Experience and Its Material," in the concluding chapter. Together, these two passages carry the book's central argument about cinema and experience. Since the latter section spells this argument out most explicitly, I turn here to Kracauer's conclusions from *Theory of Film*, reserving the discussion of spectatorship for the next chapter.

The keystone in Kracauer's discussion of the cinema's experiential dimension is the final chapter, titled "Film in Our Time." Even though it appears as the book's epilogue, Kracauer considered it the "masterkey to all that precedes it."[93] His argument here turns on the claim that the world of modernity—the postwar, post-Holocaust, post-Stalinist, nuclear age—is governed by the loss of reliable, binding belief systems and by "abstraction." The former claim is in keeping with Kracauer's long-held "lapsarian" view of modernity that characterized his earliest works (influenced by *Lebensphilosophie* and specifically his teacher Simmel),[94] and which he would theorize repeatedly by invoking Lukács's notion of "geistige Obdachlosigkeit." However, against the backdrop of his own analyses of Nazi propaganda from the late 1930s onward, and in keeping with his indictment of Hollywood for ideological apathy during the 1940s, this notion now takes on a specific historical valence. The Cold War forces an ideological breach into which cinema springs by restoring experience.

The concern with abstraction likewise pre-dates work on *Theory of Film*, where it, too, is transformed. In essays like "The Mass Ornament," it will be recalled, Kracauer had theorized the inherently *ambivalent* nature of abstraction, locating the remedy to its ills dialectically in the phenomenon itself and advocating *more* rather than less rationalization. The argument in *Theory of Film* appears, by contrast, to conceive abstraction in binary opposition to the concrete. Rather than advocating a way out of increased abstraction that leads *through* the mass ornament, he now theorizes film as a medium that affords concrete experience *against* the abstraction of everyday life under capitalism.

And yet Kracauer significantly refuses to equate the concrete with empirical sense data. Nor is the abstract simply immaterial. Abstraction, Kracauer specifies in *Theory of Film,* "refers us to physical phenomena, while at the same time luring us away from their *qualities.* Hence the urgency of grasping precisely these *given and yet ungiven* phenomena in their concreteness."[95] What looks like equivocation—how can a concrete phenomenon be "given and yet ungiven"?—is in fact a dialectical assumption at the heart of Kracauer's experiential realism. In a line of thinking that reaches from Marx to Brecht and Benjamin, the concrete only has explanatory power as "a synthesis of determinations" that begins not with sense data, but with abstract determinations that lead "to the reproduction of the concrete."[96] Given as the physical reality of Kracauer's title, phenomena yet remain "ungiven"—that is, abstract and uncomprehended—until they reach the spectator as a concrete synthesis of determinations in the medium of film. Consequently, the cinematic concrete is for Kracauer not an ontological fact but an experiential one that relies, precisely, on mediation.

In the epilogue to *Theory of Film,* Kracauer exemplifies his own method by a reference to Alfred North Whitehead. To understand the workings of a factory, Whitehead suggests, it is not sufficient to deal "merely in terms of economic abstractions." What we want to train, rather, is "the habit of apprehending such an organism in its completeness."[97] Kracauer quotes this passage approvingly but goes on to note that "perhaps the term 'completeness' is not quite adequate. In experiencing an object, we not only broaden our knowledge of its diverse qualities but in a manner of speaking incorporate it into us so that we grasp its being and its dynamics from within—a sort of blood transfusion, as it were."[98] The organicist vocabulary here is intriguing for what it suggests about the phenomenology of the film experience. By the same token, it can be deceiving in that it suggests a form of immediacy where Kracauer is in fact attempting to work out a series of complicated mediations. For what is at stake in this image of introjection and blood transfusion is the dialectics of subject and object, the concrete and abstract. Film has the power to mediate between these poles; it is able to represent (rather than simply reproduce) reality—the diverse qualities of the object, its abstract dynamics as much as its sensible surface appearance—as a concrete perceptual object for the spectator, who in turn experiences that object as a synthesis of determinations.

In this reading of *Theory of Film,* the medium's appointed task to record and reveal is itself a dialectical one. For merely to record would be to reproduce the false concrete, just as unmediated revelation would yield a false abstraction. The cross-section films of the Weimar Republic, Kracauer had already complained in *From Caligari to Hitler,* excelled at "showing much and revealing nothing."[99] True cinema, by contrast—or what Kracauer liked to call "cinematic films"—"blast the prison of conventional reality," "disclos[e] new aspects of physical reality," and reveal "things normally unseen."[100] In its recording function, the cinema is partial, as Kracauer would put it in the subsequent book on history, to "objectives and modes of being which still lack a name and hence are overlooked or misjudged."[101] Less a theological category than a phenomenological one, the titular "redemption" depends precisely on this dialectics of recording and revealing, of concretion and abstraction, of the given and yet ungiven. It is perhaps worth noting again in this context that for the German version of the book Kracauer decided to translate *redemption* not as *Erlösung* (salvation) but as *Errettung* (literally, rescue): film's redemptive powers, then, consist in the medium's ability to rescue from oblivion unseen or overlooked objects and phenomena and to make them available—to experience.

Consequently, Kracauer proposes that film provides a "remedy" for abstractness by allowing spectators to "experience . . . things in their concreteness."[102] What is unavailable in everyday life, where experience itself has come under threat, film facilitates. By gravitating toward the unstaged, the fortuitous, and the "flow of life," the cinema allows the modern subject to reconnect to, indeed to reconstitute itself in, forms of experience that lend significance to transience and indeterminacy in the face of reification. In view of the scripted forms of experience promulgated, according to Warshow, by middlebrow culture, it is no accident that Kracauer's theory—like that of Bazin, who reached similar conclusions working independently in France—ultimately amounts to a defense of ambiguity. This is his way of locating the resistance of experience to reification.[103]

In the photographic medium of film and in the stylistic commitment to realism, Kracauer sees the promise of breaking through the reification of everyday life by confronting viewers with the estranged fragments of their existence and allowing them to recoup these fragments in the medium of experience. Film, according to the underlying argument, at once estranges us from our ingrained habits of (alienated) perception and overcomes alienation, reinstating what Kracauer calls "the humane" as the measure of experience. In this sense, Kracauer's is a profoundly humanist theory of film—even if, as we shall see in the following chapter, his is also a curious humanism, bound to a realist aesthetic whose emphasis on the materiality of objects occasionally appears to write the human out of the picture. Can there be such a thing as nonanthropocentric humanism?

9. The Curious Humanist

> The thinking promoted by capitalism resists culminating in that reason which arises from the basis of man.
>
> SIEGFRIED KRACAUER, "The Mass Ornament"

First conceptualized in French exile at the beginning of the 1940s and finally published in 1960, *Theory of Film* ends, in a sense, where Kracauer's American career began: at MoMA. The book's final section is titled "The Family of Man" in explicit reference to Edward Steichen's blockbuster 1955 exhibit at the Museum of Modern Art. The closing nod to this photography show harks back to the opening chapters of the book, in which Kracauer had derived his theory of film from the history and "nature" of photography. In the book's final pages, he again links the "photographic nature" of film to the power of photographs "to authenticate the reality of the vision they feature."[1]

Film comes into its own as a realist medium that inherits and expands on photography's affinities with physical reality—its indeterminacy, its endlessness, its unstaged, fortuitous configurations. This, in a nutshell, is the central argument of *Theory of Film*. But more is at stake in the book's parting glance at *The Family of Man*, whose relevance to Kracauer's project is hardly exhausted by its turn to photography as a realist medium. For Steichen's exhibit was also an emblem of a particular politics of the image at the height of the Cold War. By appealing to its exemplary function as a purveyor of liberal humanist values, Kracauer in turn begs the question of how we might read the politics of his late film theory.

To explore this question, the present chapter first inquires into the place of *Family of Man* in *Theory of Film*, noting how Kracauer explicitly aligns himself, via Erich Auerbach's *Mimesis*, with the universal humanism that characterized Steichen's show. But Kracauer also complicates the ideological premises that he invokes—for in significant ways, his realist film theory appears to be premised on the very absence of humanism's core tenet: the individual human subject. Cinema's domain, according to Kracauer, is an alienated, nonanthropocentric world of "camera reality" that radically decenters human subjectivity and at times seems to do away with it altogether. In this regard, I read *Theory of Film* as a critique of the more blandly universalizing gestures of Steichen's photographic humanism. Despite its patently antitotalitarian intentions, *Family of Man* papers over the unraveling of long-held humanist beliefs in the face of totalitarianism and the camps; Kracauer's *Theory of Film*, by contrast, registers this unraveling in the way its cinematic ontology and even its phenomenological claims marginalize the human subject.

And yet, I argue, Kracauer remains wedded—like the other members of the Frankfurt School—to the unfinished project of enlightenment that he, like the Institut für Sozialforschung, began to critique as early as the 1920s. Despite some theoretical motifs that he may share with more recent object-oriented ontologies and new realisms,[2] it would be entirely misleading to think of Kracauer as a (proto-)posthumanist thinker.[3] To adapt Adorno's influential description of his erstwhile mentor's "curious" *(wunderlich)* realism, I propose instead that we consider Kracauer a "curious humanist"—a film theorist who leads us through a nonanthropocentric and occasionally postapocalyptic universe of "camera reality" and "historical reality" back to the promise of a weak but renewed faith in human subjectivity and experience.

Kracauer critiques humanist assumptions from within, in the name of what his posthumous book on history calls "the humane." That book was intended explicitly as a sequel of sorts to *Theory of Film*. If we take this claim seriously and read Kracauer's historiography as film theory, I propose, we can trace the reconstruction of human subjectivity from its postwar ruins. Kracauer's central figure for this postwar subject, I will argue, is the spectator: a cinephilic subject that bears the marks of its prior decentering but holds out the promise of a renewed receptivity and openness to the world, the possibility of experience after the age of the crisis of man.[4]

MIDCENTURY MIDDLEBROW: *THE FAMILY OF MAN*

The Family of Man featured 503 photographs from around the globe, organized around putatively universal subjects such as love and marriage, children, work, birth and death. Visitors were invited to recognize the differences among cultures, to be sure; but they were also entreated to subsume those differences under the family resemblances implied by the title. The images of *The Family of Man*, in other words, were designed to reflect back both the viewing subject's own likeness and the shared bonds of humanity—including its shared fate. Famously, the show featured one single color photograph: it depicted an atomic mushroom cloud and was accompanied by a quotation from Bertrand Russell linking nuclear bombs to the "end of the human race."

The universalism of the show's message echoed the curator's conviction that photography, the chosen medium for the exhibit, "gave visual communication its most simple, direct, universal language."[5] In an article published the same year *Theory of Film* appeared, Steichen noted that "the importance of the art of photography as mass communication [had] been amply demonstrated" by *The Family of Man*. The show's mass audiences, he claimed, "not only understand this visual presentation, they also participate in it, and identify themselves with the images, as if in corroboration of the words of a Japanese poet, 'When you look into a mirror, you do not see your reflection, your reflection sees you.'"[6] The experience afforded by the exhibit, Steichen's reference seems to imply, should lead to a recognition of the universal similarity between self and other.

The Family of Man ran for four months in New York in early 1955 and then traveled around the world for the following eight years under the auspices of MoMA's Rockefeller-funded International Program and the recently founded United States Information Agency.[7] Replicating the global reach of its subject matter in its marketing, the exhibit showed at over 150 museums in thirty-seven countries on six continents before it was permanently installed at Clervaux Castle in Steichen's native country of Luxemburg. *The Family of Man* is now estimated to have been viewed by over ten million visitors, not counting the further millions who encountered its images in the affordable, best-selling catalogue. Even prior to the recent restoration of the original photographs and a newly designed installation replete with tablet guides, the show was entered into the UNESCO Memory of the World register.[8]

The exhibit's broad, international reach has been accompanied almost since its opening by an equally robust critique. To the New York Intellectuals, *Family of Man* was the epitome of the middlebrow "culture-pattern." In his influential *Partisan Review* essay "Masscult and Midcult" (published, like *Theory of Film*, in 1960), Macdonald wrote:

> The Midcult mind aspires toward Universality above all. A good example was that "Family of Man" show of photographs Edward Steichen put on several years ago at the Museum of Modern Art to great applause. (The following summer it was the hit of the American exhibition in Moscow, showing that a touch of Midcult makes the whole world kin.) The title was typical—actually it should have been called Photorama. There were many excellent photographs, but they were

arranged under the most pretentious and idiotic titles [. . .] and the whole effect was of a specially pompous issue of *Life*. [. . .] The editorializing was insistent—the Midcult audience always wants to be Told—and the photographs were marshaled to demonstrate that although there are real problems (death, for instance), it's a pretty good old world after all.[9]

Macdonald frequently voiced his disdain for the leveling effects of the *Life* aesthetic ("masscult," he averred with typical irony, "is very, very democratic; it refuses to discriminate against or between anything or anybody").[10] His comments on "that show" at MoMA amplify this contempt through his characteristically acerbic style, his sarcastic tone, right down to the clever capitalizations. But for all its idiosyncrasies, Macdonald's take on *The Family of Man* strikes a note that is common to many critiques of the show. The latter is widely recognized today as exhibit A for American postwar humanism at the height of the Cold War. Certainly by the time MoMA and the USIA sent it on its Coca-Cola–sponsored world tour—which began, significantly, in West Berlin and Guatemala—*Family of Man* had become the poster child of American "public diplomacy."[11] As such, this "cold war extravaganza," as Allan Sekula called it, has also become a flashpoint for the critique of midcentury middlebrow aesthetics and for the universalizing claims of a liberal humanist view that would enthrone an essentially abstract notion of (the family of) man at the center of the world.[12]

For this the show has been lambasted by critics such as Macdonald and, perhaps even more famously, Roland Barthes, who first saw it in Paris and wrote an incisive critique of the show's underlying ideology.[13] To Barthes, the exhibit (retitled "The Great Family of Man" in French) exemplified precisely those operations of culture that he aimed to unmask in *Mythologies*. As Steichen himself never tired of repeating, the show was designed to offer a "mirror of the universal elements and emotions in the everydayness of life— . . . a mirror of the essential oneness of mankind through the world."[14] Barthes countered that the emphasis on the supposedly universal constants, or "a human essence" undergirding human differences, elided the constitutive role of history and the social. In their place, the photos of birth, death, and human work appealed to the ostensibly timeless and unifying forces of religion, nature—and myth.

Other critics have fleshed out exactly what aspects of history and society the show's universalism mythologized. They have reconstructed its imbrication in the discourses and geopolitical practices of American cold war imperialism, queried the omission of the Holocaust, skewered its naive treatment of race and class, and unpacked its normative assumptions about the nuclear family and the domestic ideal of the Eisenhower era.[15] Fundamentally, these critiques all agree that the exhibit's universalism manifests in sentimental strategies of decontextualization and naturalization; it marks "the epitome of American cold war liberalism," appears naive in its "familial humanism," and papers over the unequal distribution of political power by erasing particularity and difference.[16] These shortcomings appear endemic to the show's liberal humanist ethos; to undo them would have required what Barthes calls a "progressive humanism" that would "constantly scour nature, its 'laws' and its 'limits' in order to discover History there, and at last to establish Nature itself as historical."[17] For such critics, however, this would have involved an entirely different approach to the selection of photographs, to the editorializing comment, and to the very arrangement of the exhibit as it was displayed in New York and throughout the world.

THE FAMILY OF MAN IN THEORY OF FILM

When Kracauer references *The Family of Man* at the close of *Theory of Film*, he certainly appears to buy into the show's universal humanism and its ostensibly non- or postideological aspirations. Having outlined a "material aesthetics" of film and theorized its promise as an inherently realist, photographic medium, Kracauer concludes with a brief glance at the power of cinema to effect change. In a cold war gesture, he first dismisses claims that tie cinema to revolutionary causes. But he also refuses to limit the function of cinema to "promoting responsible citizenship" or to prioritize any other instrumentalization of the medium: the range of "equally legitimate propositions," he claims, "is inexhaustible."[18] And yet, drawing on Auerbach's now famous account of realism in Western literature in *Mimesis*, Kracauer does venture a thesis of his own. A scholar with deeply held humanist convictions and training, Auerbach had concluded his recently translated book with an outlook toward a near future when human differences would yield to a "common life of mankind on earth."[19] Of this future he found inklings in the modern realist novel's attention to the commonality of the everyday—to the "wealth of reality and depth of life in every moment to which one submits without intentionality."[20]

Kracauer adopts this argument and applies it to the photographic media. To him, cinema represents the apogee of this line of reasoning, whose premise dates back to Lessing's *Laocoön:* able to "record the material aspects of common daily life in many places," to reveal their meaningfulness and connect them through editing, films "authenticate the reality" of the humanist vision in ways specific to the medium.[21] Kracauer exemplifies this claim by referring to documentaries such as Paul Rotha and Basil Wright's *World without End* (1953), commissioned by the same UNESCO that had only recently included Steichen's exhibit in its register. The two eminent British documentarians had teamed up to direct a poetic paean to international development by editing together material shot in Siam and Mexico. To Kracauer, the film's composite image of remote regions—what Rotha himself labeled its "humanism of internationalism"—represents the "one-world idea within the visual dimension."[22] In this regard, it is easy to see the parallels between Rotha and Wright's aesthetic choices and Steichen's selection and arrangement of photographs for the MoMA exhibit.

Similarly, when Kracauer quotes a letter writer enthusing about Satyajit Ray's *Aparajito* (1956) to the *New York Times,* he might as well be referring to the ideological message of *The Family of Man:* what seems remarkable about the film, writes the reader, "is that you see this story happening in a remote land and see these faces with their exotic beauty and still feel that the same thing is happening every day somewhere in Manhattan or Brooklyn or the Bronx."[23] Underlying social and cultural differences, we find a common human essence. Little wonder that a German reviewer of *Theory of Film* described its basic tenor as "a pedagogically minded humanism."[24]

"The key question posed by any humanism or universalism is point of view," remarks Marianne Hirsch in discussing Steichen's exhibit.[25] In this respect, the wording of the letter quoted by Kracauer is revealing: the parallels and mirrorings recall Steichen's emphasis on photography's ability to "mirror the essential oneness of mankind through the world"; but there is a profound asymmetry between the "exotic beauty" of a "remote" India and the perspective of a New Yorker looking from an American vantage point at the changing world (or at Ray's film). Shrinking worlds and the gradual leveling of differences among humans are perforce imagined differently from distinct geopolitical, historical, cultural, and social perspectives. Postwar liberal humanism, by contrast, has come under critique for eliding such differences and universalizing an American point of view that remains unmarked as such, even as it becomes instrumentalized in the geopolitics of the Cold War.

The key question is point of view, and we should ask it of Kracauer's film theory. Back in 1941, we recall, the American vantage point had been marked explicitly in the recollection of the immigrant's arrival in New York Harbor and in the first person plural of "Why France Liked Our Films." And even as Kracauer's enthusiasm for Hollywood waned over the course of his first American decade, articles on Preston Sturges, pseudo-liberal trends in the movies, and Hollywood's "terror films" had taken up a reflexive subject position from which to critique the shortcomings of American mass culture. As numerous critics have pointed out, little of this reflexivity remains in the seemingly more detached tone of *Theory of Film*—let alone in its concluding vision of a common humanity and of films that "make the world our home."[26]

What, then, are the politics of film theory in Kracauer's late American writings? An implicit critical consensus becomes explicit in Eric Rentschler's claim that, given Cold War circumstances, the émigré author "made certain that all traces of his former political convictions vanished from his work."[27] Worse still, the turn to *Family of Man* might even suggest the adoption of a new set of political convictions, all the more insipid for remaining unmarked: are we to conclude that by 1960 Kracauer had adopted the imperialist, Cold War perspective that informed Steichen's exhibit and the USIA's "public diplomacy" for American democracy? Moreover, if *Theory of Film* really elides both Kracauer's own intellectual history and the historical dimension of film as a mass medium, as Miriam Hansen suggests, does it thereby espouse the ahistorical humanism that Barthes and others have critiqued as *Family of Man*'s governing ideology?[28]

The answer that I propose in this chapter and the next is a qualified no: Kracauer's engagement with humanism is far more nuanced and more deeply inscribed into the trajectory of his thinking from Weimar to New York than these questions imply. But before I explain why and how, let me state the qualifications up front: First, as is evident from his endorsement of Steichen's exhibit, Kracauer indisputably participated in the Cold War humanist discourse that the MoMA show championed, and it would be difficult (and wrong) to confuse his film theory with the kind of ideology critique championed by Barthes—or by some of the critical theorists with whom Kracauer was certainly in communication at the time, for that matter. *Theory of Film*'s realist aesthetic, as we shall see, exudes at certain points a postideological fatigue that is decidedly of a piece with the universalizing gestures in *Family of Man*. Second, the language of *Theory of Film* does place it at a great distance from the ironic engagement and dialectical nuance with which Kracauer had analyzed film and photography during the 1920s and in his native German. While Pauline Kael overreached in her scathing critique of Kracauer's occasionally ponderous language, she was arguably right to sense that "Kracauer's best stuff isn't in English."[29]

And yet, two aspects complicate this reading of *Theory of Film* as simply another midcentury middlebrow text. First, as I elaborate below, Kracauer's is a curious humanism: a humanism with a difference, one considerably less certain of the human subject's essential sovereignty. The specific contours of this curious humanism emerge, secondly, if we historicize Kracauer's late works. Which is to say: we must again situate the culminating humanist vision of *Theory of Film* within the larger context of his American writings that I have been sketching in this book. In that sense, Kracauer still writes both his film aesthetics and his final book on historiography against the backdrop of totalitarian terror, which he and others had found to result in the erasure of experience, the liquidation of subjectivity, and the annihilation of difference in the name of racial antisemitism. As Hirsch points out in defense of Steichen's tendency to subsume difference under an ostensibly postideological notion of common humanity in *The Family of Man*, "we must remember the political context in which difference had so recently been used as a justification for genocide."[30] The same holds true for Kracauer's attempts to theorize film as a way out of atomization, abstraction, and a "creeping apathy."[31] In this regard, historicizing *Theory of Film* also means reading it as a response to the question raised by the previous book, *From Caligari to Hitler*: how to rekindle the promise of cinema after Hitler, the Holocaust, and Hiroshima, but also in the face of the illiberal tendencies Kracauer attributed to Hollywood in his essays of the 1940s.

DECENTERING THE SUBJECT: *THEORY OF FILM'S* NONANTHROPOCENTRIC UNIVERSE

A close look at the central theoretical motifs of Kracauer's book reveals something counterintuitive about the humanist turn at its close. Here, too, the comparison with *Family of Man* is instructive. Steichen's exhibit assumes and celebrates the universal centrality of "man" as the measure of all things; the entire conception of the show, from its title to the selection and arrangement of photos in MoMA, centers on the commensurability of human experience and subjectivity: "man" is the subject of these images in both senses of the word, aesthetic and humanist. Steichen's exhibit admittedly includes a number of strategically placed images that do not display the human face or figure: enormous reproductions of landscape and nature photography featuring mountain ranges, tree formations, or the glistening drops of water formed by a cresting wave—not to mention the image of outer space at the entrance to the New York exhibit. However, with the exception of the latter (which serves more as an invitation to enter than as part of the show's curated "argument" about a human family), what is striking about the nonhuman subject matter in the show is how insistently it is "humanized": the belly and breasts of a pregnant woman are imposed on an image featuring a round sun over a fertile landscape; images of loggers turn nature photography into a depiction of natural resources for human labor; waves become an object for the play of children featured on the surrounding photographs under the Shakespeare quote "O wonderful, wonderful, and most wonderful! And yet again wonderful . . ." Moreover, nature photography—including the opening shot of the universe—is consistently instrumentalized for syntactic purposes: it generally recurs as a way of transitioning among the various themes of the exhibit. The purview of *Family of Man* emphatically does not include any notion of nature as independent of the human subject.

Theory of Film, by contrast, conceptualizes film as a medium that profoundly decenters the human subject in favor of an object-oriented notion of "physical reality"—or what at one point Kracauer calls "crude existence."[32] "Camera reality," as Kracauer defines it here, is tied time and again to a world all but independent of human subjectivity. Instead, inanimate objects loom large and the medium provides access to those aspects that are inaccessible to perception and consciousness: objects and phenomena that exceed our grasp by virtue of their excessive or diminutive size; fleeting, transitory moments that lie in the "blind spots of the mind."[33] It is as if the physical reality favored and represented by photographic media came into being precisely by the subtraction of human agency, consciousness, and subjectivity.

Time and again, we find Kracauer constructing scenarios that diminish the human and increase the stature of the object world. Cinema, he argues, is a "garbage-minded" medium that gravitates to a lower world, a ragpicker among the "crude and unnegotiated presence of natural objects."[34] It is a medium endowed with an a-subjective gaze that fixes not on the party but on its aftermath, when the people are gone and only the crumpled tablecloth and half-empty glasses remain. In outlining the "photographic approach" from which he derives his film theory, Kracauer singles out images from Talbot to Atget that feature abandoned spaces: a broom in an open door, a granite canyon, the empty streets of Paris.

In contrast to Steichen's teeming photographs, then, Kracauer's cinematic world can appear strangely depopulated. The aesthetics of cinematic realism, in other words, consist in mechanically reproducing a reality from which the human dimension is always in some measure absent—what Miriam Hansen describes as a "strange, nonanthropocentric landscape."[35] In this world of "camera reality," any remainder of human interiority is derivative of materiality and the "thicket of material life," and wholeness is displaced by cinema's "tendency toward decomposing given wholes."[36] To the degree that cinema does provide a time-image of the "flow of life," it is

9. William Henry Fox Talbot (1800–1877), *The Open Door*, 1844. (Digital image courtesy of the Getty's Open Content Program)

"a kind of life which is still intimately connected, as if by an umbilical cord, with the material phenomena from which its emotional and intellectual contents emerge." The flow of life, Kracauer consequently insists, "is predominantly a material rather than a mental continuum."[37]

From this antihumanist impulse Kracauer derives the medium's defining powers of alienation. A favorite passage from Proust that Kracauer cites early on sets the stage for his theory of cinematic realism as a form of estrangement: Proust's narrator enters his grandmother's living room unnoticed by her and suddenly sees the scene as if through a camera. Instead of the close relative whose loving gaze is structured by memory and daily contact, the narrator becomes "identical with the camera lens"—a witness, an observer, a stranger, in every way "the opposite of the unseeing lover." As a consequence, the grandmother suddenly appears completely alien, "a dejected old woman whom I did not know."[38]

Nothing could be further from the subject Steichen and his collaborators imagined as the ideal viewer of *Family of Man*. In his prologue to the exhibition catalogue, the poet Carl Sandburg speaks directly of and to the viewer, addressing her in the second person but also anticipating and

10. Eugène Atget, *Rue St. Rustique*, 1922. (The Metropolitan Museum of Art, David Hunter McAlpin Fund, 1956. www.metmuseum.org)

ventriloquizing an expected response. This imaginary visitor moves through the show as a tourist fully at home in the global village: "you travel and see what the camera saw. The wonder of human mind, heart, wit and instinct, is here. You might catch yourself saying 'I'm not a stranger here.'"[39]

As if in explicit opposition to the show's identificatory approach to photography and its universalist emphasis on human kinship, photographic media are to Kracauer "the product of complete alienation." Where Steichen wants audiences to perceive common universals in even the most remote or exotic subjects, Kracauer holds that "the way leads toward the unfamiliar in the familiar."[40] Close-ups turn human bodies back onto their sheer materiality. Even human eyes offer no window into the soul; rather, "skin textures [become] reminiscent of aerial photographs, eyes turn into lakes or volcanic craters. Such images [. . .] blast the prison of conventional reality, opening up expanses which we have explored at best in dreams before."[41] Rather than bringing home the likeness of all human pursuits as in *The Family of Man*, *Theory of Film* prizes the photographic media's power to make "the most familiar . . . appear as the most alien."[42]

As both the tool and the product of alienation, cinema "protests its peculiar requirement to explore all of physical existence, human or nonhuman." In the process, the human is decentered. Of the actor, Kracauer remarks that he appears most effective and comes into his own as a cinematic presence precisely to the degree that he sheds his humanity and becomes "an object among objects," no more than "a detail, a fragment of the matter of the world."[43] Indeed, Kracauer goes so far as to call uncinematic any film "in which the inanimate merely serves as a background to self-contained dialogue and the closed circuit of human relationships."[44] Cinematic realism involves breaking open that circuit through the power of the medium and integrating it into a larger notion of physical existence, a world that is not cut to the measure of man, familial or otherwise, but rather rendered in its "virgin indeterminacy." What emerges here, as in Kracauer's writings on photography, is a peculiar form of natural history in which the world appears either independent of human intervention or abandoned by humans. It appears "inchoate, cocoon-like" as an "anonymous state of reality."[45]

While it would be wrong to call this world postapocalyptic, there is a strong sense in which Kracauer maps at least the possibility of a universe devoid of human subjectivity onto photographic media. Indeed, Kracauer had long anticipated such a posthumanist world in which reason had succumbed to the irrational forces of nature. Already in 1927, the "blizzard" of photography in the illustrated magazines had been the occasion to posit a stark alternative between enlightenment humanism and a posthumanist, capitalist mode of production in which society "has fallen prey to a mute nature which has no meaning." In his well-known photography essay, this had been precisely the all-out gamble with history: whether the world could come to its senses and restore human reason and "liberated consciousness" as the arbiter of human affairs—or whether "mute nature" would eradicate consciousness altogether and "sit down at the very table that consciousness had abandoned."[46]

As we have seen in previous chapters, by the time Kracauer writes *Theory of Film*, that gamble has in an important sense been lost—and the utopian hope he had invested in photographic media appears all but smothered under totalitarianism, war, and the illiberal turn of the twentieth century. Consciousness, reason, enlightenment, and indeed humanism itself appear to have failed; subjectivity has been eroded, authoritarianism has triumphed, and, in the words of Adorno and Horkheimer's *Dialectic of Enlightenment*, the "wholly enlightened world is radiant with triumphant calamity."[47]

At this historical juncture, the theoretical motif of nonanthropocentric, a-subjective ontology that one can trace all the way back to Kracauer's Weimar writings assumes far more sinister undertones. In 1927, there was still something Chaplinesque about Ginster, the reticent protagonist of Kracauer's eponymous novel, who dreams of dissolving into the furniture, hopes to trickle away or to be "gaseous."[48] After the experience of exile, World War II, and the camps, and faced with the threat of nuclear annihilation, the playful escape hatches for human subjectivity that *Ginster* still envisioned have become all too real. Humanism is compromised, and Kracauer does not share Steichen's almost naive faith in human universals. On the contrary, the photographic media register the evaporation of human subjectivity, intimating what W. G. Sebald would later describe as a "natural history of destruction."[49] In photography's ruin aesthetic, consciousness has all but abandoned the table at which the go-for-broke game of history was to play out.[50]

SPECTATORSHIP AND THE SUBJECT OF EXPERIENCE

And yet, from the ruins of subjectivity a tenuous, new subject emerges. Although the conception of "physical reality" that anchors *Theory of Film* is nonanthropocentric in the ways just described, it is not devoid of human subjectivity altogether. Kracauer's realist film theory implies a posttotalitarian critique of the universal, sovereign subject as humanism's grounding figure; but Kracauer ultimately reinstates a "weak" version of this figure, I now want to suggest, in the guise of a properly cinematic, if not cinephilic subject: the spectator.

Kracauer's writings are populated with characters and protagonists of various types who may be (and have been) seen as identificatory projections of the author—whether the little shopgirls of the essays from the 1920s, Offenbach in Paris, the humanist Erasmus in the preface to the posthumous *History*, or that book's figurations of the historian as "stranger" and "exile." This is not even to mention the (dis)avowedly autobiographical protagonists of his novels.[51] Of equal significance in this set of identifications, however, is "the inveterate moviegoer" himself, a figure that has gone relatively unnoticed in Kracauer's oeuvre.[52] This figure assumes enormous theoretical weight once we recognize that it recurs in various guises throughout the final two books on film theory and history, respectively. Spectatorship, as we shall see, defines not only the moviegoer but also the historian; reappearing in Kracauer's late writings as the characteristic attribute of various crucial mythological figures (Ahasuerus, Orpheus, Perseus), a particular form of cinephilic spectatorship becomes the defining trait in the restoration of humanist subjectivity.

The figure of the spectator makes its appearance in the remarkable and pivotal chapter devoted to the topic in *Theory of Film*. Here Kracauer modulates insights borrowed from critics such as Balázs and Benjamin, takes up contemporary concerns with the "immediate experience" of film and mass culture, and also anticipates far more recent discussions in film theory. What binds together his wide-ranging insights in this chapter is the underlying attempt to draw out the characteristic subjectivity of the "inveterate moviegoer." It is a decentered subjectivity to match the decentered world, and while Kracauer at one point explicitly imagines this subject to be "as little humanistic or humanitarian as possible," this chapter begins to reintroduce spectatorship as a form of "the humane." This is a line of thinking on which Kracauer intended to follow through in *History*, had he lived to complete the book. But even in the version compiled posthumously from drafts and notes, he ties a notion of dispassionate spectatorship and the cinema's power to restore experience to the humanism of figures like Erasmus or Jakob Burckhardt. His film theory prepares the nonanthropocentric ground for this new humanism. It is, then, in both senses of the word a curious subject that emerges from Kracauer's theory of spectatorship. Let us briefly review the contours of that theory.

Drawing explicitly on work by the affiliates of the French *filmologie* movement, Kracauer first describes the spectator as a sensory being that responds physiologically to visual stimuli.[53] His emphasis on the role of movement and what he calls the spectator's "kinesthetic responses" continues a line of reasoning he had already explored in the Marseille Notebooks, according to which the cinema "undermines idealist and anthropocentric positions on the level of reception, in the ways it engages the material reality of the spectator—the human being 'with skin and hair.'"[54] Yet in his emphasis on involuntary sensory, somatic responses, Kracauer also anticipates far more recent theorizations of spectatorship, whether from the standpoint of cognitivism, evolutionary biology, or neophenomenology.[55]

Unlike the cognitivists, however, Kracauer makes a fairly sharp distinction between cognition and affect, reserving the former for processes of "reasoning" and locating the latter in "dimensions where sense impressions are all-important"—notably in the spectator's dreamlike state.[56] When Kracauer moves from his discussion of the sensory impact of cinema to the spectator's "lowered consciousness," he consequently shifts from the vocabulary of evolutionary biology and physiology to the language of psychoanalysis. The reflections that follow from here predate the turn to psychoanalysis in screen theory by over a decade, but they sound many of that approach's central motifs. Like the later Christian Metz, who considers cinema as "more perceptual, if the phrase is allowable, than many other means of expression," Kracauer begins with the perceptual qualities of the medium, and of the spectator's experience in particular.[57] From here, he takes the step into what Metz would define as the imaginary dimension of cinema and spectatorship. For Kracauer, as for the later French critics,[58] this dimension is linked to altered psychological states, whether of hypnosis, trance, or dreaming (all of which Kracauer mentions).

In these states, the subject both expands and contracts. In a section entitled "the two directions of dreaming," Kracauer distinguishes between an object-driven and a subject-driven form of spectatorship, both of which resonate again with subsequent conceptualizations of the spectator in screen theory. The latter notably drew attention to the ego-effect of cinema, the illusion of perceptual mastery that enthrones the subject as the imaginary origin and telos of the images onscreen.[59] Just as Jean-Louis Baudry would later emphasize the narcissistic and regressive aspects of this process, for example, Kracauer, too, speaks of the "child-like omnipotence" of the spectator and explicitly labels this omnipotence "imaginary" (though without reference to Lacan's understanding of the term).[60] But Kracauer adds a social dimension to this ontogenetic explanation that is missing in Baudry, even where Baudry explicitly critiques the ideological effects of the cinematic apparatus: for Kracauer, the regressive moment of spectatorship is a compensatory satisfaction, prompted by a world that "has grown so complex, politically and otherwise, that it can no longer be simplified." Deprived of "binding norms and beliefs and [confronted with] a loss of concreteness," the spectator comes home to the cinema where "the frustrated may turn into the kings of creation."[61] To Kracauer, the cinema promises to renew experience where it has become impoverished in the world.

Now, as apparatus theory would also insist, spectatorship entails a loss, a diminution of the self, a relinquishing of autonomy: after all, for critics writing in the wake of Lacan, the spectator's narcissistic aggrandizement is unmasked as an illusion, a mis-recognition.[62] Kracauer speaks in this respect of the "shrinking self," of the spectator who responds to the lure of the image. The resulting effect amounts not merely to a diminution but to the virtual disappearance of the subject: "So he drifts toward and into the objects—much like the legendary Chinese painter who, longing for the peace of the landscape he had created, moved into it, walked toward the faraway mountains suggested by his brush strokes and disappeared in them never to be seen again."[63]

This account of the film experience records a sense of "losing oneself" at the movies, which at some level remains profoundly familiar to anyone who remembers "snapping out" of a particularly suspenseful scene, an engrossing emotional twist, or a captivating action sequence—as if returning to reality from that Chinese painter's faraway mountains. Film theory has devised numerous ways to interpret this experience. To Béla Balázs, who invoked the same orientalist legend, it encapsulated the cinema's romantic promise of overcoming the subject/object split;[64] to 1970s "screen theory," the same experience amounts to a dangerous, regressive illusion, a failure of reality testing akin to the narcissistic wish-fulfillment of a dream. Consequently, apparatus theory would sharply criticize the dual subject-effect of cinema, the double power of the *dispositif* to endow the transcendental subject with imaginary omnipotence and to reduce it to a mere ideological effect. In Kracauer, however, we find another reading of the spectator's characteristic film experience, which prizes this diminution of subjectivity in the face of a world of objects—that "physical reality" that he deems the proper domain of cinema.

This diminished subjectivity becomes explicit, finally, in the figure of the "film addict," whose peculiar cinephilia is of enormous consequence to Kracauer's thinking.[65] The film addict is a curious, emblematic figure, endowed with traits that Kracauer consistently valorized in writings from vastly different time periods. Like "those who wait" from his 1921 article by that title, and like the distracted, unfulfilled city dweller of the Weimar Republic whose "body takes root in the asphalt" while his spirit "roams ceaselessly out of the night and into the night," the film addict is at once active and passive—a paradoxical tension that returns, notably, in the final book on history.[66] Quoting a French critic from the 1920s to whom he attributes "all the earmarks of genuine first-hand experience," Kracauer describes the sensibility of the film addict as "passive, personal, as little humanistic or humanitarian as possible; diffuse, unorganized, and unselfconscious like an amoeba; deprived of an object or rather, attached to all of them like fog, and penetrant like rain; heavy to bear, easy to satisfy, impossible to restrain; displaying everywhere, like a roused dream, that contemplation . . . which incessantly hoards without rendering anything."[67]

Endowed with these traits, the film addict has an eye for detail, for the wind in the trees or the reflections of "the trembling upper world in the dirty puddle."[68] The cinephilic experience "hoards" what others overlook; like the camera that enables it, cinephilic viewing has the power to defamiliarize our habitual, ethnocentric gaze.[69] It owes this power precisely to the diminution of the subject who undergoes this experience: a subject that yields its autonomy and sovereignty and gains a new openness and receptivity in return. Wandering, in Kracauer's terms, through the film experience, the spectator happens upon the unexpected. "All his senses strained," he enters into a synaesthetic relation to the image, where "images begin to sound, and the sounds are again images."[70] The name that Kracauer gives to the content of this synaesthetic experience—which he calls the "confused" and "indeterminate . . . murmur of existence" and which he considers the supreme and unattainable telos of the film addict's active passivity—references precisely the nonanthropocentric universe from which subjectivity has withdrawn, except as a receptive surface. In this encounter, facilitated by cinema between a weak subjectivity and the "murmur" of the object world, alienation becomes productive.

This emphasis on defamiliarization is consequently as central to Kracauer's conception of the spectatorial experience as it is to the world of "camera reality" itself; in the discussion of spectatorship, however, it takes on subjective dimensions as a form of self-estrangement hovering, in his terms, "between self-absorption and self-abandonment."[71] Again we may note how Kracauer's argument could not be further removed from Steichen's familial humanism. *Family of Man* gave a perfunctory nod to difference, but its explicit goal was to foster the recognition of the self in the other and thereby to drive home its liberal message of a common humanity. Kracauer, by contrast, makes strange not only the world around us, but the viewing subject as well.[72] That subject's curious, nonanthropocentric humanism would continue to occupy Kracauer as he turned, at the end of his life, from film to history.

10. *History* and Humanist Subjectivity

> The spectacle before the spectator—enacted, as it were, for his judgment—is history as a whole.
> HANNAH ARENDT, *Lectures on Kant's Political Philosophy*

Kracauer's humanist politics remain somewhat oblique in *Theory of Film*, decipherable largely through references to exhibits such as *The Family of Man* or films such as *World without End*, and implicit, as we saw in the last chapter, in the central role of spectatorship and experience for his film theory. When Kracauer turns, at the end of his life, from film to history, the humanist stance becomes fully explicit, exemplified by the two unmistakable heroes of his posthumous book, *History: The Last Things before the Last:* the nineteenth-century historian Jakob Burckhardt and the sixteenth-century humanist reformer Erasmus of Rotterdam. Burckhardt, in particular, becomes the "model case" for what Kracauer labels "anteroom thinking"—a form of theorizing situated between the universal abstractions of philosophical speculation and the positivist facticity of empiricism and the natural sciences. Kracauer prizes Burckhardt's resistance to preconceived notions and his sensitivity to historical detail, which he approaches in the spirit of an "amateur" and an "archdilettante," with a "compassionate urge to uncover lost causes in history." As such, Burckhardt is "not only historical-minded but also profoundly humane."[1]

The importance that Kracauer attaches to this historiographical humanism becomes even more explicit in his paean to Erasmus in the introduction to the book. Situating him between the warring fronts of the Reformation era, Kracauer sees in Erasmus an exemplary anti-ideological figure, one who thought and acted in the "interstices" between Catholic dogma and Protestant zeal. Erasmus is defined for Kracauer by his all-pervading "fear of the fixed" that placed him in opposition to the "hardening creeds" and "fixed causes" on both sides of the Reformation.[2] Countering the rigidity of religious belief systems, Erasmus identified ambiguity as the marker of truth and operated on precisely the middle ground that Kracauer describes as the "anteroom" in the final chapter of *History*. But already in the opening pages of the book, he is at pains to distinguish this middle ground from mere compromise or vacillation by defining it instead as "the way of the humane." Erasmus is an exemplary figure for Kracauer because "all that he did and was had a bearing on the humane."[3]

The image that Kracauer paints of the sixteenth-century humanist is a thinly veiled self-portrait of the intellectual at midcentury. In other words, even though work on *History* took Kracauer back to Europe for conferences and conversations toward the end of his life, like *Theory of Film* the posthumous volume bears distinct traces of the place and time of its conceptualization. Thus, it is difficult not to hear the echoes of the Cold War in the description of Reformation Europe as "a world split into two camps," riven with ideological strife between Rome and Wittenberg. And just as Erasmus vindicates the "fear of the fixed" by refusing to assume a partisan, engaged stance in the world, so does Kracauer resist taking sides in the Cold War world, preferring instead to withdraw to the ostensibly nonideological, middle ground of humanism.

In considering Kracauer's nod to Steichen's *Family of Man* in the previous chapter, we noted not only the topicality but also the shortcomings of such a conception of "the humane," which short-circuits the question of politics and begs that of point of view. But Kracauer's historiography, no less than his film theory, merits a closer look for the way it specifically modulates its Cold War premises. Indeed, like the earlier book, *History* espouses a humanist outlook only to draw into question its fundamental tenets. And again, the central figure in this curious humanism is defined by its look: the humanist subject of history, it turns out, is a spectator.

This continuity between the two books is not accidental. Kracauer devotes ample space to rehearsing the links that connect *Theory of Film* to *History*. And yet, as I demonstrate below, there is something incongruous about the move from film theory to historiography as Kracauer himself construes it. After briefly reviewing his own arguments about the relation between his two final books, I therefore address the limitations of locating the analogies between film theory and historiography at the level of shared tropes (the "close-up" of microhistory, the shared dedication to reality, etc.). The more substantial continuities between the two books, I suggest, are instead to be sought at the level of theory, where *History* does indeed continue the curious humanist project that undergirds *Theory of Film*. Like the latter, Kracauer's posthumous work advances a spectral humanism that dethrones the autonomous subject but reinstates it as a receptive subject of experience. Significantly, Kracauer's treatise on historiography defines this subject in the same visual terms as his work on cinema: like Hannah Arendt's posthumous work on judgment, Kracauer's posthumous work on history culminates in the figure of the spectator.

FROM FILM THEORY TO HISTORY

When Kracauer turns to the topic of history at the end of his life, he describes the move as an all but organic development of his earlier work. "My interest in history," he writes in a letter to his friend Leo Löwenthal, "actually grew out of the ideas I tried to implement in my *Theory of Film*," the book he had only recently completed and published with Oxford University Press. This insight, which he still reports with a sense of discovery in the introduction to *History*, had dawned on him during the early stages of work on the new book when he realized that the latter would be "a direct continuation of my theory of film: the historian has traits of the photographer, and historical reality resembles camera reality. The similarities are really startling; I had gone on this route completely unconsciously."[4] Indeed, to his own surprise Kracauer now finds that his historical pursuits follow an inner necessity that derives from his writings on photography dating back as far as the 1920s. "So at long last," he notes with an almost audible sigh of contentment, "all my main efforts, so incoherent on the surface, fall into line—they all have served, and continue to serve, a single purpose."[5]

There is something striking about this retrospective discovery of coherence.[6] As an epistemological gesture it is vaguely familiar, to be sure: we have seen a similar logic at work in the way *From Caligari to Hitler* was conceived in "the blinding light of hindsight." However, in Kracauer's final book the coherence derives not from the discovery of a teleology that binds together a nation's films and its "psychological predispositions," but from the ostensible unity of an individual's migratory intellectual pursuits. The corresponding passages in the book read as if Kracauer, the "intellectual nomad," had found his way home. Here the septuagenarian secures what, in the 1927 essay on photography, he had called a person's "last image"; describing this particular kind of memory image as a person's "actual *history*," he had likened it to a "*monogram* that condenses the name into a single graphic figure which is meaningful as an ornament."[7] In the introduction to *History*, then, we find Kracauer engraving his own monogram. No wonder that the posthumous book has been classified in more than a chronological sense as an exemplar of Kracauer's "late works" *(Alterswerk).*[8]

What, though, is the monogram's specific trait, the "single purpose" that Kracauer now recognizes as his own? And how is this purpose borne out in similar ways by the theorization of film as a medium for the "redemption of physical existence," on the one hand, and of an "aesthetic approach" to history, on the other?[9] The broader argument about this comparison is anchored in various analogies between history and cinema, which Kracauer spells out explicitly at several junctures. In *Theory of Film*, we recall, he had advanced an argument about the power of photographic media to record and reveal physical reality. In the introductory chapters to that book, on which he relies heavily in *History* (sometimes reproducing passages verbatim), Kracauer had argued that for their subject matter, photography and film gravitate toward what he calls "camera reality." By this, as we saw, he means a primordial "murmur of existence," an unshaped reality defined by its endlessness, its indeterminacy, its ongoing flow, its unstaged and fortuitous configurations.[10] These same configurations return in the history book, where they are now taken to define "historical reality." What *Theory of Film* had described as "the transitory world we live in" now becomes simply the *Lebenswelt*, a term Kracauer explicitly borrows from Husserl's phenomenology.[11] Like cinema, he now argues, history gravitates toward a universe that "is full of intrinsic contingencies, . . . is virtually endless . . . [and] is indeterminate as to meaning."[12] The comparison with the prior theorization of film's characteristic affinities challenges us to think of camera reality and historical reality as two signifiers with the same referent: both concepts refer to a common, experiential, "endless, fortuitous, and indeterminate *Lebenswelt*" that constitutes the profilmic (or "prohistorical") universe from which the camera and the historian select and construct their representations.[13]

On the basis of this fundamental link between "camera reality" and "historical reality," Kracauer proceeds to outline several further analogies: between film's and photography's power to generate a defamiliarizing view of the world, and history as "a means of alienation";[14] between Leopold von Ranke's idea of history as an account of "wie es eigentlich gewesen" (how it really was) and the photographic media's automatic inscription of things as they really exist; between aerial photography or the long shot and macrohistory—and consequently also between microhistory and the close-up.[15] Kracauer even analogizes the place of cinema and history within the broader scheme of the arts and sciences, respectively, suggesting that history is a science "with a difference," just as photography and film are "art with a difference." Both occupy an intermediary place—the anteroom—between two extremes: philosophy and empiricism on the one hand, exalted art and mere reproduction on the other. In other words, both film and history have the power to undo the traditional hierarchy of aesthetic valuation and scientific inquiry, respectively.[16]

Foundational though these analogies may be to the arguments put forth in *History*, however, they do not in themselves add up to the coherent project that Kracauer claims to have discovered in his life's work in retrospect. The unifying perspective that he does identify in turn is somewhat surprising, for it is not immediately apparent how it condenses either Kracauer's work on film and photography or his newly discovered (but ostensibly long-standing) interest in history. Instead Kracauer claims that all his intellectual efforts share a commitment to "the rehabilitation of objectives and modes of being which still lack a name and hence are overlooked or misjudged."[17] To shore up this claim, he neither adduces the book in which it appears (though we may infer that *History* is designed to show in what sense historical reality might qualify as such a nameless, overlooked, or misjudged object), nor does he mention here his two major books on film. Rather, Kracauer refers the reader to an early novel, a sociological treatise from the late Weimar Republic, and a biography written in French exile. Admittedly, each of these works in some sense illustrates the commitment to "rehabilitate" and gives voice to the nameless and to previously invisible forms—whether in the shape of the vanishing protagonist Ginster in the novel by that title; of the salaried masses of *Die Angestellten* who desperately attempt to hide their material proletarianization behind outmoded bourgeois forms; or of the overlooked Jewish émigré composer Jacques Offenbach, whose biography allows Kracauer to portray the second Empire as a dance on the volcano with palpable parallels to the twilight of the Weimar Republic. Intriguing though these books may be, it is difficult to recognize in them the coherent project Kracauer would have us see. More significantly, and contrary to the claim that an interest in history and photography/film has been central to this project from the start, concerns with visual media and historiography are hardly at the forefront of these three texts, with the possible exception of the Offenbach biography and its manifest interest in nineteenth-century Paris.

In fact, the appeal to continuity masks a number of further incongruities regarding Kracauer's turn to history at the end of his life, particularly when measured against his two earlier books on cinema. Thus, in an introduction meant to highlight the relationship between history and film, he fails to mention his one work explicitly devoted to this relationship, *From Caligari to Hitler*. Not only does that book make the interest in history and film explicit in its subtitle, but as we have seen, it also offers a far more reflexive articulation of the film/history relationship than is often assumed—including, one is inclined to think, by the author. Why else would he decide not to bring it up as evidence for his belated realization that "the many existing parallels between history and the photographic media" had been intrinsic to his thinking all along?[18]

Yet as we have already noted, Kracauer does bring up *Theory of Film*, claiming that his interest in film developed precisely "along the lines manifest in that book."[19] It will, of course, be the task of the history book to bear out this claim by pursuing the various analogies I enumerated above. But we might note that *Theory of Film* constitutes an odd starting point in this regard. For had Kracauer not all but evacuated the category of history from the consideration of modern visual media in *Theory of Film*? Particularly when measured against early drafts of the project in the "Marseille Notebooks" from the late 1930s, the final version of that book almost seems at pains to avoid the connection between film and history that Kracauer claims to have discovered. As Miriam Hansen puts it, "History disappears from *Theory of Film* in a double repression," both at the level of theory and at the level of Kracauer's own intellectual biography.[20] In its attention to "physical reality," Inka Mülder-Bach similarly suggests, *Theory of Film* "phenomenologized history" and thereby "dehistoricized the phenomenal."[21] Where the book does deal with questions of history, it argues the irreconcilability of historical representation with cinematic ontology, or what Kracauer calls film's specific "affinities." History, he flatly concludes, is an "uncinematic area."[22] *Theory of Film* would seem particularly unsuited to ground the claim that, in turning his attention to history, Kracauer "just continued to think along the lines manifest in that [earlier] book."[23]

At the outset of an argument about the analogy between film and history, we are thus confronted with a series of claims and precedents in Kracauer's own work that appear to undercut this very relation. How, then, are we to make sense of Kracauer's ostensible intellectual "monogram"? Given the limitations of the direct analogy, which are only reinforced by Kracauer's own misgivings about analogical reasoning elsewhere in the book,[24] we must locate the continuity of his late film theoretical and historiographical work, I suggest, in a horizon that subsumes and justifies the otherwise tenuous links.[25] That horizon, I now want to suggest, is the one we began mapping in the previous chapter. Both *Theory of Film* and *History*, in other words, outline a humanist subjectivity whose autonomy is reduced to a seismographic membrane that registers an infinite, indeterminate object world—whether the latter be defined in terms of cinematic realism or as the historical *Lebenswelt*. Above, we already noted the centrality of the humanist outlook that Kracauer attributes to Burckhardt and Erasmus. Its peculiar politics of spectating subjectivity come into focus if we track other figurations of the historian in *History*.

FIGURATIONS OF THE HISTORIAN

Kracauer's concern in his posthumous book is with the writing, or "doing," of history—and with the subjectivity of the one doing the writing. It is a mobile subjectivity in the sense that the book, which Kracauer at one point considered titling *The Historian's Journey*, fundamentally casts (the writing of) history as a form of travel.[26] In the published book, the itinerant figure of the historian appears in many guises. Indeed, one might argue that *History* encircles its object by rehearsing different figurations of the historian as she journeys into the past. In doing so, the book assembles a cast of characters who range from the fictional to the autobiographical, the historical to the mythological. Thus, we find not only Laurence Sterne and, again, Marcel Proust but also Tristram Shandy and Proust's Marcel standing in for particular aspects of the historian's craft and of historical consciousness; they take their place alongside historical practitioners of the craft from Thucydides to Hayden White and from Burckhardt to Reinhart Koselleck.

Some of Kracauer's references, such as the above-mentioned Erasmus, bear perceptibly autobiographical traits. These become virtually explicit, in turn, in the figure of the stranger and the exile, whom Kracauer famously introduces as particularly suitable figurations of the historian's epistemological position. It is difficult, for example, not to detect Kracauer's own subjectivity behind his examples of "great historians" like Thucydides and Namier, "who owe much of their greatness to the fact that they were expatriates."[27] Drawing on the same passage on photography in Proust that he had adduced in *Theory of Film*, Kracauer locates the historian-as-stranger in the same space—"the near-vacuum of extra-territoriality"—that he liked to claim for himself from his early Weimar writings up through his late New York years. In *History*, however, he overlays the stranger with the figure of the exile, whose "state of self-effacement, or homelessness" becomes a precondition for the writing of history.

More important than the autobiographical traits of this exilic subjectivity, then, is once again its characteristic diminution, which we traced in *Theory of Film* and in the figure of cinephilic spectatorship as well. If *History* similarly seeks to define a humanist subject, or what Kracauer calls "the humane," that subject is likewise defined by a curious reticence. In describing the historian's journey into the past, Kracauer offers countless formulations that recall the amoebalike receptive spectator of cinema, who "wavers between self-abandonment and self-absorption."

This is most obvious, perhaps, in his take on historicism, whose claim to objectivity relies on the historian's ability to "blot out his self so that only the things themselves may do the talking."[28] Although Kracauer is fully aware of the objective fallacy of this approach (which he had critiqued as early as the 1920s), he notes of the towering nineteenth-century historicist Leopold von Ranke that his "yearnings point in the right direction." That direction becomes abundantly clear in Kracauer's further descriptions of the historian's "flexible and manipulable self," a pliable subjectivity that always appears to erase itself as it approaches its object.[29] Abandoning autonomy and self-assertion, it adopts a purely receptive attitude toward an object world alien to it.

The real hero of Kracauer's last book, the collective protagonist that congeals into the figure of the humane historian, is consequently one who "withdraws" from the scenario she observes on her travels into the past. In what Kracauer describes as a "productive absent-mindedness" that again recalls descriptions of cinematic spectatorship from Kracauer to screen theory, the subject all but vanishes in the "self-forgetting immersion in the texts and remains" of history.[30] Even the association of diminished consciousness with sleep and dreaming, familiar from a long history of psychoanalytic and other film theories, recurs in Kracauer's notion of the historian's self as one that has been "put to sleep"—the better to register the historical material before it. At times, indeed, the historian appears to resemble not so much the spectator but the film strip itself. Like the latter, Kracauer's ideal historian is a passive, "sensitive" surface that "gathers evidence [and] palpably favors the influx of minutiae."[31]

Like the cinema experience, however, the self-effacing, protocinematic "stay in the past" produces a "change in identity."[32] Having withdrawn from the scene of history, the subject returns "at a low pitch." In what amounts to a humanist ethics, *History* outlines a mode of subjectivity that asserts its humanity by adopting a stance of "active passivity," turning the self into a "sheer receiving instrument" in order to (re)engage with the historical *Lebenswelt*.[33] Kracauer describes the "historian's journey," in other words, as one that leads from near (self-)extinction to a cautious reassertion of subjectivity. While this trajectory is linked explicitly to the plight of the exile and might thus be read biographically, it also acquires broader relevance as a diagnosis of the posttotalitarian, post-Holocaust subjectivity that we have been tracing in Kracauer's American writings. The stakes of this journey become clear in the cast of mythological characters Kracauer mobilizes in the context of his two final books.

ORPHEUS, AHASUERUS, PERSEUS: MYTHOLOGICAL "IMAGE-WATCHERS"

In its search for "the humane," *History* glosses countless histories and discusses notable historians from the Roman era through Kracauer's present day. But the most memorable figures in the book's cast of historian characters are mythological. Two in particular emblematize the historian's journey and reveal its ethical stakes. The first is Orpheus, who descends to Tartarus to retrieve Eurydice from the dead. Like the mythic musician with his lyre, Kracauer suggests, "the historian must descend into the nether world to bring the dead back to life."[34] In this analogy, Eurydice and the underworld stand for the historical past, giving a rather different inflection to the experiential world Kracauer had defined as the realm of "historical reality." Rather than in the daylight of the *Lebenswelt*, we now move in the underworld, the shadowy realm of the dead. This scenario casts the historian as a traveler who journeys to the dead past to retrieve the stuff of history. But in keeping with the mythological narrative, the historiographical act—akin to the moment at which Orpheus turns to reassure himself that Eurydice is still with him—incurs the loss of the past, which is replaced by narrativization and writing. As if to emphasize the precariousness of historical knowledge, in other words, Kracauer chooses a figure whose attempt to bring the past into the present is doomed. It is perhaps no coincidence, then, that he equivocates at one point and (mis?)labels the orphic figure a "Pied Piper," thereby overlaying the mythic story about curative music with the folktale of a musical lure.

As I suggest below, however, the ability to coax the minutiae of history from the flow of time is arguably less significant to Kracauer's epistemology of history than the issue of how to access those minutiae in the first place. This becomes evident in the introduction of a second and crucial mythological figure, to whom Kracauer devotes a later chapter: Ahasuerus, the wandering Jew, "the only reliable informant" on the question of historical temporality.[35] Having witnessed all historical periods in his own, eternal present, he looks back at the historical process with a synthetic and synoptic glance. This enables Ahasuerus to perceive structures and differentiations where we sense nothing but chronological time. Instead, he contemplates a "cataract of times," with "pockets and voids amidst these temporal currents."[36] Unlike Orpheus, who journeys to the underworld and returns, albeit empty-handed, Ahasuerus roams about without a specific itinerary. Standing above time, so to speak, he occupies a vantage point from which temporality itself—what Kracauer calls "the riddle of time"—comes into view.

In opposing Ahasuerus's grasp of temporality to linear notions of chronology and progress, Kracauer draws explicitly on Walter Benjamin's "Theses on the Philosophy of History," in particular on his diatribe against the historicist notion of a "homogeneous, empty time."[37]. In this context, then, it is difficult not to see in Ahasuerus Kracauer's response to Benjamin's Angelus Novus—the angel of history, as Benjamin interpreted Klee's painting by that title.[38] Both Ahasuerus and Benjamin's angel are messianic figures, engaged in a redemptive struggle against the inexorable flow of time and history. Both could arrest this flow only at "the end of Time," which Kracauer defines as "the imaginary moment at which Ahasuerus, before disintegrating, may for the first time be able to look back on his wanderings through the periods."[39] For Benjamin, this is the moment when the wind of progress might cease, allowing the angel finally "to stay, awaken the dead, and make whole what has been smashed."[40] In this sense, the reference to the legendary, wandering Jew and the ekphrastic passage on Klee's angel both ground the critical projection of the unreconciled historical world that confronts the historian.

While they are in this sense strictly metaphorical and somewhat abstract figures, Ahasuerus and Angelus Novus assume strikingly concrete features in the two authors' respective descriptions, which both center on the face. Ageless and beyond time, these figures take on an arresting countenance. For Benjamin, Klee's painting shows "an angel looking as though he is about to move away from something he is fixedly contemplating." Benjamin comments explicitly on the angel's staring eyes, face turned toward the past, where "he sees one single catastrophe which keeps piling wreckage upon wreckage and hurls it in front of his feet."[41] Ahasuerus, for Kracauer, is similarly defined by his gaze back at the "process of becoming and decaying" that is history—a gaze that distorts his features: "how unspeakably terrible he must look!" In a rare use of the first person, Kracauer notes of the angel's physiognomy: "I imagine it to be many faces, each reflecting one of the periods which he traversed, all of them combining into ever new patterns, as he restlessly, and vainly, tries on his wanderings to reconstruct out of the times that shaped him the one time he is doomed to incarnate."[42]

The emphasis on the face, and—in Adorno's memorable formulation—on the angel's "enigmatic eyes" in particular, is at the same time an emphasis on the gaze.[43] Ahasuerus, who will at one point "look back on his wanderings through the periods," and the angel, who stares wide eyed and open mouthed at the wreckage of the past, are defined by their look in both senses of the word. In keeping with the "primacy of the optical" that Adorno had recognized as defining Kracauer's work, the central figures in

History are theoretical figures in the etymological sense:[44] they grasp the world by looking. In a word, they are spectators. By attending more closely to the deployment of mythical figures in *History*, we can flesh out the centrality of spectatorship to Kracauer's conception of history and of historical consciousness, if not of subjectivity itself.

The same holds true, of course, for Orpheus, the subject of not one but two scopic scenarios.[45] Most familiar is his fateful look back at Eurydice. But Kracauer's interest in Orpheus as a figure for the historian is arguably motivated primarily by the act of looking that precedes this moment in the myth: prior to the second gaze at Eurydice, we first encounter him looking for her in the underworld. His journey to the kingdom of the dead, his *katabasis*, is for Kracauer that of the historian as sightseer: with wide-open eyes, Orpheus perambulates among the dead who are the subjects of history.

As a number of critics have suggested, there is a historical specificity to Kracauer's figurations of the historian as wandering Jew and as Orpheus.[46] Julia Hell has shown that the proliferation of orphic scenarios after World War II in particular indexes an aporetic realist project invested (perhaps even overinvested) in the "literary production of visibility" and in fantasies of reenactment.[47] At once political and aesthetic, that project envisages, in W. G. Sebald's terms, a "synoptic and artificial view" of the horrors of aerial bombing and the Holocaust.[48] Caught between the horrified, photographic gaze of Benjamin's detached angel and the empathic, participant observation of the historian, the postwar turn to realism bespeaks a conflicted subjectivity: the confrontation with the Holocaust and the ruinscapes of World War II evinces a strong scopophilic desire and an equally powerful impulse to look away.

This tension is clearly inscribed in the figure of Orpheus, both in his "first" look at the shades and all manner of terrifying sights in the underworld, and in his second, longing look at Eurydice. But in Kracauer's oeuvre, it is perhaps even more powerfully embodied in a further mythological figure that rounds out the quartet of Orpheus, Ahasuerus, and Benjamin's angel: I am referring, of course, to Perseus, who makes his appearance toward the end of *Theory of Film* in the section titled "The Head of Medusa." He, too, is defined by a look—a look of terror and of domination. Knowing that the sight of the Medusa will turn anyone, man or beast, to stone, he deflects the monster's image by mirroring it in Athena's shield. Looking at the reflection, Perseus is able to slay the Medusa.

As is well known to readers of *Theory of Film*, Kracauer introduces the shield as a metaphor for the screen ("The film screen is Athena's polished shield") and makes explicit the underlying concern with Holocaust representation in particular by noting that "in experiencing . . . the litter of tortured human bodies in the films made of the Nazi concentration camps, we redeem horror from its invisibility behind the veils of panic and imagination."[49] This striking reversal of the trope of the unrepresentability of Auschwitz has been noted by numerous scholars. In the context of Kracauer's figurations of the historian's gaze, however, what principally concerns me here is neither the shield/screen nor the reflections/representations that it enables, but Perseus himself as a member of the mythological quartet that populates Kracauer's and Benjamin's writings on history and film. For Perseus is yet another figure defined by his gaze. Although he acts on this vision in ways that are distinct from the variously petrified, contemplative, and fateful acts of the other figures, Perseus, too, confronts horrific images that are at once historical and cinematic—and he confronts them first and foremost as a spectator. Significantly, Kracauer speaks of the mythic figure, slayer of the Medusa, as "Perseus, the image watcher."[50]

If Kracauer and Benjamin theorize historical consciousness as a form of spectatorship above all, we must reconsider the relationship of *Theory of Film* to *History*. Whereas Kracauer had claimed the continuity of his thinking derived from the analogies between camera reality and historical reality, between the ontology of the photographic image and the epistemology of history, I want to suggest that the comparison ultimately centers on shared notions of looking, spectatorship, and subjectivity. The analogous structures of history and film converge not simply on "realism" and "historicism," let alone on shared tropes of historical and shot scales, but on a notion of subjectivity best exemplified, for Kracauer, in the nature of film spectatorship. Unlike the explicit cross-references between the two books, this link remains comparatively unmarked, but it is palpable in direct borrowings, too. Thus, when Kracauer describes the requisite "active passivity" of the historian, he is not only reinvoking a theoretical motif that he first developed in his own Weimar essays, but also rehearsing a stance that he had attributed explicitly to the cinephilic "film addict" in *Theory of Film:* tracing his routes within the material of history, the historian must "let himself drift along, and take in, with all his senses strained, the various messages that happen to reach him."[51] That disposition is precisely the stance of the film addict "listening, with all his senses strained, to [the] confused murmur" of existence.

Kracauer alerts us to the significance of the spectator's gaze in his choice of mythological figures. But if we return now from these to the "model case" of Jakob Burckhardt, we find him translating the love etymologically inscribed in cinephilia from its Greek to its Latin roots: what moves Kracauer about Burckhardt's humanist approach to history is its *amateurism*. Like the cinephile "rag-picker," Burckhardt is "deliberately unsystematic, repudiating anything that looks like a construction imposed form without. [. . .] Of the past he picks up what attracts and interests him, as he strolls through the world of history." Like Erasmus, that other humanist with whom Kracauer begins his book, Burckhardt appears at its end as a champion of the essential flow of history, its openness toward reconfiguration, its refusal to submit to Hegelian teleology, Christian theology, or any other unifying concept. This openness is only available, according to Kracauer, to the loving gaze of an "amateur who follows his inclinations."[52] This is the same eye that the theorist Kracauer casts on "objectives and modes of being which still lack a name and hence are overlooked or misjudged."[53] It is a rehabilitating, redemptive gaze; in its cinephilic and amateurish dimension, it is, like Orpheus's glance at Eurydice, a loving gaze. Helmuth Lethen rightly speaks in this context of Kracauer's "doctrine of love" *(Liebeslehre)*.[54]

By the same token, Kracauer has been accused of idealizing the objects of this gaze—which is to say, physical reality, the *Lebenswelt*, cinema, history. In Adorno's formulation, he fails to produce the requisite indignation against reification, and in the eyes of the ideological critics who followed in his wake, he fails to grasp the fact that what the camera and the gaze of the cinephile both register is the world as construed through the dominant ideology. From this perspective, Kracauer's cinephilic realism is profoundly conservative, to say the least. Worse yet, Kracauer's late works have been seen as trumpeting the cause of an "end of ideology" altogether—and indeed, his Erasmus is, as we have seen, an exemplary humanist for "delineating a way of living free from ideological constraints."[55]

None of these critiques should be dismissed out of hand. But if we look for Kracauer's politics, as I have suggested, in the fundamental, cinephilic subjectivity that he outlines, an alternative assessment emerges. That subjectivity is culturally significant in ways that reach well beyond the cinema and into the realms of history and politics, where Kracauer is not so easily consigned to the corner of reaction. For if we historicize the loving gaze of the cinephile and the amateur historian and place it in the context of Kracauer's American writings in particular, we recognize that it is mobilized precisely against the most conservative and reactionary politics of the day—against the terror of fascism as much as the schematisms of Cold War block mentality.

Nor is this simply a liberal, individualist view, as should be evident from the intense solidarity that animates the loving gaze of the cinephile/amateur—a solidarity not only with the overlooked and the nameless, but also with collectivity. Adopting the classic position that cinephilia takes hold below the level of plot and intrigue and consequently pays little heed to the individual hero in a scripted drama,[56] Kracauer notes: "What redeems the film addict from his isolation is not so much the spectacle of an individual destiny which might again isolate him as the sight of people mingling and communing with each other according to ever-changing patterns."[57] If Kracauer's political subject is a liberal humanist one, as it undoubtedly is, then it is one that refuses the liberal humanist fixation on the freedom of the individual at the cost of solidarity, of "mingling and communing with each other according to ever-changing patterns." While this cinephilic subjectivity may originate in exilic feelings of isolation, or in Kracauer's vaunted "extraterritoriality," it is emphatically worldly; and where it withdraws or shrinks, in a gesture typical of Kracauer's writings from *Ginster* onward, this subject does so in order to "grab in history not always only himself, but rather the Other, that which does not relate to him as well."[58] Wavering, in Kracauer's terms, between absorption and self-abandonment, cinephilic subjectivity, and by extension historical consciousness and the subject of humanism itself, are profoundly invested in alterity.

Epilogue

Siegfried Kracauer and the Emergence of Film Studies

The initial phase of an accepted idea appears to have a significance of its own which distinguishes it from all subsequent phases.

SIEGFRIED KRACAUER, *History*

Upon Siegfried Kracauer's death in November 1966, *Cinema Journal*—the recently rechristened annual publication of the Society of Cinematologists—ran a rare obituary paying tribute to "one of its most eminent members." Kracauer, the council of the society noted, "responded to the challenge of film scholarship before there was group organization or governmental support." As an example of his pioneering work, which "stands as an inspiration for those who came after him," the obituary singled out the American writings we have discussed in this book—his work on Nazi propaganda, *From Caligari to Hitler*, and his "monumental work in film aesthetics," *Theory of Film*.[1]

To be sure, these references no longer fully define our image of Kracauer today. Even at the time of his death, his essays and books from the Weimar period were gradually being rediscovered, thanks in large part to Adorno's advocacy in post-Nazi Germany on behalf of his all-but-forgotten friend and to the efforts of Siegfried Unseld of the Suhrkamp Verlag. A carefully curated collection of essays under the title *Das Ornament der Masse* appeared in 1963, followed by *Straßen in Berlin und anderswo* one year later.[2] Those who read these essays carefully could discover in them not only Kracauer's unique voice from the Weimar Republic but also a (pre)history of Frankfurt School Critical Theory, whose reception was particularly intense around 1968 and which remains, in Miriam Hansen's words, "unthinkable without Kracauer."[3] Although Karsten Witte had begun editing Kracauer's collected works in 1971, this project remained incomplete at the time of Witte's untimely death in 1995. It was only in the wake of the centennial of his birth in 1989 and the "bibliographic recovery effort" led by Tom Levin that a full reevaluation of Kracauer's contributions to cultural theory in the broadest sense got under way—further fueled, for the

English-speaking world, by Levin's translation of *The Mass Ornament* in 1996.[4]

Since then we have seen the completion of the superb Suhrkamp edition of Kracauer's collected works under the aegis of Inka Mülder-Bach and Ingrid Belke, together with a team of excellent editors, as well as new translations of selected works into multiple languages. As numerous conferences and anthologies demonstrate, Kracauer has become familiar not only as a film critic and theorist but also in his many cross-disciplinary guises, as a "thinker of history," a sociologist, a *feuilletonist*, a novelist, not to mention the architect he was by training.[5] We have come to think of him as a modernist and a theorist of modernism, but also as the prescient critic of a postmodern culture of surfaces;[6] as the mentor and friend to prominent members of the Frankfurt School and as a participant in 1960s debates on poetics and hermeneutics; as a Kantian, a Warburgian, a "critical" and a "curious" realist, and even as a "magical nominalist."[7] And as we saw in the introduction, readers have come to value Kracauer's reflections on exile and on the stranger as a guide to the values of "extraterritorial" subjectivity.

From our contemporary vantage point, then, and certainly to anyone familiar with this booming Kracauer reception of late, the references in the *Cinema Journal* obituary will now appear, a half century later, as a curiously incomplete and conspicuously Americanized list; the obituary is oblivious to the Weimar essays, the novels, the sociological treatises and essays, and even to those works—like Kracauer's *Offenbach*—that had long been available in English. And yet I want to suggest that the obituary remains a valuable source for precisely this reason. For as I have argued throughout this book, even as we recover the richness of Kracauer's thinking, we should keep its historical dimensions in our sights. To the degree that they overlap with his American exile, these are dimensions I have sought to restore. This not only includes the specificity of Kracauer's own exile, his growing self-identification as an American citizen who made his home in New York, and his theorization of humanist subjectivity in the Cold War context; it includes also, finally, Kracauer's role in the history of film studies, for which his American writings became crucial touchstones.

FILM STUDIES: THE SHAPE OF THINGS TO COME

Kracauer's two monographs on Weimar cinema and film theory, in particular, remain deeply familiar to scholars in the field of film studies. Generations of students have been taught to consider them as paradigmatic texts of "classical film theory"—with all the variously reverent, revisionist, critical, iconoclastic, or (worst of all) routinized responses that classic texts tend to elicit from subsequent generations of readers. The notice in *Cinema Journal*, however, invites us to contextualize and to historicize these responses. It reminds us that the conception and publication of these texts "responded to the challenge of film scholarship before there was group organization or governmental support" (not that there has been much of the latter since then).

In this context, Kracauer's two monographs were immediately recognized as important interventions, particularly given that, as Rick Altman now reminds us in looking back on cinema studies half a century after its institutionalization, "during the sixties . . . , the film studies bibliography was limited indeed."[8] Indeed, the very notion of a "film studies bibliography" is something of an anachronism for the period. As Dana Polan points out, "Even as late as the 1960s, film studies found its useful literature not in the efforts of film *scholars* . . . but in works of criticism . . . or in scholarly writings by people in other fields."[9] During the two and a half decades Siegfried Kracauer spent working on film in the United States, film studies was a protean field *in statu nascendi*.

As such, the field has attracted the interest of a number of scholars who have begun to write the history of the discipline. Prompted in part by the half centennials in 2010 of both the Society for Cinema and Media Studies in the United States and the influential British journal *Screen*, these authors have drawn our attention to the "historically contingent ways in which [the] varied ideas and practices of film study came to be assembled into a discipline."[10] This work has led to a significant revision of the accepted narrative, according to which film studies emerged in conjunction with the social movements of the late 1960s and the canonizing impulses of the *auteur* theory, culminating in the founding of the Society of Cinematologists at the beginning of the 1960s and the first doctoral program in cinema studies at New York University at the end of the decade. This account, which Dana Polan describes as the "heroic narrative" of film studies' history as a discipline and which Lee Grieveson and Haidee Wasson have critiqued as "nostalgic,"[11] has been dislodged through recent historical work: on film pedagogy from the 1910s onward, by Polan himself; on the productive relation between Hollywood and the "culture elite" at Harvard and Columbia Universities, among others, by Peter Decherney; on the profound impact that the MoMA film library exerted on film study in this country (as we have also seen here), by Haidee Wasson; and on the many other tributaries feeding the "invention of film studies," as described in a recent collection of essays under that title.[12]

This is to say nothing of the Anglo-centric version of film studies that the "heroic narrative" endorses, which could and should be rewritten in a transnational perspective.[13] The transatlantic dimensions of Kracauer's work that this book has mapped might provide one angle for such a perspective. The place of exile in his work, and the negotiation of multiple discursive influences both proximate and distant, are echoed in the "traveling theories" of any number of other critics who contributed foundational texts to the film studies bibliography—from Hugo Münsterberg, the German professor who discovered his passion for film late in life at Harvard University; through Béla Balázs, whose prolific writings on film were doubtless shaped by the multiple displacements that led him from his native Hungary through Vienna and Berlin to exile in the Soviet Union; to Hans Richter, whose work in and on documentary was profoundly shaped by the time he spent in New York (where he overlapped with Kracauer and Luis Buñuel, among others, at MoMA); to Rudolf Arnheim, who wrote *Film as Art* at the end of the Weimar Republic but gained a reputation as a foremost formalist film theorist on the basis of a truncated version of that book published in 1955, when he had settled in the United States after periods of exile in Italy and Great Britain.[14] The examples could be multiplied, and ongoing efforts at translating seminal texts will doubtless help to round out this picture.[15] But again, we should not confuse transnationalism with dislocation. Rather, we should bear in mind the local contexts that shape and tether even the most global of discourses. And so we return, one more time, to Manhattan, where the members of the newly founded Society of Cinematologists convened over two days in April 1960 at the faculty club of NYU for their first annual meeting.

KRACAUER AMONG THE CINEMATOLOGISTS

Kracauer joined them at that meeting. Among his well-organized papers at the German Literary Archives, in a folder labeled "Accompanying Materials: Society of Cinematologists," one can find the one-page program. It accompanied a letter by the society's president, Robert Gessner, who had recruited Kracauer as a "charter member" of SOC.[16] On the program, Gessner noted by hand that he was "glad you will be with us" and instructed Kracauer on where to send his membership dues. The carrot to accompany that stick, it appears, was the presentation of an honorary membership to Erwin Panofsky, Kracauer's friend of two decades, who, Gessner indicated, would be present at the meeting.

Kracauer thus traveled the short distance from his Upper West Side apartment, subsequently noting his own attendance at the luncheon and

S.K.— Glad you will be with us! R.G.

The Society of Cinematologists

THE FIRST NATIONAL MEETING

April 11-12, 1960

New York University Faculty Club
22 Washington Square North
New York City

ROBERT GESSNER, President
NEW YORK UNIVERSITY
HUGH GRAY, Secretary
UNIVERSITY OF CALIFORNIA AT LOS ANGELES
GERALD NOXON, Treasurer
BOSTON UNIVERSITY

COUNCIL
Erik Barnouw, 1963
COLUMBIA UNIVERSITY
George Amberg, 1962
UNIVERSITY OF MINNESOTA
Richard Griffith, 1961
MUSEUM OF MODERN ART
Arthur Knight, 1960
CITY COLLEGE OF NEW YORK

Send dues here!

Monday, April 11, Green Room:

2:00 p.m.   **Old Business:** Reports by the President, Secretary and Treasurer.

2:30   **Report** by George Amberg, Conference Director, S.O.C. Conference, University of Minnesota, March 19-21: "A Definition of Cinema: Relative Values in Narrative, Dramatic, Pictorial and Cinematic Illusion."

Discussion: Significance of the Minnesota Conference for the interdiscipline curriculum, Hugh Gray, U.C.L.A.; for the communications curriculum, Gerald Noxon, B.U.

"Raising Standards in a New Field," George D. Stoddard, Chancellor, N.Y.U.

Refreshments will be served.

Tuesday, April 12, Madden Room:

10:00 a.m.   **Panel on Sources:**

Thomas Brandon, Brandon Films
Leo Dratfield, Contemporary Films
George Pratt, George Eastman House
Robert Gardner, Harvard University
Richard Griffith, Museum of Modern Art
Rosalind Kossoff, Film Images
Herman Weinberg, International Critic

12:30   **Luncheon**

Presentation of Honorary Membership to Erwin Panofsky

Speakers: Eric Larrabee, American Heritage
          "Learned and Unlearned Societies."
Dwight Macdonald, Critic
          "Taste and Judgment."
Robert Gessner, President
          "Cinema and Scholarship."

Discussion

3:30   **New Business:**   Plans for 1960-61
           Publications
           Election of new members
           Election of officers

Attendance invitational, except business sessions.
Registration fee: $2.00
Luncheon: $2.75 and includes morning refreshments.

11. Kracauer's program of the first meeting of the Society of Cinematologists, April 11–12, 1960. (Deutsches Literaturarchiv Marbach)

several talks in the program's margins: it appears that he arrived in time for a presentation by Herman Weinberg (a critic to whom he was indebted for having reviewed *From Caligari to Hitler* as "perhaps the greatest book on the films ever written");[17] stayed for lunch and the presentation of the honorary membership to Panofsky; and remained until the conclusion of the afternoon presentations by Eric Larrabee, Dwight Macdonald (who, we recall, had lauded Kracauer's work on fascist propaganda but had far less patience for the "totalitarian method" of *Caligari*), and Gessner himself, who lectured on "cinema and scholarship."

Kracauer's decision to stay through the end of the presidential address may have been more than a matter of courtesy to his host. Having recently completed *Theory of Film* in the explicit hopes of contributing a definitive aesthetics to the field, having been involved with the spate of film journals that were cropping up in the United States during the 1950s, and having followed with interest the development of *filmologie* in France, Kracauer would have had a keen interest in the professionalization and institutionalization of film scholarship.[18] To be sure, his film book had been a long time in the making, and one might be tempted to consider the close proximity between the first meeting of the Society of Cinematologists in April and the publication of *Theory of Film* in October of 1960 a mere coincidence. In concluding our reconsideration of Kracauer's American writings, however, I would like to take these events, as well as Kracauer's presence at this society's first annual meeting, as a starting point for considering his place in the institutionalization of film studies.

Retracing Kracauer's contributions to the field as well as his reception among the fledgling cinematologists, I submit two interrelated claims about Kracauer's role in inventing film studies: First, we should consider the importance of Kracauer's contribution as *theory* to a field largely founded on history, analysis, pedagogy, and practice. Second, as I have argued throughout this book, this contribution must be defined, in contradistinction to some of the social science contexts in which it evolved, as a humanistic approach to cinema.

BETWEEN NOMENCLATURE AND THEORY:
EARLY AMERICAN CINEMATOLOGY

As president of the new society, Gessner struck a programmatic tone in his address to the cinematologists at the NYU faculty club that April, taking aim at "nothing less, nor more fundamental, than the first article of our Constitution: our purpose," he said, "is 'the study of the moving image.'"[19]

Manifestolike, Gessner launched into a rhetorical flourish, merrily mixing his metaphors:

> For us, there can be as yet no luxury of monopolies on some obscure corner in the field, no indulgence in abstractions, no esoteric pursuits. These are the sinecures of our senile brothers; in all due time we shall get there! A cinema scholar today needs to be triple-gaited to move in so virginal a territory. He needs to be able to plod peasant-like with plow in hand, furrowing out fact. He needs to be a cross-country runner, capable of judging distance. Finally, he needs to be a pilot with a capacity for interpreting landscape, weather, and wind-drift.[20]

When Gessner goes on to unpack this landscape of film scholarship, the peasant somewhat confusingly becomes the "scholar-as-clerk," the runner the "scholar-as-judge," and the pilot the "scholar-as-interpreter." But the impetus of his remarks is clear enough: given the precarious state of cinema studies, and given the "confusion over fact coupled with the lack of critical standards" in the field, Gessner insists, first, on careful historical spadework (he goes on to exemplify this by discussing questions of dating and attribution); and second, on scholarly rigor in the evaluation of factual evidence (which he illustrates by comparing two extant prints of Edwin S. Porter's *Life of an American Fireman* [1903] and enumerating the questions the comparison raises). He concludes his programmatic remarks on the disciplining of film scholarship with a proposal on nomenclature: a standardized vocabulary for film study.

Gessner's nomenclature represented a curious attempt at systematicity. Under three main headings ("objective elements," "coordinative factors," and "subjective qualities"), he grouped aspects of subject matter, film style, narrative form, and rhetoric.[21] It is difficult to see how this project, to which Gessner devoted considerable energy during the early 1960s and which occupied an entire standing committee of cinematologists, would have helped to chart a path through the thicket of cinema's audiovisual forms and meanings. Though Gessner claimed self-servingly that Panofsky considered this list to represent "the *Grundbegriffe* of cinematology," it was perceived even at the time as "surely one of the oddest specimens of classificatory logic ever set on paper."[22] But the performative aspect of the scheme was doubtless more important to Gessner than its internal logical coherence. His real interest in addressing the question of "cinema and scholarship" was in "disciplining" film studies, and in this his efforts at taxonomy or nomenclature followed other attempts—from Rudolf Arnheim's *Film as Art* to the contemporary French *filmologie* movement, whose example Gessner was copying.

In keeping with this aim, Gessner's talk rather self-consciously mapped out the central coordinates of disciplinary knowledge production. Not only does his nomenclature proposal imply the need for a specialized vocabulary on a par with the natural sciences' self-evident use of technical terms,[23] but Gessner's tripartite scheme of plodding, running, flying—or of clerk, judge, and interpreter—also plainly suggests the constitutive concern of any given discipline with history, analysis, theory. Symptomatically, however, the sequence also denotes a hierarchy in keeping with the tenets of the contemporary New Criticism.[24] According to these tenets, disciplinary knowledge concerns, first and foremost, the facts (to be garnered, according to the New Critics, through the vaunted practice of "close reading");[25] second, their critical evaluation with the help of the correct, medium-specific nomenclature—which Gessner explicitly conceived as tools for "empirical analysis," in contradistinction to Kracauer's approach in *Theory of Film*;[26] and third—as an afterthought treated in one brief paragraph and without examples—theory, which Gessner essentially positions *beyond* the boundaries of the field. Seemingly reluctant to grant it a role at all in his disciplinary architecture, he describes theory as a matter of taste: "The scholar-as-interpreter is the most difficult role to fulfill because it involves more than tangible tools. Once facts and factual evaluations are in order, once the house is built, the question of taste cannot be avoided. The scholar-as-interpreter is a man with a private lantern. He occupies a room from which he has a personal view of the world, and it is more aesthetic than black-and-white or CinemaScope."[27]

It is difficult to imagine much enthusiasm on Kracauer's part for this relegation of theoretical concerns and aesthetic judgment to the realm of private taste. Nor would the seventy-one-year-old author of *Theory of Film* have been likely to appreciate Gessner's pragmatist rallying cry against "abstraction" and "esoteric pursuits" as "the sinecures of our senile brothers." For Kracauer's labors of the previous decades (dating back to the early drafts in the late 1930s) had been devoted precisely to charting an aesthetics of the medium. The two books that resulted have been faulted, as we have seen, for a number of shortcomings, but *not* for lack of a normative account that sought to raise the study of film above the level of private appreciation. In a sense, Pauline Kael got it just right even as she tried to drive the last nail into the coffin of Kracauer's film theory with her review of his book: Kracauer, she complained, "must think we read books on the movies to get our knowledge of history and philosophy."[28] Full of disdain for anything but the kind of pragmatic (and often highly entertaining), pop-cultural criticism that she herself championed, Kael scorned the idea that one might study film academically—which is to say, as part of a humanistic, interdisciplinary enterprise. Yet this was precisely what Kracauer had advocated in *Theory of Film*, where film, avowedly, served merely as a "pretext" *(Vorwand)* for treatment of larger historical and philosophical questions.[29] Those questions related, as we have seen, to pressing political issues such as totalitarianism, democracy, and the authoritarian personality; to the place of ideology and abstraction in contemporary society; to the fate of experience and human subjectivity lost and regained—in other words, to the emerging institutional discourse on film.

Kracauer had not only contributed analyses of German propaganda, a psychological history of the German film, and a realist theory of the medium. Through his many interventions, he had also made a lasting case for the place of theory in any future configuration that "cinema and scholarship" might take. David Rodowick has noted that among the most striking paradoxes of the period leading up to the founding of the Society of Cinematologists is "the absence of theory as a regulative concept in the 1950s, even as the discursive and institutional contexts that frame its conditions of possibility rapidly emerge and settle into place."[30] This was a situation still lamented explicitly in 1963 by Jerzy Toeplitz, then director of the International Federation of Film Archives (FIAF), in whose review of the state of the discipline Kracauer featured prominently; and Peter Harcourt would still warn at the end of the same decade that "without *some* interest in theoretical matters, without an awareness of the relevance of film theory both to criticism *and* creation, the critic simply has to assert the supremacy of his own taste."[31]

In this context, even to title a book *Theory of Film* was a significant intervention. As theory, in other words, Kracauer's work was in some sense untimely. Not only did it not fit squarely, at least initially, into the brief that Gessner issued to the newly institutionalized discipline; it also came at a period when that discipline's very notion of what constituted "theory" in the first place was up for grabs, as Rodowick has shown. Responding to the "new and welcome fascination with the history of film theory," Rodowick has helpfully reconstructed its fate as a shifting concept, thereby restoring to our awareness the "*strangeness* of this word" after its reification as "Theory" in the 1970s and 1980s and its devolution into "post-theory" after the turn of the millennium.

This also involves, fundamentally, recalling the "rarity of theory" in the first half of the twentieth century.[32] Only after World War II, Rodowick notes, can we identify a shift "that involved a new set of criteria for identifying theory as a concept allied to a distinct set of institutional practices." For Rodowick, that shift is inaugurated by Guido Aristarco's *Storia delle teoriche del film* (1951) as the first synoptic account of what we now consider classical film theory. But we should situate Kracauer's American writings in this genealogy as well—as Rodowick indeed does when he places Kracauer at the close of the classical period (which he relabels "aesthetic" to highlight its abiding links with an earlier philosophical tradition), "undoubtedly the richest and most complex period of writing on film."[33] Although he thus considers Kracauer to represent "the closure of a certain kind of thought," Rodowick simultaneously finds him, along with Stanley Cavell, to open up "new philosophical vistas to which we still have not properly adjusted our vision."[34] In this sense, he explicitly and emphatically considers Kracauer's work "untimely."

Rodowick is joined in this assessment by Dudley Andrew, who considers Kracauer's work in the context of Critical Theory's contributions to media studies. Describing *Theory of Film* as "the most ambitious treatise on the cinema written by anyone from this school of thought," Andrew notes that the impact of Critical Theory perhaps "could only be felt when American film studies began to realize that media was integral to a discipline no longer bounded by dates or by specific technologies."[35] With this (re)assessment, Andrew implicitly reinforces Rodowick's description of *Theory of Film* as an "untimely" work, as well as the sense that Kracauer's contribution to film studies should be seen in his insistence on a theoretical dimension. This view also characterizes Miriam Hansen's lifelong work and her challenge to rethink the history of film theory itself through a rereading of figures like Kracauer, Adorno, and Benjamin.[36]

But as I have been insisting throughout this book, that history is not one of isolated thinkers single-handedly innovating entire fields of research by conceptualizing and publishing monographs; nor is Gessner's image of the scholar-as-interpreter appropriate if we wish to grasp the genealogy of film studies and theory. To be sure, the idea subsequent generations would have of Kracauer corresponded rather closely to Gessner's image of the private intellectual occupying a room from which he shines his aesthetic light on the world, and on the medium of film in particular. Recall the descriptions of Kracauer enclosing his workspace in the MoMA film library behind a wall of books. And yet, as I have argued, such anecdotal accounts fall short of the vibrant discursive networks within which Kracauer's theory of film developed. Rather, Kracauer was a recognized voice in a period that Haden Guest rightly considers "formative [for] the evolution of film study in the United States."[37]

By 1952, *Harper's* ranged Kracauer explicitly alongside Manny Farber and James Agee as one of "the good critics today [who] long to get back to

12. Undated Polaroid photo of Siegfried Kracauer, Lili Kracauer, and Maya Deren. (Deutsches Literaturarchiv Marbach)

the free and gay concern with unorganized experience for its own sake, the sort of thing you got in the silent comedies. They saw this all along."[38] Other film circles in which Kracauer moved included his participation in the annual Flaherty Seminar, and later in the University Seminars at Columbia. He became involved in Amos Vogel's influential Cinema 16, where he was "a mainstay" and where Amos's wife, Marcia, remembers him, along with his wife, as "one of the particularly strong presences."[39] An undated Polaroid showing Kracauer and his wife, Lili, together with the avant-garde filmmaker Maya Deren may well stem from this context. Within Kracauer's photographic archive, it stands out not only for the questions of provenance that it raises, but also as a reminder of Kracauer's sociability—a trace of the company Kracauer kept.[40]

Other traces include, of course, his wide-ranging correspondence with film critics and scholars from James Agee to Paul Rotha to Gessner himself. But perhaps most importantly here, we should note Kracauer's contributions to the fledgling film journals of the decade: beginning with a fascinating article on Preston Sturges for the inaugural issue of *Films in Review* (1950), he would go on to prepublish various parts of *Theory of Film* in the same journal and in *Film Culture*.[41] In 1955, Gideon Bachmann, editor of the short-lived but influential *Cinemages*, conducted an extensive interview with Kracauer for an issue on G.W. Pabst (though Kracauer ended up contributing material on the director from the *Caligari* book).[42] This is to say nothing of Kracauer's contributions to British, French, and Italian journals, including numerous articles in *Cinema nuovo* and the placement of the introduction to *From Caligari to Hitler* in the influential *Revue internationale de filmologie* under the aegis of Gilbert Cohen-Séat.[43]

As far the American context is concerned, Haden Guest has argued persuasively that *Film Culture, Films in Review*, and *Cinemages* were central to the transformation of film scholarship and criticism during the 1950s. Kracauer, I suggest, was centrally involved in this transformation, even if he was not one of the frequent contributors like Jonas Mekas, Theodore Huff, or Herman Weinberg. Guest discerns two important trends in these journals: first, in various ways—especially by publishing film lists and filmographies—they helped to establish rigorous standards of film history (with an emphasis on silent cinema); second, these journals pushed the limits of film criticism, allowing authors such as Agee, Otis Ferguson, Robert Warshow, Jonas Mekas, and Andrew Sarris to carve out a "type of expansive and deeply personal artistic practice."[44] Kracauer, who had developed precisely such a practice during his Weimar years, did not join the American historical and critical debates directly, even though he did contribute to the same journals; instead, he helped to move the field as a whole toward a concern with theory.

FILM THEORY AND THE HUMANITIES

Just as Kracauer's role as a film theorist would have positioned him beyond the purview of Gessner's emphasis on the role of history and analysis in film scholarship, so would his contributions on stage and screen acting for *Films in Review* or on filmed opera for *Film Culture* appear to have been outliers in a field plowed by some of the more prominent critics mentioned above. By the same token, however, Kracauer's work toward a *Theory of Film* contributed centrally to the ongoing elaboration of what would constitute film studies as a discipline in years to come. Although he was certainly attuned to the importance of historical work (he would, after all, go on to write a book on historiography), and although he clearly had the concerns of criticism and analysis in mind, his work was geared toward establishing the study of film as a branch of the humanities, where it would have to prove its social relevance.

As early as 1932 Kracauer had insisted, in an address at the convention of cinema owners, that "the film critic of note is conceivable only as a social critic. His mission is to unveil the social images and ideologies hidden in mainstream films and through this unveiling to undermine the influence of the films themselves wherever necessary."[45] This critical stance derived from Kracauer's own work as film critic for the *Frankfurter Zeitung*, which had prepared the ground for his writings in the United States, most notably *From Caligari to Hitler*, which put into practice the method of "unveiling the social images and ideologies" hidden in the films of the Weimar era. He would continue to work in this vein in subsequent publications—"National Types as Hollywood Presents Them," for example, or his exploration of the ideological implications of what we think of today as film noir in "Hollywood's Terror Films."

We can trace Kracauer's interest in linking social and aesthetic critique through an exchange prompted, characteristically, by an article in one of the decade's film magazines. It was in the pages of *Film Culture* that Kracauer came across a contribution by Enno Patalas titled "The Contemporary West German Film as a Social Symptom."[46] Kracauer seized the opportunity to strike up a conversation, congratulating the young critic in a letter from September 1955. Patalas had Kracauer to thank, in turn, for inspiring himself and a whole generation of critics, such as those who would go on to found the influential journal *Filmkritik*. Having received the first copy of that journal's short-lived forerunner, *film 56*, Kracauer responded to Patalas with a theoretical credo of his own: "I consider this sociological take on film production absolutely necessary; I would only wish that in the future you would try more systematically to discern what is sociopolitically wrong or right in the aesthetic domain as well. At first glance, it appears that you have placed too much emphasis on *the manifest content*. But the manner of photography, the camera take, and the editing contribute much that should be considered in the overall evaluation. In other words, I am advocating a melding of the sociological and the aesthetic approach."[47]

This "meld" sounds retrospectively like a blend of the sociopsychological approach of *From Caligari to Hitler* with the "material aesthetics" of *Theory of Film*. It was a theoretical position that seemed to have little traction among the early cinematologists, who focused instead on historical fact-gathering, nomenclature, and formalist leanings in the vein of the New Criticism. By 1968, however, we find the renamed Society for Cinema Studies using language rather similar to Kracauer's credo. The announcement that *Cinema Journal* would increase its frequency from one to two issues per year was accompanied by an editorial statement. Though the tone is already more self-confidently academic than that struck by Gessner in his lecture on "cinema and scholarship" eight years prior, the editorial still expresses a good degree of trepidation: "Cinema," the editors submit, "is unlike any other field of study. Its source material is shadowy, unsteady, indescribable. We are searching for our best approach, our discipline. A journal is a familiar American way of doing it right out in the open with everyone watching." When they offer their own basic tenets in this search for a disciplinary approach, it is in keeping with Kracauer's "meld." Having paid tribute to more social scientific approaches, the editors note that "the social implications of cinema are never far from our thoughts. But most of the time," they continue, "we shall . . . emphasize film as an art and the criticism of it as one of the humanities."[48] Here, I suggest, Kracauer's two monographs as well as his scattered publications in the journals and little magazines of the 1950s resonate in the annals of the society of which he was a founding member and which has emerged as the discipline's premier professional organization.

During the 1940s and '50s, many of Kracauer's own studies and articles were not merely pieces of (social) film criticism, but occasionally had social scientific aims in mind, as suggested in the introduction to *From Caligari to Hitler* or in the study Kracauer did for UNESCO on National Types. Like the work of many émigrés at the time, as we have seen, his contributed to the urgent need to elucidate "the German Question." The resulting studies on the origins of totalitarianism, on wartime communication (i.e. propaganda), and on the authoritarian personality have come to be seen as the founding texts of social science disciplines such as political science and communication studies. Kracauer himself contributed to those disciplines with a book-length study of public opinion behind the Iron Curtain,[49] a critical assessment of quantitative methods for *Public Opinion Quarterly*,[50] and through his work on propaganda in the context of Ernst Kris and Hans Speier's project on wartime communication at the New School.[51]

As we have seen, such projects were frequently funded by the Rockefeller Foundation, where the emerging discipline of communication studies was championed by John Marshall, a Harvard-educated humanist and director of the foundation's Division of Humanities. As I argued earlier, the distinctions between social scientific and humanities research were secondary to the shared sense of political purpose. But if we adopt a retrospective view from our current institutional landscape, where disciplines such as film studies and communication studies are housed in separate divisions and occasionally compete over funding, students, and even the very objects that they study (not to mention the methods with which to study them), the historical juncture of the 1940s seems profoundly consequential. For from the wartime collaboration among institutions and personnel as different in purpose and temperament as the Museum of Modern Art, the Rockefeller "Communications Group," the American Jewish Congress, the Office of Strategic Services, the Bureau of Applied Social Research, the various radio research projects, and many more, certain paths bifurcated. The study of film, which was integral to research on propaganda, communication, public opinion, and even to the Studies in Prejudice, might easily have taken the turn toward the social sciences. As Lee Grieveson rightly notes, film studies emerged out of social scientific interests as much as from the arts-centered pedagogy charted by Polan and the political machinations chronicled by Decherney. Kracauer's work in New York hovered precisely around this bifurcation, but his sensibilities as a humanist did not: despite his occasional interest in instrumentalizing his own insights, he never considered that the latter could be generated in any other way than through an interpretive, theoretically reflexive form. Kracauer was and remained a humanist first and a social scientist a distant second. Like Hannah Arendt, he held that "understanding will never be the product of questionnaires, interviews, statistics, and their scientific evaluation."[52] Such forms of quantification, in Kracauer's opinion, confused living textures with the "dead matter" of scientific research.[53] As he put it at the close of an incisive critique of quantitative methods in the early 1950s,

> Documents which are not simply agglomerations of facts participate in the process of living, and every word in them vibrates with the intentions in which they originate and simultaneously foreshadows the indefinite effects they may produce. Their content is no longer their content if it is detached from the texture of intimations and implications to which it belongs and taken literally; it exists only with and within this texture—a still fragmentary manifestation of life, which depends upon response to evolve its properties. Most communications are not so much fixed entities as ambivalent challenges. They challenge the reader or the analyst to absorb them and react to them. Only in approaching these wholes with his own whole being will the analyst be able both to discover and determine their meaning—or one of their meanings—and thus help them to fulfill themselves.[54]

Here, at the close of an article in a journal devoted to social scientific research on public opinion, we find Kracauer almost defiantly sounding his themes as a humanist: the commitment to the minute, to "every word" that "vibrates with intentions"; the emphasis on hermeneutics, on the constant interaction between subjectivity and objectivity, between the scholar and his/her material; and even the language of redemption, of a care of the world that allows "documents"—which for Kracauer may be anything form verbal communications, to physical objects, to art works, to "material reality" and the screen image—to "fulfill themselves."

Once *Theory of Film* had been published in October 1960, half a year after the first meeting of the cinematologists at the NYU faculty club, the book was taken up by another member of the society. At its second meeting, Gerald Noxon delivered a paper titled "The Anatomy of the Close-up," which began by asserting agreement with Kracauer on the centrality of still photography for any understanding of the cinematic medium and then proceeded to read Proust—Kracauer's star witness for the alienating power of photography—as the writer of the close-up. Noxon's presentation concluded by politely disagreeing with Kracauer's emphasis on film's specificity as an artform compared to literature, painting, and other forms of human communication (a point made far more vehemently by Kael in her review for *Sight and Sound*).[55] According to the minutes of the meeting, the controversial discussion about film aesthetics that followed Noxon's presentation centered on "the new Kracauer book," which some considered "a major work and a major statement," whereas others accused Kracauer of having chosen "an illusory medium with which to redeem reality."[56] Although Kracauer himself appears to have abandoned his interest in the society's proceedings (but hardly in photography and film themselves) as he turned his attention to his book on historiography, his name and his work from this point on were an indelible part of the conversation about "cinema and scholarship."

CODA: KRACAUER'S ANONYMITY

Perhaps Adorno had something like this status in mind when, in his obituary for Kracauer, he offered a striking assessment of his friend's lifelong work as a film critic and theorist. By the time of his death, Adorno claimed, Kracauer's approach to film had "long since become anonymous." As he was quick to qualify, the line was meant as a compliment on one of Kracauer's principal accomplishments *(Errungenschaften)*, the notion of anonymity signifying recognition of the pervasive influence of Kracauer's way of thinking. In this view, Kracauer's writings on cinema from the 1920s through the 1960s had receded by the time of his death into the very fabric of film theory and criticism, woven into its DNA as the "self-evident condition, as it were, for all reflection on the medium."[57] Today, we take for granted Kracauer's original insights on the task of the film critic, on the relationship between the social and aesthetic dimensions of cinema, and on the specificity of film's relation to reality.

But Adorno's tribute remains ambivalent, unable fully to rein in the implication that, having become anonymous, Kracauer was invisible. From this perspective, Adorno's presumably well intentioned remark suggests that Kracauer's work on film had dissipated into the ether of cultural criticism, lacking any consequence that would attach to an authorial name. Even though Kracauer indisputably helped to bring film theory and criticism into its own, and although his early essays may have outlined a "proleptic physiognomics of [the] culture industry" (as Adorno somewhat self-servingly admits),[58] the world had moved on to find itself occupied with other issues and discourses at the time of Kracauer's death. Though his passing did not escape notice (in addition to the notice in *Cinema Journal*, the *New York Times* also ran an obituary), compared to towering figures such as Hannah Arendt, Herbert Marcuse, or Adorno himself, Siegfried Kracauer was virtually anonymous indeed.

Curiously, both of the assessments that resonate in Adorno's description of Kracauer's anonymity capture something important about Kracauer's work. For he was almost deliberately anonymous in many ways; indeed, he prized the virtues of remaining unidentified, incognito. But Kracauer also plainly longed for recognition; starting out as a freelancer, and then again in exile, his livelihood depended on it.[59] Consequently, as we have seen, Kracauer's first order of business in exile was to network, introduce, and make a name for himself—activities hardly designed to achieve anonymity. As for his contributions to film criticism and theory, Kracauer's own hopes were hardly that they would dissolve into generally accepted premises but rather, as he had written to Löwenthal shortly before publication of his summa, that *Theory of Film* would "become a classic."[60]

To speak of Kracauer's anonymity, then, is at once flattering and flawed. Flattering because it is sensitive to an avowedly idiosyncratic trait of Kracauer's character and because it indexes the degree to which some of his pioneering insights now appear to us as received wisdom. Flawed because to speak of Kracauer's anonymity is somewhat disingenuous today, when Berlin has named a square—the *Kracauerplatz*—after Siegfried and Lili, who had lived there in the 1930s, and when Kracauer appears alongside the likes of Asta Nielsen, Billy Wilder, and Marlene Dietrich on the "Boulevard der Stars" in front of the *Filmhaus* at Potsdamer Platz. Kracauer's name is by now firmly established in pantheons of intellectual history alongside (depending on the angle from which you consider his work) Theodor W. Adorno and Walter Benjamin;[61] Rudolf Arnheim, André Bazin, and Christian Metz;[62] Aby Warburg and Erwin Panofsky;[63] or, as I have argued in this book, the key figures on the New York scene in the 1940s and '50s—from the members of the Institute for Social Research uptown, to the scholars in the Rockefeller "Communications Group," to Hannah Arendt, to the New York Intellectuals and their "little magazines" downtown.

Accordingly, the task of the present book has been twofold: to rescue Kracauer from anonymity and at the same time restore him to it. To the degree that Kracauer's work has become routinized and amounts to a set of unexamined premises for film criticism and cultural theory, I have sought to shine a bright light on the logic, the contradictions, and especially the historical specificity of his influential work during the quarter century he spent in New York. Returning to the sociopolitical moments of their formulation and following roughly the chronology of the development of Kracauer's thinking from his arrival in Manhattan in 1941 until his death in 1966, I have argued the coherence of his cultural critique and outlined the broadly humanist, yet nonanthropocentric politics of subjectivity that underpin it.

But to shore up this authorial signature is simultaneously to dissolve its contours and return to it the contextual, historical energies that coursed through the conception of Kracauer's works.[64] By placing him in the vibrant intellectual scene of New York at midcentury, home to both his Frankfurt friends and acquaintances and to the loose-knit "tribe" of New York Intellectuals among whom he sought new contacts and fora for publication and intellectual exchange, I have sought to paint the picture of a specific kind of anonymity for Kracauer: that of a transatlantic mediator between Frankfurt and New York, between (film) criticism and (cultural) theory, between high and low culture, between differing intellectual traditions—none of which bear his name, but all of which might be imagined counterfactually to communicate through his oeuvre.

The contradiction between the two aims of this book is more apparent than real, for both projects—at once diminishing and increasing Kracauer's anonymity—have derived from the same, underlying methodological impulse to *historicize* Kracauer's work. Although I have insisted on the relevance of Kracauer's contributions as a cultural critic and film theorist, I am wary of reclamatory gestures that short-circuit different historical moments to claim the "actuality" of an oeuvre, let alone the perennial (which is to say: ahistorical) value of a classic. Instead, we should steep Kracauer's texts, like those of classical film theory more broadly, in their historical moments, where, like an exposed strip of film in a chemical bath, they may begin to reveal previously unseen contours and tonalities.[65] In

13. Scenes of instruction: Siegfried Kracauer and an unidentified boy, Wilmington, Vermont, 1958. (Deutsches Literaturarchiv Marbach)

this way, the texts themselves become newly legible, not only for the ways in which they amount to a coherent authorial project, but also in terms of the historical discourses in which they participated.

For this kind of approach, we have a model in Kracauer's own teachings—to which Adorno attested in a far less ambivalent accolade than the one cited above. "I am not exaggerating in the slightest," Adorno said in the 1964 radio address later published as "The Curious Realist," "when I say that I owe more to [Kracauer] than to my academic teachers." Extolling Kracauer as an "exceptionally gifted pedagogue," Adorno recalled Saturday afternoons that the two men spent together reading Kant, whom Kracauer made "come alive for me. Under his guidance I experienced the work from the beginning not as mere epistemology, not as an analysis of the conditions of scientifically valid judgments, but as a kind of coded text from which the historical situation of spirit *(Geist)* could be read, with the vague expectation that in doing so one could acquire something of truth itself."[66] Even if we leave aside the Hegelian notion of *Geist* and an emphatic notion of "truth itself," I submit, we may apply Kracauer's lesson in reading Kant to our reading of Kracauer himself. In this view, Kracauer's American writings, too, appear as a kind of coded text, to be read as part of various

Manhattan networks of émigré scholars, Frankfurt friends, New York Intellectuals, editors, publishers, and film scholars. If I have succeeded in thus bringing Kracauer's writings to life, it is my hope that we may now decipher in them the historical situation of film, theory, and politics around midcentury, and that we may yet discover in them some truths for our own digital, posthumanist, and neoliberal present.

Notes

INTRODUCTION

1. "Der Denkende in der Emigration sollte sich nicht vormachen, ein neues Leben zu beginnen, sondern die Konsequenz aus dem vergangenen, aus seiner ganzen Erfahrung ziehen, die europäische Katastrophe und die Schwierigkeiten im neuen Lande inbegriffen." Theodor W. Adorno, "Fragen an die intellektuelle Emigration," in *Gesammelte Schriften* 20.1, *Vermischte Schriften* I (Frankfurt am Main: Suhrkamp, 1986), 357.

2. "Tiny Liner Brings 816 from Europe," *New York Times*, April 26, 1941; "Keine Zwischenfälle auf der 'Nyassa,'" *Aufbau*, May 2, 1941, 4.

3. Letter from Siegfried and Lili Kracauer to Eugen and Marlise Schüfftan, April 22, 1944, in *Nachrichten aus Hollywood, New York und anderswo. Der Briefwechsel Eugen und Marlise Schüfftans mit Siegfried und Lili Kracauer*, ed. Kathinka Dittrich van Weringh and Helmut G. Asper (Trier: WVT [Wissenschaftlicher Verlag Trier], 2003), 57. The cameraman Eugen Schüfftan had made the crossing together with his wife Marlise on the same ship as the Kracauers; the Schüfftans and the Kracauers became close friends in the process, socializing often during their first six months in New York and exchanging numerous affectionate letters over the next two decades. On the first anniversary of their crossing, the Kracauers remembered "the marvelous time we spent together on deck and then our arrival here that marked the end of so many sufferings and the beginning of a new life for you and us." Schüfftan, however, reminded the couple of the journey's "shady sides," even if "the light sides are paramount" in retrospect. See letters of April 21 and April 25, 1945, respectively; ibid., 38–39.

4. Siegfried Kracauer, "Why France Liked Our Films," in *Siegfried Kracauer's American Writings: Essays on Film and Popular Culture*, ed. Johannes von Moltke and Kristy Rawson (Berkeley: University of California Press, 2012), 33–40.

5. Siegfried Kracauer, Letter to Theodor W. Adorno, March 28, 1941, in Adorno and Kracauer, *"Der Riß der Welt geht auch durch mich ..."* Theodor

W. Adorno/Siegfried Kracauer, *Briefwechsel 1923–1966*, ed. Wolfgang Schopf (Frankfurt am Main: Suhrkamp, 2008), 527.

6. *Soziologie als Wissenschaft* was originally published in 1922 and is now available in Werke 1.1 (Frankfurt am Main: Suhrkamp, 2006). *Ginster. Von ihm selbst geschrieben* was serialized in the *Frankfurter Zeitung* and published by S. Fischer in 1928; it now appears in Werke 7 / *Romane und Erzählungen*, ed. Inka Mülder-Bach (Frankfurt am Main: Suhrkamp, 2004). *Die Angestellten. Aus dem neuesten Deutschland* similarly appeared in serialized form in the *Frankfurter Zeitung* and as a monograph in 1930; it, too, is included in Werke 7, and has been translated as Siegfried Kracauer, *The Salaried Masses: Duty and Distraction in Weimar Germany*, trans. Quentin Hoare (London: Verso, 1998).

7. Letter to Adorno, in Adorno and Kracauer, "Der Riß der Welt . . . ," 232.

8. Ibid.

9. Both books appeared with Suhrkamp: *Das Ornament der Masse: Essays* (1963), subsequently translated by Thomas Y. Levin as *The Mass Ornament: Weimar Essays* (Cambridge, Mass.: Harvard University Press, 1995); *Straßen in Berlin und anderswo* (1964).

10. Siegfried Kracauer, "Pariser Kunstchronik," in *Essays, Feuilletons, Rezensionen, 1932–1965*, ed. Inka Mülder-Bach, Werke 5.4 (Frankfurt am Main: Suhrkamp, 2011), 551–53; idem, "Americana: Glossen zur Ausstellung 'Trois Siècles d'Art aux États-Unis,'" ibid., 554–65; idem, "Ausstellung der New-Yorker Film Library," in *Kleine Schriften zum Film, 1932–1961*, ed. Inka Mülder-Bach, Werke 6.3 (Frankfurt am Main: Suhrkamp, 2004), 215–17.

11. Beginning with two trips in 1956 and 1958, and then on annual visits from 1960 until his death in 1966, Kracauer would return to Europe regularly during the summers, combining research on behalf of the Bollingen Foundation with vacation time spent primarily in Italy and the Alps.

12. Both books have recently been reprinted, with new introductions by Leonardo Quaresima and Miriam Bratu Hansen, respectively, by Princeton University Press: Siegfried Kracauer, *Theory of Film: The Redemption of Physical Reality* (1997) and *From Caligari to Hitler: A Psychological History of the German Film* (2004). Of the latter, Hermann Kappelhoff notes with some justification: "there is hardly another book that has so fundamentally influenced the discourse of modern film studies" (Kapplehoff, *The Politics and Poetics of Cinematic Realism* [New York: Columbia University Press, 2015], 62).

13. Rotha is quoted in *Siegfried Kracauer, 1889–1996*, ed. Ingrid Belke and Irina Renz, *Marbacher Magazin*, no. 17 (1988): 107. The reception history of *Caligari* is too broad to recapitulate here—though as with *Theory of Film*, one would need to distinguish and compare its English-language reception with respect to the book's impact in Germany and elsewhere. For the former, see Leonardo Quaresima, "Introduction," in *From Caligari to Hitler*. See also Patrice Petro, "From Lukács to Kracauer and Beyond: Social Film Histories and the German Cinema," *Cinema Journal* 22, no. 3 (1983): 47. See also the pathbreaking bibliographic work by Thomas Y. Levin: "Siegfried Kracauer in English: A Bibliography," *New German Critique*, no. 41 (April 1987): 140–50;

Siegfried Kracauer. Eine Bibliographie seiner Schriften (Marbach am Neckar: Deutsche Schillergesellschaft, 1989); and "The English-Language Reception of Kracauer's Work: A Bibliography," *New German Critique*, no. 54 (October 1991): 183–89. For the impact Kracauer had on an entire generation of film critics in Germany, see Enno Patalas, "Siegfried Kracauer," *Filmkritik* 11, no. 1 (January 1967): 5. For the divergent reception of *Theory of Film* in Germany and the United States, see Eric Rentschler, "Kracauer, Spectatorship, and the Seventies," in *Culture in the Anteroom: The Legacies of Siegfried Kracauer*, ed. Gerd Gemünden and Johannes von Moltke (Ann Arbor: University of Michigan Press, 2012), 61–75.

14. See David Culbert, "The Rockefeller Foundation, the Museum of Modern Art Film Library, and Siegfried Kracauer, 1941," *Historical Journal of Film, Radio, and Television* 13, no. 4 (January 1993): 495–511; Quaresima, "Introduction"; Noah W. Isenberg, "This Pen for Hire: Siegfried Kracauer as American Cultural Critic," in Gemünden and von Moltke (eds.), *Culture in the Anteroom*, 29–41.

15. "Dumbo," *The Nation*, November 8, 1941, 463.

16. As Ingrid Belke puts it in a recent intellectual portrait of Kracauer, "exile marked a break in Kracauer's work: in place of up-to-date social criticism and trenchant and original linguistic form, we find scientific analyses, principally works on the new and internationally understood medium of film" (Ingrid Belke, "Siegfried Kracauer [1889–1966]—Ein Portrait," *Galerie—Revue culturelle et pédagogique* 30, no. 3 [2012]: 244).

17. "I can't shed the superstition," Adorno wrote in one of several letters that touched on the use of German or English in his own and Kracauer's writings, "that we can only say the decisive things in our own language" (Letter to Siegfried Kracauer, July 19, 1951, in Adorno and Kracauer, *Briefwechsel*, 461).

18. Miriam Hansen, "'With Skin and Hair': Kracauer's Theory of Film, Marseille 1940," *Critical Inquiry* 19 (Spring 1995): 438.

19. Gertrud Koch retells the anecdote of Kracauer's self-constructed isolation behind a "veritable tower of books," which she attributes to Annette Michelson, in Gertrud Koch, *Siegfried Kracauer: An Introduction*, trans. Jeremy Gaines (Princeton, N.J.: Princeton University Press, 2000), 76.

20. Peter Harcourt, "What, Indeed, Is Cinema?" *Cinema Journal* 8, no. 1 (1968): 22. Harcourt freely admits that he deduces his impression entirely from Kracauer's writing, "for I know nothing at all about his personal life" (25).

21. Dudley Andrew, *The Major Film Theories: An Introduction* (London: Oxford University Press, 1976), 107.

22. Dudley Andrew, "The Core and the Flow of Film Studies," *Critical Inquiry* 35, no. 4 (January 2009): 908.

23. Kracauer, in particular, appears to have encountered antisemitism even from his most well-meaning benefactors. While John Marshall, the associate director for Humanities at the Rockefeller Foundation who championed Kracauer's "unique grasp of the film in the general social scene," merely considered him "personally most unprepossessing" (John Marshall, diary of July

19, 1946, Rockefeller Archive Center, Rockefeller Foundation Collection, RG 1.1 [Projects], Series 200 R, Box 250, Folder 2993), Iris Barry made no bones about her prejudice. The influential curator of the MoMA film library, Barry is rightly remembered as Kracauer's patron who provided refuge to the errant exile and repeatedly served as a reference and a reviewer on Kracauer's behalf. Judging by the notes to her unpublished memoir, however, it appears she was less than enthusiastic in this role. In barely veiled racist terms, Barry vividly recalls their first meeting in Paris: "I thought at once of Toulouse Lautrec, for here was a very small, hideous short man with black golliwog hair, vividly red lips and a hare-lip which emitted with dignity a considerable stammer (defect of speech)." The dubious portrait is overlaid, in the immediate context of Barry's notes, with more than a hint of antisemitism: "So when the Jewish refugees came to one's cognizance it was difficult to react. Across the Red Sea? The circumcised? . . . Pawnbrokers? Something to do with finance and money and the Rothschilds . . . ? [. . .] Thus a Jewish refugee—and I had to cope [with] many of them later—was weird and disturbing and what was one to do about it?" In the same vein, she recollects fretting over how to react to Kracauer's arrival in New York later on and considers him, in retrospect, "a nightmare."

Perhaps owing to the impromptu nature of the draft (handwritten on small sheets of paper), Barry's remarks are confounding in their mix of naiveté, gross caricature, racism, and reflection; they also corroborate the anecdotal evidence of his "defensive" working habits at the film library: "To me he seemed so profoundly German, which was an inimical thing and irritating, too: 'I vill ezplain everting!' Perhaps he thought that when I avoided or evaded him it was because he was a Jew (once persecuted, thrice wary) or difficult (and goodness knows he was immensely proud and difficult). In fact I was mostly ashamed of myself for not responding better to his nature and his needs. To me he was a sort of nightmare. Nevertheless in the shelter of the R[ockefeller] F[oundation] and at the Museum he wrote, but the librarian found him difficult, hedged in for months by a wall of books which he would not cede to anyone like a dog in the manger. He worked hard, did his job well, was praised for it, but I do not judge that he was contented. To me he was a nightmare." Whatever her motives, Barry did support Kracauer's work at MoMA for a number of years, though she made no efforts to regularize his employment after grants from the Rockefeller Foundation ran out. Museum of Modern Art, Film Study Center, Department of Film and Media Records, Box 5, file 5.14. See also Robert Sitton, *Lady in the Dark: Iris Barry and the Art of Film* (New York: Columbia University Press, 2014).

24. Miriam Bratu Hansen, *Cinema and Experience: Siegfried Kracauer, Walter Benjamin, and Theodor W. Adorno* (Berkeley: University of California Press, 2012), chap. 1.

25. Both quoted phrases appear as subheadings in the final chapter to Kracauer, *Theory of Film*, 287, 291.

26. Ibid., 288. In the same section (291), Kracauer invokes David Riesman's well-known diagnosis of the "lonely crowd" to further explain this motif.

27. Letter to Adorno, November 8, 1963, in Adorno and Kracauer, *"Der Riß der Welt . . . ,"* 621.

28. Siegfried Kracauer, *History: The Last Things before the Last* (New York: Oxford University Press, 1969), 81.

29. Erich Auerbach, *Mimesis: The Representation of Reality in Western Literature* (Princeton: Princeton University Press, 1953), 557. Along with related concepts of nomadism, displacement, travel, and the "transnational," this notion of exile as estrangement has been central to recent theoretical developments in fields ranging from anthropology and history to literary and cultural studies. For an excellent overview, see John Durham Peters, "Exile, Nomadism, and Diaspora: The Stakes of Mobility in the Western Canon," in *Home, Exile, Homeland: Film, Media, and the Politics of Place,* ed. Hamid Naficy (New York: Routledge, 1999), 17–41.

30. Kracauer, *History,* 93.

31. See, in particular, Martin Jay, "The Extraterritorial Life of Siegfried Kracauer," in *Permanent Exiles: Essays on the Intellectual Migration from Germany to America* (New York: Columbia University Press, 1986), 152–97; and Enzo Traverso, *Siegfried Kracauer: Itinéraire d'un intellectuel nomade* (Paris: Éd. la Découverte, 1994).

32. Koch, *Siegfried Kracauer,* 5.

33. Jay, "Extraterritorial Life of Siegfried Kracauer."

34. Traverso, *Siegfried Kracauer,* 188, 191.

35. Hamid Naficy, "Introduction. Framing Exile: From Homeland to Homepage," in Naficy (ed.), *Home, Exile, Homeland,* 4. Kader Konuk has recently proposed just such a perspective on the exile of Kracauer's friend Erich Auerbach in Turkey, advocating a view of exile as a "condition of multiple attachments" (Konuk, *East West Mimesis: Auerbach in Turkey* [Stanford, Calif.: Stanford University Press, 2010], 13). This allows her to show how Auerbach's work on *Mimesis* was steeped not only in the reality of Europe but also in that of Istanbul, and how the philologist found there a complexly mediated Hellenic culture whose history he would trace along the notion of realism (eventually influencing Kracauer's understanding of film through this work). Konuk explicitly sets out to question

> one of the important premises of exile studies, namely, that exile is synonymous with isolation and that isolation is, in and of itself, intellectually and artistically productive. For many contemporary critics, exile still represents a state of critical detachment and superior insight that is supposed to arise when intellectuals are expelled from their homes and forced to take up residence elsewhere. It concerns me, however, that this line of thought too readily reduces exile to a mere metaphor for uprootedness: disconnected from his or her social and political context, the exile is coupled with possibilities for cultural transfer and transnational exchange. Too easily does the exilic condition acquire almost utopian possibilities: the exile is suddenly unencumbered by indigenous tradition, emerging instead as

the new mediator between systems, a perspicuous commentator on both the endogenous and exogenous. I argue that this view of exile distorts the historical record. (12–13)

Consequently, Konuk calls for a "new approach to the study of exile, one that recognizes both the historicity of exile and the exile's material existence" (13).

36. See Konuk, *East West Mimesis;* Richard King, *Arendt and America* (Chicago: University of Chicago Press, 2015); David Jenemann, *Adorno in America* (Minneapolis: University of Minnesota Press, 2007); Thomas Wheatland, *The Frankfurt School in Exile* (Minneapolis: University of Minnesota Press, 2009); Detlev Claussen, "Intellectual Transfer: Theodor W. Adorno's American Experience," *New German Critique,* no. 97 (January 2006): 5–14. King's book appeared as my own was going into print. Rather than fully engage its reassessment of Arendt's work in light of her American affiliations, here I can only note that *The Curious Humanist* very much aims to do for Kracauer what King does for Arendt when he writes: "Put most strongly, the United States was not just where she lived and where her thought was first published. It was a crucial theme and concern *of* her thought. This means that I have stressed Arendt's interaction with American intellectuals, with American thought and culture, and with America as a place and set of institutions rather than treat her life and thought as detached from where she actually lived, as though the life of the mind was lived no place particularly" (4).

37. Jenemann, *Adorno in America,* 109.

38. See Vilém Flusser, *The Freedom of the Migrant: Objections to Nationalism,* ed. Kenneth Kronenberg and Anke K. Finger (Urbana: University of Illinois Press, 2003), for an unabashedly celebratory account of the productivity of exilic detachment or *Heimatlosigkeit.*

39. Wheatland, *Frankfurt School in Exile,* 142.

40. Theodor W. Adorno, "The Curious Realist: On Siegfried Kracauer," *New German Critique,* no. 54 (Autumn 1991): 159–77.

41. Momme Brodersen, *Siegfried Kracauer* (Reinbek bei Hamburg: Rowohlt Taschenbuch Verlag, 2001), 120.

42. Siegfried Kracauer, Letter to Eugen Schüfftan, January 1, 1948, in Dittrich van Weringh and Asper (eds.), *Nachrichten aus Hollywood, New York und anderswo,* 73.

43. We can measure the progress of Kracauer's facility with the English language in two letters he wrote to his friends Meyer Schapiro and Theodor Adorno, respectively. In August of 1941 he still noted, in halting and self-critical sentences, that "English writing means yet hard work to me, and I only hope you will not be too sensible with respect to my funny style. [. . .] accordingly to my disordered live during the last year I have no practice more in putting phrases together. What a pity! Each little step forward, formerly performed without any pain, is now the result of a tremendous effort. I have to train myself again" (Letter to Meyer Shapiro, August 6, 1941; Deutsches Literaturarchiv Marbach [repository of Kracauer's files; hereafter cited as DLA]). Two years later he would

write to Adorno in California, "I've made rather good progress with writing in English; I'm passionate about it" (Letter to Adorno, May 1, 1943, in *"Der Riß der Welt . . . ,"* 431). While Adorno would famously criticize Kracauer's decision virtually to abandon the German language (see "The Curious Realist"), Max Horkheimer explicitly commended him for retaining his "old style, sober as well as loaded with allusions; as a matter of fact it withstands the transfer into English much better than Teddie's or my own way of expression" (letter of May 1, 1943, in *"Der Riß der Welt . . . ,"* 433).

44. These writings are now available in *Siegfried Kracauer's American Writings: Essays on Film and Popular Culture,* ed. Johannes von Moltke and Kristy Rawson (Berkeley: University of California Press, 2012). See also Isenberg, "This Pen for Hire."

45. Quotes: Kracauer, *Theory of Film,* 196; and *Siegfried Kracauer's American Writings,* 40.

46. Hannah Arendt, *The Origins of Totalitarianism* (New York: Harcourt, Brace & World, 1966), xxiv.

47. Raffaele Laudani, ed., *Secret Reports on Nazi Germany: The Frankfurt School Contribution to the War Effort* (Princeton, N.J.: Princeton University Press, 2013).

48. Siegfried Kracauer, "Those Movies with a Message," in *Siegfried Kracauer's American Writings,* 72–80.

49. Siegfried Kracauer, "Hollywood's Terror Films," in *Siegfried Kracauer's American Writings,* 41–6; Leo Löwenthal and Norbert Guterman, *Prophets of Deceit: A Study of Techniques of the American Agitator* (New York: Harper, 1949); Theodor W. Adorno et al., *The Authoritarian Personality* (New York: Harper, 1950).

50. One can chart these debates, for example, in the pages of *Partisan Review,* where they led to editorial defections and the founding of new, opposing journals. When the principal editors Phillip Rahv and William Phillips came out in support of the U.S. declaration of war after Pearl Harbor, both Dwight Macdonald and Clement Greenberg openly distanced themselves from the policy of the editors. After internal struggles over control, Macdonald left *Partisan Review* in 1943 to found *Politics,* wherein he would argue for a third-camp model as an alternative to both U.S. capitalism and fascist as well as communist totalitarianism—until he surprisingly proclaimed his unequivocal alignment with the Western Bloc in a 1952 article flatly entitled "I Choose the West" (reprinted in *The New York Intellectuals Reader,* ed. Neil Jumonville [New York: Routledge, 2007], 63–68).

51. It is interesting to note that Kracauer's promiscuous interests during the Weimar years, when he wrote on architecture, exhibitions, and the arts as much as on cinema, mass culture, and the metropolis, seem drastically reduced during his American years. If his published writings are anything to go by, he focused almost entirely on film despite the fact that he asked friends not to think of him exclusively (or at all) as a "film man." On the other hand, the archival record shows that the published writings are *not* all we should go by, as he continued

to read and converse about a vast array of subjects, both as author of reports for agencies such as the Bureau of Applied Social Research or the Voice of America and as a consultant for the Bollingen Foundation.

52. Lionel Trilling, *The Liberal Imagination: Essays on Literature and Society* (New York: Viking Press, 1950), xvii.

53. Lionel Trilling, "Reality in America," ibid., 11.

54. For the reception of *Theory of Film*, see Gerd Gemünden and Johannes von Moltke, "Kracauer's Legacies," in idem (eds.), *Culture in the Anteroom*, 1–25. See also Rentschler, "Kracauer, Spectatorship, and the Seventies."

55. Robert Stam, *Film Theory: An Introduction* (Oxford: Blackwell, 2000), 77.

56. The German phrase, coined in a discussion of Bertolt Brecht's legacy, is "durchschlagende Wirkungslosigkeit eines Klassikers" (Max Frisch, *Öffentlichkeit als Partner* [Frankfurt am Main: Suhrkamp, 1967], 73).

57. Dana Polan, *Scenes of Instruction: The Beginnings of the U.S. Study of Film* (Berkeley: University of California Press, 2007), 4–5.

58. The work of Christian Metz constitutes the watershed in Andrew's account *(Major Film Theories)*, which, after surveying realist and formalist theories in the first two parts of the book, devotes considerable space to Metz in the concluding section, "Contemporary French Film Theory."

59. Editors, "Cinema/Ideology/Criticism," *Cahiers du cinéma*, November 1969, 25.

60. Eric Rentschler, "Rudolf Arnheim's Early Passage between Social and Aesthetic Film Criticism," in *Arnheim for Film and Media Studies*, ed. Scott Higgins (New York: Routledge, 2011), 51–68, at 63.

61. Ibid.

62. Siegfried Kracauer, "The Little Shopgirls Go to the Movies," in *The Mass Ornament*, 290–304; Kracauer, *The Salaried Masses*.

63. Hansen, *Cinema and Experience*, 75.

64. Wendy Brown, "Untimeliness and Punctuality: Critical Theory in Dark Times," in *Edgework: Critical Essays on Knowledge and Politics* (Princeton, N.J.; Princeton University Press, 2006), 15.

65. David Rodowick similarly notes the untimeliness of Kracauer's work in *The Virtual Life of Film* (Cambridge, Mass.: Harvard University Press, 2007) and again in *Elegy for Theory* (Cambridge, Mass.: Harvard University Press, 2014).

66. Kracauer, *From Caligari to Hitler*, 11.

67. Mark Greif, *The Age of the Crisis of Man: Thought and Fiction in America, 1933–1973* (Princeton, N.J.: Princeton University Press, 2015).

68. On nervous liberals, see Brett Gary's excellent book *The Nervous Liberals: Propaganda Anxieties from World War I to the Cold War* (New York: Columbia University Press, 1999).

69. On the notion of "bleak liberalism," see Amanda Anderson, "Character and Ideology: The Case of Cold War Liberalism," *New Literary History* 42, no. 2 (2011): 209–29.

70. Robert Warshow, *The Immediate Experience: Movies, Comics, Theatre, and Other Aspects of Popular Culture* (Cambridge, Mass.: Harvard University Press, 2002)

71. Peter Decherney, *Hollywood and the Culture Elite: How the Movies Became* American (New York: Columbia University Press, 2005); Saverio Giovacchni, *Hollywood Modernism: Film and Politics in the Age of the New Deal* (Philadelphia: Temple University Press, 2001); Haden Guest, "Experimentation and Innovation in Three American Film Journals of the 1950s," in *Inventing Film Studies*, ed. Lee Grieveson and Haidee Wasson (Durham, N.C.: Duke University Press, 2008): 235–63; Polan, *Scenes of Instruction;* Haidee Wasson, *Museum Movies: The Museum of Modern Art and the Birth of Art Cinema* (Berkeley: University of California Press, 2005).

CHAPTER 1

1. Siegfried Kracauer, "Dumbo (1941)," in *Siegfried Kracauer's American Writings*, 139–40. Unless otherwise indicated, subsequent quotations are from this short piece. This chapter draws on the work I undertook together with Kristy Rawson in preparing Siegfried Kracauer's American Writings, which in many ways provided the original impetus for the present book as well. I remain grateful to Kristy for her role in sparking this inquiry, for the many conversations we had about Kracauer in New York, and for her permission to use this material here.

2. Disney had figured previously in Kracauer's reflections on broader film-theoretical and -historical concerns such as the advent of sound and color. See Siegfried Kracauer, "Internationaler Tonfilm? (1931)," in *Kleine Schriften zum Film, 1928–1931*, ed. Inka Mülder-Bach, Werke 6.2 (Frankfurt am Main: Suhrkamp, 2004), 475–79; idem, "Zur Ästhetik des Farbenfilms (1937)," in *Kleine Schriften zum Film, 1932–1961*, 194–98.

3. Hansen, *Cinema and Experience*, 170.

4. Ibid.

5. Siegfried Kracauer, "Hollywood's Terror Films: Do They Reflect an American State of Mind? (1946)," in *Siegfried Kracauer's American Writings*, 45.

6. Barbara Deming, "The Artlessness of Walt Disney," *Film Chronicle : A New Magazine of Film Criticism and Research* 12, no. 2 (1945): 226–31. Deming's article clearly owes a great debt in turn to Kracauer's thinking on film—one she acknowledged explicitly in later publications.

7. Kracauer, "Hollywood's Terror Films," 45.

8. Max Horkheimer and Theodor W. Adorno, *Dialectic of Enlightenment: Philosophical Fragments* (Stanford: Stanford University Press, 2002), 112.

9. Walter Benjamin, "The Work of Art in the Age of Its Technological Reproducibility," in *Walter Benjamin: Selected Writings*, vol. 3: *1935–1938*, ed. Howard Eiland and Michael W. Jennings, trans. Edmund Jephcott (Cambridge, Mass.: Belknap Press of Harvard University Press, 2002), 117.

10. See the discussion of laughter and fun in Horkheimer and Adorno, *Dialectic of Enlightenment* (112): " . . . There is nothing to laugh about.

Laughter, whether reconciled or terrible, always accompanies the moment when a fear is ended. It indicates a release, whether from physical danger or from the grip of logic. Reconciled laughter resounds with the echo of escape from power; wrong laughter copes with fear by defecting to the agencies which inspire it. It echoes the inescapability of power. Fun is a medicinal bath which the entertainment industry never ceases to prescribe."

11. Ibid., 1.

12. Siegfried Kracauer, "Preston Sturges, or Laughter Betrayed (1950)," in *Siegfried Kracauer's American Writings*, 112. As the article points out, *Sullivan's Travels*, "the turning point in Sturges' career," pivots on the protagonist's experience watching a Mickey Mouse cartoon with fellow prisoners during a stint in jail. Once freed, Sullivan—a Hollywood film director by trade—returns to his trademark comedies without any further thoughts about social critique such as had originally set him off on his travels. Kracauer reads the self-reflexive film as symptomatic, detecting in the fictional traveler's journey the arc of Sturges's career: "There was something Aristophanic about Sturges' beginnings, but in *Sullivan's Travels* he betrayed what was best in his laughter" (113).

13. Mark Greif, *The Age of the Crisis of Man: Thought and Fiction in America, 1933–1973* (Princeton, N.J.: Princeton University Press, 2015).

14. Already in a 1923 review of *Die närrische Wette des Lord Aldini*, we find Kracauer plumbing this "amusing prank" for a "metaphysics of film"— which he locates in the power of laughter: "The deeper meaning of the amusing gag consists in the fact that it reveals the triviality of a world that can be set in motion by trivialities, and in the fact that it conjures laughter at the defanged seriousness of this world" (Kracauer, "Wetter und Retter," in *Kleine Schriften zum Film*, ed. Inka Mülder-Bach, Werke 6.1 [Frankfurt am Main: Suhrkamp, 2004], 43).

15. Patrice Petro notes a similar dialectic in the relation between the two film books; see Petro, "Kracauer's Epistemological Shift," *New German Critique*, no. 54 (October 1991): 137.

16. Kracauer, *Theory of Film*, 287. For the critique of Disney, see 89–90.

17. See Petro, "Kracauer's Epistemological Shift."

18. One recalls the famous phrase that "the process leads directly through the mass ornament, not away from it" (Kracauer, "The Mass Ornament," in *The Mass Ornament*, 86).

19. Siegfried Kracauer, "Bemerkungen zum französischen Film," in *Kleine Schriften zum Film, 1932–1961*, 282–86.

20. Kracauer, "Why France Liked Our Films," in *Siegfried Kracauer's American Writings*, 33–40. Unless otherwise indicated, subsequent quotations are from this essay.

21. Speaking of Kracauer's early writings from the Weimar years, Hansen (*Cinema and Experience*, 19) observes that "Kracauer needs the distinctions between personal pronouns for a particular rhetorical strategy—a shifting of perspectives from a third-person, impersonal distance to a more personal voice, whether first-person plural or second-person singular. . . . This rhetorical strat-

egy more often than not signals a shift in the critic's attitude toward the phenomenon or mode of behavior described, a revaluation of an earlier negative stance." As we shall see, a similar rhetorical strategy governs the composition of "Why France Liked Our Films."

22. Although Kracauer tends to essentialize the devotion to "delicacy of literary language" as a specifically French trait, he adumbrates a critique that François Truffaut would pick up over a decade later in his now famous article "A Certain Tendency of the French Cinema," originally published in *Cahiers du cinéma* in 1954. In terms strikingly similar to Truffaut's blazing indictment of the "tradition of quality" which treated directors as mere "metteurs-en-scène" tasked with supplying appropriate images for the all-important words of the script, Kracauer complains that in recent French films, "the flood of words submerged the pictures.... In consequence, the screen approached the stage and the pictures functioned as mere illustrations. Whereas the development of a true film depends upon the meaning of its pictures, in these films the dialogue alone determined the progress of the action.... [French films] simply followed the course of the words instead of directing it" (Kracauer, "Why France Liked Our Films," 34–35). Cf. François Truffaut, "A Certain Tendency of the French Cinema," in *Movies and Methods*, ed. Bill Nichols (Berkeley: University of California Press, 1976), 224–37.

23. Miriam Bratu Hansen, Introduction to Kracauer, *Theory of Film*, vii–xlv. Cf. Klaus Michael, "Vor dem Café: Walter Benjamin und Siegfried Kracauer in Marseille," in *Aber ein Sturm weht vom Paradiese her: Texte zu Walter Benjamin*, ed. Michael Opitz and Erdmut Wizisla (Leipzig: Reclam, 1992), 203–21.

24. This phrase reappears almost verbatim in *Theory of Film* (297), where Kracauer sounds one of Critical Theory's perennial motifs, the waning of experience: "The geometric pattern of New York streets is a well-known fact, but this fact becomes concrete only if we realize, for instance, that all the cross streets end in the nothingness of the blank sky."

25. See, for example, his report to Löwenthal upon returning from a trip to Germany on October 27, 1958: "The fact that there never has been any society [*Gesellschaft*] in Germany is frighteningly apparent. The people are utterly formless and unchanneled, they have no exterior (and a disorderly interior). Everything is there, but nothing in its place. Hence the inauthentic, artificial comportment, the *stilted language*, the complete insecurity. The people are *not so much human beings as raw material for human beings*. In a word: I don't trust them. And I don't even dare to imagine what would result in the case of an economic or political crisis" (Leo Lowenthal and Siegfried Kracauer, *In steter Freundschaft: Leo Löwenthal–Siegfried Kracauer, Briefwechsel 1921–1966* [Springe: zu Klampen, 2003], 211–13). Though of a later date, Kracauer's observations echo some of Hannah Arendt's impressions from an earlier visit, published in *Commentary* in 1950; see Arendt, "The Aftermath of Nazi Rule: Report from Germany," in *Essays in Understanding, 1930–1954: Formation, Exile, and Totalitarianism* (New York: Schocken, 1994), 248–69.

26. On Kracauer as writer of "urban miniatures" see Andreas Huyssen, *Miniature Metropolis*, chap. 4.

27. Neil Jumonville, "Introduction," in *New York Intellectuals Reader*, 3.

28. Irving Howe, "New York in the Thirties: Some Fragments of Memory," *Dissent*, Summer 1961, quoted from Jumonville, *New York Intellectuals Reader*, 29.

29. Irving Howe, "The New York Intellectuals: A Chronicle and a Critique," *Commentary* 46, no. 4 (October 1968): 29; David Denby, "Robert Warshow: Life and Works," in *The Immediate Experience: Movies, Comics, Theatre, and Other Aspects of Popular Culture* (Cambridge, Mass.: Harvard University Press, 2002). See also Stanley Cavell, "Epilogue: After Half a Century," ibid., 291.

30. Enzo Traverso formulates Kracauer's position among the New York Intellectuals paradoxically: "without identifying with it completely, both because of his cultural trajectory as a German Jewish émigré and his distance from the squabbles of the American left, Kracauer situated himself, albeit in a marginal position, at the heart of this milieu" (Traverso, *Siegfried Kracauer: Itinéraire d'un intellectuel nomade* [Paris: Éd. la Découverte, 1994], 168). Howe describes the "loose and unacknowledged tribe" in his retrospect, "The New York Intellectuals," 30.

31. Dwight Macdonald, "'The Conquest of Europe on the Screen: The Nazi Newsreel, 1939–1940,' by Siegfried Kracauer, *Social Research*, September 1943," *Politics*, May 1944, 118. Greenberg invited Kracauer to contribute to *Commentary* in a letter dated March 27, 1946. "We are familiar with your writing," he notes, "and should very much desire to have you contribute to *Commentary*" (letter in DLA).

32. Howe, "New York Intellectuals." On his relationship with Schapiro, see Mark M. Anderson, "Siegfried Kracauer and Meyer Schapiro: A Friendship," *New German Critique*, no. 54 (October 1991): 19–29.

33. Schapiro had already asked Kracauer (with Krautheimer as a reference) to write something for his journal, *Marxist Quarterly*, in 1937. Kracauer responded (February 12, 1937) with excerpts from the *Offenbach* book (letters in DLA).

34. Adorno, "The Curious Realist," 172.

35. The importance of form, presentation, or *Darstellung* was recognized by many critics in the orbit of the Frankfurt School; it was certainly a defining aspect of Adorno's demanding style, though the latter arguably honed his philosophical language in part through his exchanges with Kracauer. In their correspondence, the two men debate the importance of form, for example, in the discussion of Kracauer's then recently published study of white-collar culture, *The Salaried Masses*.

36. Lionel Trilling, "The Function of the Little Magazine," in *The Liberal Imagination: Essays on Literature and Society* (New York: Viking Press, 1950), 100.

37. Hugh Wilford's account of the New York Intellectuals' transition "from vanguard to institution" convincingly demonstrates that institutionalization

was in fact part and parcel of the Intellectuals' definition as a group. In addition to the magazines, other established institutions and patrons also played a role from the very earliest days—among them the American Communist Party and affiliated organizations such as the John Reed Club (the original sponsor of *Partisan Review*) or City College, where many of the New York Intellectuals were educated in the 1930s. See Hugh Wilford, *The New York Intellectuals: From Vanguard to Institution* (Manchester: Manchester University Press, 1995).

38. Karl Schapiro, quoted ibid., 33.

39. "Who could have dreamt that in the eighties everyone would want to know what happened in those early decades?" mused William Phillips in his memoirs (Phillips, *A Partisan View: Five Decades of the Literary Life* [New York: Stein & Day, 1983], 12). The New York Intellectuals have been the object of numerous studies. Especially from the mid-1980s on, there was a decade of steady publications on the group, initiated by Alexander Bloom, *Prodigal Sons: The New York Intellectuals and Their World* (New York: Oxford University Press, 1986); Terry A. Cooney, *The Rise of the New York Intellectuals: "Partisan Review" and Its Circle* (Madison: University of Wisconsin Press, 1986); Alan M. Wald, *The New York Intellectuals: The Rise and Decline of the Anti-Stalinist Left from the 1930s to the 1980s* (Chapel Hill: University of North Carolina Press, 1987); Neil Jumonville, *Critical Crossings: The New York Intellectuals in Postwar America* (Berkeley: University of California Press, 1991). Later publications had the benefit of being able to build on these texts and offer new, revisionist perspectives, such as Wilford, *The New York Intellectuals;* and Harvey M. Teres, *Renewing the Left: Politics, Imagination, and the New York Intellectuals* (New York: Oxford University Press, 1996).

40. Hannah Arendt, *Rahel Varnhagen: The Life of a Jewish Woman.* (New York: Harcourt Brace Jovanovich, 1974); cf. Siegfried Kracauer, *Orpheus in Paris: Offenbach and the Paris of His Time* (New York: Alfred A. Knopf, 1938). For a comparison, see Sabina Loriga, "L'histoire mode de vie: Reflexions autour de Hannah Arendt et Siegfried Kracauer," in *Penser l'histoire: De Marx aux siècles des catastrophes,* ed. Christophe Bouton and Bruce Bégout (Paris: Éd. de l'Éclat, 2011).

41. Letter from Hannah Arendt to Lili and Siegfried Kracauer, November 24, 1939, DLA.

42. To my knowledge, the only other archival cross-reference comes in the form of a newspaper clipping from the *Aufbau* in Kracauer's files of Arendt's appointment as the first female professor in 212 years at Princeton University. The clipping is noted by Volker Breidecker in his edition of the correspondence between Panofsky and Kracauer: *Siegfried Kracauer, Erwin Panofsky: Briefwechsel 1941–1966* (Berlin: Akademie Verlag, 1996), 41.

43. Hannah Arendt, *Denktagebuch 1950–1973,* 2 vols., ed. Ursula Ludz and Ingeborg Nordmann (Munich: Piper, 2002); Hannah Arendt, *Das private Adressbuch 1951–1975,* ed. Christine Fischer-Defoy (Leipzig: Koehler & Amelang, 2007). Arendt's handbag, containing her previous address book, was

stolen in 1945. There is no way of knowing whether the Kracauers were listed in that book.

After the war ended, their paths would similarly converge without coinciding, back in Europe. On his first return trip in the summer of 1956, Kracauer paid a visit to the eminent philosopher Karl Jaspers in Basel; in a letter of October 28, 1956, to his friend Leo Löwenthal, Kracauer reports having had a long conversation with the philosopher—though he neglects to say anything about the subjects they discussed (*In steter Freundschaft*, 183). Besides Heidegger, Jaspers was of course Arendt's most important mentor; he became something of a father figure whom she visited annually after she herself had begun returning to Europe. And so, in 1956, she passed through Jaspers's house within weeks of Kracauer's visit (see Elisabeth Young-Bruehl, *Hannah Arendt: For Love of the World* [New Haven: Yale University Press, 1982], 299–300). One imagines that Kracauer would have been a topic of conversation, even if other philosophical and geopolitical issues may have predominated.

44. Elliot Cohen, "Jewish Culture in America," *Commentary* 3, no. 5 (May 1947): 412–20. Arendt's response appeared a few months later as part of "Jewish Culture in This Time and Place: A Symposium," *Commentary* 4, no. 5 (November 1947): 424–26. Kracauer's submission now appears as "On Jewish Culture" in *Siegfried Kracauer's American Writings*, 54–56.

45. Rudolf Arnheim, Review of *Siegfried Kracauer, Erwin Panofsky: Briefwechsel 1941–1966, Leonardo* 31, no. 1 (January 1998): 74.

46. Letter to Heinrich Blücher, August 2, 1941, in Hannah Arendt and Heinrich Blücher, *Within Four Walls: The Correspondence between Hannah Arendt and Heinrich Blücher, 1936–1968*, ed. Lotte Köhler, trans. Peter Constantine (New York: Harcourt, 2000), 72.

47. The terms *Schweinebande* and *Hornochsen* stem from the bitter dispute over Benjamin's legacy that she had with Adorno and Horkheimer after Benjamin's suicide. While cordial in her letters to the members of the Institute, she did not hold back in her complaints to her husband, to whom she said she was "so terribly furious that I could murder the whole lot of them" (ibid.). The English version translates both the two different German words as "bastards."

48. Lars Rensmann and Samir Suresh Gandesha, *Arendt and Adorno: Political and Philosophical Investigations* (Stanford, Calif.: Stanford University Press, 2012), 9.

49. Letter from Max Horkheimer to Siegfried Kracauer, June 26, 1943, DLA.

50. Edward W. Said, "Traveling Theory," in *The World, the Text, and the Critic* (Cambridge, Mass.: Harvard University Press, 1983), 226–47.

CHAPTER 2

1. "Film News and Comment," *New York Times*, May 18, 1941.
2. "Anti-Nazi League Seeks Ban on 'Sieg im Westen' Film," *Christian Science Monitor*, May 9, 1941.

3. "Anti-Nazis Picket Uptown Theatre Here As German Propaganda Newsreel Opens," *New York Times*, May 8, 1941.

4. "Pro-Nazis Cheer War Film in Theater Here," *New York Herald Tribune*, May 8, 1941.

5. The 96th Street Theater was labeled a "Nazi cinema" by *Aufbau*, New York's German-Jewish newspaper ("New Yorker Notizbuch," *Aufbau*, July 4, 1941).

6. Kracauer mentions explicitly "the six times I attended *Victory in the West* in a Yorkville theater" in "Propaganda and the Nazi War Film," in *From Caligari to Hitler*, 283.

7. Toward the end of the film's run in New York during the summer of 1941, the film library at MoMA began negotiations with the Canadian government to obtain, along with other confiscated German film material, an incomplete but substantial copy of *Sieg im Westen*. Before Kracauer completed his study the following spring, he refined and checked his analysis by reviewing the Canadian materials, once they had arrived in New York in late 1941, in the comparative solitude of a MoMA screening room. See "Memo from Richard Griffith to Iris Barry," June 16, 1941, RG 1.1, Series 200, Box 250, Folder 1989, MoMA Film Library Collection, New York.

8. The manuscript underwent two sets of revisions before being incorporated into the book. First produced as a "Preliminary Report of the Research on Totalitarian Film Propaganda" at MoMA, in collaboration with the "Totalitarian Communications Research Project" directed by Ernst Kris and Hans Speier at the New School, the text was revised, according to suggestions by John Marshall, for the mimeographed brochure, which MoMA labeled "Confidential" and circulated primarily to a small group in the State Department. The version included in *From Caligari to Hitler* is the result of another set of (largely stylistic) revisions. See Sabine Biebl, "Nachbemerkung und editorische Notiz," in Siegfried Kracauer, *Von Caligari zu Hitler: Eine Psychologische Geschichte des deutschen Films*, Werke 2.1 (Frankfurt am Main: Suhrkamp, 2012), 506–510.

9. Theodor W. Adorno, *Minima Moralia: Reflections on a Damaged Life* (London: Verso, 2005), 50.

10. Barry's comment is quoted from the extensive diaries of John Marshall at the Rockefeller Foundation. Officers like Marshall routinely kept these diaries, which served to document all meetings and conversations for the Foundation. John Marshall, Diary entry of January 28, 1942, RG 1.1, Series 200, Box 251, Folder 2990, Rockefeller Archive Center, Rockefeller Foundation, New York [hereafter RAC].

11. See Ernst Kris and Hans Speier, *German Radio Propaganda: Report on Home Broadcasts during the War* (London: Oxford University Press, 1944). The group took up its work on April 1, 1941.

12. It is interesting to note, in view of the subsequent development of communication studies and film studies as academic disciplines, that this research was pioneered by and carried out under the aegis of the *Humanities* Division at the Rockefeller Foundation. I return to this issue in the epilogue to this book.

13. Charles A. Siepmann, "Kracauer, Siegfried, *Theory of Film,*" *Public Opinion Quarterly* 25, no. 1 (Spring 1961): 153. On the so-called Communications Seminar or Communications Group at the Rockefeller Foundation, see Gary, *Nervous Liberals,* 85–128; and Decherney, *Hollywood and the Culture Elite,* 146ff. See also chapter 5, below.

14. So determined at a luncheon meeting between Lasswell, Lazarsfeld, and Marshall on June 7, 1941; Officers' Diaries, RG 12, RAC.

15. Letter from Iris Barry to John Marshall, May 14, 1941, RG 1.1, Series 200, Box 250, Folder 2989, RAC.

16. Memo in John Marshall diaries, July 7, 1941, RG 1.1, Series 200, Box 251, Folder 2990, RAC.

17. Paul Lazarsfeld, "Remarks on Adminstrative and Critical Communications Research," *Studies in Philosophy and Social Science* 9, no. 3 (Spring 1941).

18. Siegfried Kracauer, "The Challenge of Qualitative Content Analysis," *Public Opinion Quarterly* 16, no. 4 (1952): 631–42. Adorno's most explicit reflections on the meeting between critical theory and communications research appear in "Scientific Experiences of a European Scholar in America," in *Critical Models: Interventions and Catchwords,* trans. Henry W Pickford (New York: Columbia University Press, 1998), 215–42. More recently, however, Jenemann and Detlev Claussen have persuasively nuanced our received image of this "cantankerous" Adorno in favor of a more differentiated account of Adorno's positions on social research over the years—and especially after his return from the United States. See Jenemann, *Adorno in America;* and Claussen, "Intellectual Transfer: Theodor W. Adorno's American Experience," *New German Critique,* no. 97 (Winter 2006): 5–14.

19. See Jenemann, *Adorno in America,* esp. chap. 1.

20. See Kris and Speier, *German Radio Propaganda.* This project's methods relied on word counts ("words connoting bravery," mentions of Hitler's name and those of enemy leaders, etc.), the quantification of particular sentence types (such as "non-military process sentences"), and the number of references to particular topics (German culture; British vs. German morale; youth and age stereotypes; national attributes; etc.); it then correlated these findings with the course of the war and its various, specific military campaigns from the invasion of Poland to the battle of Stalingrad, to find that "the decline of Nazi propaganda [preceded] that of the German army" (vii).

21. This was specifically Charles Siepmann's concern in response to a 1940 report titled "Research in Mass Communications." See Gary, *Nervous Liberals,* 104.

22. Decherney, *Hollywood and the Culture Elite.* On the "Communications Group," see note 13 above.

23. Karsten Witte notes that the discussion of the masses in the 1937 propaganda work incontrovertibly forms "a hinge between his Weimar essay 'The Mass Ornament' of 1927 and his New York film history *From Caligari to Hitler* of 1947" (Witte, "Siegfried Kracauer im Exil," *Exilforschung* 5 [1987]: 141).

24. According to Decherney (*Hollywood and the Culture Elite*, 151), in fact, "the attention to data without general theory is largely the point. Kracauer was interested in identifying the functions of enemy propaganda for some of the same reasons that Goebbels studied *Potemkin:* both to decode it and to reapply its methods in the service of a different ideology."

25. These are section headings from the published version.

26. Marshall, Diary entry, January 28, 1942, RAC. The section outlining the concepts and scheme of the "structural analysis" is doubtless among the least important contributions of Kracauer's propaganda study, and presumably for that reason was omitted from the most recent, revised and otherwise *expanded* edition of *From Caligari to Hitler*. Although Kracauer adopted it for a later essay ("The Conquest of Europe on the Screen: The Nazi Newsreel 1939–40," *Social Research* 10, no. 1 [January 1943]: 38), and although he harbored hopes that it would be taken up by other research projects, the scheme he develops suffers from excessive and idiosyncratic coding of various "units" and an apparent attempt to bend his interpretive skills to suit the perceived demands of "process research" and the quantitative methods employed by Kris and Speier, among others. This said, it is difficult to overlook the explicit structuralist impulse, the efforts at identifying syntagmatic and paradigmatic patterns, in a study that significantly predates the structuralist turn in film theory inaugurated by figures like Umberto Eco, Roland Barthes, and especially Christian Metz. See, e.g., Metz, "Le cinéma : Langue ou langage ?" *Communications* 4, no. 1 (1964): 52–90.

27. Erwin Panofsky, Letter to Kracauer, August 18, 1942, in *Kracauer, Panofsky: Briefwechsel 1941–1966*, 11.

28. Although this approach undoubtedly derives from Kracauer's and others' explicit hopes that their findings might be operationalized for "the purposes of psychological warfare" (Kracauer, *From Caligari to Hitler*, 274), it is worth noting that Kracauer's interest here is as much in the way Nazism employed propaganda to wage psychological war against its own population, which it reduced to a "chain-gang of souls," as in the potential application of his insights by the U.S. Office of Strategic Services (the wartime precursor of the CIA), where the brochure circulated on its completion in 1942. In a letter of July 1, 1942, Charleton F. Scofield mentions having borrowed the pamphlet from Frank Capra and expresses his wish to own a copy himself (RG 1.1, Series 200R, Box 251, Folder 2992, RAC).

29. Kracauer, "Propaganda and the Nazi War Film," 281.

30. Ibid., 306.

31. Ibid., 278.

32. Siegfried Kracauer, "Totalitäre Propaganda," in *Studien zu Massenmedien und Propaganda*, ed. Christian Fleck and Bernd Stiegler, Werke 2.2 (Frankfurt am Main: Suhrkamp, 2012), 113.

33. Joseph Goebbels, "Dr. Goebbels' Speech at the Kaiserhof on March 28, 1933," in *German Essays on Film*, ed. Richard W. McCormick and Alison Guenther-Pal (New York: Continuum, 2004), 154.

34. Kracauer, "Propaganda and the Nazi War Film," 279; Hans Speier, "Magic Geography," *Social Research* 8, no. 3 (Fall 1941): 310–30.

35. Kracauer, "Propaganda and the Nazi War Film," 298. "Although Kracauer emphasizes from the start that the newsreel and for the most part the campaign films, too, draw almost exclusively on authentic footage from the front, his main reproach—that they are lacking in 'reality'—runs through the study from beginning to end" (Ingrid Belke, "Das 'Geheimnis' des Faschismus liegt in der Weimarer Republik: Der Kunsthistoriker Meyer Schapiro über Kracauers erstes Film-Buch," *Filmexil* 4 (1994): 39.

36. Kracauer, "Propaganda and the Nazi War Film," 292.

37. Ibid., 288.

38. Ibid., 299.

39. On the propaganda function of maps, see Speier, "Magic Geography," which comes out of the Research Project on Totalitarian Communication, with which Kracauer was loosely affiliated while working on "Propaganda and the Nazi War Film."

40. Kracauer, "Propaganda and the Nazi War Film," 278–88.

41. Ibid., 297.

42. Ibid., 296.

43. Ibid., 306.

44. Ibid., 295.

45. Ibid., 307.

46. See Siegfried Kracauer, "'Marseiller Entwurf': Zu einer Theorie des Films," in *Theorie des Films. Die Errettung der äußeren Wirklichkeit*, Werke 3 (Frankfurt am Main: Suhrkamp, 2005), 521–779. Cf. Miriam Hansen, "'With Skin and Hair': Kracauer's Theory of Film, Marseille 1940," *Critical Inquiry* 19 (Spring 1995): 437–69.

47. Kracauer, *Theory of Film*, 88. In this context it is worth noting, however, that an article-length study of Nazi newsreels that Kracauer published shortly after "Propaganda and the Nazi War Film" in the New School's journal *Social Research* contained a few paragraphs on cinematic realism as "a truly cinematic procedure," which appear to derive directly from the Marseille notebooks. The passage recurs almost verbatim in the introduction to *From Caligari to Hitler*, and it condenses the broader argument of *Theory of Film*. See Kracauer, "Conquest of Europe on the Screen."

48. Kracauer, "Propaganda and the Nazi War Film," 281.

49. Ibid., 305. Referencing William Shirer's *Berlin Diary*, Kracauer does note, however, that the Nazis screened footage detailing death and destruction for foreign journalists, as if to taunt the world with the "war horrors" that the German army was capable of inflicting. For a radically different way of treating death in a campaign film, see the famous sequence—one of the most famous in Japanese film history—of the dying horse in Kamei Fumio's 1939 war documentary *Fighting Soldiers*. As Markus Nornes points out, the scene "provokes our recognition of the ontological difference of the documentary image of

death" (Nornes, *Japanese Documentary Film: The Meiji Era through Hiroshima* [Minneapolis: University of Minnesota Press, 2003], 166–67).

50. André Bazin, "Death Every Afternoon," in *Rites of Realism: Essays on Corporeal Cinema*, ed. Ivone Margulies, trans. Mark A. Cohen (Durham, N.C.: Duke University Press, 2003), 30.

51. Kracauer, "'Marseiller Entwurf'"; on this motif, see also Hansen, "'With Skin and Hair.'"

52. Kracauer, "Propaganda and the Nazi War Film," 306.

53. "Leningrad Hailed by Soviet Writers," *New York Times*, February 26, 1942, cited in Kracauer, "Propaganda and the Nazi War Film," 296.

54. Kracauer, "Propaganda and the Nazi War Film," 288.

55. Ibid., 298.

56. Ibid., 295.

57. Ibid., 303.

58. Ibid. Sontag at one point adopts verbatim (without citing) and at others draws liberally on Kracauer's analysis in "Propaganda and the Nazi War Film." Sontag's version of Kracauer's mirror maze reads: "*Triumph of the Will* represents an already achieved and radical transformation of reality: history become theater. How the 1934 Party convention was staged was partly determined by the decision to produce *Triumph of the Will*—the historic event serving as the set of a film which was then to assume the character of an authentic documentary" (Sontag, "Fascinating Facism," in *Under the Sign of Saturn* [New York: Farrar, Straus & Giroux, 1980], 83).

59. In Adorno's assessment for the *Zeitschrift*, the gloves come off: "The study is neither of actual theoretical value nor is it sufficiently founded in empirical material, but it does occasionally express certain experiences and observations in eminently useful literary formulations; these are valid above and beyond the outsider [*outsiderhafte*] position of the author" (Adorno, "Gutachten über die Arbeit 'Die totalitäre Propaganda Deutschlands und Italiens,' S. 1 bis S. 106, von Siegfried Kracauer," in Kracauer, *Studien zu Massenmedien und Propaganda*, 821).

60. Letter from Kracauer to Adorno, August 20, 1938, in Adorno and Kracauer, "*Der Riß der Welt . . . ,*" 398.

61. Letter from Adorno to Kracauer, September 12, 1938," ibid., 401.

62. Although the typescript that Kracauer sent to Adorno and Horkheimer in New York is considered lost, the editors of Kracauer's collected works were able to painstakingly reconstruct a complete version of the text from a surviving manuscript and Kracauer's systematic bibliographical work. See Kracauer, "Totalitäre Propaganda."

63. Siegfried Kracauer, "Hollywood's Terror Films: Do They Reflect an American State of Mind? (1946)" and "Those Movies with a Message (1948)," in *Siegfried Kracauer's American Writings*, 41–46 and 72–80, respectively.

64. "Kracauer neither belongs to us in any binding way as far as his theoretical disposition is concerned, nor can he be considered a scholarly author at

all as far as his working methods are concerned" (Adorno, "Gutachten über die Arbeit 'Die totalitäre Propaganda Deutschlands und Italiens,'" 821). Given the at times tenuous relations between the two men, I am inclined to take Adorno's demurral as symptomatic, an effect deriving from the narcissism of small differences.

65. Kracauer, "The Mass Ornament," 75.

66. Kracauer, "Totalitäre Propaganda," 20.

67. "Many measures of totalitarian propaganda are calculated purely to fascinate aesthetically. [It] takes care to pique visual pleasure and seduce into contemplation. It continually transforms solvable problems into unproblematic images [. . .] and strikes ornamental effects from questionable situations—effects that are too beautiful to still permit the situations to produce any effects. The aestheticizing of propaganda aims at anesthetizing the masses" (ibid., 75).

68. The link to the Institute project is further strengthened by Adorno's extensive reworking of "Totalitäre Propaganda," which he significantly retitles "Zur Theorie der autoritären Propaganda"—the "authoritarian" personality being the central concern of the later Studies in Prejudice. See Theodor Adorno, "Zusammenfassung der gekürzten Fassung von 'Totalitäre Propaganda,'" in Kracauer, *Studien zu Massenmedien und Propaganda*, 825–26.

69. Kracauer, "Totalitäre Propaganda," 72.

70. Adorno, "Zusammenfassung der gekürzten Fassung," 826.

71. Kracauer, "Totalitäre Propaganda," 90.

72. Ibid., 80.

73. Kracauer draws the notion of unpredictability from Erich Fromm's contributions to *Studien über Autorität und Familie*; see ibid., 80–81.

74. See Kracauer, "Conquest of Europe on the Screen"; Siegfried Kracauer and Joseph Lyford, "A Duck Crosses Main Street," *New Republic*, December 13, 1938.

CHAPTER 3

1. "An fremdem Ort erscheint, was aufs eigene Konto zu setzen ware." Kracauer, *Studien zu Massenmedien und Propaganda*, 70.

2. Kracauer, "Totalitäre Propaganda," 71.

3. Kracauer's synopses are reproduced in "Deutsche Filme," *Studien zu Massenmedien und Propaganda* 409–31..

4. Robespierre's terror, Danton suggests in the film, proceeds by "intoxicat[ing] people with blood . . . to suppress in them the memory of freedom, to change them into drunken slaves of . . . dictatorship."

5. The others were *Ohm Krüger* (1941), for which the predicate was invented; *Der große König* (1942); *Die Entlassung* (1942); and the infamous, last-ditch *Kolberg* (1945).

6. Details on the film can be found in Gerald Trimmel's monograph *Heimkehr: Strategien eines nationalsozialistischen Films* (Vienna: W. Eichbauer Verlag, 1998). While the following analysis is indebted to Trimmel's book for a

number of facts, his quantifying and somewhat positivistic approach tends to block, rather than reveal, insights into the historical logic of images with which I am concerned here—and which, I argue, Kracauer's propaganda analysis helps to pinpoint.

7. "Großes Zeitdokument," in *Filmwoche* 47/48 (1941), quoted in Rolf Giesen and Manfred Hobsch, *Hitlerjunge Quex, Jud Süss und Kolberg. Die Propagandafilme des Dritten Reiches: Dokumente und Materialien zum NS-Film* (Berlin: Schwarzkopf & Schwarzkopf, 2005), 349. "Staatspolitisch und künstlerisch besonders wertvoll" (especially valuable in terms of state policy and aesthetics) was an official designation handed out by the state along with its system of *Prädikate*, or ratings, for major films. For more on this system, see David Welch, *Propaganda and the German Cinema, 1933–1945* (London: I.B. Tauris, 2001), 15–16.

8. Quoted in Trimmel, *Heimkehr*, 63.

9. Notably, these resettlements did *not* bring the Germans back to the so-called *Altreich*, Germany in the borders of 1933, but to the German-occupied western part of Poland. To the degree that *Heimkehr* is designed to quell any political discontent over these resettlement policies, it could be compared to Wolfgang Liebeneiner's notorious *Ich klage an*. Liebeneiner's melodrama was designed among other things to put to rest public concerns over the so-called T4 euthanasia program, which had come under pressure after its existence became public knowledge. I thank Phillip Stiasny for pointing this out to me.

10. This scene consequently picks up where the immensely successful *Wunschkonzert* (1940) had left off: narration, sound, and editing in the latter film had been carefully designed to illustrate (and emulate) the role of radio in the formation of the *Volksgemeinschaft*. See David Bathrick, "Making a National Family with the Radio: The Nazi *Wunschkonzert*," *Modernism/Modernity* 4, no. 1 (1997): 115–27.

11. On the function of Heimat in *Heimkehr*, see Johannes von Moltke, *No Place Like Home: Locations of Heimat in German Cinema* (Berkeley: University of California Press, 2005).

12. Goebbels, quoted in Trimmel, *Heimkehr*, 63.

13. Kracauer emphasizes the formal qualities of propaganda and their subject-effects: "'Original power of rhythm.' [. . .] One shapes arbitrary material to produce shocks to stave off any slackening of tension, and transmits propaganda waves that can be made to rise gradually or ebb suddenly as needed; in any event, one ensures the effective coordination of tempos. It is the rhythmic aspect of their development that lends propagandistic significance to these events: the artistic sequence of rest and action, pressure and attraction. If in the past the proclamation of appealing substantive goals was crucial, today one attempts to accomplish the psychophysical constitution appropriate to pseudo-reality through the forms in which propaganda instantiates the requisite actions and claims" (Kracauer, "Totalitäre Propaganda," 169).

14. This is not to suggest that the mistreatment of Germans by Poles is a freely invented fiction and that the latter were blameless. Poles did invalidate

German land leases, they closed German private schools and arrested several hundred German men at the beginning of the war, deporting them as far as the Berez Kartuska concentration camp. See Ortfried Kotzian, *Die Umsiedler. Die Deutschen aus West-Wolhynien, Galizien, der Bukowina, Bessarbien, der Dobrudscha und in der Karpatenukraine* (Munich: Langen Müller, 2005), 54. The brazen and cynical nature of *Heimkehr* as a propaganda film, then, lies in the way it puts pressure on these historical realities, dramatically exaggerates and illustrates them through particular visual material—and suppresses the fact that the increasing pressure on Germans in Poland was itself a reaction to German war mongering.

15. Kracauer, "Totalitäre Propaganda," 69.

16. Ibid., 69–70.

17. The first transport of Polish prisoners arrived in Auschwitz on July 14, 1940. See Bogdan Musial, "Das Schlachtfeld zweier totalitärer Systeme: Polen unter deutscher und sowjetischer Herrschaft 1939–1941," in *Genesis des Genozids. Polen 1939–1941*, ed. Klaus-Michael Mallmann and Bogdan Musial (Darmstadt: Wissenschaftliche Buchgesellschaft, 2004).

18. Trimmel, *Heimkehr*, 53.

19. "An fremden Orten erscheint, was aufs eigene Konto zu setzen wäre" (Kracauer, "Totalitäre Propaganda," 70).

20. See Eric Rentschler, *The Ministry of Illusion: Nazi Cinema and Its Afterlife* (Cambridge, Mass.: Harvard University Press, 1996), 125–40.

21. This logic is not restricted to the cinema or to film analysis; it has also been confirmed by historical investigations of Nazi propaganda, which have found similar projections of fantasies of guilt and fear, according to which enemy deeds ostensibly repeat the Nazis' own atrocities. Particularly in the final phase of the war, both official discourse and the secret reports on German mentality gathered by the Sicherheitsdienst establish a connection between German war crimes and genocide, on the one hand, and the acts—imagined or real—of the enemy, on the other. In September 1944, Goebbels instructs the press to continue spreading antisemitic propaganda, but emphasizes that it would be "unhelpful to speak of 'Jewish revenge,'" for this could lead weaker minds to the impression that there might be a correspondence to the Germans' own deeds. Goebbels's instructions unwittingly betray a repressed knowledge of the logic that he wishes to censure: "As is well known, revenge assumes a previously inflicted injustice. Consequently, we will only speak of a Jewish annihilation campaign and consistently point out that the Jews have always been the aggressor and that our own measures were merely designed as a defense for our survival" (Peter Longerich, *"Davon haben wir nichts gewusst!" Die Deutschen und die Judenverfolgung 1933–1945* [Munich: Siedler, 2006], 309). Shortly thereafter, the Soviet advance into eastern Prussia led to the murder of German civilians. But when German propagandists attempted to capitalize on these murders by making them public and criticizing them, the German population considered this "shameless," according to secret reports; for they did not fail to see the relation between precedent German acts and the reactions of

the wartime enemy: "Any thinking person who sees these blood sacrifices [i.e., murdered German civilians] will immediately think of the atrocities we have committed in enemy territory and even in Germany. Haven't we slaughtered the Jews by the thousands? [. . .] The Jews are also human beings. So we showed the enemy what they can do to us should they carry the victory" (ibid., 310). If, as Adorno and Horkheimer had claimed, the Nazis unconsciously "expressed their own essence" in the image of the Jew, we could rephrase the same logic with regard to the relation between film and history in *Heimkehr*: in its image of the ethnic Germans, the filmmakers unconsciously express the essence of antisemitism. It represents the latter allegorically, in the distorting mirror of Polish atrocities enacted upon German minorities. *Heimkehr* in this sense operates a rather frightening reversal of the projection of self onto other—it is a perfidious film that finds the images for the persecution of Germans precisely in the iconographic repertoire that now constitutes the visual archive of the Holocaust.

22. Linda Schulte-Sasse, *Entertaining the Third Reich: Illusions of Wholeness in Nazi Cinema* (Durham, N.C.: Duke University Press, 1996), 48.

23. Rentschler, *Ministry of Illusion*, 163. If we follow this logic of projection as well as the corresponding aesthetic strategies in Harlan's film, it is difficult to avoid concluding, as Rentschler does, that "in order to feel their own existence and confirm their won reality, the Nazis needed the Jews" (154).

24. Joseph Goebbels, "Mimicry," in *Die Zeit ohne Beispiel. Reden und Aufsätze aus den Jahren 1939/40/41* (Munich: Zentralverlag der NSDAP, 1941), 526–31.

25. Horkheimer and Adorno, *Dialectic of Enlightenment*, 151.

26. Ibid., 154. As they put it, "Hitler can gesticulate like a clown, Mussolini risk false notes like a provincial tenor, Goebbels talk as glibly as the Jewish agent whose murder he is recommending" (152). Drawing on Freudian categories, Adorno and Horkheimer reveal the logic of projection at work in the antisemitic construction of self and other. Pathic projection, they note, involves the "transference of socially tabooed impulses from the subject to the object"; antisemitic projection, which takes the Jews as its object, is "false" in the sense that subject and object crowd each other out: "The disorder lies in the subject's faulty distinction between his own contribution to the projected material and that of others" (154).

27. Ibid., 137.

28. In a letter of July 9, 1942, to Hans Speier, who had recently moved from the New School to Washington, D.C., Kracauer notes that the Office of Strategic Services was "seriously interested in my report." Correspondence to this effect made Kracauer "hopeful as to the consequences of my report, and I dream of the possibility that people at Washington ask my services as an expert" (DLA).

29. John Marshall, memo of March 12, 1942 Record Group 1.1, Series 200, Box 251, Folder 2990, RAC.

30. "I am shocked to read of the 'natural inclination of Germans for thinking in anti-rational mythological terms.' That is what the Nazis want the people to believe. [. . .] Your explanation of the superiority of German organization

by the passivity of the German people is another bit of ethno-psychology that I can't swallow; it is almost an inversion of the Nazi theory (which distinguishes active and passive peoples in history)" (Letter from Meyer Schapiro, August 12, 1942, reprinted in Belke, "Das 'Geheimnis' des Faschismus," 41).

31. Ibid., 40.

32. Hans Speier, "On Propaganda," *Social Research* 1, no. 3 (1934): 377.

33. Kracauer, Letter to Adorno, August 20, 1938, in Adorno and Kracauer, "*Der Riß der Welt...,*" 398.

34. For this insight I draw heavily on Belke, "Das 'Geheimnis' des Faschismus."

35. Kracauer, "Propaganda and the Nazi War Film," 305.

36. Kracauer, *From Caligari to Hitler*, 8, 9.

37. Brett Gary points out that the "sharp distinction between education (the pursuit of truth) and propaganda (never adequate as the truth and usually deceptive)" was endemic to communications research under the aegis of the Rockefeller Foundation in the 1940s. However, as Gary also notes, important figures such as Harold Lasswell could and did argue in favor of what they conceived as "a *genuinely democratic propaganda.*" See Gary, *Nervous Liberals*, 91, 93 (emphasis in original).

38. This and the following quotes are from a letter to Paul Lazarsfeld, November 23, 1942, DLA.

39. Hannah Arendt, "Understanding and Politics (The Difficulties of Understanding)," in *Essays in Understanding, 1930–1954: Formation, Exile, and Totalitarianism* (New York: Schocken, 1944), 309–10.

40. Letter to Robert Van Gelder at the *New York Times*, June 28, 1943, DLA. Already a year earlier he had confided to Hans Speier, one of the founders of the University in Exile at the New School for Social Research, that he "dream[t] of the possibility that people at [sic] Washington ask my services as an expert." See also Kracauer's letter of May 12, 1945, to Donald Slesinger at the American Film Center, in which he outlines plans for future work and indicates that his work on Nazi film propaganda was "of some help for the production of our Army Morale films" (DLA).

41. Kracauer, *From Caligari to Hitler*, v. This passage was added late in the editing process (Kracauer, Letter to Jean Maclachlan, Princeton University Press, August 29, 1946, Princeton University Press Archives); like much of Kracauer's work at the time, it has both a theoretical and a pragmatic dimension in that it is designed not only to outline a horizon for the approach that he sketches in the book, but also to suggest ways in which Kracauer himself might be employed.

42. Orville Prescott, reviewing Brickner, *Is Germany Incurable?*, in "Books of the Times" *New York Times*, April 28, 1943, 21. Kracauer was familiar with both Brickner's book and Prescott's review, of which he kept a copy among his clippings for the work on *From Caligari to Hitler*.

43. "Preliminary Report on My Project, 'The History of German Film,'" typescript in DLA.

CHAPTER 4

1. Elliot Cohen, "An Act of Affirmation: Editorial Statement." *Commentary* 1, no. 1 (November 1945): 1.

2. Ibid.

3. In this, *Commentary* could draw during its early years on the army of qualified freelance writers without regular jobs; and it benefited from the contacts and patterns established by the *Contemporary Jewish Record*, which it incorporated. The AJC sponsorship, moreover, helped to ensure not only a readership but also a community from which to draw authors. See Nathan Glazer, "*Commentary:* The Early Years," in *"Commentary" in American Life*, ed. Murray Friedman (Philadelphia: Temple University Press, 2005), 45.

4. Cohen, "Act of Affirmation," 3. Robert Warshow would join the group in July 1946; see Glazer, "*Commentary:* The Early Years," 44.

5. Glazer, "*Commentary:* The Early Years," 42. Authors included, among others, George Orwell; the distinguished Jewish historian Salo Baron, professor at Columbia University; Percy Corbett, professor of political science at Yale; the philosopher Franz Rosenzweig (posthumously), whose 1920 open letter to Hermann Cohen, "On Being a Jewish Person," was translated here for the first time; the journalists Sidney Hertzberg, formerly of the *New York Times* and *Time* magazine, and James Rorty—the latter reporting on an AJC-sponsored project on antisemitism being carried out by the Institute for Social Research under the aegis of Max Horkheimer and Leo Löwenthal; the influential art critic Harold Rosenberg; the Austrian émigré writer Hertha Pauli; novelist and *Esquire* movie critic Meyer Levin; the novelist and critic Mary McCarthy; the poet Randall Jarrell, critically reviewing poetry that satirized the perpetrators of the Holocaust; and, from the editorial team, the young Nathan Glazer, who inaugurated a regular column titled "The Study of Man."

6. "*Commentary* would be a Jewish magazine—after all, the AJC was paying for it—but it was at the same time to be a general magazine" (ibid., 41).

7. Letter from Clement Greenberg, March 27, 1946, DLA.

8. The original manuscript entitled "Freedom from Fear: An Analysis of Popular Film Trends" is reproduced in Siegfried Kracauer, *Kleine Schriften zum Film, 1932–1961*, 479–85. As I discuss below, the prominent reference to Roosevelt's 1941 "Four Freedoms" speech (see n. 20 below) in the original title was deliberate, given the article's underlying contention that the "movies . . . reflect popular tendencies and inclinations," that the cinema is a seismograph of the soul, and that Hollywood unwittingly paints a picture of politics.

9. Warshow, who died young at age thirty-eight in 1955, would correspond with Kracauer on numerous occasions in his role on the editorial boards of both *Commentary* and *Partisan Review;* he would also become a reader of Kracauer's manuscript for *Theory of Film*. By 1953, relations had clearly warmed to the point where Kracauer could describe the younger man as "my friend Warshow" in a letter to the editor James Laughlin (April 1, 1953, DLA).

10. Kracauer, "Hollywood's Terror Films," 41.

11. Ibid.

12. Ibid.

13. Ibid., 42, 46.

14. Edward Dimendberg, "Down These Seen Streets a Man Must Go: Siegfried Kracauer, 'Hollywood's Terror Films,' and the Spatiality of Film Noir," *New German Critique* 89 (2003): 124. Kracauer thus inaugurates an important, historicizing approach to *film noir* even before the authors of *Panorama du film noir américain*, the first book-length treatment of the subject, hold that "film noir is noir for us, that's to say, for Western and American audiences of the 1950s. It responds to a certain kind of emotional resonance as singular in time as it is in space" (Raymond Borde, Etienne Chaumeton, and Marcel Duhamel, *Panorama du film noir américain, 1941–1953* [Paris: Flammarion, 1988], quoted in William Luhr, *Film Noir*, [Chichester, West Sussex: Wiley-Blackwell, 2012], 53). In subsequent work in this vein, to pick two examples, Dimendberg historicizes *films noirs* by locating them in relationship to contemporary developments/discourses in architecture and urban development; and Polan links its narratives specifically to wartime political conditions. See Edward Dimendberg, *Film Noir and the Spaces of Modernity* (Cambridge, Mass.: Harvard University Press, 2004); and Dana Polan, *Power and Paranoia: History, Narrative, and the American Cinema, 1940–1950* (New York: Columbia University Press, 1986).

15. Kracauer, "Hollywood's Terror Films," 44–45.

16. Ibid., 45.

17. Ibid.

18. Dimendberg, "Down These Seen Streets."

19. Hannah Arendt, "No Longer and Not Yet," in *Essays in Understanding*, 159.

20. Roosevelt's 1941 State of the Union address to Congress was designed to articulate the values on behalf of which the United States was "meeting the foreign peril" by increasing its arms production and its involvement in international conflict, before joining WWII itself later that year in the wake of Pearl Harbor. The address has become known as the "Four Freedoms" speech for articulating four "essential human freedoms" as the basis for the "future days which we seek to make secure: freedom of speech, freedom of religion, freedom from want, and freedom from fear." (Ironically, in an argument for ramping up wartime production, FDR defines "freedom from fear" largely in terms of arms reduction.) For the text of Roosevelt's speech, see www.fdrlibrary.marist.edu/pdfs/ffreadingcopy.pdf.

21. Hannah Arendt, "Home to Roost: A Bicentennial Address," *New York Review of Books*, June 26, 1975; quoted in Ira Katznelson, *Fear Itself: The New Deal and the Origins of Our Time* (W.W. Norton, 2013), 7.

22. E. B. White, Letter to the *New York Herald Tribune*, quoted in the epigraph to Katznelson, *Fear Itself*.

23. Katznelson, *Fear Itself*, 50.

24. See Leo Lowenthal and Norbert Guterman, *Prophets of Deceit: A Study of the Techniques of the American Agitator* (New York: Harper, 1949), which in

the preface explicitly thanks Kracauer for his "valuable suggestions on methodological and sociological problems" (xvii).

25. Mark Greif, *The Age of the Crisis of Man: Thought and Fiction in America, 1933–1973* (Princeton, N.J.: Princeton University Press, 2015).

26. Kracauer, *From Caligari to Hitler*, 11.

27. To the degree that these debates centered on Germany, they often took the diagnostic form of a sociomedical problem in search of a "cure," as in Richard Brickner's influential 1943 book *Is Germany Incurable?* But as Anton Kaes points out, the various proposals put forward in this extensive reeducation debate (prior to the implementation of any postwar policies) "shed light on a cultural dynamic that had as much to do with the construction of an American identity . . . as with the German national character" (Kaes, "What to Do with Germany?" *German Politics and Society* 13, no. 3 [Fall 1995]: 132). For extensive discussions of this dynamic, see also Jennifer Fay, *Theaters of Occupation* (Minneapolis: University of Minnesota Press, 2008); and Jennifer M. Kapczynski, *The German Patient: Crisis and Recovery in Postwar Culture* (Ann Arbor: University of Michigan Press, 2011).

28. For the following, see Benjamin Alpers, *Dictators, Democracy, and American Public Culture: Envisioning the Totalitarian Enemy, 1920s–1950s* (Chapel Hill: University of North Carolina Press, 2003). I am grateful to Giorgio Bertellini for emphasizing the importance of Mussolini to these developments, which has arguably been overshadowed by, though it predated, the role that German Nazism played in the American consciousness.

29. On the anti-Nazi film, see Sabine Hake, *Screen Nazis: Cinema, History, and Democracy* (Madison: University of Wisconsin Press, 2012), 32–65.

30. I will discuss the most influential of these, *The Authoritarian Personality*, in the following chapter. For a contemporary overview and assessment of four representative studies, see Himelhoch, "Is There a Bigot Personality? A Report on Some Preliminary Studies," *Commentary*, January 1947, 277–84.

31. Himelhoch, "Is There a Bigot Personality?," 284.

32. Max Horkheimer, "Introduction," in Lowenthal and Guterman, *Prophets of Deceit*, xiii.

33. Ibid., xi.

34. Lowenthal and Guterman, *Prophets of Deceit*, 140.

35. Quoted in Ben Urwand, *The Collaboration: Hollywood's Pact with Hitler* (Cambridge, Mass.: Belknap Press, 2013), 165; originally in "Lewis Says Hays Bans Film of Book," *New York Times*, February 16, 1936. For more on the Hollywood fate of Lewis's novel, see ibid., 161–77.

36. Gary, *Nervous Liberals*, 5.

37. Lasswell, "The Garrison State," *American Journal of Sociology* 46, no. 4 (1941): 459.

38. Editors, "The Crisis of the Individual: A Series," *Commentary* 1, no. 2 (December 1945): 1–2.

39. Sidney Hook, "Intelligence and Evil in Human History: An Answer to Intellectual Defeatism," *Commentary* 3, no. 3 (March 1947): 210–21. For

conservative positions, see in particular Hans Kohn, "This Century of Betrayal: Can America Lead a New Struggle for Independence?" *Commentary* 2, no. 3 (September 1946): 201–8; and William A. Orton, "Everyman amid the Stereotypes," *Commentary* 1, no. 7 (May 1946): 9–16. Taking an unabashedly humanist position, the Nobel laureate Pearl Buck saw "the human being today [as] more unhappy, more lost, than he has ever been in all history.... He feels that life is increasingly threatened, and the miracles which he works only leave him more sad and more fearful for himself.... He is only terrified by what he has done" (Buck, "The Solitary," *Commentary* 1, no. 6 [April 1946]: 8). The historian Hans Kohn drew on Valéry to highlight the same motifs of uncertainty and fear; see Kohn, "This Century of Betrayal," 203.

40. John Dewey, "The Crisis in Human History," *Commentary* 1, no. 5 (March 1946): 5.

41. Hannah Arendt, "Imperialism: Road to Suicide," *Commentary* 1, no. 2 (December 1945): 31. See also Arendt, *Origins of Totalitarianism*, 139–47.

42. Paul Valéry, Address delivered at the University of Zurich, November 15, 1922, in *Sources of European History: Since 1900*, ed. By Marvin Perry, Matthew Berg and James Krukones, 2nd ed. (Boston: Wadsworth, 2011), 78.

43. Löwenthal, "Terror's Atomization of Man," *Commentary* 1, no. 3 (January 1946): 1–8.

44. Ibid., 3. Orton's contribution sounds a similar motif, the "thinness of the average individual life experience" and the loss of memory, albeit from a differently inflected political perspective: although he draws on Alfred North Whitehead's analysis, just as Kracauer will in *Theory of Film*, unlike Kracauer he faults precisely the movies for this demise, and holds out hope for a profoundly conservative restoration of the humanist tradition, calling for a "training" that integrates the "developing personality within a coherent system of values, manners and morals" (Orton, "Everyman amid the Stereotypes," 14).

45. Löwenthal, "Terror's Atomization of Man," 7. Indeed, even Arendt had gestured in this direction when, in her contribution to the *Commentary* series ("Imperialism"), she located at least the potential for terror in the liberal social contract as theorized by Hobbes.

46. Löwenthal, "Terror's Atomization of Man," 7.

47. Katznelson, *Fear Itself*, 43, 30. Katznelson identifies three acute sources of fear in this era: the worry that liberal democracy could not compete successfully with the dictatorships; the fear unleashed by exponential growth in sophisticated weaponry; and fears stemming from the racial structure of the South.

48. Ibid., 92.

49. Cf. Beck, *Risk Society*; Giddens, *The Consequences of Modernity*.

50. Reddy, *The Navigation of Feeling*, 124.

51. Katznelson, *Fear Itself*, 33.

52. Kracauer, "Hollywood's Terror Films," 46.

53. See, e.g., Reinhold Niebuhr's opening volley in *Commentary*'s series "The Crisis of the Individual," where he locates that crisis between two forms of secularized religion—one of which "made the individual self-sufficient to

the point of making man the idolatrous end of his own existence. The other religion made society the idolatrous end of the existence of the individual" (Niebuhr, "Will Civilization Survive Technics?" *Commentary* 1, no. 2 [December 1945]: 6). Unlike Kracauer, Niebuhr ultimately seeks a spiritual solution to this dichotomy.

54. Kracauer, "Those Movies with a Message," 78.
55. Kracauer, "Hollywood's Terror Films," 43, 44.

CHAPTER 5

1. This ambiguity was erased in the first, tendentious translation of the text into German as "Von Caligari bis Hitler" (i.e., from Caligari *until* Hitler).
2. Kappelhoff, *Realismus*, 59.
3. Eric Bentley, "The Cinema: Its Art and Techniques," *New York Times Book Review*, May 18, 1947.
4. See "Geschichtsschreibung und Geschichtsphilosophie," a presumably unpublished 1926 review for the *Frankfurter Zeitung*, in *Essays, Feuilletons, Rezensionen, 1924—1927*, ed. Inka Mülder-Bach, Werke 5.2 (Berlin: Suhrkamp, 2011), 512–17. Notably, Kracauer's own 1927 essay on photography, which he would reference in the introduction to *History*, engaged in important ways with question of historicity, historicism, and historiography; see Kracauer, "Photography," in *The Mass Ornament*, 47–64. See also Nicholas Baer, "Historical Turns: On Caligari, Kracauer, and New Film History," in *Film und Geschichte. Produktion und Erfahrung von Geschichte durch Bewegtbild und Ton*, ed. Delia González de Reufels, Rasmus Greiner, and Winfried Pauleit (Berlin: Bertz + Fischer, 2015), 127–37.
5. Kracauer, *History*, 87.
6. Siegfried Kracauer, "Climate of Doom," review of *The Dragon in the Forest* by Richard Plant, *New Republic*, March 7, 1949. Noah Isenberg points out the echoes between Plant's novel and *From Caligari to Hitler* in "This Pen for Hire," 37.
7. Gertrud Koch, "'Not Yet Accepted Anywhere': Exile, Memory, and Image in Kracauer's Conception of History," trans. Jeremy Gaines, *New German Critique*, no. 54 (October 1991): 97.
8. Thomas Elsaesser, *Das Weimarer Kino. Aufgeklärt und doppelbödig* (Berlin: Vorwerk 8, 1999), 10.
9. Arendt, "Understanding and Politics," 309.
10. Arendt, *Origins of Totalitarianism*, preface to part III, xxiv.
11. Arendt, "Understanding and Politics," 319.
12. Ibid.
13. Sabina Loriga draws a connection between Arendt's and Kracauer's historiographic projects in their early works, showing how her biography on Rahel Varnhagen and his on Jacques Offenbach are "founded on a reading against the grain *[à rebours]*" that is "resolutely anachronistic" (Loriga, "L'histoire mode de vie. Reflexions autour de Hannah Arendt et Siegfried Kracauer," in *Penser*

l'histoire: De Marx aux siècles des catastrophes, ed. Christophe Bouton and Bruce Bégout [Paris: Éd. de l'Éclat, 2011], 213).

14. Kracauer, *From Caligari to Hitler,* 11.

15. For the former, see Kappelhoff, *Realismus;* see also his description of *From Caligari to Hitler* as "eines der wirkungsmächtigsten Zeugnisse für ein historisches Verfahren . . . , das nicht zu rekonstruieren vorgibt, sondern von den Notwendigkeiten und Nöten der Gegenwart ausgehend die Genealogie dieser Gegenwart zu entwerfen versucht" (58). Also see Dagmar Barnouw's considerably less sanguine assessment in *Critical Realism: History, Photography, and the Work of Siegfried Kracauer* (Baltimore: Johns Hopkins University Press, 1994).

16. Quaresima, Introduction to *From Caligari to Hitler,* xxxix.

17. Ibid., xlii, xxxix.

18. Kracauer, *From Caligari to Hitler,* 93.

19. Kracauer, Letter to Erwin Panofsky, May 2, 1947, in *Kracauer, Panofsky: Briefwechsel 1941–1966,* 47.

20. "As Kracauer returns to his own past through the movies, he performs what war psychoanalyst Ernst Simmel suggested in 1918 that shell shock victims do in hypnosis: to let the past run by repeatedly—like a movie—in order to understand what caused the traumatic event. Were there signs in Weimar cinema that pointed to this catastrophic outcome? Were there hints he had overlooked? Although Kracauer before all critics had detected protofascist tendencies in Weimar cinema already in the late 1920s, his *post factum* readings are sealed with a certainty that leaves no alternatives or ambiguities. What critics have decried as teleological fallacy in his approach was nothing less than the frantic attempt to find the origins of what happened to him and his country. The original plan to write a social history of film became an opportunity to work through a personal and national trauma" (Anton Kaes, "Siegfried Kracauer: The Film Historian in Exile," in *"Escape to Life": German Intellectuals in New York; A Compendium on Exile after 1933,* ed. Eckart Goebel and Sigrid Weigel [Berlin: Walter de Gruyter, 2012], 244).

21. "Wichtig und einzukalkulieren: die Zeitbedingtheit der Interpretation selber" (Kracauer, "'Marseiller Entwurf' zu einer Theorie des Films," 529).

22. Unlike Barnouw, who considers *From Caligari to Hitler* to be "too directly influenced by Kracauer's work on Nazi film propaganda" (*Critical Realism,* 95–96), I contend that we must first understand the nature of this influence and evaluate it in the context of contemporary work on culture, politics, and society before dismissing the later book as too selective and narrow.

23. Quaresima, Introduction to *From Caligari to Hitler,* xviii. The absence of any reference to *From Caligari to Hitler* is as glaring in Miriam Hansen's *Cinema and Experience* as it is in the French collection that Quaresima mentions in this context, Nia Perivolaropoulou and Philippe Despoix, *Culture de masse et modernité. Siegfried Kracauer: Sociologue, critique, écrivain* (Paris: Éd. de la Maison des sciences de l'homme, 2001). Within Kracauer scholarship, only Gertrud Koch has sought to probe beneath the patina of critical neglect

that *From Caligari to Hitler* has accumulated over the years; see Koch, *Siegfried Kracauer: An Introduction*, 75–94. See also Michael Mack, "Film as Memory: Siegfried Kracauer's Psychological History of German 'National Culture,'" *Journal of European Studies* 30, no. 118 (June 2000): 157–81.

24. Erwin Panofsky, "Style and Medium in the Motion Pictures," in *Three Essays on Style*, ed. Irving Lavin (Cambridge, Mass.: MIT Press, 1995), 91–128. On the history of Panofsky's engagement with the movies and his relation to Kracauer, see Thomas Y. Levin, "Iconology at the Movies: Panofsky's Film Theory," *Yale Journal of Criticism* 9, no. 1 (Spring 1996): 27–55.

25. Panofsky, "Style and Medium," quoted in Kracauer, *From Caligari to Hitler*, 6.

26. Note that Kracauer at this point derives this "innate mission" of film *not* from its photographic properties, as he will later in *Theory of Film*, but from the particular malleability of the space-time-continuum in which "space itself moves, changing, turning, dissolving and recrystallizing" (*From Caligari to Hitler*, 6). In its emphasis on movement, scale, and duration, this is a far cry from the ontological realism that some have attributed to Kracauer.

27. Kracauer, *From Caligari to Hitler*, 75.

28. Kracauer, "Why France Liked Our Films," 35.

29. Panofsky, "Style and Medium," quoted in Kracauer, *From Caligari to Hitler*, 6.

30. Jules Romains, "The Crowd at the Cinematograph," in *French Film Theory and Criticism: A History/Anthology, 1907–1939*, ed. Ricahrd Abel, vol. 1: *1907–1929* (Princeton, N.J.: Princeton University Press, 1988), 53, excerpted from "La foule au cinématographe, in *Les puissances de Paris* (Paris: Eugène Figuière, 1911).

31. Kracauer, *From Caligari to Hitler*, 74.

32. Kracauer analyzed this brilliantly as a decaying form of second nature in the 1926 article "Calico World," in *The Mass Ornament*, 281–88.

33. Kracauer, *From Caligari to Hitler*, 186.

34. Ibid., 56–57.

35. Ibid., 91.

36. Ibid., 80–81.

37. Ibid., 74.

38. Ibid., 137.

39. Ibid., 138–52.

40. Ibid., 93.

41. One might usefully trace this analysis back to the spatial investigations of Kracauer's *Feuilleton* essays of the 1920s, with their interest in center and periphery ("Zur Analyse eines Stadtplans"), threatening urban spaces ("Straße ohne Erinnerung"), and the fear of enclosure that he discovers in Kafka's writings ("Foolish expectation—to be able to slip out in spite of it all! The doors have no keys, and any holes that might open are immediately walled up again" ["Zu Franz Kafkas nachgelassenen Schriften," in Kracauer, *Essays, Feuilletons, Rezensionen, 1924–1927*, 625]).

42. Kracauer explicitly diagnoses an entire "period of introvert films" in the early postwar era (see Kracauer, *From Caligari to Hitler*, 55), but in keeping with the spatial logics outlined above, the "two disparate tendencies" of introversion and extroversion continue to structure his account throughout the book.

43. Ibid., 165.

44. Ibid., 76.

45. Erich Fromm, *Escape from Freedom* (New York: Farrar & Rinehart, 1941). Kracauer cites Fromm in the introduction, and he indirectly quotes Fromm's analysis when he describes the enthusiasm of young men enlisting in the German army at the beginning of World War I as an "escape from vain freedom into a life under compelling pressure" (ibid., 20). For a detailed discussion of the role Fromm's psychoanalytic framework plays in Kracauer's book, see chapter 6 below.

46. Ibid.

47. Ibid., 166.

48. For a related account of centripetal and centrifugal organizations of urban and cinematic space, see Dimendberg, *Film Noir and the Spaces of Modernity*, which draws in part on Kracauer's earlier writings.

49. Thomas Elsaesser, *Weimar Cinema and After: Germany's Historical Imaginary* (London: Routledge, 2000), 31. Anton Kaes similarly notes that "in order to sustain the master narrative from Caligari to Hitler, Kracauer must downplay not only the diversity of Weimar production but also the aesthetic complexity of individual works. Films are never organic, unified wholes carrying a single message. Rather, they are fractured entities that must be read, like products of the unconscious, by means of their omissions and silences" *Shell Shock Cinema: Weimar Culture and the Wounds of War* (Princeton, N.J.: Princeton University Press, 2009), 5.

50. Polan, *Power and Paranoia*, 31.

51. Ibid.

52. "Was he writing about American movies after World War II," asks Kaes (*Shell Shock Cinema*, 214), "or rather about German cinema at the end of World War I, the subject of his study *From Caligari to* Hitler?"

53. Kracauer, *From Caligari to Hitler*, 74.

54. Kracauer, "Those Who Wait," in *The Mass Ornament*, 129–42.

55. Letter to C. Wright Mills, August 26, 1945, DLA.

56. Kracauer, *From Caligari to Hitler*, 116.

57. Ibid., 19. And see Max Horkheimer, *Eclipse of Reason* (New York: Seabury Press, 1974).

58. Kracauer, "Preliminary Report on my Project 'History of the German Film . . .' (1944)," DLA.

59. Such a critique is occasionally advanced even by well-meaning critics. Thus, for example, Leonardo Quaresima writes that Kracauer's "central, unequivocal position stifles the multiplicity of voices and the dynamic of his subjects" (Introduction to *From Caligari to Hitler*, xxxiii).

60. See Hansen, *Cinema and Experience*, 3–39.
61. See Arendt, "Understanding and Politics."

CHAPTER 6

1. Letter to Datus Smith, March 18, 1946, Princeton University Press Archives.
2. Kracauer, *From Caligari to Hitler*, 2004.
3. Ibid., 11.
4. See Fay, *Theaters of Occupation*, for how these approaches led to an understanding of film as a curative, pedagogical medium—indeed *the* medium of reeducation in Germany. See also Kaes, "What to Do with Germany?"; and Kapczynski, *The German Patient*.
5. C. Wright Mills, "The Nazi Behemoth Dissected," *Partisan Review* 9, no. 5 (September 1942): 432–37. Neumann subsequently moved to the Office of Strategic Services, where he joined other leading scholars of the time, including his Frankfurt School colleagues Herbert Marcuse and Otto Kirchheimer in the Research and Analysis Branch. This astonishing though short-lived unit in the predecessor organization to the CIA has been described as "the biggest American research institution in the first half of the twentieth century" (Raffaele Laudani, "Introduction," in *Secret Reports on Nazi Germany*, 2). Tim B. Müller likewise finds that "the expert knowledge in the strategic state apparatuses was far more precise and open to unexpected results than broad swaths of university-based research at the time" (Müller, *Krieger und Gelehrte: Herbert Marcuse und die Denksysteme im kalten Krieg* [Hamburg: Hamburger Edition, 2013], 118). The Research and Analysis Branch united an eclectic group of scholars whose political leanings covered the entire ideological spectrum; among these, the Frankfurt group distinguished itself by its progressive philosophical analyses. As one contemporary collaborator later recalled, "it was as if the left-Hegelian *Weltgeist* had taken up temporary residence in . . . the OSS" (John Herz, quoted in Laudani, "Introduction," 9). Devoted to topics ranging from antisemitism as the "spearhead of universal terror" (in Neumann's influential but controversial formulation) to the significance of Prussian militarism and German social stratification (Marcuse), these studies coincided with Kracauer's work in their attempts to elucidate the rise of fascism, its preconditions, and its effects. Though resulting from wide-ranging and politically open-ended discussions, they were part of a secret service epistemology (Müller, *Krieger und Gelehrte*, 49–59) that was clearly aimed at implementing both reeducation policy abroad and preventive measures against the rise of fascism in the United States.
6. Kracauer was also familiar, however, with Fromm's earlier elaboration of some of the psychoanalytic motifs of *Escape from Freedom* in "Theoretische Entwürfe über Autorität und Familie," his contribution to the Institut für Sozialforschung's first published study, Max Horkheimer, ed., *Studien über Autorität und Familie. Forschungsberichte aus dem Institut für Sozialforschung* (Paris: F. Alcan, 1936), 77–135. Kracauer cites and discusses Fromm's "interesting

treatment of the socio-psychological functions of an authoritarian regime" in "Totalitäre Propaganda," 86.

7. See Rolf Wiggershaus, *The Frankfurt School: Its History, Theories, and Political Significance* (Cambridge, Mass.: MIT Press, 1995); Martin Jay, *The Dialectical Imagination: A History of the Frankfurt School and the Institute of Social Research, 1923–1950* (Boston: Little, Brown, 1973).

8. Fromm, *Escape from Freedom*, 30. See also 260–61.

9. Ibid., 104.

10. Ibid., 158.

11. Ibid., 164. Fromm originally developed the notion of the authoritarian character in the context of the Frankfurt School's *Studien über Autorität und Familie*.

12. Fromm, *Escape from Freedom*, 164.

13. Ibid., 170.

14. Kracauer, *From Caligari to Hitler*, 122, chap. 6 (77–87).

15. Ibid., 60.

16. Ibid., 160.

17. Ibid., 162.

18. Ibid., 115. Problematically, Kracauer subsumes even *Die Straße*, an early favorite of his from the Weimar years, under this analysis, now treating the film as a thwarted rebellion that ends in submission.

19. Ibid., 118.

20. Ibid., 100.

21. I am not the first to draw these connections. See, e.g., Noah W. Isenberg, "Investigations of Character: Jewish Exiles Face the German Question," *German Politics and Society* 13, no. 3 (Fall 1995): 81–88, which links *Caligari* and *The Authoritarian Personality* as contributions to "the German Question." However, whereas Isenberg ultimately is concerned with the different degrees of explicitness with which Adorno and Kracauer indict the Weimar Republic and the Germans for the rise of fascism, I am more interested in shared questions of interpretation and method.

22. Theodor W. Adorno, Else Frenkel-Brunswik, Daniel J. Levinson, and R. Nevitt Sanford, *The Authoritarian Personality*, Studies in Prejudice 33 (New York: Harper, 1950), 2.

23. For the following, see Siegfried Kracauer, "Caligari," *Partisan Review* 14, no. 2 (March 1947): 160–73.

24. All quotes in this paragraph are from Kracauer, *From Caligari to Hitler*, 64–65.

25. Fromm (*Escape from Freedom*, 75) explicitly mentions the role of transference and the analyst (along with other authority figures such as physicians, ministers, teachers) in this connection.

26. Kracauer, *From Caligari to Hitler*, 67.

27. As Anton Kaes (*Shell Shock Cinema*, 53) points out, the flashback structure of the film, too, follows this logic: "The master narrative—Francis's psychoanalytic talking cure—situates his own story in relation to that of

Dr. Caligari. Caligari's story, in turn, is also told in flashbacks, resulting in a Chinese box effect."

28. Subsequent historiography has shown that Kracauer relied too heavily on Janowitz's self-serving account in attributing to the screenwriters a revolutionary inner story that was framed/tamed by the intervention of a draconian director (it turns out that the original script already contained a framing device). See Helga Belach and Hans-Michael Bock, eds., *Das Cabinet des Dr. Caligari. Drehbuch von Carl Mayer und Hans Janowitz zu Robert Wienes Film von 1919/20* (Munich: Edition Text+Kritik, 1995); and Olaf Brill, *Der Caligari-Komplex* (Munich: Belleville, 2012).

29. Kracauer, *From Caligari to Hitler*, 66.

30. Ibid., 67.

31. Ibid., 9.

32. Neither Caligari nor Hitler was always going to be in the title of what Kracauer for a long term planned as a "History of the German Film." With his publisher, Kracauer subsequently batted about formulations involving "Shadows of the Mass Mind" and "The German Film and the German Mind" before settling on *From Caligari to Hitler* against the initial objections of the press, which was reticent to include Hitler in the title. With help from his friend Erwin Panofsky, Kracauer ultimately prevailed. For more on the publication history, see Kaes, "Kracauer: Film Historian in Exile."

33. The others were Else Frenkel-Brunswik, Daniel J. Levinson, and R. Nevitt Sanford; Betty Aron, Maria Hertz Levinson and William Morrow were listed as collaborators; Horkheimer and Flowerman served as editors of the entire series of publications to come out of the Studies in Prejudice.

34. Kaes, "Kracauer: Film Historian in Exile," 262.

35. Adorno et al., *Authoritarian Personality*, 224.

36. Ibid., 1.

37. Ibid., 223.

38. Kracauer, *From Caligari to Hitler*, 72.

39. Fred I. Greenstein, "Personality and Political Socialization: The Theories of Authoritarian and Democratic Character," *Annals of the American Academy of Political and Social Science* 361, no. 1 (1965): 82–83.

40. Adorno et al., *Authoritarian Personality*, 489. The "thematic apperception test" is the subject of chapter 14 (489–544), authored by Betty Aron.

41. Ibid., 489–90.

42. Kracauer, "Challenge of Qualitative Content Analysis."

43. Kracauer, *From Caligari to Hitler*, 7.

44. Volker Breidecker, "'Ferne Nähe': Kracauer, Panofsky und 'The Warburg Tradition,'" in Breidecker (ed.), *Kracauer, Panofsky: Briefwechsel 1941–1966*, 129–226; Detlev Schöttker, "Bild, Kultur und Theorie: Siegfried Kracauer und der Warburg Kreis," in *Denken durch die Dinge. Siegfried Kracauer im Kontext*, ed. Frank Grunert and Dorothee Kimmich (Munich: Fink, 2009), 207–24.

45. For the following, see Gertrud Koch, "Die kritische Theorie in Hollywood," in *Die Einstellung ist die Einstellung. Visuelle Konstruktionen des*

Judentums (Frankfurt am Main: Suhrkamp, 1992), 54–256; G. Gilloch and J. Kang, "Below the Surface: Antisemitism, Prejudice, and Siegfried Kracauer's 'Test Film' Project," *New Formations* 61, no. 2 (July 2007): 149–160; and Jenemann, *Adorno in America*, 105–47.

46. Scientific Research Advisory Council, Minutes and Memoranda, January–March 1945; available online at www.ajcarchives.org/AJCArchive/DigitalArchive.aspx. A German translation of the materials on the test film that can be found in the Kracauer archives in DLA appears in Siegfried Kracauer, "Projekt eines Testfilms," in *Studien zu Massenmedien und Propaganda*, 470–99.

47. Gertrud Koch, *Die Einstellung ist die Einstellung. Visuelle Konstruktionen des Judentums* (Frankfurt am Main: Suhrkamp, 1992), 61.

48. Kracauer, *From Caligari to Hitler*, 8.

49. Gilloch and Kang, "Below the Surface," 155.

50. Kracauer, *From Caligari to Hitler*, 7.

51. Isenberg, "Investigations of Character."

52. Kracauer, *From Caligari to Hitler*, 149–50, 153.

53. Ibid., 162.

54. First quote: Thomas Elsaesser, *Metropolis* (London: BFI Publications, 2000), 16; second quote: from Kaes, "Metropolis," 174.

55. Kracauer, *From Caligari to Hitler*, 163.

56. Anton Kaes ("Metropolis," 162) reads Rotwang's death as the excision of a Jewish presence from the plot and the final reconciliation.

57. See Kracauer, *From Caligari to Hitler*, 272. Quaresima ("Introduction," xxxix) considers this "undoubtedly the book's weakest point," noting that anticipationist hypotheses and "notions such as 'pre-Fascism' and 'proto-Nazism' (not to mention premonition or vision) . . . are incongruous and have no basis in historiography or criticism." However, as we have seen, the diagnosis of fascist potential is as much a contemporary interest in line with *The Autoritarian Pesonality*'s identification of the "potentially Fascist individual" as it is a prophecy in retrospect. In the context of the 1940s, Kracauer's approach proved influential, cropping up even in places as unlikely as *The Dialectic of Enlightenment*, where Horkheimer and Adorno note that "in Germany even the most carefree films of democracy were overhung already by the graveyard stillness of dictatorship," 99.

58. This procedure, which recurs somewhat tediously throughout the book, might be explained as a methodological necessity: Kracauer was writing about many films that only he had (re)viewed; to make a plausible argument about them in an era when only a minuscule group of scholars and museum practitioners would have access to sources with which to verify that argument, Kracauer could hardly avoid summarizing the contents of films before proceeding to make claims about them.

59. Quaresima, "Introduction," xxxv.

60. Kracauer, *From Caligari to Hitler*, 164.

61. On the link between femininity and technology in the film, see Andreas Huyssen, "The Vamp and the Machine: Technology and Sexuality in Fritz

Lang's Metropolis," *New German Critique*, nos. 24/25 (1981): 221–37. On the "vaguely connoted 'Jewish' influence" associated with Rotwang, see Kaes, "Metropolis."

62. Kracauer, *From Caligari to Hitler*, 164.

63. Kracauer, "The Mass Ornament," 78. In this sense, I would dispute Quaresima's claim that Kracauer's "motif of ornamentation, or the decorative, epitomizes the narrowness that afflicts *From Caligari to Hitler*" ("Introduction," xxxiii). While Quaresima is right to claim that Kracauer reduces the dialectics, or "openness," that had informed the 1927 essay, his attentiveness to the truth value of ornamentation indicates a greater continuity between the Weimar writings and the book about Weimar than Quaresima allows.

64. Kracauer, "The Mass Ornament," 78.

65. "Both proliferations of organic forms and the emanations of spiritual life remain excluded" in the mass ornament, according to Kracauer (ibid.). As Kracauer points out, however, Lang does assemble his masses of extras into ornamental patterns at certain moments even during the climactic flight from the rising waters, leading him to conclude: "Cinematically an incomparable achievement, this inundation sequence is humanly a shocking failure" (*From Caligari to Hitler*, 150).

66. Klaus Theweleit, *Male Fantasies: Psychoanalyzing the White Terror*, trans. Chris Turner, vol. 2 (Cambridge: Polity Press; Minneapolis: Regents of the University of Minnesota, 1989), 3–7.

67. Kracauer, *From Caligari to Hitler*, 164.

68. Ibid.

69. Arendt, *Origins of Totalitarianism*, 325.

70. Kracauer, *From Caligari to Hitler*, 164.

71. Note also that this is a purely formal relationship, not determined by the will to power: "In substance, the totalitarian leader is nothing more nor less than the functionary of the masses he leads; he is not a power-hungry individual imposing a tyrannical and arbitrary will upon his subjects. Being a mere functionary, he can be replaced at any time, and he depends just as much on the 'will' of the masses he embodies as the masses depend on him" (Arendt, *Origins of Totalitarianism*, 325).

72. "The term masses applies only where we deal with people who either because of sheer numbers, or indifference, or a combination of both, cannot be integrated into any organization based on common interest, into political parties or municipal governments or professional organizations or trade unions" (ibid., 311).

73. Ibid., 308.

74. Ibid., 323, 352.

75. Kracauer, *From Caligari to Hitler*, 257.

76. Ibid., 258.

77. Ibid., 54.

78. Ibid., 55.

79. David Frisby, *Fragments of Modernity: Theories of Modernity in the Work of Simmel, Kracauer, and Benjamin* (Cambridge, Mass.: MIT Press, 1986); Graeme Gilloch, *Siegfried Kracauer* (Malden, Mass.: Polity, 2015).

80. Arendt, *Origins of Totalitarianism*, 334.

81. Ibid., 334, 330.

82. Kracauer, *From Caligari to Hitler*, 53.

83. Ibid., 107.

84. Kracauer, "Those Who Wait," 138–39.

85. Kracauer, *From Caligari to Hitler*, 107–8.

86. Ibid., 165.

87. Ibid., 75.

88. Arendt, *Origins of Totalitarianism*, 338.

89. Ibid., 318.

90. Ibid., 332.

91. Ibid., 338.

92. For the gender politics of *Caligari*, see Patrice Petro, *Joyless Streets: Women and Melodramatic Representation in Weimar Germany* (Princeton, N.J.: Princeton University Press, 1989).

93. Arendt, *Origins of Totalitarianism*, 466. See also Hannah Arendt, "Mankind and Terror," in *Essays in Understanding*, 297–306.

94. Arendt, "Mankind and Terror," 302.

95. Kracauer, *From Caligari to Hitler*, 11.

96. Ibid., 10, 11. In his early notes toward what would become *Theory of Film*, composed largely during the months he spent in Marseille, Kracauer had formulated the claim that "the dimension in which the phenomenon of film really hits home lies beneath the dimension in which political and social events occur. To be sure, the mission of film is bound to its time . . . " ("'Marseiller Entwurf,'" 529).

CHAPTER 7

1. David T. Bazelon, "The Hidden Movie: Siegfried Kracauer, *From Caligari to Hitler* (Book Review)," *Commentary* 4, no. 2 (August 1947).

2. Iris Barry, "The German Film," *New Republic*, May 19, 1947.

3. Kaes, "Kracauer: Film Historian in Exile," 244.

4. See Hayden Guest, "Experimentation and Innovation in Three American Film Journals of the 1950s," in Lee Grieveson and Haidee Wasson, *Inventing Film Studies*, ed. Lee Grieveson and Haidee Wasson (Durham, N.C.: Duke University Press, 2008), 235–63; as well as epilogue, below. On the novelty of Kracauer's method, see Christoph Brecht, "Strom der Freiheit und Strudel des Chaos," *Marbacher Magazin*, no. 105 (2004): 5–52.

5. "A Nation and Its Movies," *Time*, May 19, 1947.

6. See, e.g., Dwight Macdonald, "Through the Lens Darkly," *Partisan Review* 14, no. 5 (1947): 526–28; Martha Wolfenstein and Nathan Leites, *Movies: A Psychological Study* (Glencoe, Ill.: Free Press, 1950).

7. Reviewers, too, suggested this line of inquiry: with *From Caligari to Hitler,* declared one reviewer, "an operational plan now exists to be utilized by persons understanding American cine-symbolic patterns" (Karl W. Hinkle, "Films and Nations: Siegfried Kracauer, *From Caligari to Hitler* [Book Review]," *ETC: A Review of General Semantics* 5, no. 2 [Winter 1948]: 132–35). For an "application" of Kracauer's method to the postwar German case, see Barbara Bongartz, *Von Caligari zu Hitler, von Hitler zu Dr. Mabuse? Eine psychologische Geschichte des deutschen Films von 1946 bis 1960* (Münster: MakS, 1992).

8. Siegfried Kracauer, "Movie Mirror (1950)," in *Siegfried Kracauer's American Writings,* 195–96. Other reviews of Wolfenstein/Leites picked up on this overlap as well. Writing in *Hollywood Quarterly* (for which he had already reviewed *From Caligari to Hitler*), Franklin Fearing noted that Wolfenstein and Leites "are concerned with the same problem and utilize essentially the same method as that of Siegfried Kracauer in *From Caligari to Hitler.* The problem is concerned with the relations between the content of films and existing patterns of culture. The method consists in the analysis of the manifest content of films for the purpose of detecting recurrent or typical themes. The assumption is that in these themes will be found reflections of the daydreams and conscious and unconscious wishes, of the mass audience, and that somehow the producers have tapped this reservoir of material" (Fearing, "A Bibliography for the Quarter," *Quarterly of Film, Radio, and Television* 5, no. 1 [Autumn 1950]: 101).

9. See Janna Jones, "The Library of Congress Film Project: Film Collecting and a United State(s) of Mind," *Moving Image* 6, no. 2 (2006): 30–51; and Barbara Deming, "The Library of Congress Film Project: Exposition of a Method," *Chimera: A Literary Quarterly* 3, no. 2 (Winter 1945): 3–21, and no. 3 (Spring 1945): 6–26, which concludes with the following note: "I want to acknowledge a friendly debt to the critic, Siegfried Kracauer, for many of the thoughts expressed in this paper have crystallized after conversations with him" (26). From extant correspondence it appears that Deming assisted Kracauer extensively in preparing the manuscript of *Caligari,* providing the eye and ear of a native speaker for the German-accented English in which Kracauer composed the book.

10. Patalas, "Siegfried Kracauer," 5.

11. Andrew Higson, "The Concept of National Cinema," *Screen* 30, no. 4 (1989): 36–46.

12. See Andrew Higson, "The Limiting Imagination of National Cinema," in *Cinema and Nation,* ed. Mette Hjort and Scott MacKenzie (London: Routledge, 2000), 63–74.

13. "The conviction that the mass medium of film serves as a reliable seismograph of socio-psychological dispositions and as an indicator for mental displacements in modern societies has long become accepted so generally that it now forms the self-evident common sense of criticsm and is part of the latter's rhetorical tool kit" (Brecht, "Strom der Freiheit und Strudel des Chaos," 8). Both Routledge and Indiana University Press maintain lists in "National Cinemas" and "New Directions in National Cinemas," respectively.

14. Macdonald, "Through the Lens Darkly," 526.

15. Seymour Stern, "Political History of the German Film: *From Caligari to Hitler* (Book Review)," *New Leader*, June 28, 1947.

16. See Michael Wreszin, *A Rebel in Defense of Tradition: The Life and Politics of Dwight Macdonald* (New York: Basic Books, 1994), xviii.

17. Though these are hardly communist, Kracauer does measure the value of numerous films by how close they come to realizing the ideal of social democracy, repeatedly invoking socialism as a norm and citing Meyer Schapiro to critique mere social reformism, as opposed to real structural (not to say revolutionary) change. See, e.g., Kracauer, *From Caligari to Hitler*, 166.

18. Robert Warshow, "The German Film," *New Leader*, August 9, 1947, 14. Warshow went on to refute Stern's claims about Kracauer's communism by citing passages from the book that are unmistakably critical of the German Communist Party; but this response only engaged the red-baiting charges and not the question that both Stern's and Macdonald's critiques flag as a central issue: the politics of Kracauer's method.

19. Quaresima, "Introduction," xvii. Quaresima now speaks of the "discomfort and embarrassment" that the book tends to elicit among critics.

20. Kracauer, "The Mass Ornament," 86; idem, "Photography," 62.

21. Kracauer, "Photography," 62–63. As Thomas Levin puts it, "The problem is not the advanced state of disenchantment but rather the fact that this disenchantment has not advanced far enough. The alienation of *Ratio* here becomes an intermediate stage in the process of liberation from myth. [. . .] It is this drama of enlightenment—the wavering between utopian possibility and apocalyptic threat—that structures the title essay of *The Mass Ornament* and, by extension, the entire book" (Levin, "Introduction," in Kracauer, *The Mass Ornament*, 17).

22. Kracauer, "Wetter und Retter," 43.

23. "Echtes Kinospiel [hat] die Aufgabe [. . .], durch Übersteigerung der Unwirklichkeit unseres Lebens seine Scheinhaftigkeit zu ironisieren und derart auf die wahre Wirklichkeit hinzudeuten" (ibid.).

24. For a detailed reading of the photography essay, see Hansen, *Cinema and Experience*, 27–39.

25. Kracauer, *From Caligari to Hitler*, 186.

26. The photography essay had critiqued the factographic inventory provided by the illustrated magazines during the Weimar Republic, likening it to a historicist "*general inventory* of a nature that cannot be further reduced" (Kracauer, "Photography," 61); but then Kracauer saw in this inventory a tool to explore the previously "unexamined *foundation of nature*. For the first time in history, photography brings to light the entire natural cocoon; for the first time, the inert world presents itself in its independence from human beings" (62). Written at the height of the "New Objectivity," this sanguine assessment differs drastically from the assessment of the same period in *From Caligari to Hitler* (166), where the "new realism" paralyzes the subject in a meaningless "ocean of facts."

27. Kracauer, "Photography," 61.

28. When Adorno (*Authoritarian Personality*, 781) attempts to outline this character with reference to one of the interview subjects, the multiplication of clichés is hard to take. See also Greenstein, "Personality and Political Socialization"; and Harold Dwight Lasswell, "Democratic Character," in *The Political Writings of Harold D. Lasswell* (Glencoe Ill.: Free Press, 1951), 465–525.

29. Adorno, *Authoritarian Personality*, 976.

30. Arendt, *Origins of Totalitarianism*, 479.

31. Kracauer, *From Caligari to Hitler*, 272.

32. "The genesis of *Caligari* reaches far back into the time of French exile in Paris and Marseille. For many years, it was closely allied with initial reflections and preliminary work on another 'film book' that Kracauer would only bring to conclusion over a decade later in *Theory of Film*. The paths of the two projects only diverged in the USA, when the topic for his research assignment at the film library was finalized" (Biebl, "Nachbemerkung und Editorische Notiz," 499–500).

33. In an article devoted to the genesis of *From Caligari to Hitler*, Anton Kaes ("Kracauer: Film Historian in Exile," 254) claims that "the political project of [Kracauer's] *Caligari* is stated more clearly in the research proposals and correspondence than in the published book itself."

34. Siegfried Kracauer, "Notes on the Planned History of the German Film," in Breidecker (ed.), *Kracauer, Panofsky: Briefwechsel 1941–1966*, 15–18.

35. Kracauer, "The Mass Ornament," 75.

36. Kracauer, *Theory of Film*, 97.

37. Kracauer, "Notes," 16.

38. Kracauer, *History*, 83.

39. Aside from the *locus classicus* for such figures of thought in "The Mass Ornament," consider for example the claim in Kracauer's essay on Simmel that "the core of mankind's essence is accessible through even the smallest side door" (Kracauer, "Georg Simmel," in *The Mass Ornament*, 237).

40. See Kracauer, *History*, 8–15; the formulation comes in the portrait of Erasmus that anchors the introduction to his posthumous book on history, but it can also be read as a thinly veiled self-portrait of Kracauer's own "fear of all that is definitely fixed," his interest in how "the humane" may be located in the interstices of any given era rather than in its outwardly defining movements. Kracauer the exile who constantly had to work for recognition likely also projected himself into the ways in which "Erasmus remained largely invisible" (ibid., 12).

41. For a new evaluation of the kind of *Kulturkritik* adumbrated by Kracauer's early writings in particular, see Olivier Agard, *Kracauer: Le chiffonnier mélancolique* (Paris: CNRS, 2010), 17–48.

42. Hansen, *Cinema and Experience*, 81.

43. Kracauer, *From Caligari to Hitler*, 187, 94.

44. Ibid., 74.

45. Brecht, "Strom der Freiheit und Strudel des Chaos," 47. See also Mack, "Film as Memory," 158.

46. "Not the slightest allusion of true freedom interferes with the persistent alternative of tyranny or chaos" (Kracauer, *From Caligari to Hitler*, 83).

47. Ibid., 169.

48. Ibid., 73.

49. The equivocation continues in the following paragraph, which turns to the visualization of circularity, ubiquitous in *Caligari*'s many irises as well as in the motif of the spinning carousel at the fair. Again, Kracauer is forthright in stating his argument: the circle symbolizes chaos, the false alternative to tyranny and the dark side of freedom. But again we might ask what distinguishes the circle-as-chaos from the circle as a geometrical symbol for perfection, wholeness, unity, infinity, etc.?

50. Letter from Kracauer to Panofsky, February 4, 1947, in Breidecker (ed.), *Kracauer, Panofsky: Briefwechsel 1941–1966*, 44.

51. Kracauer, *From Caligari to Hitler*, 16.

52. Hermann Kappelhoff writes about Kracauer's approach in *Caligari* and elsewhere: "Tracing such images of space, dreams of society, and using them to lift social reality into the realm of the visible denotes the aesthetic potential of cinema. The visual spaces of the cinema open up external reality as a field of the possible experience of social reality. A reality of society represented in the stances and gestures of the body, in the spatial configurations of surfaces as well as in the emotional atmospheres, in the modes of perception and modulations of the gaze carried out by the camera's position. It is presented as the experience of reality in the mode of possibility" (Kappelhoff, *The Politics and Poetics of Cinematic Realism*, trans. Daniel Hendrickson [New York: Columbia University Press, 2015], 65–66).

53. Kracauer, *From Caligari to Hitler*, 100.

54. Ibid., 189.

55. Ibid., 121.

56. Ibid., 176, 175.

57. Ibid., 178.

58. Ibid., 104.

59. Ibid., 7.

60. Kracauer writes of *Der letzte Mann*: "This irresistible tendency to involve inanimate objects in the action springs from the intrinsic nature of Mayer's instinct-possessed characters. Incapable of sublimating their impulses, they inhabit a region determined by physical sensations and material stimulants—a region in which objects loom high, taking on the function of stumbling-blocks or signal-posts, enemies or partners" (ibid., 103).

61. Ibid., 102.

62. Ibid., 194.

63. A number of recent contributions point in this direction, including Martin Jay's elaboration of Kracauer's "magical nominalism" (constructivism with a magical rest of ontology) in "Kracauer, the Magical Nominalist," in *Siegfried Kracauer's American Writings*, 227–36. Drehli Robnik suggests that Kracauer may profitably be reread through the works of Agamben and Rancière, in Robnik,

"Among Other Things—a Miraculous Realist: Political Perspectives on the Theoretical Entanglement of Cinema and History in Siegfried Kracauer," in Gemünden and von Moltke (eds.), *Culture in the Anteroom*, 258–75. Kappelhoff similarly revaluates Kracauer's rancierian politics of the aesthetic. In *The Politics and Poetics of Realism*, he demonstrates how Kracauer conceives of the cinematic image "not as a depiction of social reality, but as a medium with which this reality is disclosed as a physical=sensory being-in-the-world" (64). Privileging social gesture over plot, and surface ornamentation over manifest content, Kracauer's contributions from the 1920s onward center on cinema as a medium for a redistribution of the sensible; if the social becomes fully intuitable in the cinema, it is only as a profoundly aesthetic effect, not as a merely ontological or mimetic fact. Rather than reflectionist and plot centered, this line of argument goes, Kracauer's approach to cinema in *From Caligari to Hitler* is constructivist and visually based.

64. It is a romantic ideal of cinema as an art that "gives the political community that form of visible commonality that, in contrast to the abstraction of the law, places people in living relation to one another" (Jacques Rancière, "L'historicité du cinéma," quoted in Kappelhoff, *Politics and Poetics of Cinematic Realism*, 8).

65. Kappelhoff, *Politics and Poetics of Cinematic Realism*, 69.

66. Adorno et al., *Authoritarian Personality*, 973.

67. Only then is Kracauer able to integrate the horrific into his theory of cinema, not as something extraneous or atavistic, but as central to its aesthetic mission. See Kracauer, *Theory of Film*, 305–6.

CHAPTER 8

1. "Eine entscheidende theoretische Arbeit über den Film ist von der allergrößten Bedeutung und zwar im höchst belasteten, keineswegs bloß dem üblichen soziologischen Sinn, weil hier die tiefsten Schichten der Veränderung des Erfahrens, bis in die Wahrnehmung hinein, sich niedergeschlagen haben." Adorno and Kracauer, "Der Riß der Welt . . . ," 453.

2. For the latter, see D.N. Rodowick, *The Crisis of Political Modernism: Criticism and Ideology in Contemporary Film Theory* (Berkeley: University of California Press, 1994).

3. Rodowick, *Elegy for Theory*, 74.

4. Stam, *Film Theory*, 77.

5. On the tenuous relations between Kracauer and the *filmologie* movement, see Leonardo Quaresima's insightful article "De faux amis: Kracauer et la filmologie," *Cinémas* 19, no. 2/3 (Spring 2009): 333–58.

6. See "Nachbemerkung und editorische Notiz," in Kracauer, *Theorie des Films*, 858, 873. My thanks to the late Miriam Hansen for sharing details of her archival work on this question.

7. Robert Warshow, *The Immediate Experience: Movies, Comics, Theatre, and Other Aspects of Popular Culture* (Cambridge, Mass.: Harvard University Press, 2002), 165.

8. Thomas L. Jeffers, "What They Talked about When They Talked about Literature: *Commentary* in Its First Three Decades," in Friedman (ed.), *"Commentary" in American Life*, 121.

9. Warshow's writings were recently reissued in an "enlarged edition," with a biographical essay by David Denby and an epilogue by Stanley Cavell, as *The Immediate Experience* (Cambridge, Mass.: Harvard University Press, 2011).

10. The question obsessing the editors of *Partisan Review* from its founding years on was How can literature maintain a revolutionary attitude and yet incorporate the discoveries of modernism? See Serge Guilbaut, *How New York Stole the Idea of Modern Art: Abstract Expressionism, Freedom, and the Cold War* (Chicago: University of Chicago Press, 1983), 23. Or in Teres's words (*Renewing the Left*, 21): *Partisan Review* "involved bringing the cultural avant-garde and the political vanguard into some form of productive mutual relation for the first time since the 1910s."

11. "Like the Frankfurt critics Adorno and Horkheimer, Clement Greenberg . . . and Dwight Macdonald . . . allowed their dispute with Stalinism and their understanding of fascism in Europe to obscure their vision of popular culture in the United States. By equating the populism of the Communist Party with mass-produced, commodified culture in general, which they considered fascistic, they unrealistically saw the specter of advancing totalitarianism in a range of cultural practices, including publishing, moviemaking, and television" (Teres, *Renewing the Left*, 16).

12. See Warshow, "Father and Son—and the FBI," in *The Immediate Experience*, 133–41; Irving Howe, "The New York Intellectuals," 38ff.

13. Irving Howe, "Notes on Mass Culture," *Politics*, March 1948, 120–22.

14. Andrew Ross, "Containing Culture in the Cold War," in *No Respect: Intellectuals and Popular Culture* (New York: Routledge, 1989), 42–64; the Kennan quote appears on p. 47.

15. Clement Greenberg, "Avant-Garde and Kitsch," *Partisan Review* 6, no. 5 (1939): 34–49.

16. Ibid., 38, 39.

17. Serge Guilbaut, in *How New York Stole the Idea of Modern Art*, 17–47, provides an excellent overview of how this "de-Marxization" played out with and against Trotsky's involvement in the pages of *Partisan Review*.

18. Dwight Macdonald, "A Theory of Mass Culture," in *Mass Culture: The Popular Arts in America*, ed. Bernard Rosenberg and David Manning White (Glencoe, Ill.: Free Press, 1957), 59.

19. Ibid., 64.

20. Ibid., 69.

21. Ibid., 63–64.

22. Dwight Macdonald, "The Soviet Cinema: 1930–1938" (parts I and II), *Partisan Review* 5, no. 2 (July 1938): 37–50; no. 3 (August 1938): 35–62.

23. Daniel Bell, "The Theory of Mass Society," *Commentary* 22, no. 1 (July 1956): 81.

24. See his "The Liberal Conscience of *The Crucible,*" in *The Immediate Experience,* 189–203.
25. Leo Löwenthal, "As I Remember Friedel," *New German Critique,* no. 54 (October 1991): 10.
26. Macdonald, "Theory of Mass Culture," 60.
27. Looking back from the radically changed cultural landscape of 1968, Irving Howe ("The New York Intellectuals," 35) noticed that "the theory advanced by Greenberg and Macdonald turned out to be static; it could be stated, but apparently not developed."
28. Dwight MacDonald, "Lowbrow Thinking," *Politics* 1, no. 7 (August 1944): 217.
29. Dwight Macdonald, "Masscult and Midcult," in *Masscult and Midcult: Essays against the American Grain,* ed. John Summers (New York: New York Review Books, 2011), 66.
30. Macdonald, "Theory of Mass Culture," 66.
31. Terry Teachout, "The Experience of America: Robert Warshow, the Critic Who Did Pop Culture Right," *Weekly Standard,* March 25, 2002, www.weeklystandard.com/article/2308 (accessed December 15, 2015).
32. Ernest Callenbach, Review of *The Immediate Experience* by Robert Warshow, *Film Quarterly* 16, no. 2 (December 1962): 56. See also Denby, "Robert Warshow: Life and Works," ix–xxiv.
33. Herbert Marcuse, "The Affirmative Character of Culture (1937)," in *Negations: Essays in Critical Theory* (Boston: Beacon Press, 1968), 88–133.
34. Warshow, "Woofed with Dreams," in *The Immediate Experience,* 19–23; and "Re-viewing the Russian Movies," ibid., 241.
35. Warshow, "The Legacy of the 30s," in *The Immediate Experience,* 9.
36. Warshow, "Author's Preface," in *The Immediate Experience,* xlii.
37. Ibid., xl. In his overview of different approaches to the cinema, Warshow lists Kracauer—the author not (yet) of *Theory of Film,* but of *From Caligari to Hitler*—as an "excellent example" of sociological criticism (xxxix).
38. Ibid., xl.
39. Warshow, *"Paisan,"* in *The Immediate Experience,* 221.
40. "While being an acknowledged master of the *feuilleton* form," Martin Jay notes, Kracauer "never narcissistically foregrounded his own sensibility in the manner of many other writers in that tradition" (Jay, "Kracauer, the Magical Nominalist," 229).
41. Kracauer, *Theory of Film,* xi.
42. On spectatorship in *Theory of Film,* see 157–72 and my discussion below; on the experience of fully silent cinema, see 134.
43. Warshow, "Movie Chronicle: The Westerner," in *The Immediate Experience,* 106.
44. "The 'Idealism' of Julius and Ethel Rosenberg" and "E. B. White and the *New Yorker,*" in *The Immediate Experience,* 46, 75, respectively.

45. See Martin Jay, *Songs of Experience: Modern American and European Variations on a Universal Theme* (Berkeley: University of California Press, 2006), 404.

46. Susan Sontag, "Against Interpretation," in *Against Interpretation, and Other Essays* (New York: Farrar, Straus & Giroux, 1966), 7.

47. Ibid., 11.

48. See Rentschler, "Kracauer, Spectatorship and the Seventies."

49. Siegfried Kracauer, "Letter to *film 56*," in *Siegfried Kracauer's American Writings*, 226. See also Johannes von Moltke, "2 February, 1956. Siegfried Kracauer Advocates a Socio-Aesthetic Approach to Film in a Letter to Enno Patalas," in *A New History of German Cinema*, ed. Jennifer M Kapczynski and Michael David Richardson (Rochester, N.Y.: Camden House, 2012), 359–64.

50. Warshow, "Author's Preface," in *The Immediate Experience*, xli.

51. Sontag, "Against Interpretation," 13.

52. Warshow, "Author's Preface," in *The Immediate Experience*, xxxvii–xliii.

53. See, e.g., Wallace Phelps (William Phillips) and Philip Rahv, "Criticism," *Partisan Review and Anvil* 2, no. 7 (April 1935); also Wallace Phelps (William Phillips), "Sensibility and Modern Poetry," *Dynamo* 1, no. 3 (Summer 1934).

54. When the journal resumed publication after a short intermezzo in December 1937, the editorial statement set the tone for a magazine that "aspire[d] to a place in the vanguard of literature" but would be "unequivocally independent" from any political party. Rejecting that "totalitarian trend" within the Communist Party in particular, the editorial nonetheless embraced "Marxism in culture" as "an instrument of analysis and evaluation." Against the genteel traditions of the old Left and its "literature of good cheer," the editors championed the "cause of revolutionary literature" for a "new and dissident generation in American letters" ("Editorial Statement," *Partisan Review* 4, no. 1 [December 1937]). This shift significantly enhanced the profile of the magazine, aligning it with modernism over the traditional forms of aesthetic commitment espoused by the Communist Party that had sponsored its earlier incarnation. But *Partisan Review* would remain under the sway of political developments leading up to the U.S. entry into World War II. United, if not identified, by their anti-Stalinism in the wake of the 1936 Moscow trials, the members of the *Partisan Review* circle were starkly divided on whether to support the American war effort. When Rahv and Phillips came out in support of the U.S. declaration of war after Pearl Harbor, both Dwight Macdonald and Clement Greenberg openly distanced themselves from the policy of the editors. After internal struggles over control, Macdonald left *Partisan Review* in 1943 to found *Politics*, wherein he would argue for a third-camp model as an alternative to both U.S. capitalism and fascist as well as communist totalitarianism—until he surprisingly proclaimed his unequivocal alignment with the Western Bloc in a 1952 article flatly entitled "I Choose the West." See Cooney, *Rise of the New York Intellectuals*, 167–95.

55. Philip Rahv, "The Cult of Experience in American Writing," *Partisan Review* 7 (January 1940): 420.

56. Teres, *Renewing the Left*, 13.
57. Ibid.
58. Macdonald, "Masscult and Midcult," 42n.
59. Warshow, "The Legacy of the 30s," in *The Immediate Experience*, 18.
60. See letter from Philipp Rahv, editor, *Partisan Review*, March 24, 1948: "Dear Dr. Kracauer, We do like this piece quite a bit, but it appears impossible to use it in view of the fact that another film chronicle by Warshow is scheduled for the May issue and we cannot print more than one film piece in any given issue. If, in a few weeks, you have not placed this review elsewhere, do let me know and we will take the matter up again" (DLA).
61. For an argument about Kracauer and cinephilia, see Christian Keathley, *Cinephilia and History; or, The Wind in the Trees* (Bloomington: Indiana University Press, 2006), chap. 5.
62. See Kracauer, *Theory of Film*, 282.
63. Warshow, *The Immediate Experience*, 120.
64. André Bazin, *What Is Cinema?*, vol. 2 (Berkeley: University of California Press, 2005), 27.
65. Kracauer, "Those Movies with a Message," 78.
66. Warshow, "Paisan," 222.
67. Kracauer, "Those Movies with a Message," 79. Interestingly, this is also how Bazin tentatively defines the "fundamental humanism" of *Paisan*, which renders Italian Neorealist cinema "more sociological than political. By that I mean that such concrete social realities as poverty, the black market, the administration, prostitution and unemployment do not seem to have given place in the public conscience to the *a priori* values of politics. Italian films rarely tell us the political party of the director or whom he is intending to flatter" (Bazin, *What Is Cinema*, 2:21–22).
68. Warshow, "Paisan," 222.
69. Ibid., 226.
70. Ibid., 221. Warshow goes on to liken the evidentiary power of *Paisan* to the iconic documentary images of the age: "Like the stacked dry corpses of Buchenwald or the clownish figure of Mussolini hanging by the heels, these images have an autonomy that makes them stronger and more important than any ideas one can attach to them."
71. Kracauer, "Those Movies with a Message," 78, 79. "Profoundly concerned with the actual existence of humaneness," Kracauer notes, "the film never so much as mentions the 'cause' of humanity" (79).
72. Warshow, "Paisan," 226–27.
73. Kracauer, "Paisan," in *Siegfried Kracauer's American Writings*, 153.
74. Kracauer, *Theory of Film*, 248, 253, 257.
75. *Theory of Film* "may deal with film, but it concerns a general aesthetics and leads to a philosophy of our times" *(handelt zwar vom Film, betrifft aber die allgemeine Aesthetik und muendet in eine Philosophie unserer Zeit ein)* (Kracauer, Letter to Siegfried Unseld, December 23, 1962, DLA).
76. Kracauer, *Theory of Film*, 285.

77. Ibid., 40.

78. Ibid., 296.

79. Ibid., 297. This formulation derives almost verbatim from Kracauer's moving account of his own first experience of the United States during his entry into New York Harbor aboard the steamship that had carried him and his wife to safety from Lisbon in 1941. See the discussion in chapter 1 above; and Kracauer, "Why France Liked Our Films," 40.

80. Miriam Hansen, "Introduction," in Kracauer, *Theory of Film*, vii–xlv, x. Also see Rentschler, "Kracauer, Spectatorship, and the Seventies."Gertrud Koch, in *Siegfried Kracauer: An Introduction*, argues that the three strands she identifies as central to *Theory of Film*—its sensualist aesthetics, its existential ontology, and its aesthetics of reconciliation—all "take recourse to a concept of experience, albeit one that is not always conceived in a unified way" (138). See also Hermann Kappelhoff, "Realität Lesen: Das Kino und die Politik des Ästhetischen," in *Unerhörte Erfahrung: Texte zum Kino*, ed. Doris Kern and Sabine Nessel (Frankfurt am Main: Stroemfeld, 2008), 39.

81. Hansen, *Cinema and Experience*, 10.

82. Adorno et al., *Authoritarian Personality*, 973, 1.

83. Löwenthal, "Terror's Atomization of Man," 3.

84. See Katznelson, *Fear Itself*.

85. Arendt, *Origins of Totalitarianism*, 308.

86. "Once it has established its premise, its point of departure, experiences no longer interfere with ideological thinking, nor can it be taught by reality" (ibid., 471).

87. Ibid., 474.

88. "Not least to blame for the withering of experience is the fact that things, under the law of pure functionality, assume a form that limits contact with them to mere operation, and tolerates no surplus, either in freedom of conduct or in autonomy of things, which would survive as the core of experience, because it is not consumed by the moment of action" (Theodor W. Adorno, *Minima Moralia: Reflections from Damaged Life* [London: Verso, 1974], 40). Numerous commentators have picked up on this notion that "the experience of the loss of experience is one of the oldest motifs of Critical Theory" (Detlev Claussen, *Theodor W. Adorno: One Last Genius* [Cambridge, Mass.: Belknap Press of Harvard University Press, 2008], 7). See, among others, Martin Jay, "Lamenting the Crisis of Experience: Benjamin and Adorno," chapter 8 in *Songs of Experience*; Miriam Hansen, "Benjamin, Cinema, and Experience: 'The Blue Flower in the Land of Technology,'" *New German Critique*, no. 40 (Winter 1987): 179–224; Howard Caygill, *Walter Benjamin: The Colour of Experience* (London: Routledge, 1998).

89. See Jay, *Songs of Experience*, 199–211.

90. "It is not individuals who have experiences, but subjects who are constituted through experience" (Joan Scott, "The Evidence of Experience," *Critical Inquiry* 17, no. 4 [Summer 1991]: 779).

91. Martin Jay, "Experience without a Subject," in *Cultural Semantics: Keywords of Our Time* (Amherst: University of Massachusetts Press, 1998), 47–61, 51.

92. Kracauer, *Theory of Film*, 172.

93. Letter to Barbara Deming, November 16, 1960, DLA.

94. On the role of Simmel and *Lebensphilosophie* for early Kracauer, see Gilloch, *Kracauer*, esp. 19–56.

95. Kracauer, *Theory of Film*, 298; emphasis added.

96. Karl Marx and Friedrich Engels, *Collected Works*, vol. 28 (New York: International Publishers, 1986), 36.

97. Kracauer, *Theory of Film*, 297, citing A. N. Whitehead.

98. Ibid.

99. Kracauer, *From Caligari to Hitler*, 188.

100. Kracauer, *Theory of Film*, 46, 48.

101. Kracauer, *History*, 4.

102. Kracauer, *Theory of Film*, 296.

103. *Theory of Film*'s term for ambiguity is "the indeterminate"; but he will elaborate this emphasis in defining the "intermediary area" of film, culture, and history in his final book, where "ambiguity is of the essence." Bazin famously opined that "depth of focus reintroduced ambiguity into the structure of the image." Like Kracauer and Warshow, he found this promise enacted most compellingly by the Italian Neorealist films, which were able, in his estimation, "to give back to the cinema a sense of the ambiguity of reality" (André Bazin, *What Is Cinema?* vol. 1, trans. Hugh Gray (Berkeley: University of California Press, 2005), 28, 37.

CHAPTER 9

1. Kracauer, *Theory of Film*, 310.

2. See, for example, Steven Shaviro's recent *The Universe of Things* (Minneapolis: University of Minnesota Press, 2014), which usefully references some recent work on "object-oriented ontologies," but draws specifically on Alfred North Whitehead, whose work Kracauer cites prominently at the close of *Theory of Film*.

3. That said, there have been some productive explorations in this direction, notably by Drehli Robnik in "Among Other Things."

4. See Greif, *The Age of the Crisis of Man*.

5. Edward Steichen, "On Photography," *Daedalus* 89, no. 1 (January 1960): 136.

6. Ibid., 137.

7. USIA was established by the Eisenhower administration in 1955.

8. "Edward Steichen at *The Family of Man*, 1955," MoMA, *Archive Highlights*, available at www.moma.org/learn/resources/archives/archives_highlights_06_1955 (accessed January 25, 2016).

9. Dwight Macdonald, "Masscult and Midcult," in *Masscult and Midcult: Essays against the American Grain*, ed. John Summers (New York: New York Review Books, 2011), 42n.

10. Ibid., 11; Macdonald, "A Theory of Mass Culture," 62. *The Family of Man* drew heavily from the pool—and consequently, it has been claimed, from the aesthetic—of photographers working for *Life* magazine. At the same time, it enlisted some of the best-known names in photography and helped launch the career of others. Artists included Ansel Adams, Edward Weston, and Dorothy Lange as well as the up-and-coming Robert Frank, Diane Arbus, and Bill Brandt. Some of the images that hung in various sizes on the walls and from the ceilings of the carefully designed exhibition space at MoMA, where the show occupied an entire floor, have become iconic in the history of photography—among them Lange's *Migrant Mother* and August Sander's *Young Farmers*.

11. West Berlin was, of course, the "Frontstadt" of the Cold War; USIA figures indicate that a quarter of the 44,000 visitors came from the Eastern sector. Guatemala had recently seen the CIA-backed coup of the democratically elected, pro-Communist government. See Sarah E. James, "A Post-Fascist Family of Man? Cold War Humanism, Democracy, and Photography in Germany," *Oxford Art Journal* 35, no. 3 (December 2012): 315–36, on Germany; and Allan Sekula, "The Traffic in Photographs," *Art Journal* 41, no. 1 (1981): 15, on Guatemala. See also John O'Brian, "The Nuclear Family of Man," *Asia-Pacific Journal: Japan Focus*, July 11, 2008, available at http://japanfocus.org/-john-o_brian/2816/article.html (accessed January 25, 2016).

12. Sekula, "Traffic in Photographs"; see also Fred Turner, "*The Family of Man* and the Politics of Attention in Cold War America," *Public Culture* 24, no. 1 (January 2012): 55–84.

13. Roland Barthes, "The Great Family of Man," in *Mythologies*, trans. Annette Lavers (New York: Hill & Wang, 1972), 100–103.

14. Edward Steichen, quoted in Marianne Hirsch, *Family Frames: Photography, Narrative, and Postmemory* (Cambridge, Mass.: Harvard University Press, 1997), 49.

15. According to Allan Sekula in "Traffic in Photographs" (94), "The peaceful world envisioned by *The Family of Man* is merely a smoothly functioning international market economy, in which economic bonds have been translated into spurious sentimental ties, and in which the overt racism appropriate to earlier forms of colonial enterprise has been supplanted by the 'humanization of the other' so central to the discourse of neocolonialism." Viktoria Schmidt-Linsenhoff analyzes the repression of the Holocaust in "Denied Images: The Family of Man and the Shoa," in *The Family of Man 1955–2001. Humanismus und Postmoderne: Eine Revision von Edward Steichens Fotoausstellung*, ed. Jean Back and Viktoria Schmidt-Linsenhoff (Marburg: Jonas Verlag, 2004), 81–99. On race and class, see Christopher Phillips, "The Judgment Seat of Photography," *October* 22 (1982): 27; John Berger, *About Looking* (New York: Pantheon Books, 1980); and Abigail Solomon-Godeau, "Den Humanismus für ein postmodernes Zeitalter aufpolieren," in Back and Schmidt-Linsenhoff

(eds.), *The Family of Man 1955–2001*, 28–55. Marianne Hirsch critiques the "familial humanism" of *The Family of Man* in *Family Frames*.

16. Sekula, "Traffic in Photographs," 21, 19; Hirsch, *Family Frames*, 50.
17. Barthes, *Mythologies*, 101.
18. Kracauer, *Theory of Film*, 310.
19. On the specific location of Auerbach's humanism and its exilic contexts, see Konuk, *East West Mimesis*, chaps. 1 and 2.
20. Auerbach, *Mimesis*, 488.
21. Kracauer, *Theory of Film*, 210.
22. Paul Rotha, *The Film till Now: A Survey of World Cinema* (London: Spring Books, 1967), 735; Kracauer, *Theory of Film*, 205.
23. Kracauer, *Theory of Film*, 311.
24. Heidi Pataki, "Das Kino Und Die Wirklichkeit," *Frankfurter Allgemeine Zeitung*, September 6, 1973.
25. Hirsch, *Family Frames*, 71.
26. Kracauer, *Theory of Film*, 304.
27. Rentschler, "Arnheim's Early Passage," 63.
28. "It could be argued that history disappears from *Theory of Film* in a double repression: both at the level of theory, inasmuch as the specifically modern and modernist moment of film and cinema is transmuted into a medium-specific affinity with visible, physical, or external reality; and, in the same move, at the level of intellectual biography, in that Kracauer seems to have cut himself off completely from his Weimar persona and the radical 'love of cinema' that inspired him then" (Hansen, *Cinema and Experience*, 256). It should be noted that Hansen proceeds from here to "restore [the] dimension of history in and to the book"—in part by looking "at the history *of* the book," its origins in the so-called Marseille Notebooks in particular (257).
29. Pauline Kael, "Is There a Cure for Film Criticism?" *Sight and Sound* 31, no. 2 (Spring 1962): 56.
30. Hirsch, *Family Frames*, 50.
31. Kracauer, *Theory of Film*, 294.
32. Ibid., 64.
33. Ibid., 53.
34. Ibid., 164.
35. Hansen, *Cinema and Experience*, 276.
36. Kracauer, *Theory of Film*, 48, 50.
37. Ibid., 71.
38. Quoted ibid., 14.
39. Museum of Modern Art (New York), *The Family of Man: The Greatest Photographic Exhibition of All Time—503 Pictures from 68 Countries* (New York: Published for the Museum of Modern Art by the Maco Magaine Corp., 1955), 2.
40. Kracauer, *Theory of Film*, 55.
41. Ibid., 48. Kracauer is referring explicitly to Benjamin, from whom he borrows the notion of "blasting the prison of reality."

42. Ibid., 57.
43. Ibid., 45.
44. Ibid., 46.
45. Ibid., 56, 69.
46. Kracauer, "Photography," 61.
47. Horkheimer and Adorno, *Dialectic of Enlightenment*, 1.
48. Kracauer, *Ginster: Von ihm selbst geschrieben*, in *Romane und Erzählungen*, ed. Inka Mülder-Bach and Sabine Biebl, Werke 7 (Frankfurt am Main: Suhrkamp, 2004), 140. For more on the film theoretical implications of Kracauer's novel, see Johannes von Moltke, "Theory of the Novel: The Literary Imagination of Classical Film Theory," *October*, no. 144 (Spring 2013): 49–72.
49. W.G. Sebald, *On the Natural History of Destruction: With Essays on Alfred Andersch, Jean Améry, and Peter Weiss*, trans. Anthea Bell (New York: Modern Library, 2004).
50. Siegfried Kracauer, *The Past's Threshold: Essays on Photography*, ed. Philippe Despoix and Maria Zinfert (Zurich: Diaphanes, 2014), 16. See also *Ruins of Modernity*, ed. Julia Hell and Andreas Schönle (Durham, N.C.: Duke University Press, 2010).
51. On the exile/stranger, see esp. Inka Mülder-Bach, "The Exile of Modernity: Kracauer's Figurations of the Stranger," in Gemünden and von Moltke (eds.), *Culture in the Anteroom*, 276–92. On the anonymity of the autobiographical characters, see Christian Rogowski, "'Written By Himself': Siegfried Kracauer's 'Auto-Biographical' Novels," ibid., 199–212.
52. Kracauer, *Theory of Film*, 169.
53. On Kracauer's relationship to *filmologie*, see Quaresima, "De faux amis." See also his letter of October 5, 1947, to Lotte Eisner, whom he thanks for attending the convention of "these 'filmologists'" in Paris. "I hope you were not too much bored. And I find it just wonderful that you took the floor to insist on cooperation between any new 'centres de documentation' and the existing film libraries in Paris, New York, and elsewhere. For the rest, I entirely agree to what you say about Cohen-Seat and his set. I read his pamphlet and skimmed through the material they sent. And all this gave me the impression that they are more interested in philosophy than in the cinema itself. I wrote to them in this sense, politely indicating that I expected them to become more concrete in the near future. You see we are of the same opinion. Do you think they will be able to get down to brass tacks? It would be good to try to keep them close to the real thing, for they are certainly willing to do something useful" (DLA).
54. Hansen, "Introduction,"' in Kracauer, *Theory of Film*, xvii.
55. Kracauer refers explicitly to "our biological heritage" to explain the penchant for responding to motion and moving images (ibid., 168).
56. Ibid., 159.
57. Christian Metz, *The Imaginary Signifier: Psychoanalysis and the Cinema* (Bloomington: Indiana University Press, 1981), 43.
58. Ibid.; Jean-Louis Baudry, "The Apparatus: Metapsychological Approaches to the Impression of Reality in the Cinema," in *Film Theory and*

Criticism: Introductory Readings, ed. Leo Braudy and Marshall Cohen (Oxford: Oxford University Press, 1998), 760–77; Roland Barthes, "Leaving the Movie Theater," in *The Rustle of Language* (New York: Hill & Wang, 1986), 345–49.

59. See Baudry, "The Apparatus." This is what Metz calls "primary cinematic identification" (*Imaginary Signifier*, 56).

60. Kracauer, *Theory of Film*, 171.

61. Ibid.

62. This is spelled out most notably in Baudry's analogy between the cinema and Plato's cave: the apparatus takes hold of the subject; instead of its delusional sense of mastery, of being the origin and telos of the image, we discover that the subject is nothing but an ideological effect.

63. Kracauer, *Theory of Film*, 165.

64. See von Moltke, "Theory of the Novel," 56–60.

65. See Keathley, *Cinephilia and History*.

66. Siegfried Kracauer, "Boredom," in *The Mass Ornament*, 332. The notion of active passivity is formulated as a "hesitant openness" that Kracauer endorses in "Those Who Wait," 138; in *History* (84), it is likened to the patient attitude of the photographer and, by implication, to the chemical reaction of the passive film strip.

67. Kracauer, *Theory of Film*, 165. One is tempted here to recognize echoes of the "cinematic condition" of the spectator that Roland Barthes describes in his utterly cinephilic "Leaving the Movie Theater" (345): already before entering, he finds the spectator to bring "a feeling of emptiness, idleness, inactivity"; afterward, "he is stiff, a little numb, bundled up, chilly: he is sleepy . . . his body has turned into something soft, peaceful, sopitive; limp as a sleepy cat, he feels a little out of joint."

68. Keathley, *Cinephilia and History*, li.

69. Kracauer (*Theory of Film*, 53) references the power of the cinema to undo "cultural standards and traditions" through the example of a group of African spectators who detect a chicken in an ethnographic film that had escaped even the filmmaker's attention. The example is drawn from an article by Maddison in *Revue internationale de filmologie*. See also Helmut Lethen, "Sichtbarkeit: Kracauer's Liebeslehre," in *Siegfried Kracauer. Neue Interpretationen*, ed. Michael Kessler and Thomas Y. Levin (Tübingen: Stauffenburg, 1990), 195–228.

70. Kracauer, *Theory of Film*, 165.

71. Ibid., 166.

72. But perhaps we might now enlist Kracauer as a reader of the spectatorial address of Steichen's exhibit and inquire whether *The Family of Man* could not also permit other readings than those apparently favored by the curator himself—readings that would align more closely with the critical power of cinematic realism and weakened subjectivity Kracauer held cinema to offer the Cold War audience. This appears to be the impetus of more recent, revisionist accounts of *The Family of Man* that situate the show in the same contexts in which, I have been suggesting, we must see *Theory of Film*. See in particular

the discussions by Turner, "*Family of Man* and the Politics of Attention"; and Blake Stimson, *The Pivot of the World: Photography and Its Nation* (Cambridge, Mass.: MIT Press, 2006).

CHAPTER 10

1. Kracauer, *History*, 209, 208.
2. Ibid., 15.
3. Ibid., 9.
4. Letter to Leo Löwenthal, quoted in Jay, *Permanent Exiles*, 184.
5. Kracauer, *History*, 4.
6. Other commentators have similarly picked up on some of the incongruities I go on to trace. See, in particular, Inka Mülder-Bach, "History as Autobiography: The Last Things before the Last," trans. Gail Finney, *New German Critique*, no. 54 (1991): 139–57; and Ingrid Belke, "Nachbemerkung und editorische Notiz," in Siegfried Kracauer, *Geschichte—Vor den letzten Dingen*, ed. Ingrid Belke with Sabine Biebl, Werke 4 (Frankfurt am Main: Suhrkamp, 2009), 435–627.
7. Kracauer, "Photography," 51
8. Lethen, "Sichtbarkeit," 220.
9. Kracauer, *History*, chap. "Aesthetic Approach."
10. Kracauer, *Theory of Film*, 165.
11. Ibid., 28; Kracauer, *History*, 46, 58.
12. Kracauer, *History*, 45.
13. Ibid., 194. Consequently, this is not a matter of comparing history films with other forms of historical representation—the subject of much writing on the relation between film and history. Kracauer's analysis aims not at competing representations by film and historians, nor at the representation of history on film, but at the shared ground for representation.
14. Kracauer, *Theory of Film*, 14–16; idem, *History*, 5. Kracauer substantiates both of these claims by referring to the same example from Proust's *The Guermantes Way*.
15. Kracauer historicizes his own analogy by pointing to the proximity between the publication of Ranke's influential writings on historiography and the invention of photography—a connection for which he finds further evidence in Heinrich Heine's notion of a "daguerreotypic history book" that would contain the record of passing days in the form of pictures (*History*, 49).
16. Ingrid Belke discusses these and other analogies in "Nachbemerkung und editorische Notiz," 606. See also Jay, *Permanent Exiles*, 185.
17. Kracauer, *History*, 4.
18. Perhaps this isn't a matter of deciding consciously whether to bring up *Caligari* or not; referring to his recent rediscovery of his own 1927 essay on photography, in which he had "compared historicism with photography already ... in the 'twenties," Kracauer asks himself: "Had I been struck with blindness up to this moment? Strange power of the subconscious which keeps hidden

from you what is so obvious and crystal-clear when it eventually reveals itself" (*History*, 4). The same might be said for the relevance of *Caligari* to *History*.

19. Kracauer, *History*, 3.

20. Hansen, "Introduction," xiii. Hansen does note subsequently that "there are traces, and more than traces, of history—both of the earlier project [outlined in the "Marseille Notebooks"] and of history—in the published book" (xxiv); her reading of the *Theory of Film*'s genesis from the 1940s to its publication in 1960 consequently aims to "restore the dimension of history *in and to* the book" (xiv).

21. Mülder-Bach, "History as Autobiography," 151.

22. Kracauer, *Theory of Film*, 82. "As matters stand, the historian's quest and history on the screen are at cross-purposes" (80).

23. Kracauer, *History*, 3.

24. Ibid., 59–60.

25. We may wish to recall in this context that Kracauer had considered film merely a "pretext" for a broader philosophical discussion in *Theory of Film*, just as he would later describe his interest in history as nothing more than an occasion for working out the contours of what he calls "anteroom thinking." See letter to Adorno, February 12, 1949, in Adorno and Kracauer, "Der Riß der Welt...," 444.

26. Indeed, Kracauer attached great enough importance to the "Historian's Journey" chapter, which introduces the figures of the exile and the stranger, to consider using that title for the book as a whole. See Belke, "Nachbemerkung und editorische Notiz," 590.

27. Kracauer, *History*, 84. See also Mülder-Bach, "History as Autobiography."

28. Kracauer, *History*, 81.

29. Ibid., 82.

30. Ibid., 92, 89.

31. Ibid., 89.

32. Ibid., 91.

33. Ibid., 85.

34. Ibid., 75.

35. Ibid., 157.

36. Ibid., 198.

37. Walter Benjamin, "Theses on the Philosophy of History," in *Illuminations*, ed. Hannah Arendt, trans. Harry Zohn (New York: Schocken, 1968), 262.

38. I am not the first to make this connection; see also Nia Perivolaropoulou and Philippe Despoix, "Postface: 'L'histoire est un amusement de vieillard,'" in Kracauer, *L'histoire—Des avant-dernières choses* (Paris: Stock, 2008), 308. By contrast, Dagmar Barnouw (*Critical Realism*, 258) argues that any reference to Benjamin "gravely distorts the meanings of Kracauer's concept of history and thus the contribution of his work to cultural modernity. Unless one sets out deliberately to read Kracauer 'against himself,' one would be hard put to hear 'Benjamin's voice' in Kracauer's text." Given the extensive relations between the two men as well as the explicit citations of Benjamin in Kracauer's footnotes, it

is difficult to grant Barnouw's irreconcilable stance, let alone her accusation of scholars like D.N. Rodowick for having pointed out echoes of Benjamin in the hopes of making Kracauer "more easily marketable."

39. Kracauer, *History*, 163. For an argument against Kracauer's messianism, however weak, see Carlo Ginzburg, "Details, Plans, Microanalysis: Thoughts on a Book by Siegfried Kracauer," in *Threads and Traces: True, False, Fictive* (Berkeley: University of California Press 2012), 180–92.

40. Benjamin, "Theses," 257.

41. Ibid.

42. Kracauer, *History*, 157.

43. Julia Hell, "The Angel's Enigmatic Eyes; or, The Gothic Beauty of Catastrophic History in W.G. Sebald's 'Air War and Literature,'" *Criticism* 46, no. 3 (2004): 361–92.

44. On the changing notions of theory, and the etymological ramifications of the original Greek *theorein*, see Rodowick, *Elegy for Theory*, 8n.7.

45. For the following, see Alan Itkin, "Orpheus, Perseus, Ahasuerus: Reflection and Representation in Siegfried Kracauer's Underworlds of History," *Germanic Review: Literature, Culture, Theory* 87, no. 2 (2012): 175–202. In Virgil's telling, as Itkin points out, Orpheus sees "mothers and husbands and the bodies, devoid of life, of great-souled heroes, unmarried boys and girls, and youths placed on pyres before the eyes of their parents" (Virgil, *Aeneid*, quoted in Itkin, "Orpheus," 180).

46. Gertrud Koch (*Siegfried Kracauer zur Einführung* [Hamburg: Junius, 2012], 151) detects in the wandering Jew the guilt-ridden gaze of the survivor. Itkin has linked both Ahasuerus and Orpheus to some of the central concerns of Holocaust representation. In doing so, he draws especially on Julia Hell's work on the ubiquity of orphic scenarios in postwar German literature. See Julia Hell, "Ruins Travel: Orphic Journeys through 1940s Germany," in *Writing Travel: The Poetics and Politics of the Modern Journey*, ed. John Zilcosky (Toronto: University of Toronto Press, 2008), 123–60; idem, "Modernity and the Holocaust; or, Listening to Eurydice," *Theory, Culture, and Society* 27, no. 6 (November 2010): 125–54; idem, "The Angel's Enigmatic Eyes."

47. Hell, "The Angel's Enigmatic Eyes."

48. Sebald, *On the Natural History of Destruction*, 26.

49. Kracauer, *Theory of Film*, 306.

50. Ibid., 305.

51. Kracauer, *History*, 81.

52. Ibid., 208.

53. Ibid., 4.

54. Lethen, "Sichtbarkeit."

55. Kracauer, *History*, 9.

56. "The delight [the spectator] takes in films does not, or need not, stem from their intrigue proper" (Kracauer, *Theory of Film*, 170).

57. Ibid., 170–71.

58. Mülder-Bach, "History as Autobiography," 141.

EPILOGUE

1. "Obituary [of Siegfried Kracauer]," *Cinema Journal* 6 (1966): 32. The Society of Cinematologists was the precursor to the Society for Cinema Studies, which was in turn renamed Society for Cinema and Media Studies (SCMS) in 2002; on its history, see Lee Grieveson, "Discipline and Publish: The Birth of Cinematology," *Cinema Journal* 49, no. 1 (2009): 168–76.

2. On the detailed, and for Kracauer enormously gratifying, attention that the Suhrkamp editor Klaus Michel lavished on *Das Ornament der Masse*, see Belke, "Kracauer (1889–1966)—Ein Portrait."

3. Hansen quoted in Eric Rentschler, "Cinema and the Legacies of Critical Theory: Roundtable Discussion," *New German Critique*, no. 122 (Summer 2014): 20.

4. Levin's bibliography was instrumental in unlocking the riches still housed by the Marbach archives prior to the completion of the critical edition. The term "bibliographic recovery effort" is Dudley Andrew's; see "Core and Flow," 908.

5. See Michael Kessler and Thomas Y. Levin, eds., *Siegfried Kracauer. Neue Interpretationen* (Tübingen: Stauffenburg, 1990); Philippe Despoix and Peter Schöttler, eds., *Siegfried Kracauer, penseur de l'histoire* (Paris: Éd. de la Maison des sciences de l'homme, 2006); Gemünden and von Moltke (eds.), *Culture in the Anteroom*.

6. On modernism, see Hansen, *Cinema and Experience*; on postmodernism, see Petro, "Kracauer's Epistemological Shift."

7. On poetics and hermeneutics, see, most recently, Ahlrich Meyer, "'Der Wunsch, die Augen zu verschliessen—wovor?' Siegfried Kracauer und die Forschungsgruppe 'Poetik und Hermeneutik,'" *Neue Zürcher Zeitung*, January 23, 2016, 50; on Kant, see Ian Aitken, *European Film Theory and Cinema: A Critical Introduction* (Bloomington: Indiana University Press, 2001); on Warburg, see Breidecker (ed.), *Kracauer, Panofsky Briefwechsel*; on critical realism, see Barnouw, *Critical Realism*; on magical nominalism, see Jay, "Kracauer, the Magical Nominalist."

8. Rick Altman, "Whither Film Studies (in a Post–Film Studies World)?" *Cinema Journal* 49, no. 1 (2009): 131

9. Dana B. Polan, *Scenes of Instruction: The Beginnings of the U.S. Study of Film* (Berkeley: University of California Press, 2007), 20.

10. Lee Grieveson and Haidee Wasson, "The Academy and Motion Pictures," in *Inventing Film Studies* (Durham: Duke University Press, 2008), xii. On the fiftieth anniversary of *Screen* (originally *Screen Education*), see the special issue edited by Annette Kuhn, "Screen and Screen Theorizing Today," *Screen* 50, no. 1 (March 20, 2009): 1–12; on the fiftieth anniversary of SCMS (originally the Society of Cinematologists), see Lucy Fisher, ed., "In Focus: SCMS at Fifty," *Cinema Journal* 49, no. 1 (Fall 2009): 128–76.

11. Polan, *Scenes of Instruction*, 4–6; Grieveson and Wasson, *Inventing Film Studies*, xxxin.20.

12. Polan, *Scenes of Instruction*; Decherney, *Hollywood and the Culture Elite*; Haidee Wasson, *Museum Movies: The Museum of Modern Art and the Birth of Art Cinema* (Berkeley: University of California Press, 2005); Grieveson and Wasson, *Inventing Film Studies*.

13. For some gestures toward a more international genealogy, see Andrew, "Core and Flow." Masha Salazkina has adopted a compelling transnational framework to reconstruct the trajectory of materialist film theory from Soviet cinema to Italy and Brazil; see "Moscow-Rome-Havana: A Film-Theory Road Map," *October*, no. 139 (2012): 97–116.

14. On the "exilic" dimension of Kracauer's, Arnheim's, and Balázs's writings, see von Moltke, "Theory of the Novel." On Balázs, see Hanno Loewy, *Béla Balázs. Märchen, Ritual und Film* (Berlin: Vorwerk 8, 2003); and Erica Carter's introduction to Béla Balázs, *Early Film Theory: Visible Man and the Spirit of Film*, ed. Erica Carter (New York: Berghahn Books, 2010), xv–xlvi. For Richter, see Yvonne Zimmerman, *Hans Richter and the Transatlantic Exchange of Film Culture* (forthcoming).

15. Important anthologies include Richard Abel, *French Film Theory and Criticism: A History/Anthology, 1907–1939* (Princeton, N.J.: Princeton University Press, 1988); Sarah Keller and Jason N. Paul, eds., *Jean Epstein: Critical Essays and New Translations* (Amsterdam: Amsterdam University Press, 2012); Aaron Gerouw, *Decentering Theory: Reconsidering the History of Japanese Film Theory* (Saitama-ken Sakado-shi, Japan: Center for Inter-cultural Studies and Education, Josai University, 2010); Anton Kaes, Nicholas W. Baer, and Michael Cowan, eds., *The Promise of Cinema: German Film Theory, 1907–1933*, annotated ed. (Berkeley: University of California Press, 2015). See also the Translation Project of the Permanent Seminar on Histories of Film Theories, http://filmtheories.org/translation-project.

16. See letter from Robert Gessner, March 21, 1960, and Kracauer's acceptance in response, March 24, 1960, both in DLA.

17. Herman Weinburg, "The Film and Humanity," *Sight and Sound* 16 (Summer 1947): 78–79.

18. On Kracauer's relation with *Film Culture* and *Cinemages*, see below. On his interest in *filmologie*, see his letter of October 5, 1947, to Lotte Eisner (DLA, cited in chap. 9, n. 52), as well as the many references in *Theory of Film*; see also Quaresima, "De faux amis." On the place of *filmologie* in the history of film studies as a discipline, see Rodowick, *Elegy for Theory*, 112–30; and Andrew, "Core and Flow," esp. 888–97.

19. Robert Gessner, "Cinema and Scholarship," *Journal of the Society of Cinematologists* 3 (January 1963): 74.

20. Ibid., 74–75.

21. Under "objective elements," for example, we find "animate life (actors, persons, animals)" next to "makeup," "voice," "music," and "sound," among others. The entry for "perspective" under the same rubric is subdivided into "a) Linear (line, point, mass, depth)" and "b) Optical (lenses)." It is anyone's guess how Gessner wanted scholars to parse "subjective qualities" as "descriptive,"

"narrative," "informational," and "symbolic." See ibid., 79; also Robert Gessner, "'The Parts of Cinema': A Definition," *Journal of the Society of Cinematologists* 1 (1961): 25–39.

22. Henry Breitrose, "Review of the *Journal of the Society of Cinematologists*, vols. 1 and 2," *Film Quarterly* 16, no. 2 (Winter 1962): 55.

23. This relationship to the sciences, too, was modeled by French *filmologie*, in whose *Revue* Étienne Souriau had proclaimed explicitly in 1950: "Filmology is, must be, wants to be a science. And if a science is not uniquely, according to the celebrated formula of Condillac, 'a well-made language,' it at least requires and supposes such a language" (Souriau, "La structure de l'univers filmique et le vocabulaire de la filmologie," *Revue internationale de filmologie* 2, nos. 7–8 [1951]: 213; quoted in and translated by Rodowick, *Elegy for Theory*, 125).

24. On the relevance of New Criticism for the formation of film studies during the 1950s, see Grieveson, "Discipline and Publish," 169.

25. See Andrew Dubois, "Introduction," in Frank Lentricchia and Andrew DuBois, eds., *Close Reading: The Reader* (Durham, N.C.: Duke University Press, 2003), 1–41.

26. See letter from Robert Gessner, December 12, 1960, which praises *Theory of Film* as "the final word on the philosophy of film and as such it is monumental for all time. Congratulations. My project is in another vein, the empirical analysis. My chart of 19 Plus [i.e., another iteration of the nomenclature categories] is different from the one I gave you in June, thanks again to our mentor, Erwin Panofsky!" (DLA).

27. Gessner, "Cinema and Scholarship," 78.

28. Kael, "Is There a Cure for Film Criticism?," 63.

29. Letter to Adorno, February 12, 1949, in Adorno and Kracauer, *"Der Riß der Welt . . . ,"* 444.

30. Rodowick, *Elegy for Theory*, 91.

31. Harcourt, "What, Indeed, Is Cinema?," 27. See also Jerzy Toeplitz, "Film Scholarship: Present and Prospective," *Film Quarterly* 16, no. 3 (Spring 1963): 27–37.

32. Rare titles such as Lukács's *Theory of the Novel* (1920) or Eikhenbaum's "Theory of The 'Formal Method'" (1926), or the explicit discussion of theory as a "compass" in Balázs's *Visible Man*, are the exceptions that prove Rodowick's rule of rarity.

33. Rodowick, *Elegy for Theory*, 68, 73.

34. Ibid., 74. See also the discussion of Kracauer in Rodowick, *Virtual Life of Film*, 73–74.

35. Andrew, "Core and Flow," 909.

36. Hansen, *Cinema and Experience*. On the challenge to "theorize history and historicize theory" as a way of "rethink[ing] the history of film theory" itself, see Rentschler, "Cinema and the Legacies of Critical Theory."

37. Haden Guest, "Experimentation and Innovation in Three American Film Journals of the 1950s," in *Inventing Film Studies*, ed. Lee Grieveson and Haidee Wasson (Durham, N.C.: Duke University Press, 2008), 235.

38. Mr. Harper, "After Hours: Dialogue in Distress," *Harper's Magazine*, August 1, 1952, 95.

39. Kracauer is identified as a "mainstay" of Cinema 16 in a notice in "After Hours," *Harper's Magazine*, July 1, 1949, 102. See also "Interview with Marcia Vogel" in Scott MacDonald, ed., *Cinema 16: Documents toward a History of the Film Society* (Philadelphia: Temple University Press, 2002), 67. In a brief article for the *Saturday Review*, Amos Vogel listed Kracauer as one of the "sponsors" of the society ("Film Dos and Don'ts", August 20, 1949), and the following year, in response to Vogel's request for a letter of introduction to film people in Europe, Kracauer would return the favor: "I welcome this opportunity to tell you that in my opinion your CINEMA 16 is one of the living forces in a field which had been badly neglected before you took over. You have created this unique organization out of nothing and you have shown us, within its framework, a number of educational, scientific, experimental and socially interesting documentaries which we would have never seen were it not for your untiring initiative. Through your activities many young people who confused films with Hollywood films and perhaps were fed up with them, have for the first time realized the inherent potentialities of the medium. Whenever I attended the screenings of CINEMA 16, I felt elated about the intensity with which a huge audience watched the spectacles you offered them—films in a daring mood, films with a serious purpose. You yourself are an educator, and your own passion for the cinema is contagious" (Letter from Kracauer to Vogel, May 28, 1950, quoted in Macdonald [ed.], *Cinema 16*, 24).

40. On Kracauer's photographs, including Lili's prominent role in producing and securing these traces, see Maria Zinfert, ed., *Kracauer: Photographic Archive* (Zurich: Diaphanes, 2015).

41. Siegfried Kracauer, "Stage vs. Screen Acting: The Theoretical Differences Are Fundamental," *Films in Review* 1, no. 9 (December 1950): 7–11; idem, "Opera on the Screen," *Film Culture* 1, no. 2 (March–April 1955): 19–21.

42. [Siegfried Kracauer on G.W. Pabst], *Cinemages* 3 (1955): 79–93.

43. Siegfried Kracauer, "Cinéma et sociologie (sur l'exemple du cinéma de l'Allemagne pré-Hitlerienne)," *Revue internationale de filmologie* 1, nos. 3–4 (October 1948): 311–18. By April 1957 we find Kracauer withdrawing from journal publication and devoting what little time he has entirely to the completion of *Theory of Film*. In a letter to Edgar Morin dated April 1, 1957, he writes: "I have not contributed to magazines, except for pages from the synopsis of my book which appeared in *Film Culture* and *Cinema Nuovo*. My association with the Bureau of Applied Social Research, Columbia University and my job as a consultant to a Foundation do not permit me excursions into the literary field. What time I have on my hands is given over to the completion of my film aesthetics" (DLA).

44. Haden Guest, "Experimentation and Innovation in Three American Film Journals of the 1950's," in Grieveson and Wasson, *Inventing Film Studies*, 236.

45. Siegfried Kracauer, "The Task of the Film Critic," in *The Weimar Republic Sourcebook*, ed. Anton Kaes, Martin Jay, and Edward Dimendberg (Berkeley: University of California Press, 1994), 635.

46. Enno Patalas, "The Contemporary West German Film as a Social Symptom," *Film Culture* 1, no. 4 (Summer 1955): 9–22.

47. [Letter to the editor], *film 56* 1, no. 3 (March 1956): 155; reprinted in Kracauer, *Kleine Schriften zum Film, 1932–1961*, 470–71. Italicized phrase is English in the original. The complete letter, dated February 12, 1956, is in DLA.

48. "Front Matter," *Cinema Journal* 8, no. 1 (October 1968): 1.

49. *Satellite Mentality: Political Attitudes and Propaganda Susceptibilities of Non-Communists in Hungary, Poland, and Czechoslovakia* (New York: F.A. Praeger, 1956), co-authored with Paul Berkman under the aegis of the Bureau for Applied Social Research, was based on interviews with East Bloc citizens who had fled to the West.

50. Kracauer, "Challenge of Qualitative Content Analysis."

51. Kris and Speier, *German Radio Propaganda*.

52. Hannah Arendt, "On the Nature of Totalitarianism: An Essay in Understanding," n.d., Speeches and Writings File, 1923–1975, Hannah Arendt Papers, Library of Congress, http://memory.loc.gov/cgi-bin/ampage?collId=m harendt&fileName=05/051930/051930page.db&recNum=0.

53. Kracauer, "Challenge of Qualitative Content Analysis," 642.

54. Ibid., 641–42.

55. Gerald Noxon, "The Anatomy of the Close-up: Some Literary Origins in the Works of Flaubert, Huysmans, and Proust," *Journal of the Society of Cinematologists* 1 (1961): 1–24.

56. See Minutes of Second National Meeting of the Society of Cinematologists, March 27–28, 1961, in Rochester (NYU Robert Gessner Archives). Noxon's paper was subsequently published as the first article in the opening issue of the *Journal of Cinematologists* (1961).

57. Theodor W. Adorno, "Nach Kracauers Tod," in *Vermischte Schriften I. Theorien und Theoretiker, Gesellschaft, Unterricht, Politik*, Gesammelte Schriften 20.1 (Frankfurt am Main: Suhrkamp, 1986), 195.

58. Ibid.

59. See Gemünden and von Moltke (eds.), *Culture in the Anteroom*.

60. "Ich bin entschlossen, das soll ein classic werden" (Letter to Löwenthal, February 16, 1957, in Löwenthal and Kracauer, *In steter Freundschaft*, 188). And indeed, three years after its publication, the book was included on Andries Deinum's list "Thirty Fundamental Books on Film," *Film Quarterly* 16, no. 2 (1962): 60.

61. Hansen, *Cinema and Experience*.

62. Andrew, *The Major Film Theories*.

63. Detlev Schöttker, "Bild, Kultur und Theorie: Siegfried Kracauer und der Warburg Kreis," in *Denken durch die Dinge: Siegfried Kracauer im Kontext*, ed. Frank Grunert and Dorothee Kimmich (Munich: Fink, 2009), 207–24; Breidecker (ed.), *Kracauer, Panofsky Briefwechsel;* .

64. As Adorno puts it in a letter critiquing Kracauer's book on Offenbach, the goal here would be to "dissolve the figure-ground dualism" (Adorno,

Letter to Kracauer, May 13, 1937, in Adorno and Kracauer, "Der Riß der Welt...," 355.

65. For a discussion of the methodological implications of various recent returns to classical film theory—including my own in this project—see the recent dossier in *Screen* titled "What's New in Classical Film Theory" (*Screen* 55, no. 3 [Autumn 2014]: 396–420). In my contribution, "Out of the Past: Classical Film Theory" (ibid., 398–403), I set off the historicizing approach I outline here from other ways of engaging the film-theoretical "canon" according to today's ostensibly postphotographic, if not posttheoretical, vantage point.

66. Adorno, "The Curious Realist," 160.

Bibliography

Abel, Richard. *French Film Theory and Criticism: A History/Anthology, 1907–1939*. Princeton, N.J.: Princeton University Press, 1988.
Adorno, Theodor W. "The Curious Realist: On Siegfried Kracauer." *New German Critique*, no. 54 (Autumn 1991): 159–77.
———. "Fragen an die intellektuelle Emigration." In *Vermischte Schriften I: Theorien und Theoretiker, Gesellschaft, Unterricht, Politik,* Gesammelte Schriften 20.1, 352–59. Frankfurt am Main: Suhrkamp, 1986.
———. "Gutachten über die Arbeit 'Die Totalitäre Propaganda Deutschlands und Italiens,' S. 1 bis S. 106, von Siegfried Kracauer." In Siegfried Kracauer, *Studien zu Massenmedien und Propaganda,* ed. Christian Fleck and Bernd Stiegler, Werke 2.2, 821–24. Frankfurt am Main: Suhrkamp, 2012.
———. *Minima Moralia: Reflections on a Damaged Life*. London: Verso, 2005.
———. "Nach Kracauers Tod." In *Vermischte Schriften I. Theorien und Theoretiker, Gesellschaft, Unterricht, Politik,* Gesammelte Schriften 20.1, 194–96. Frankfurt am Main: Suhrkamp, 1986.
———. "Scientific Experiences of a European Scholar in America." In *Critical Models: Interventions and Catchwords,* trans. Henry W Pickford, 215–42. New York: Columbia University Press, 1998.
———. "Zusammenfassung der gekürzten Fassung von 'Totalitäre Propaganda.'" In Siegfried Kracauer, *Studien zu Massenmedien und Propaganda,* ed. Christian Fleck and Bernd Stiegler, Werke 2.2, 825–826. Frankfurt am Main: Suhrkamp, 2012.
Adorno, Theodor W., and Siegfried Kracauer. *"Der Riß der Welt geht auch durch mich ... " Theodor W. Adorno/Siegfried Kracauer, Briefwechsel 1923–1966*. Ed. Wolfgang Schopf. Frankfurt am Main: Suhrkamp, 2008.
Adorno, Theodor W., Else Frenkel-Brunswik, Daniel J. Levinson, and R. Nevitt Sanford. *The Authoritarian Personality*. Studies in Prejudice 33. New York: Harper, 1950.
Agard, Olivier. *Kracauer: Le chiffonnier mélancolique*. Paris: CNRS, 2010.

Aitken, Ian. *European Film Theory and Cinema: A Critical Introduction*. Bloomington: Indiana University Press, 2001.

Alpers, Benjamin Leontief. *Dictators, Democracy, and American Public Culture: Envisioning the Totalitarian Enemy, 1920s–1950s*. Chapel Hill: University of North Carolina Press, 2003.

Altman, Rick. "Whither Film Studies (in a Post–Film Studies World)?" *Cinema Journal* 49, no. 1 (2009): 131–35.

Anderson, Amanda. "Character and Ideology: The Case of Cold War Liberalism." *New Literary History* 42, no. 2 (2011): 209–29.

Anderson, Mark M. "Siegfried Kracauer and Meyer Schapiro: A Friendship." *New German Critique*, no. 54 (October 1, 1991): 19–29.

Andrew, Dudley. "The Core and the Flow of Film Studies." *Critical Inquiry* 35, no. 4 (January 2009): 879–915.

———. *The Major Film Theories: An Introduction*. London: Oxford University Press, 1976.

"Anti-Nazi League Seeks Ban on 'Sieg im Westen' Film." *Christian Science Monitor*, May 9, 1941.

"Anti-Nazis Picket Uptown Theatre Here as German Propaganda Newsreel Opens." *New York Times*, May 8, 1941.

Arendt, Hannah. "The Aftermath of Nazi Rule: Report from Germany." In *Essays in Understanding*, 248–69.

———. *Denktagebuch 1950–1973*. 2 vols. Ed. Ursula Ludz and Ingeborg Nordmann. Munich: Piper, 2002.

———. *Essays in Understanding, 1930–1954: Formation, Exile, and Totalitarianism*. New York: Schocken, 1994.

———. *Hannah Arendt: The Recovery of the Public World*. Ed. Melvyn A. Hill. New York: St. Martin's Press, 1979.

———. "Home to Roost: A Bicentennial Address." *New York Review of Books*, June 26, 1975.

———. "Imperialism: Road to Suicide." *Commentary* 1, no. 2 (December 1945): 27–35.

———. *Lectures on Kant's Political Philosophy*. Chicago: University of Chicago Press, 1989.

———. "Mankind and Terror." In *Essays in Understanding*, 297–306.

———. "No Longer and Not Yet." In *Essays in Understanding*, 158–62.

———. "On the Nature of Totalitarianism: An Essay in Understanding." Speeches and Writings File, 1923–75, Hannah Arendt Papers, Library of Congress, http://memory.loc.gov/cgi-bin/ampage?collId=mharendt&fileName=05/051930/051930page.db&recNum=0.

———. *The Origins of Totalitarianism*. New York: Harcourt, Brace & World, 1966.

———. *Das private Adressbuch 1951–1975*. Ed. Christine Fischer-Defoy. Leipzig: Koehler & Amelang, 2007.

———. *Rahel Varnhagen: The Life of a Jewish Woman*. New York: Harcourt Brace Jovanovich, 1974.

---. "Social Science Techniques and the Study of Concentration Camps." In *Essays in Understanding*, 232–47.
---. "Understanding and Politics (The Difficulties of Understanding)." In *Essays in Understanding*, 307–27.
---. *Within Four Walls: The Correspondence between Hannah Arendt and Heinrich Blücher, 1936–1968*. Ed. Lotte Köhler, trans. Peter Constantine. New York: Harcourt, 2000.
Arendt, Hannah, and Heinrich Blücher. *Hannah Arendt/Heinrich Blücher. Briefe 1936–1968*. Ed. Lotte Köhler. Munich: Piper, 1996.
Arnheim, Rudolf. Review of *Siegfried Kracauer, Erwin Panofsky: Briefwechsel 1941–1966*. *Leonardo* 31, no. 1 (January 1, 1998): 74–75.
Auerbach, Erich. *Mimesis: The Representation of Reality in Western Literature*. Princeton, N.J.: Princeton University Press, 1953.
Back, Jean, and Viktoria Schmidt-Linsenhoff, eds. *The Family of Man, 1955–2001. Humanismus und Postmoderne; Eine Revision von Edward Steichens Fotoausstellung*. Marburg: Jonas Verlag, 2004.
Baer, Nicholas. "Historical Turns: On *Caligari*, Kracauer, and New Film History." In *Film und Geschichte. Produktion und Erfahrung von Geschichte durch Bewegtbild und Ton*, ed. Delia González de Reufels, Rasmus Greiner, and Winfried Pauleit, 127–37. Berlin: Bertz & Fischer, 2015.
Balázs, Béla. *Early Film Theory: Visible Man and the Spirit of Film*. Ed. Erica Carter. New York: Berghahn Books, 2010.
Barnouw, Dagmar. *Critical Realism: History, Photography, and the Work of Siegfried Kracauer*. Baltimore: Johns Hopkins University Press, 1994.
Barry, Iris. "The German Film." *New Republic*, May 19, 1947.
Barthes, Roland. "Leaving the Movie Theater." In *The Rustle of Language*, 345–49. New York: Hill & Wang, 1986.
---. *Mythologies*. Trans. Annette Lavers. New York: Hill & Wang, 1972.
Bathrick, David. "Making a National Family with the Radio: The Nazi Wunschkonzert." *Modernism/Modernity* 4, no. 1 (1997): 115–27.
Baudry, Jean-Louis. "The Apparatus: Metapsychological Approaches to the Impression of Reality in the Cinema." In *Film Theory and Criticism: Introductory Readings*, ed. Leo Braudy and Marshall Cohen, 760–77. Oxford: Oxford University Press, 1998.
Bazelon, David T. "The Hidden Movie: Siegfried Kracauer, *From Caligari to Hitler* (Book Review)." *Commentary* 4, no. 2 (August 1947).
Bazin, André. "Death Every Afternoon." In *Rites of Realism: Essays on Corporeal Cinema*, ed. Ivone Margulies, trans. Mark A. Cohen, 27–31. Durham, N.C.: Duke University Press, 2003.
---. *What Is Cinema?* 2 vols. Trans. Hugh Gray. Berkeley: University of California Press, 2005.
Beck, Ulrich. *Risk Society: Towards a New Modernity*. London: Sage, 2010.
Belach, Helga, and Hans-Michael Bock, eds. *Das Cabinet des Dr. Caligari. Drehbuch von Carl Mayer und Hans Janowitz zu Robert Wienes Film von 1919/20*. Munich: Edition Text + Kritik, 1995.

Belke, Ingrid. "Das 'Geheimnis' des Faschismus liegt in der Weimarer Republik: Der Kunsthistoriker Meyer Schapiro über Kracauers erstes Film-Buch." *Filmexil* 4 (1994): 35–49.

———. "Nachbemerkung und editorische Notiz." In Siegfried Kracauer, *Geschichte—Vor den letzten Dingen*, ed. Ingrid Belke with Sabine Biebl, Werke 4, 435–627. Frankfurt am Main: Suhrkamp, 2009.

———. "Siegfried Kracauer (1889–1966)—Ein Portrait" (parts 1–3). *Galerie—Revue culturelle et pédagogique* 30, no. 3 (2012): 536–68; 31, no. 1 (2013): 91–130; 31, no. 2 (2013): 226–257.

Belke, Ingrid, and Irina Renz. *Siegfried Kracauer 1989–1966*. Marbacher Magazin 47. Marbach: Schiller Nationalmuseum, 1988.

Bell, Daniel. "The Theory of Mass Society." *Commentary* 22, no. 1 (July 1956): 75–84.

Benjamin, Walter. *Illuminations*. Ed. Hannah Arendt, trans. Harry Zohn. New York: Schocken, 1968.

———. "The Work of Art in the Age of Its Technological Reproducibility." In *Walter Benjamin: Selected Writings*, vol. 3: *1935–1938*, ed. Howard Eiland and Michael W Jennings, trans. Edmund Jephcott, 101–33. Cambridge, Mass.: Belknap Press of Harvard University Press, 2002.

———. "Theses on the Philosophy of History." In Benjamin, *Illuminations*, ed. Hannah Arendt, trans. Harry Zohn, 253–263. New York: Schocken, 1968.

Bentley, Eric. "The Cinema: Its Art and Techniques." *New York Times Book Review*, May 18, 1947.

Berger, John. *About Looking*. New York: Pantheon Books, 1980.

Biebl, Sabine. "Nachbemerkung und editorische Notiz." In Siegfried Kracauer, *Von Caligari zu Hitler*, ed. Sabine Biebl, Werke 2.1, 499–532. Frankfurt am Main: Suhrkamp, 2012.

Bloom, Alexander. *Prodigal Sons: The New York Intellectuals and Their World*. New York: Oxford University Press, 1986.

Bongartz, Barbara. *Von Caligari zu Hitler, von Hitler zu Dr. Mabuse? Eine psychologische Geschichte des deutschen Films von 1946 bis 1960*. Münster: MakS, 1992.

Borde, Raymond, Etienne Chaumeton, and Marcel Duhamel. *Panorama du film noir américain, 1941–1953*. Paris: Flammarion, 1988.

Brecht, Christoph. "Strom der Freiheit und Strudel des Chaos." *Marbacher Magazin*, no. 105 (2004): 5–52.

Breidecker, Volker. "'Ferne Nähe': Kracauer, Panofsky und 'The Warburg Tradition.'" In *Siegfried Kracauer, Erwin Panofsky: Briefwechsel 1941–1966*, ed. Volker Breidecker, 129–226. Berlin: Akademie Verlag, 1996.

Breitrose, Henry. Review of the *Journal of the Society of Cinematologists*, vols. 1 and 2. *Film Quarterly* 16, no. 2 (Winter 1962): 54–55.

Brill, Olaf. *Der Caligari-Komplex*. Munich: Belleville, 2012.

Brodersen, Momme. *Siegfried Kracauer*. Reinbek bei Hamburg: Rowohlt Taschenbuch Verlag, 2001.

Brown, Wendy. "Untimeliness and Punctuality: Critical Theory in Dark Times." In *Edgework: Critical Essays on Knowledge and Politics*, 1–16. Princeton, N.J.; Princeton University Press, 2006.
Buck, Pearl. "The Solitary." *Commentary* 1, no. 6 (April 1946): 7–11.
Callenbach, Ernest. Review of *The Immediate Experience* by Robert Warshow. *Film Quarterly* 16, no. 2 (December 1962): 56.
Cavell, Stanley. "Epilogue: After Half a Century." In Robert Warshow, *The Immediate Experience: Movies, Comics, Theatre, and Other Aspects of Popular Culture*, 289–300. Cambridge, Mass.: Harvard University Press, 2002.
Caygill, Howard. *Walter Benjamin: The Colour of Experience*. London: Routledge, 1998.
Claussen, Detlev. "Intellectual Transfer: Theodor W. Adorno's American Experience." *New German Critique*, no. 97 (January 2006): 5–14.
———. *Theodor W. Adorno: One Last Genius*. Cambridge, Mass.: Belknap Press of Harvard University Press, 2008.
Cohen, Elliot. "An Act of Affirmation: Editorial Statement." *Commentary* 1, no. 1 (November 1945): 1.
———. "Jewish Culture in America: Some Speculations by an Editor." *Commentary* 3, no. 5 (May 1947): 412–20.
Cooney, Terry A. *The Rise of the New York Intellectuals: "Partisan Review" and Its Circle*. Madison: University of Wisconsin Press, 1986.
Culbert, David. "The Rockefeller Foundation, the Museum of Modern Art Film Library, and Siegfried Kracauer, 1941." *Historical Journal of Film, Radio, and Television* 13, no. 4 (January 1993): 495–511.
Decherney, Peter. *Hollywood and the Culture Elite: How the Movies Became American*. New York: Columbia University Press, 2005.
Deinum, Andries. "Thirty Fundamental Books on Film." *Film Quarterly* 16, no. 2 (1962): 60.
Deming, Barbara. "The Artlessness of Walt Disney." *Film Chronicle: A New Magazine of Film Criticism and Research* 12, no. 2 (1945): 226–31.
———. "The Library of Congress Film Project: Exposition of a Method." *Chimera: A Literary Quarterly* 3, no. 2 (Winter 1945): 3–21; 3, no. 3 (Spring 1945): 6–26.
———. *Running Away From Myself: A Dream Portrait of America Drawn from the Films of the Forties*. New York: Grossman, 1969.
Denby, David. "Robert Warshow: Life and Works." In Warshow, *The Immediate Experience: Movies, Comics, Theatre, and Other Aspects of Popular Culture*, ix–xxi. Cambridge, Mass.: Harvard University Press, 2002.
Despoix, Philippe, and Peter Schöttler, eds. *Siegfried Kracauer, penseur de l'histoire*. Paris: Éd. de la Maison des sciences de l'homme, 2006.
Dewey, John. "The Crisis in Human History." *Commentary* 1, no. 5 (March 1946): 1–9.
Dimendberg, Edward. "Down These Seen Streets a Man Must Go: Siegfried Kracauer, 'Hollywood's Terror Films,' and the Spatiality of Film Noir." *New German Critique* 89 (2003): 113–43.

———. *Film Noir and the Spaces of Modernity.* Cambridge, Mass.: Harvard University Press, 2004.
Dittrich van Weringh, Kathinka, and Helmut G. Asper, eds. *Nachrichten aus Hollywood, New York und anderswo. Der Briefwechsel Eugen und Marlise Schüfftans mit Siegfried und Lili Kracauer.* Trier: WVT (Wissenschaftlicher Verlag Trier), 2003.
Durham Peters, John. "Exile, Nomadism, and Diaspora: The Stakes of Mobility in the Western Canon." In *Home, Exile, Homeland: Film, Media, and the Politics of Place,* ed. Hamid Naficy, 17–41. New York: Routledge, 1999.
Editors. "The Crisis of the Individual: A Series." *Commentary* 1, no. 2 (December 1945): 1–2.
"Edward Steichen at *The Family of Man,* 1955." MoMA, *Archive Highlights.* Available at www.moma.org/learn/resources/archives/archives_highlights_06_1955 (accessed January 30, 2016).
Elsaesser, Thomas. *Metropolis.* London: BFI Publications, 2000.
———. *Weimar Cinema and After: Germany's Historical Imaginary.* London: Routledge, 2000.
———. *Das Weimarer Kino. Aufgeklärt und doppelbödig.* Berlin: Vorwerk 8, 1999.
Fay, Jennifer. *Theaters of Occupation.* Minneapolis: University of Minnesota Press, 2008.
Fearing, Franklin. "A Bibliography for the Quarter." *Quarterly of Film, Radio, and Television* 5, no. 1 (Autumn 1950): 100–103.
Fisher, Lucy, ed. "In Focus: SCMS at Fifty." *Cinema Journal* 49, no .1 (Fall 2009): 128–76.
Flusser, Vilém. *The Freedom of the Migrant: Objections to Nationalism.* Ed. Kenneth Kronenberg and Anke K. Finger. Urbana: University of Illinois Press, 2003.
Friedman, Murray, ed. *Commentary in American Life.* Philadelphia: Temple University Press, 2005.
Frisby, David. *Fragments of Modernity: Theories of Modernity in the Work of Simmel, Kracauer, and Benjamin.* Cambridge, Mass.: MIT Press, 1986.
Fromm, Erich. *Escape from Freedom.* New York: Farrar & Rinehart, 1941.
Gary, Brett. "Mobilizing for the War on Words: The Rockefeller Foundation, Communication Scholars, and the State." In *The Nervous Liberals: Propaganda Anxieties from World War I to the Cold War.* New York: Columbia University Press, 1999.
———. *The Nervous Liberals: Propaganda Anxieties from World War I to the Cold War.* New York: Columbia University Press, 1999.
Gemünden, Gerd, and Johannes von Moltke, eds. *Culture in the Anteroom: The Legacies of Siegfried Kracauer.* Ann Arbor: University of Michigan Press, 2012.
———. "Kracauer's Legacies." In *Culture in the Anteroom: The Legacies of Siegfried Kracauer,* ed. Gerd Gemünden and Johannes von Moltke, 1–25. Ann Arbor: University of Michigan Press, 2012.

Gerow, Aaron. *Decentering Theory: Reconsidering the History of Japanese Film Theory.* Saitama-ken, Sakado-shi, Japan: Center for Inter-cultural Studies and Education, Josai University, 2010.

Gessner, Robert. "Cinema and Scholarship." *Journal of the Society of Cinematologists* 3 (1963): 73–80.

———. "'The Parts of Cinema': A Definition." *Journal of the Society of Cinematologists* 1 (1961): 25–39.

Ginzburg, Carlo. "Details, Plans, Microanalysis: Thoughts on a Book by Siegfried Kracauer." In *Threads and Traces: True, False, Fictive,* 180–192. Berkeley: University of California Press, 2012.

Giovacchni, Saverio. *Hollywood Modernism: Film and Politics in the Age of the New Deal.* Philadelphia: Temple University Press, 2001.

Giddens, Anthony. *The Consequences of Modernity.* Stanford, Calif.: Stanford University Press, 1990.

Giesen, Rolf, and Manfred Hobsch. *Hitlerjunge Quex, Jud Süiss und Kolberg. Die Propagandafilme des Dritten Reiches: Dokumente und Materialien zum NS-Film.* Berlin: Schwarzkopf & Schwarzkopf, 2005.

Gilloch, Graeme. *Siegfried Kracauer.* Malden, Mass.: Polity, 2015.

Gilloch, G., and J. Kang. "Below the Surface: Antisemitism, Prejudice, and Siegfried Kracauer's 'Test Film' Project." *New Formations* 61, no. 2 (July 2007): 149–60.

Glazer, Nathan. "*Commentary:* The Early Years." In *"Commentary" in American Life,* ed. Murray Friedman, 38–51. Philadelphia: Temple University Press, 2005.

Goebbels, Joseph. "Dr. Goebbels' Speech at the Kaiserhof on March 28, 1933." In *German Essays on Film,* ed. Richard W. McCormick and Alison Guenther-Pal, 153–58. New York: Continuum, 2004.

———. "Mimikry." In *Die Zeit ohne Beispiel. Reden und Aufsätze aus den Jahren 1939/40/41,* 526–31. Munich: Zentralverlag der NSDAP, 1941.

Greenberg, Clement. "Avant-Garde and Kitsch." *Partisan Review* 6, no. 5 (1939): 34–49.

Greenstein, Fred I. "Personality and Political Socialization: The Theories of Authoritarian and Democratic Character." *Annals of the American Academy of Political and Social Science* 361, no. 1 (1965): 81–95.

Greif, Mark. *The Age of the Crisis of Man: Thought and Fiction in America, 1933–1973.* Princeton, N.J.: Princeton University Press, 2015.

Grieveson, Lee. "Discipline and Publish: The Birth of Cinematology." *Cinema Journal* 49, no. 1 (2009): 168–76.

Grieveson, Lee, and Haidee Wasson. *Inventing Film Studies.* Durham, N.C.: Duke University Press, 2008.

Guest, Haden. "Experimentation and Innovation in Three American Film Journals of the 1950s." In *Inventing Film Studies,* ed. Lee Grieveson and Haidee Wasson, 235–63. Durham, N.C.: Duke University Press, 2008.

Guilbaut, Serge. *How New York Stole the Idea of Modern Art: Abstract Expressionism, Freedom, and the Cold War.* Chicago: University of Chicago Press, 1983.

Hake, Sabine. *Screen Nazis: Cinema, History, and Democracy.* Madison: University of Wisconsin Press, 2012.
Hansen, Miriam Bratu. "Benjamin, Cinema, and Experience: 'The Blue Flower in the Land of Technology.'" *New German Critique*, no. 40 (Winter 1987): 179–224.
———. *Cinema and Experience: Siegfried Kracauer, Walter Benjamin, and Theodor W. Adorno.* Berkeley: University of California Press, 2012.
———. "Introduction." In Siegfried Kracauer, *Theory of Film: The Redemption of Physical Reality*, vii–xlv. Princeton, N.J.: Princeton University Press, 1997.
———. "'With Skin and Hair': Kracauer's Theory of Film, Marseille 1940." *Critical Inquiry* 19 (Spring 1995): 437–69.
Harcourt, Peter. "What, Indeed, Is Cinema?" *Cinema Journal* 8, no. 1 (1968): 22–28.
Hell, Julia. "The Angel's Enigmatic Eyes; or, The Gothic Beauty of Catastrophic History in W.G. Sebald's 'Air War and Literature.'" *Criticism* 46, no. 3 (2004): 361–92.
———. "Modernity and the Holocaust; or, Listening to Eurydice." *Theory, Culture, and Society* 27, no. 6 (November 1, 2010): 125–54.
———. "Ruins Travel: Orphic Journeys through 1940s Germany." In *Writing Travel: The Poetics and Politics of the Modern Journey*, ed. John Zilcosky, 123–60. Toronto: University of Toronto Press, 2008.
Hell, Julia, and Andreas Schönle, eds. *Ruins of Modernity.* Durham, N.C.: Duke University Press, 2010.
Higson, Andrew. "The Concept of National Cinema." *Screen* 30, no. 4 (1989): 36–46.
———. "The Limiting Imagination of National Cinema." In *Cinema and Nation*, ed. Mette Hjort and Scott MacKenzie, 63–74. London: Routledge, 2000.
Himelhoch, Jerome. "Is There a Bigot Personality? A Report on Some Preliminary Studies." *Commentary* 3, no. 3 (March 1947): 277–84.
Hinkle, Karl W. "Films and Nations: Siegfried Kracauer, *From Caligari to Hitler* (Book Review)." *ETC: A Review of General Semantics* 5, no. 2 (1948): 132–35.
Hirsch, Marianne. *Family Frames: Photography, Narrative, and Postmemory.* Cambridge, Mass.: Harvard University Press, 1997.
Hook, Sidney. "Intelligence and Evil in Human History: An Answer to Intellectual Defeatism." *Commentary* 3, no. 3 (March 1947): 210–21.
Horkheimer, Max. *Eclipse of Reason.* New York: Seabury Press, 1974.
———. "Introduction." In Leo Löwenthal and Norbert Guterman, *Prophets of Deceit: A Study of the Techniques of the American Agitator*, xi–xii. New York: Harper, 1949.
———. *Studien über Autorität und Familie. Forschungsberichte aus dem Institut für Sozialforschung.* Paris: F. Alcan, 1936.
Horkheimer, Max, and Theodor W. Adorno. *Dialectic of Enlightenment: Philosophical Fragments.* Stanford, Calif.: Stanford University Press, 2002.

Howe, Irving. "The New York Intellectuals: A Chronicle and a Critique." *Commentary* 46, no. 4 (October 1968): 29–51.

———. "New York in the Thirties: Some Fragments of Memory." *Dissent* 8, no. 3 (Summer 1961): 241–50.

———. "Notes on Mass Culture." *Politics*, March 1948, 120–22.

Huyssen, Andreas. *Miniature Metropolis: Literature in an Age of Photography and Film*. Cambridge, Mass.: Harvard University Press, 2015. ———. "The Vamp and the Machine: Technology and Sexuality in Fritz Lang's Metropolis." *New German Critique*, nos. 24–25 (1981): 221–37.

Isenberg, Noah W. "Investigations of Character: Jewish Exiles Face the German Question." *German Politics and Society* 13, no. 3 (Fall 1995): 81–88.

———. "This Pen for Hire: Siegfried Kracauer as American Cultural Critic." In *Culture in the Anteroom: The Legacies of Siegfried Kracauer*, ed. Gerd Gemünden and Johannes von Moltke, 29–41. Ann Arbor: University of Michigan Press, 2012.

Itkin, Alan. "Orpheus, Perseus, Ahasuerus: Reflection and Representation in Siegfried Kracauer's Underworlds of History." *Germanic Review: Literature, Culture, Theory* 87, no. 2 (2012): 175–202.

James, Sarah E. "A Post-Fascist Family of Man? Cold War Humanism, Democracy, and Photography in Germany." *Oxford Art Journal* 35, no. 3 (December 1, 2012): 315–36.

Jay, Martin. *The Dialectical Imagination: A History of the Frankfurt School and the Institute of Social Research, 1923–1950*. Boston: Little, Brown, 1973.

———. "Experience without a Subject." In *Cultural Semantics: Keywords of Our Time*, 47–61. Amherst: University of Massachusetts Press, 1998.

———. "The Extraterritorial Life of Siegfried Kracauer." In *Permanent Exiles: Essays on the Intellectual Migration from Germany to America*, 152–97. New York: Columbia University Press, 1986.

———. "Kracauer, the Magical Nominalist." In *Siegfried Kracauer's American Writings*, 227–36.

———. *Songs of Experience: Modern American and European Variations on a Universal Theme*. Berkeley: University of California Press, 2006.

Jeffers, Thomas L. "What They Talked about When They Talked about Literature: *Commentary* in Its First Three Decades." In *"Commentary" in American Life*, ed. Murray Friedman, 99–126. Philadelphia: Temple University Press, 2005.

Jenemann, David. *Adorno in America*. Minneapolis: University of Minnesota Press, 2007.

Jones, Janna. "The Library of Congress Film Project: Film Collecting and a United State(s) of Mind." *Moving Image* 6, no. 2 (2006): 30–51.

Jumonville, Neil. *Critical Crossings: The New York Intellectuals in Postwar America*. Berkeley: University of California Press, 1991.

———. "Introduction." In *The New York Intellectuals Reader*, ed. Neil Jumonville, 1–11. New York: Routledge, 2007.

Kael, Pauline. "Is There a Cure for Film Criticism?" *Sight and Sound* 31, no. 2 (Spring 1962): 56–65.
Kaes, Anton. "Metropolis." In *Weimar Cinema: An Essential Guide to Classic Films of the Era*, ed. Noah Isenberg, 173–92. New York: Columbia University Press, 2009.
———. *Shell Shock Cinema: Weimar Culture and the Wounds of War*. Princeton, N.J.: Princeton University Press, 2009.
———. "Siegfried Kracauer: The Film Historian in Exile." In *"Escape to Life": German Intellectuals in New York; A Compendium on Exile after 1933*, ed. Eckart Goebel and Sigrid Weigel, 236–69. Berlin: de Gruyter, 2012.
———. "What to Do with Germany?" *German Politics and Society* 13, no. 3 (Fall 1995): 130–41.
Kaes, Anton, Nicholas W. Baer, and Michael Cowan, eds. *The Promise of Cinema: German Film Theory, 1907–1933*. Annotated ed. Berkeley: University of California Press, 2015.
Kapczynski, Jennifer M. *The German Patient: Crisis and Recovery in Postwar Culture*. Ann Arbor: University of Michigan Press, 2011.
Kappelhoff, Hermann. *The Politics and Poetics of Cinematic Realism*. Trans. Daniel Hendrickson. New York: Columbia University Press, 2015.
———. "Realität Lesen: Das Kino und die Politik des Ästhetischen." In *Unerhörte Erfahrung: Texte zum Kino*, ed. Doris Kern and Sabine Nessel, 27–65. Frankfurt am Main: Stroemfeld, 2008.
Katznelson, Ira. *Fear Itself: The New Deal and the Origins of Our Time*. W.W. Norton, 2013.
Keathley, Christian. *Cinephilia and History; or, The Wind in the Trees*. Bloomington: Indiana University Press, 2006.
"Keine Zwischenfälle auf der 'Nyassa.'" *Aufbau*, May 2, 1941, 4.
Keller, Sarah, and Jason N. Paul, eds. *Jean Epstein: Critical Essays and New Translations*. Amsterdam: Amsterdam University Press, 2012.
Kessler, Michael, and Thomas Y. Levin, eds. *Siegfried Kracauer. Neue Interpretationen*. Tübingen: Stauffenburg, 1990.
King, Richard H. *Arendt and America*. Chicago: University of Chicago Press, 2015.
Koch, Gertrud. "Die kritische Theorie in Hollywood." In Koch, *Die Einstellung ist die Einstellung. Visuelle Konstruktionen des Judentums*, 54–256. Frankfurt am Main: Suhrkamp, 1992.
———. "'Not Yet Accepted Anywhere': Exile, Memory, and Image in Kracauer's Conception of History." Trans. Jeremy Gaines. *New German Critique*, no. 54 (October 1991): 95–109.
———. *Siegfried Kracauer: An Introduction*. Trans. Jeremy Gaines. Princeton, N.J.: Princeton University Press, 2000.
———. *Siegfried Kracauer zur Einführung*. Hamburg: Junius, 2012.
Kohn, Hans. "This Century of Betrayal: Can American Lead a New Struggle for Independence?" *Commentary* 2, no. 3 (September 1946): 201–8.
Konuk, Kader. *East West Mimesis: Auerbach in Turkey*. Stanford, Calif.: Stanford University Press, 2010.

Kotzian, Ortfried. *Die Umsiedler. Die Deutschen aus West-Wolhynien, Galizien, der Bukowina, Bessarbien, der Dobrudscha und in der Karpatenukraine.* Munich: Langen Müller, 2005.

Kracauer, Siegfried. "Americana: Glossen zur Ausstellung 'Trois Siècles d'Art aux États-Unis.'" In *Essays, Feuilletons, Rezensionen, 1932–1965*, ed. Inka Mülder-Bach, 554–65. Werke 5.4. Frankfurt am Main: Suhrkamp, 2011.

———. "Ausstellung der New-Yorker Film Library." In *Kleine Schriften zum Film, 1932–1961*, 215–17.

———. "Bemerkungen zum französischen Film." In *Kleine Schriften zum Film, 1932–1961*, 282–86.

———. "Calico World." In *The Mass Ornament: Weimar Essays*, 281–88.

———. "Caligari." *Partisan Review* 14, no. 2 (March 1947): 160–73.

———. "The Challenge of Qualitative Content Analysis." *Public Opinion Quarterly* 16, no. 4 (1952): 631–42.

———. "Climate of Doom." *New Republic*, March 7, 1949, 24.

———. "The Conquest of Europe on the Screen: The Nazi Newsreel, 1939–40." *Social Research* 10, no. 1 (January 1943): 38.

———. "Dumbo (1941)." In *Siegfried Kracauer's American Writings*, 139–40.

———. *Essays, Feuilletons, Rezensionen, 1932–1965.* Ed. Inka Mülder-Bach. Werke 5. 3 vols. Frankfurt am Main: Suhrkamp, 2011.

———. "Freedom from Fear: An Analysis of Popular Film Trends." In *Kleine Schriften zum Film, 1932–1961*, 479–85.

———. *From Caligari to Hitler: A Psychological History of the German Film.* Princeton, N.J.: Princeton University Press, 2004.

———. "Georg Simmel." In *The Mass Ornament: Weimar Essays*, 225–57.

———. *Ginster: Von ihm selbst geschrieben.* In *Romane und Erzählungen.* Ed. Inka Mülder-Bach and Sabine Biebl. Werke 7, 9–256. Frankfurt am Main: Suhrkamp, 2004.

———. *History: The Last Things before the Last.* New York: Oxford University Press, 1969.

———. "Hollywood's Terror Films: Do They Reflect an American State of Mind? (1946)." In *Siegfried Kracauer's American Writings*, 41–46.

———. "Internationaler Tonfilm? (1931)." In *Kleine Schriften zum Film, 1928–1931*, ed. Inka Mülder-Bach, 475–79. Werke 6.2. Frankfurt am Main: Suhrkamp, 2004.

———. *Kleine Schriften zum Film, 1932–1961.* Ed. Inka Mülder-Bach. Werke 6. 3 vols. Frankfurt am Main: Suhrkamp, 2004.

———. "The Little Shopgirls Go to the Movies." In *The Mass Ornament: Weimar Essays*, 290–304.

———. "'Marseiller Entwurf': Zu einer Theorie des Films." In *Theorie des Films. Die Errettung der äußeren Wirklichkeit*, 521–779. Werke 3. Frankfurt am Main: Suhrkamp, 2005.

———. "The Mass Ornament." In *The Mass Ornament: Weimar Essays*, 75–88.

Kracauer, Siegfried *(continued)*. *The Mass Ornament: Weimar Essays.* Trans. and ed. Thomas Y. Levin. Cambridge, Mass: Harvard University Press, 1995.

———. "Movie Mirror (1950)." In *Siegfried Kracauer's American Writings,* 195–96.

———. *Orpheus in Paris: Offenbach and the Paris of His Time.* New York: Alfred A. Knopf, 1938.

———. "Pariser Kunstchronik." In *Essays, Feuilletons, Rezensionen, 1932– 1965.* Ed. Inka Mülder-Bach, 551–53. Werke 5.4. Frankfurt am Main: Suhrkamp, 2011.

———. *The Past's Threshold: Essays on Photography.* Ed. Philippe Despoix and Maria Zinfert. Zurich: Diaphanes, 2014.

———. "Photography." In *The Mass Ornament: Weimar Essays,* 47–64.

———. "Preston Sturges, or Laughter Betrayed (1950)." In *Siegfried Kracauer's American Writings,* 109–14.

———. "Propaganda and the Nazi War Film." In *From Caligari to Hitler: A Psychological History of the German Film,* 275–331. Princeton, N.J.: Princeton University Press, 2004.

———. *Romane und Erzählungen.* Ed. Inka Mülder-Bach. Werke 7. Frankfurt am Main: Suhrkamp, 2004.

———. *The Salaried Masses: Duty and Distraction in Weimar Germany.* Trans. Quentin Hoare. London: Verso, 1998.

———. *Siegfried Kracauer's American Writings: Essays on Film and Popular Culture.* Ed. Johannes von Moltke and Kristy Rawson. Berkeley: University of California Press, 2012.

———. *Soziologie als Wissenschaft.* Ed. Inka Mülder-Bach. Werke 1.1. Frankfurt am Main: Suhrkamp, 2006.

———. *Straßen in Berlin und anderswo.* Frankfurt am Main: Suhrkamp, 1964.

———. *Studien zu Massenmedien und Propaganda.* Ed. Christian Fleck and Bernd Stiegler. Werke 2.2. Frankfurt am Main: Suhrkamp, 2012.

———. "The Task of the Film Critic." In *The Weimar Republic Sourcebook,* ed. Anton Kaes, Martin Jay, and Edward Dimendberg, 634–35. Berkeley: University of California Press, 1994.

———. *Theorie des Films. Die Errettung der äußeren Wirklichkeit.* Ed. Inka Mülder-Bach. Werke 3. Frankfurt am Main: Suhrkamp, 2005.

———. *Theory of Film: The Redemption of Physical Reality.* Princeton, N.J.: Princeton University Press, 1997.

———. "Those Movies with a Message (1948)." In *Siegfried Kracauer's American Writings,* 72–80.

———. "Those Who Wait." In *The Mass Ornament: Weimar Essays,* 129–42.

———. "Totalitäre Propaganda." In *Studien zu Massenmedien und Propaganda,* ed. Christian Fleck and Bernd Stiegler, Werke 2.2, 17–173. Frankfurt am Main: Suhrkamp, 2012.

———. *Von Caligari zu Hitler.* Ed. Sabine Biebl. Werke 2.1. Frankfurt am Main: Suhrkamp, 2012.

———. "Wetter und Retter." In *Kleine Schriften zum Film, 1932–1961,* 43–44.

———. "Why France Liked Our Films." In *Siegfried Kracauer's American Writings*, 33–40.

———. "Wiedersehen mit alten Filmen: Pudowkin." In *Kleine Schriften zum Film, 1932–1961*, 226–228.

———. "Zur Ästhetik des Farbenfilms (1937)." In *Kleine Schriften zum Film, 1932–1961*, 194–198.

Kracauer, Siegfried, and Paul L. Berkman. *Satellite Mentality: Political Attitudes and Propaganda Susceptibilities of Non-Communists in Hungary, Poland, and Czechoslovakia*. New York: F.A. Praeger, 1956.

Kracauer, Siegfried, and Joseph Lyford. "A Duck Crosses Main Street." *New Republic*, December 13, 1938.

Kracauer, Siegfried, and Erwin Panofsky. *Siegfried Kracauer, Erwin Panofsky: Briefwechsel 1941–1966*. Ed. Volker Breidecker. Berlin: Akademie Verlag, 1996.

Kris, Ernst, and Hans Speier. *German Radio Propaganda: Report on Home Broadcasts during the War*. London: Oxford University Press, 1944.

Kuhn, Annette. "Screen and Screen Theorizing Today." *Screen* 50, no. 1 (March 20, 2009): 1–12.

Lasswell, Harold Dwight. "Democratic Character." In *The Political Writings of Harold D. Lasswell*, 465–525. Glencoe Ill.: Free Press, 1951.

———. "The Garrison State." *American Journal of Sociology* 46, no. 4 (1941): 455–68.

Laudani, Raffaele, ed. *Secret Reports on Nazi Germany: The Frankfurt School Contribution to the War Effort*. Princeton, N.J.: Princeton University Press, 2013.

Lazarsfeld, Paul. "Remarks on Adminstrative and Critical Communications Research." *Studies in Philosophy and Social Science* 9, no. 3 (Spring 1941).

"Leningrad Hailed by Soviet Writers." *New York Times*, February 26, 1942, 9.

Lentricchia, Frank, and Andrew DuBois, eds. *Close Reading: The Reader*. Durham, N.C.: Duke University Press, 2003.

Lethen, Helmut. "Sichtbarkeit: Kracauer's Liebeslehre." In *Siegfried Kracauer. Neue Interpretationen*, ed. Michael Kessler and Thomas Y. Levin, 195–228. Tübingen: Stauffenburg, 1990.

Levin, Thomas Y. "The English-Language Reception of Kracauer's Work: A Bibliography." *New German Critique*, no. 54 (Fall 1991): 183–89.

———. "Iconology at the Movies: Panofsky's Film Theory." *Yale Journal of Criticism* 9, no. 1 (Spring 1996): 27–55.

———. "Introduction." In Siegfried Kracauer, *The Mass Ornament: Weimar Essays*, trans. and ed. Thomas Y. Levin, 1–30. Cambridge, Mass.: Harvard University Press, 1996.

———. *Siegfried Kracauer. Eine Bibliographie seiner Schriften*. Marbach am Neckar: Deutsche Schillergesellschaft, 1989.

———. "Siegfried Kracauer in English: A Bibliography." *New German Critique*, no. 41 (Spring 1987): 140–50.

"Lewis Says Hays Bans Film of Book." *New York Times*, February 16, 1936, 1.

Loewy, Hanno. *Béla Balázs. Märchen, Ritual und Film.* Berlin: Vorwerk 8, 2003.
Longerich, Peter. *"Davon haben wir nichts gewusst!" Die Deutschen und die Judenverfolgung 1933–1945.* Munich: Siedler, 2006.
Loriga, Sabina. "L'histoire mode de vie: Reflexions autour de Hannah Arendt et Siegfried Kracauer." In *Penser l'histoire: De Marx aux siècles des catastrophes,* ed. Christophe Bouton and Bruce Bégout. 211–26. Paris: Éd. de l'Éclat, 2011.
Löwenthal, Leo. "As I Remember Friedel." *New German Critique,* no. 54 (October 1, 1991): 5–17.
———. "Terror's Atomization of Man." *Commentary* 1, no. 3 (January 1946): 1–8.
Löwenthal, Leo, and Norbert Guterman. *Prophets of Deceit: A Study of the Techniques of the American Agitator.* New York: Harper, 1949.
Löwenthal, Leo, and Siegfried Kracauer. *In steter Freundschaft. Leo Löwenthal–Siegfried Kracauer, Briefwechsel 1921–1966.* Springe: zu Klampen, 2003.
Luhr, William. *Film Noir.* Chichester, West Sussex: Wiley-Blackwell, 2012.
Macdonald, Dwight. "'The Conquest of Europe on the Screen: The Nazi News-Reel, 1939–1940,' by Siegfried Kracauer, *Social Research,* September 1943." *Politics,* May 1944, 118.
———. "I Choose the West" (1952). In *The New York Intellectuals Reader,* ed. Neil Jumonville, 63–68. New York: Routledge, 2007.
———. "Lowbrow Thinking." *Politics* 1, no. 7 (August 1944): 217–18.
———. "Masscult and Midcult." In Macdonald, *Masscult and Midcult: Essays against the American Grain,* ed. John Summers, 3–71. New York: New York Review Books, 2011.
———. "The Soviet Cinema: 1930–1938" (parts 1 and 2). *Partisan Review* 5, no. 2 (1938): 37–50; 5, no. 3 (1938): 35–62.
———. "A Theory of Mass Culture." In *Mass Culture: The Popular Arts in America,* ed. Bernard Rosenberg and David Manning White, 59–73. Glencoe, Ill.: Free Press, 1957.
———. "Through the Lens Darkly." *Partisan Review* 14, no. 5 (1947): 526–28.
MacDonald, Scott, ed. *Cinema 16: Documents toward a History of the Film Society.* Philadelphia: Temple University Press, 2002.
Macé, Arnaud. "Siegfried Kracauer: La critique et l'histoire, écritures de la hantise." *Cahiers du cinéma,* no. 627 (October 2007): 68–71.
Mack, Michael. "Film as Memory: Siegfried Kracauer's Psychological History of German 'National Culture.'" *Journal of European Studies* 30, no. 118 (2000): 157–81.
Marcuse, Herbert. "The Affirmative Character of Culture" (1937). In Marcuse, *Negations: Essays in Critical Theory,* 88–133. Boston: Beacon Press, 1968.
Marx, Karl, and Friedrich Engels. *Collected Works,* vol. 28. New York: International Publishers, 1986.
Metz, Christian. "Le cinéma: Langue ou langage?" *Communications* 4, no. 1 (1964): 52–90.
———. *The Imaginary Signifier: Psychoanalysis and the Cinema.* Bloomington: Indiana University Press, 1981.

Michael, Klaus. "Vor dem Café: Walter Benjamin und Siegfried Kracauer in Marseille." In *Aber ein Sturm weht vom Paradiese her: Texte zu Walter Benjamin,* ed. Michael Opitz and Erdmut Wizisla, 203–21. Leipzig: Reclam, 1992.
Mills, C. Wright. "The Nazi Behemoth Dissected." *Partisan Review* 9, no. 5 (September 1,1942): 432–37.
Mülder-Bach, Inka. "The Exile of Modernity: Kracauer's Figurations of the Stranger." In *Culture in the Anteroom: The Legacies of Siegfried Kracauer,* ed. Gerd Gemünden and Johannes von Moltke, 276–92. Ann Arbor: University of Michigan Press, 2012.
———. "History as Autobiography: The Last Things before the Last." Trans. Gail Finney. *New German Critique* 54 (1991): 139–57.
———. "Nachbemerkung und editorische Notiz." In Siegfried Kracauer, *Theorie des Films,* ed. Inka Mülder-Bach with Sabine Biebl, Werke 3, 847–74. Frankfurt am Main: Suhrkamp, 2005.
Müller, Tim. *Krieger und Gelehrte: Herbert Marcuse und die Denksysteme im kalten Krieg.* Hamburg: Hamburger Edition, 2013.
Museum of Modern Art (New York). *The Family of Man: The Greatest Photographic Exhibition of All Time—503 Pictures from 68 Countries.* New York: Pubished for the Museum of Modern Art by the Maco Magazine Corp., 1955.
Musial, Bogdan. "Das Schlachtfeld zweier totalitärer Systeme: Polen unter deutscher und sowjetischer Herrschaft 1939–1941." In *Genesis des Genozids. Polen 1939–1941,* ed. Klaus-Michael Mallmann and Bogdan Musial, 13–35 Darmstadt: Wissenschaftliche Buchgesellschaft, 2004.
Naficy, Hamid. "Introduction. Framing Exile: From Homeland to Homepage." In *Home, Exile, Homeland: Film, Media, and the Politics of Place,* ed. Hamid Naficy, 1–17. New York: Routledge, 1999.
"A Nation and Its Movies." *Time,* May 19, 1947.
"New Yorker Notizbuch." *Aufbau,* July 4, 1941.
Niebuhr, Reinhold. "Will Civilization Survive Technics?" *Commentary* 1, no. 2 (December 1945): 2–8.
Nornes, Markus. *Japanese Documentary Film: The Meiji Era through Hiroshima.* Minneapolis: University of Minnesota Press, 2003.
Noxon, Gerald. "The Anatomy of the Close-up: Some Literary Origins in the Works of Flaubert, Huysmans, and Proust." *Journal of the Society of Cinematologists* 1 (1961): 1–24.
"Obituary [of Siegfried Kracauer]." *Cinema Journal* 6 (1966): 32.
O'Brian, John. "The Nuclear Family of Man." *Asia-Pacific Journal: Japan Focus,* July 11, 2008.
Orton, William A. "Everyman amid the Stereotypes." *Commentary* 1, no. 7 (May 1946): 9–16.
Panofsky, Erwin. "Style and Medium in the Motion Pictures." In Panofsky, *Three Essays on Style,* ed. Irving Lavin, 91–128. Cambridge, Mass.: MIT Press, 1995.

Pataki, Heidi. "Das Kino und die Wirklichkeit." *Frankfurter Allgemeine Zeitung*, September 6, 1973.

Patalas, Enno. "Siegfried Kracauer." *Filmkritik* 11, no. 1 (January 1967): 5.

———. "The Contemporary West German Film as a Social Symptom." *Film Culture* 1, no. 4 (Summer 1955): 9–22.

Perivolaropoulou, Nia, and Philippe Despoix. *Culture de masse et modernité. Siegfried Kracauer: Sociologue, critique, écrivain*. Paris: Éd. de la Maison des sciences de l'homme, 2001.

———. "Postface: 'L'histoire est un amusement de vieillard.'" In Siegfried Kracauer, *L'histoire—Des avant-dernières choses*, 301–313. Paris: Stock, 2008.

Petro, Patrice. "From Lukács to Kracauer and Beyond: Social Film Histories and the German Cinema." *Cinema Journal* 22, no. 3 (1983): 47.

———. *Joyless Streets: Women and Melodramatic Representation in Weimar Germany*. Princeton, N.J.: Princeton University Press, 1989.

———. "Kracauer's Epistemological Shift." *New German Critique*, no. 54 (October 1991): 127–38.

Phelps, Wallace (William Phillips). "Sensibility and Modern Poetry." *Dynamo* 1, no. 3 (1934).

Phelps, Wallace (William Phillips), and Philip Rahv. "Criticism." *Partisan Review and Anvil* 2, no. 7 (April 1, 1935).

Phillips, Christopher. "The Judgment Seat of Photography." *October* 22 (1982): 27.

Phillips, William. *A Partisan View: Five Decades of the Literary Life*. New York: Stein & Day, 1983.

Polan, Dana. *Power and Paranoia: History, Narrative, and the American Cinema, 1940–1950*. New York: Columbia University Press, 1986.

———. *Scenes of Instruction: The Beginnings of the U.S. Study of Film*. Berkeley: University of California Press, 2007.

"Pro-Nazis Cheer War Film in Theater Here." *New York Herald Tribune*, May 8, 1941.

Quaresima, Leonardo. "De faux amis: Kracauer et la filmologie." *Cinémas* 19, nos. 2–3 (2009): 333–58.

———. "Introduction." In Siegfried Kracauer, *From Caligari to Hitler: A Psychological History of the German Film*. Princeton: Princeton University Press, 2004.

Rahv, Philip. "The Cult of Experience in American Writing." *Partisan Review* 7 (January 1940): 412–19.

Reddy, William M. *The Navigation of Feeling: A Framework for the History of Emotions*. Cambridge: Cambridge University Press, 2001.

Remarque, Erich Maria. *Night in Lisbon*. New York: Harcourt, Brace & World, 1964.

Rensmann, Lars, and Samir Suresh Gandesha. *Arendt and Adorno: Political and Philosophical Investigations*. Stanford, Calif.: Stanford University Press, 2012.

Rentschler, Eric. "Cinema and the Legacies of Critical Theory: Roundtable Discussion." *New German Critique*, no. 122 (Summer 2014): 20–28.

———. "Kracauer, Spectatorship, and the Seventies." In *Culture in the Anteroom: The Legacies of Siegfried Kracauer*, ed. Gerd Gemünden and Johannes von Moltke, 61–75. Ann Arbor: University of Michigan Press, 2012.

———. "Rudolf Arnheim's Early Passage between Social and Aesthetic Film Criticism." In *Arnheim for Film and Media Studies*, ed. Scott Higgins, 51–68. New York: Routledge, 2011.

———. *The Ministry of Illusion: Nazi Cinema and Its Afterlife*. Cambridge, Mass.: Harvard University Press, 1996.

Robnik, Drehli. "Among Other Things—a Miraculous Realist: Political Perspectives on the Theoretical Entanglement of Cinema and History in Siegfried Kracauer." In *Culture in the Anteroom: The Legacies of Siegfried Kracauer*, ed. Gerd Gemünden and Johannes von Moltke, 258–75. Ann Arbor: University of Michigan Press, 2012.

Rodowick, David Norman. *The Crisis of Political Modernism: Criticism and Ideology in Contemporary Film Theory*. Berkeley: University of California Press, 1994.

———. *Elegy for Theory*. Cambridge, Mass.: Harvard University Press, 2014.

———. *The Virtual Life of Film*. Cambridge, Mass.: Harvard University Press, 2007.

Rogowski, Christian. "'Written By Himself': Siegfried Kracauer's 'Auto-Biographical' Novels." In *Culture in the Anteroom: The Legacies of Siegfried Kracauer*, ed. Gerd Gemünden and Johannes von Moltke, 199–212. Ann Arbor: University of Michigan Press, 2012.

Ross, Andrew. "Containing Culture in the Cold War." In *No Respect: Intellectuals and Popular Culture*, 42–64. New York: Routledge, 1989.

Rotha, Paul. *The Film till Now: A Survey of World Cinema*. London: Spring Books, 1967.

Said, Edward W. "Traveling Theory." In *The World, the Text, and the Critic*, 226–47. Cambridge, Mass.: Harvard University Press, 1983.

Salazkina, Masha. "Moscow-Rome-Havana: A Film-Theory Road Map." *October*, no. 139 (2012): 97–116.

Schmidt-Linsenhoff, Viktoria. "Denied Images: The Family of Man and the Shoa." In *The Family of Man 1955–2001. Humanismus und Postmoderne: Eine Revision von Edward Steichens Fotoausstellung*, ed. Jean Back and Viktoria Schmidt-Linsenhoff, 81–99. Marburg: Jonas Verlag, 2004.

Schöttker, Detlev. "Bild, Kultur und Theorie: Siegfried Kracauer und der Warburg Kreis." In *Denken durch die Dinge. Siegfried Kracauer im Kontext*, ed. Frank Grunert and Dorothee Kimmich, 207–24. Munich: Fink, 2009.

Schulte-Sasse, Linda. *Entertaining the Third Reich: Illusions of Wholeness in Nazi Cinema*. Durham, N.C.: Duke University Press, 1996.

Scott, Joan. "The Evidence of Experience." *Critical Inquiry* 17, no. 4 (Summer 1991): 773–97.

Sebald, W.G. *On the Natural History of Destruction: With Essays on Alfred Andersch, Jean Améry, and Peter Weiss*. Trans. Anthea Bell. New York: Modern Library, 2004.

Sekula, Allan. "The Traffic in Photographs." *Art Journal* 41, no. 1 (1981): 15–25.

Shaviro, Steven. *The Universe of Things*. Minneapolis: University of Minnesota Press, 2014.

Siepmann, Charles A. "Kracauer, Siegfried, *Theory of Film*." *Public Opinion Quarterly* 25, no. 1 (Spring 1961): 153.

Sitton, Robert. *Lady in the Dark: Iris Barry and the Art of Film*. New York: Columbia University Press, 2014.

Solomon-Godeau, Abigail. "Den Humanismus für ein postmodernes Zeitalter aufpolieren." In *The Family of Man 1955–2001. Humanismus und Postmoderne: Eine Revision von Edward Steichens Fotoausstellung*, ed. Jean Back and Viktoria Schmidt-Linsenhoff, 28–55. Marburg: Jonas Verlag, 2004.

Sontag, Susan. "Against Interpretation." In *Against Interpretation, and Other Essays*, 3–14. New York: Farrar, Straus & Giroux, 1966.

———. "Fascinating Facism." In *Under the Sign of Saturn*, 73–98. New York: Farrar, Straus & Giroux, 1980.

Speier, Hans. "Magic Geography." *Social Research* 8, no. 3 (Fall 1941): 310–30.

———. "On Propaganda." *Social Research* 1, no. 3 (1934): 376–80.

Stam, Robert. *Film Theory: An Introduction*. Malden, Mass.: Wiley, 2000.

Steichen, Edward. "On Photography." *Daedalus* 89, no. 1 (January 1960): 136–37.

Stern, Seymour. "Political History of the German Film: *From Caligari to Hitler* (Book Review)." *New Leader*, June 28, 1947, 11.

Stimson, Blake. *The Pivot of the World: Photography and Its Nation*. Cambridge, Mass.: MIT Press, 2006.

Teachout, Terry. "The Experience of America: Robert Warshow, the Critic Who Did Pop Culture Right." *Weekly Standard*, March 25, 2002.

Teres, Harvey M. *Renewing the Left: Politics, Imagination, and the New York Intellectuals*. New York: Oxford University Press, 1996.

Theweleit, Klaus. *Male Fantasies: Psychoanalyzing the White Terror*. Trans. Chris Turner. Vol. 2. Cambridge: Polity Press; Minneapolis: Regents of the University of Minnesota, 1989.

"Tiny Liner Brings 816 From Europe." *New York Times*, April 26, 1941.

Toeplitz, Jerzy. "Film Scholarship: Present and Prospective." *Film Quarterly* 16, no. 3 (Spring 1963): 27–37.

Traverso, Enzo. *Siegfried Kracauer: Itinéraire d'un intellectuel nomade*. Paris: Éd. la Découverte, 1994.

Trilling, Lionel. "The Function of the Little Magazine." In *The Liberal Imagination: Essays on Literature and Society*, 93–103. New York: Viking Press, 1950.

———. *The Liberal Imagination: Essays on Literature and Society.* New York: Viking Press, 1950.

———. "Reality in America." In *The Liberal Imagination: Essays on Literature and Society,* 3–21. New York: Viking Press, 1950.

Trimmel, Gerald. *Heimkehr: Strategien eines nationalsozialistischen Films.* Vienna: W. Eichbauer Verlag, 1998.

Truffaut, François. "A Certain Tendency of the French Cinema." In *Movies and Methods,* ed. Bill Nichols, 224–37. Berkeley: University of California Press, 1976.

Turner, Fred. "*The Family of Man* and the Politics of Attention in Cold War America." *Public Culture* 24, no. 1 (January 2012): 55–84.

Urwand, Ben. *The Collaboration: Hollywood's Pact with Hitler.* Cambridge, Mass.: Belknap Press, 2013.

von Moltke, Johannes. "2 February, 1956. Siegfried Kracauer Advocates a Socio-Aesthetic Approach to Film in a Letter to Enno Patalas." In *A New History of German Cinema,* ed. Jennifer M. Kapczynski and Michael David Richardson, 359–64. Rochester, N.Y.: Camden House, 2012.

———. *No Place Like Home: Locations of Heimat in German Cinema.* Berkeley: University of California Press, 2005.

———. "Out of the Past: Classical Film Theory." *Screen* 55, no. 3 (Autumn 2014): 394–403.

———. "Theory of the Novel: The Literary Imagination of Classical Film Theory." *October,* no. 144 (Spring 2013): 49–72.

Wald, Alan M. *The New York Intellectuals: The Rise and Decline of the Anti-Stalinist Left from the 1930s to the 1980s.* Chapel Hill: University of North Carolina Press, 1987.

Warshow, Robert. *The Immediate Experience: Movies, Comics, Theatre, and Other Aspects of Popular Culture.* Cambridge, Mass.: Harvard University Press, 2002.

———. "The German Film." *The New Leader,* August 9, 1947, 14.

Wasson, Haidee. *Museum Movies: The Museum of Modern Art and the Birth of Art Cinema.* Berkeley: University of California Press, 2005.

Weinburg, Herman. "The Film and Humanity." *Sight and Sound* 16 (1947): 78–79.

Welch, David. *Propaganda and the German Cinema, 1933–1945.* London: I. B. Tauris, 20010.

Wheatland, Thomas. *The Frankfurt School in Exile.* Minneapolis: University of Minnesota Press, 2009.

Wiggershaus, Rolf. *The Frankfurt School: Its History, Theories, and Political Significance.* Cambridge, Mass.: MIT Press, 1995.

Wilford, Hugh. *The New York Intellectuals: From Vanguard to Institution.* Manchester: Manchester University Press, 1995.

Witte, Karsten. "Siegfried Kracauer im Exil." *Exilforschung* 5 (1987): 135–49.

Wolfenstein, Martha, and Nathan Leites. *Movies: A Psychological Study.* Glencoe, Ill.: Free Press, 1950.

Wreszin, Michael, ed. *A Moral Temper: The Letters of Dwight Macdonald.* Chicago: Ivan R. Dee, 2001.
———. *A Rebel in Defense of Tradition: The Life and Politics of Dwight Macdonald.* New York: Basic Books, 1994.
Young-Bruehl, Elisabeth. *Hannah Arendt: For Love of the World.* New Haven, Conn.: Yale University Press, 1982.
Zinfert, Maria, ed. *Kracauer: Photographic Archive.* Zurich: Diaphanes, 2015.

Index

abstract expressionism, 158
abstraction, 8, 136–37, 155, 160, 166–68, 176, 206–8
Abwege (dir. Pabst, 1928), 144
"active passivity" (Kracauer), 108, 193, 197, 273n66
Adorno, Theodor W., 1–3, 6, 8–10, 22–23, 35, 37, 42, 47–48, 59–61, 76, 84, 86, 148–49, 159, 164, 166, 170, 195, 198, 200, 209, 215–16, 218; on anti-Semitism, 74; "The Curious Realist," 163, 170, 218; and Horkheimer, 28, 74, 86, 110–11, 121, 152, 154, 181; *Minima Moralia*, 147, 165. See also *Authoritarian Personality, The*; Horkheimer and Adorno
aesthetics: film, 30, 55, 99–100, 137, 139, 145, 148, 153, 160, 163, 173, 176–77, 200, 205, 207, 212, 215; middlebrow, 172; montage, 52; and politics, 50; propaganda, 60
affect, 84, 90, 162, 183
affinities: film's, 4, 18, 31, 34, 50, 55, 56, 146, 163, 169, 189, 191
Agee, James, 209–11
Ahasuerus, 182, 194–96, 256n46
alienation, 7–9, 124, 128, 137, 156, 159, 164, 178–80, 185, 189
alterity, 17, 142, 199
Altman, Rick, 202
amateurism, 186, 197–98

ambiguity, 76, 103, 168, 186, 269n103
American Communist Party, 134
American culture, vii, 9, 21, 34, 75, 78, 86, 91
American film. *See* Hollywood
Americanization, 36
American Jewish Committee, 13, 79, 85–86, 112, 115; Department of Scientific Research, 115, 120
American left, 36, 150, 158, 232n30
American popular culture, 150–51, 156
American war films, 161
Andrew, Dudley, 7, 209
angel of history (Benjamin), 195–96
animation, 26–28
anteroom, 186–87, 189
anthropocene, 15
anthroposophy, 128
anti-anticommunism, 150
anticommunism, 13, 91, 154
anti-Nazi films, 80–82, 85–86
Anti-Nazi League, 44, 46
antirealism, 7, 52, 102
antisemitism, 13, 35, 38, 52, 73–74, 86, 89, 95, 112, 116, 120, 125, 176, 223n23
anti-Stalinism, 150, 266n54
Aparajito (dir. Ray, 1956), 174
apparatus theory, 183
architecture: and film, 97–102, 246n14

303

Arendt, Hannah, 9, 12–13, 19–23, 35, 38–43, 58, 60–61, 77, 82–84, 88–89, 94–95, 107, 110, 112–13, 122, 125–31, 134, 138, 149, 164–65, 186, 188, 214, 216, 217, 226n36 249n13; *Denktagebuch*, 40; *Lectures on Kant's Political Philosophy*, 186; "the masses," 126; *The Origins of Totalitarianism*, 38, 84, 88, 126; "Social Science Techniques and the Study of Concentration Camps," 122; "Understanding and Politics," 94. *See also* totalitarianism
Aristarco, Guido, 208
Aristotle, 42
Army Morale films, 65, 78, 92
Arnheim, Rudolf, 15, 16, 42, 149, 216; *Film as Art*, 203, 206
art: "with a difference" (Kracauer), 189; autonomous, 153; commercial, 151; criticism, 154; high, 158–59; film as, 14, 146, 148, 157, 213; film, 18; *film d'art*, 143; and mass culture, 150; of photography, 171; popular, 156; production of, 8
atomization, 38, 113, 127, 128, 176
Auerbach, Erich, 10; *Mimesis*, 8–9, 169, 173; on realism, 173
Aufbau (newspaper), 38
Augustine, 138
Auschwitz, 71, 197
auteur theory, 15, 202
authoritarianism, 84, 97, 103, 110, 117, 136–38, 141, 145–47, 181
authoritarian personality, 22, 86, 112, 164, 208, 213
Authoritarian Personality, The, 13, 112–13, 116–17, 118*fig.*, 119, 121, 138, 254n21
autobiography, 8
Autorenfilm, 143
avant-garde, 36, 38, 122, 150–52, 159, 210

Balázs, Béla, 15–16, 149, 182, 184, 203
Baptism by Fire (dir. Bertram, 1940), 46, 54, 60, 64
Barry, Iris, 4, 47–48, 60, 132, 134, 224n23
Barthes, Roland, 172–73, 175
Bateson, Gregory, 109
Battleship Potemkin (dir. Eisenstein, 1925), 53
Baudelaire, Charles, 165
Baudry, Jean-Louis, 183
Bauhaus, 151
Bazin, André, 6–7, 15–17, 56, 148, 168, 216, 269n103; on *Paisan*, 160–62
BBC, 48
Belke, Ingrid, viii, 201, 223n16
Bell, Daniel, 36
Benjamin, Walter, 1, 3, 17, 23, 27, 28, 32, 40, 41, 42, 60–61, 159, 165–67, 182, 195–97, 209, 216; "The Artwork in the Age of Mechanical Reproducibility," 59, 61, 165, 168; *Illuminations*, 95; "The Storyteller," 147; "Theses on the Philosophy of History," 195–97
Bentley, Eric, 134
Berlin: Symphony of a Great City (dir. Ruttmann, 1927), 100, 137
The Best Years of our Lives (dir. Wyler, 1946), 91
Blücher, Heinrich, 41
Boomerang (dir. Kazan, 1947), 91
Boulevard der Stars, 216
boxing films, 33
Brecht, Bertolt, 120, 158, 167
Brecht, Christoph, 141–42
Brickner, Richard, 109
Buñuel, Luis, 203
Burckhardt, Jakob, 182, 186, 191–92, 197–98
Bureau of Applied Social Research, 48, 214, 280n43

Cabinet of Dr. Caligari, The (dir. Wiene, 1920), 29, 95, 97, 99, 100, 106, 113–15, 137, 142; politics of, 114
Cahiers du cinéma, 15, 148, 231n22
camera, 16, 32, 33, 53, 54, 55, 68, 70, 99, 140, 144, 177–79, 185, 188–89, 212; angles, 50; and the gaze, 198

camera reality, 27, 56–57, 177–78, 185, 188–89; and historical reality, 170, 188–89, 197
Cantril, Hadley, 48
Cavell, Stanley, 209
Chaplin, Charlie, 16, 154, 159, 181
Christian theology, 198
cinema: politics of, 15; and politics, 20–21; as medium of experience, 34, 149, 155, 159, 162, 163, 166–68, 183; as tool and product of alienation, 180; utopian potential of, 18, 23, 136. *See also* film
Cinema 16 (Film Society), 210, 280n39
Cinemages, 10, 211
Cinema Journal, 200–202, 212, 216
Cinema nuovo, 211
CinemaScope, 207
cinematology, 205–206. See also *filmologie*
cinematic communication, 52
cinephilia, 160, 184, 197–99; "inveterate moviegoer," 11, 21, 35, 155, 182. *See also* subjectivity
Citizen Kane (dir. Welles, 1941), 160
City College of New York, 36, 233n37
Clair, René, 31
class, 2, 17, 32, 36, 59, 60, 76, 88, 102, 104–5, 111, 115, 121, 126, 128–30, 139, 141, 142, 144, 172; consciousness, 126, 130
classical film theory, 15–16, 23, 43, 133, 148, 201–2, 209, 217; realist tradition of, 15–17
cognitivism, 182–83
Cohen, Elliot, 36, 41, 79
Cohen-Séat, Gilbert, 211, 272n53
Cold War, 13–14, 16–17, 21, 28, 57, 86, 90–91, 106, 134, 138, 150, 166, 198, 201; and liberal humanism, 23–24, 149, 169, 172–75, 187
Columbia Office of Radio Research, 47–48, 214
Columbia University, 12, 20, 47, 202, 210
Commentary (magazine), 10, 12, 21, 27, 30, 36–38, 41–42, 78, 79–80, 83–84, 87–88, 90, 105, 112, 126, 132, 134, 149, 150, 159, 164; "Jewish Culture in America," 41
communication: authoritarian and democratic, 21; government, 56; mass, 77, 171; totalitarian, 47–48, 75; studies, 13; visual, 120. *See also* wartime communications
communications research, 48–50, 76, 214
communism, 86, 134, 151, 152, 158, 159, 165
concentration camps, 69, 71, 72, 122, 181, 197
Confessions of a Nazi Spy (dir. Litvak, 1939), 80, 86
consciousness, 122, 133, 137–38, 161, 177, 180–81, 183, 196; historical, 196–97, 199
contact zones, 11, 19, 26–43
Cooper, Gary, 160
crisis, 30, 88, 89, 101, 105; of man, 2, 23, 29, 84, 170; of the individual, 84, 87, 89, 90, 92, 126, 164
critical theory, 17–18, 23, 43, 49, 84, 116, 147, 154, 165, 175, 200, 209
critique of mass culture, 30, 152, 171, 175
critique of modernity, 23, 107–8, 127–29, 129, 136
Crossfire (dir. Dmytryk, 1947), 120
cultural expression, 22, 85
culture, 11, 12, 14, 37, 38, 59, 61, 75, 76, 84, 87, 108, 130, 143, 155, 170, 172; elite, 202; high and low, 153, 217; middlebrow, 151–52, 156, 159, 168, 171; middle-class, 2; postmodern, 201; white collar, 29. *See also* mass culture
culture industry, 146, 154, 202

Danton (dir. Buchowetzky, 1920), 127
Danton (dir. Behrendt, 1931), 65
The Dark Corner (dir. Hathaway, 1946), 81–82, 104
Das indische Grabmal (dir. May, 1959), 100

data, 119, 134, 138, 167, 237n24
Dawes Plan, 102
Deception (Anna Boleyn, dir. Lubitsch, 1920), 127
Decherney, Peter, 24, 49–50, 52, 202, 214
Deming, Barbara, 28, 133
democracy, 12, 13, 22, 23, 29, 38, 48–50, 83, 83–88, 90–92, 102–4, 108, 121, 127 138, 175, 208; and totalitarianism, 74–77; and Weimar cinema, 139, 146
denazification, 109
Denby, David, 36
Deren, Maya, 210, 210*fig.*
Destiny (Der müde Tod, dir. Lang, 1921), 100, 122
detective films, 33, 107
Detour (dir. Ulmer, 1945), 104–105
Dewey, John, 88
dialectics, 30, 37, 110–12, 126–27, 136, 138, 140, 143, 146, 163, 166–68 175. See also Horkheimer and Adorno: *Dialectic of Enlightenment*
dictatorship, 24, 75, 85, 130, 141
Dietrich, Marlene, 216
digital age, 25, 219
Dimendberg, Edward, 82
disintegration, 42, 164
Disney, 19, 26–31, 82, 147, 229n2
Dissent (magazine), 12
documentary, 50, 53–54, 58, 100, 203
Donald Duck, 27
Double Indemnity (dir. Wilder, 1944), 104
Dragon in the Forest, The (novel), 93
dreams, 90, 122, 180, 262n52; dreaming, 183, 189; daydreams, 139, 141, 259n8
Dumbo, 19, 26–27, 29, 30, 31, 43
Duvivier, Julien, 31

Eagleton, Terry, 165
Eichmann trial, 42
Einsatzgruppen, 69, 71
Eisenstein, Sergei, 15–16, 53
Elsaesser, Thomas, 94, 105
enlightenment, 74, 107, 114, 181; dialectic of, 110; humanism, 12, 19, 180; project of, 137–38, 170. See also Horkheimer and Adorno: *Dialectic of Enlightenment*
episodic narrative construction, 27, 162
epistemology, 218; of exile, 8–9; of history, 194, 197
Epstein, Jean, 15
Erasmus, 181–82, 186–87, 191–92, 198, 261n40
estrangement, 137, 178, 185. See also alienation
Eurydice, 194, 196, 198
everyday life, 32, 54, 81, 155, 168, 172–73
evolutionary biology, 182–83
ewige Jude, Der (The Eternal Jew, dir. Hippler, 1940), 64, 73
Ewiger Wald (Eternal Forest, dir. Springer, 1936), 64
exile, 4, 6–11, 17, 19, 20–22, 30–36, 38, 40–41, 42, 59–60, 91, 93, 95, 96, 140, 153, 155, 164, 169, 181, 190, 192, 193, 201, 203, 216, 223n16, 225n29, 225n35, 226n36; epistemology of, 8–9; exile culture of midcentury New York, 10–11, 41; exilic subjectivity, 8, 192, 201; intellectual-as-exile, 6–10; Kracauer in French exile, 1, 3, 6–7, 11, 17, 20, 30–32, 35, 38, 41, 49, 58–60, 91, 95, 164, 169, 190
experience, 17, 21–23, 30, 34, 103, 126, 147, 148–50, 152, 155–160, 163–68, 170, 17, 181–87, 193; Arendt on, 149; dialectics of, 163; erasure of, 176; Greenberg on, 151; impossibility of, 20; loss of, 18, 23, 83, 86, 160, 164–65; Löwenthal on, 89; Rahv on, 158; and realism, 162; and reality, 163; reification of, 160; Warshow on, 150, 153–55, 157, 159–60
expressionism, 103, 122, 139; and democracy, 147; and film noir, 104, 108; and Hollywood, 104, 106, 108
extraterritoriality, 9, 36, 43, 140 199, 201

Family of Man, The, 24, 158, 169–80, 185, 186–87, 270n10, 273n72
Fanck, Arnold, 126
Fantasia, 26
Farber, Manny, 209
fascism, 9, 13–14, 58, 61, 75–77, 86–89, 92, 93, 103, 110–11, 116, 121, 159, 162, 164, 198, 253n5
Father Coughlin, 85, 87
Ferguson, Otis, 211
Feuertaufe (dir. Bertram, 1940), 46, 54, 60, 64
Feuilleton, 40, 155, 201, 251n41, 265n40
film: addict, 63, 155, 184–85, 197, 199; and history, 187–91, 197; as illiberal medium, 18–20, 22, 29, 49, 60, 78, 96–97, 149, 176; link to reality and experience, 163; and reality, 4, 8, 14, 16, 26–27, 33, 52–58, 102, 124, 128, 137, 139, 144, 146, 153, 159, 163, 168, 169–70, 173, 177, 180–81, 184, 188–89, 197, 215; as realist medium, 56, 57, 99, 146, 162, 169
Film Culture (journal), 10, 211–12
"film devices" (Kracauer), 50, 53
film 56 (journal), 212
Filmkritik (journal), 133, 212
Film Library (MoMA), 4, 6–7, 20–22, 24, 47–49, 97, 132, 133, 202, 209, 224n23, 235n7
film noir, 20–21, 90, 108; spatiality of, 81–83, 104–5, 212. *See also* "Hollywood's Terror Films"
filmologie, 149, 182, 205–6, 272n53, 279n23. *See also* cinematology
Films in Review (journal), 10, 30, 210–11
film studies, 4, 11, 15, 23–25, 48, 133, 200–203, 205–6, 109, 211, 213–14, 222n12, 235n12
film theory, 11–12, 14–19, 23–24, 30, 43, 50, 57, 137, 148–49, 154, 169, 170, 174–75, 177, 181–82, 184, 187, 188, 201, 207–8, 210, 215–17
Flaherty Seminar, 210
flashback, 105, 114, 254n27
Flowerman, Samuel, 115

"flow of life" (Kracauer), 54, 168, 177–78
Flüchtlinge (dir. Ucicky, 1933), 65–66
Ford, John, 16
form, 53, 141, 206; dialectical significance of, 37; importance for Frankfurt School, 232n35
formalism, 137, 156, 203, 212
Fox (film company), 63
fragmentation, 164. *See also* atomization
Frankfurt School, 2, 20, 22–24, 34–36, 43, 48, 49, 59, 60, 61, 77, 84, 88, 110, 112, 129, 146–48, 151–53, 170, 200–201, 217, 219, 253n5; in exile, 9–13, 19. *See also* Institute for Social Research
Frankfurter Zeitung, 2–3, 6, 26, 29, 32, 40, 124, 137, 212, 232n35
"Freedom from Fear: An Analysis of Popular Film Trends." *See* "Hollywood's Terror Films"
French film, 31–35, 231n22
Freud, Sigmund, 55, 94, 110, 243n26
Fridericus films, 112, 144
Fridericus Rex (dir. von Cserépy, 1922), 122
Friends of Democracy, 46
Friesennot (dir. Hagen, 1935), 65
From Caligari to Hitler: A Psychological History of German Film (Kracauer), 4, 6, 7, 10, 15, 21–22, 26, 29–31, 49–50, 60, 75–78, 82, 86, 92–94, 96–97, 98*fig.*, 99–101, 103–13, 115, 119–22, 125–27, 130, 132–34, 136–37, 139, 141–47, 149, 153, 157, 159, 162, 167, 176, 188, 190, 200, 205, 211–213
Fromm, Erich, 103, 110–12, 114–15, 129; *Escape from Freedom,* 110, 252n45, 253n6
F-scale, 116–17, 138, 164

Gabriel over the White House (dir. La Cava, 1933), 99
Gandesha, Samir, 42
gangster films, 33, 156, 160
Gary, Brett, 87, 89, 244n37

gaze, 57, 177–78, 185, 198, 262n52; historian's, 195–98; looking, 154, 196–97
Geist, 218
geistige Obdachlosigkeit, 106, 107, 166. See also shelterlessness
gender, 17, 116, 123
genocide, 176, 242. See also Holocaust
genre, 33, 81, 99, 122
Gentleman's Agreement (dir. Kazan, 1947), 91
George circle, 128
German American Bund, 46,
German-American Congress for Democracy, 46
German film, 48, 76, 82, 96, 102, 107, 121, 139, 208
German reeducation, 109
German problem, 130, 136
German question, 22, 95, 97, 138, 147, 213
German victimization, 44, 64, 69, 73. See also Nazi propaganda
Gessner, Robert, 203, 205–211, 213
ghettos, 69
Giovacchini, Saverio, 24
Glazer, Nathan, 36, 79–80
Goebbels, Joseph, 53, 65, 66, 68, 123, 242n21; "Mimicry," 73–74
Good Neighbor Policy, 27
Göring, Hermann, 71
Great Depression, 13, 85
Greenberg, Clement, 36–38, 79, 80, 88; "Avant-Garde and Kitsch," 151–52, 156, 158
Greif, Mark, 29–30, 84
Grieveson, Lee, 24, 202, 214
große Liebe, Die (dir. Hansen, 1942), 64
Guest, Haden, 38, 209, 211
Guggenheim Foundation, 140, 157, 160
Guterman, Norbert, 86–87, 90, 116

Hansen, Miriam, 6–8, 23, 27, 32, 107, 141, 163–64, 175, 177, 191, 200, 209, 230n21; Cinema and Experience, 136, 250n23
Harcourt, Peter, 6, 208

Harper's, 10, 30, 209
Harvard University, 202, 203, 213
Heimatlosigkeit, 9, 226n38. See also exile
Heimkehr (dir. Ucicky, 1941) 21, 63–72, 74, 240n6, 241n9, 242n14, 243n21
Hegel, G.W.F., 94, 198, 218
hermeneutics, 201, 214
Heydrich, Reinhard, 71
Higson, Andrew, 133
Himmler, Heinrich, 129
Hiroshima, 30, 82, 176
Hirsch, Marianne, 174, 176
"historian, the" (Kracauer), 8, 95–96, 140, 181–82, 188–89, 191–97
historicism, 136, 193, 197, 249n4, 274n18
history, 8, 17, 23–24, 94–96, 109, 124, 140, 164, 168, 186–199, 201; and aesthetics, 65; and politics, 198. See also History: The Last Things before the Last
History: The Last Things before the Last (Kracauer), 8, 23–24, 32, 33, 43, 141, 153, 168, 170, 182, 184–194, 196–97, 200
Hitchcock, Alfred, 21, 106
Hitler, Adolf, 18, 22, 41, 44, 46, 52, 67–69, 80, 82, 84, 93–94, 96, 109–11, 125–26, 129–30, 138, 141–42, 176
Hitler-Stalin pact, 66, 151
Hitler Youth Quex (dir. Steinhoff, 1933), 65
Hobbes, John, 88, 248n45
Hoffmann, E.T.A., 113
Hollywood, 7, 11, 12, 13, 18, 19, 23, 28–30, 32–35, 43, 48–49, 78, 80–83, 87, 91, 99, 104, 105–8, 120, 132, 146, 150–51, 161–62, 166, 174–76, 202; and democracy, 87, 92, 106, 138; and terror, 20–22, 57, 60, 79, 90, 104, 175
"Hollywood's Terror Films" (Kracauer), 13, 27, 78, 80, 82–83, 86, 91–92, 96–97, 105–6, 108, 164, 212
Holocaust, 12, 13, 21, 30, 64, 79, 87, 89, 94–96, 138, 165, 166, 172, 176, 193, 196

Hook, Sidney, 36, 88
Hörbiger, Attila, 65
Horkheimer, Max, 3, 28, 35, 42, 43, 60, 74, 86, 107, 110–11, 115–17, 120–21, 152, 154, 181
Horkheimer and Adorno, 28, 42, 74, 110, 152, 154, 181, 229n10, 234n47, 243n21, 256n57; *Dialectic of Enlightenment*, 28, 74, 86, 110–11, 121, 152, 154, 181
horror, 79, 81, 91, 106, 113–14
Howe, Irving, 36–37, 151
Huff, Theodore, 211
human and technology: relationship between, 29, 165
"the humane" (Kracauer), 17, 23–24, 168, 170, 182, 187, 192, 194, 261n40
humanism, 12, 18, 145, 160, 174–75, 181–82, 187, 199; ahistorical, 175; curious, 7, 18, 23, 168, 185; enlightenment, 19, 180; "familial," 173, 185; Kracauer and, 14, 17, 149, 175–76, 181, 187, 199; liberal, 23, 158; nonanthropocentric, 168, 185; photographic, 170; postwar, 172; "progressive," 173; universal, 23, 169, 173
humanist politics, 24, 186
humanities, 140; and film theory, 211–15
human subject, 23, 56, 85, 108, 169–70, 176–77
human subjectivity, 17, 29, 89, 170, 177, 180–81, 208

ideology, 60, 121, 148, 160; and class, 76; critique, 15, 17, 60, 134; dominant, 16; fascist, 60–61; Nazi, 65, 73; and personality, 86; totalitarian, 125, 164–65; and experience, 156; of *Family of Man*, 172, 175
immediacy, 153, 155–57, 165, 167
imperial Germany, 87, 111, 129
imperialism, 38, 88, 89, 95, 122; American cold war, 172
indexicality, 54–55, 82, 90, 91, 108, 127
individuation, 110, 112, 115

inside/outside distinction, 101
Institute for Social Research, 2–4, 20, 85–86, 120, 217; *Studies in Philosophy and Social Science* (journal), 120–21. See also Frankfurt School
Institut für Sozialforschung, 3, 10–12, 34, 42, 59, 61, 88, 110, 115, 170
instrumentalization, 17, 53, 77, 109, 174
International Federation of Film Archives (FIAF), 208
inversions, 64, 74
irrationality, 145, 180
Isenberg, Noah, 121
Italian fascism, 86
Italian Neorealism, 30, 34, 147, 159, 160, 162, 267n67, 269n103

Janowitz, Hans, 114, 255n28
Jaspers, Karl, 42, 234
Jay, Martin, 8, 265n40; *Songs of Experience*, 156
Jeffers, Thomas, 150
Jetztzeit, (Benjamin), 95
Jewish question, 71
John Reed Club, 158, 233n37
journalism, 3; film, 133; Kracauer's journalistic work, 3, 6, 27. See also *Feuilleton*
Joyce, James, 158
Joyless Street, The (dir. Pabst, 1925), 142
Jud Süß (dir. Harlan, 1941), 65, 73, 243n23

Kael, Pauline, 175, 207, 215
Kaes, Anton, 96–97, 116, 132, 247n2, 252n49, 254n27
Kafka, Franz, 137, 158, 251n41
Kaiserreich, 87, 111, 129
Kammerspielfilm, 100–101
Kant, Immanuel, 42, 201, 218
Kappelhoff, Hermann, 145, 262n52
katabasis, 196
Katznelson, Ira, 84, 89–90, 248n47
Kazan, Elia, 134
Kennan, George F., 151

Killers, The (dir. Siodmak, 1946), 104–5
Kinoreformbewegung, 111, 143
Kirchheimer, Otto, 13, 88, 253n5
kitsch, 38, 151–52. 156
Klee, Paul, 195
Koch, Gertrud, 94, 121, 250n23, 268n80, 276n46
Koselleck, Reinhart, 192
Kracauer, Lili, 1, 2, 38, 80, 210fig., 216
Kracauer, Siegfried: reception, 7, 20, 47, 157, 200–201, 205, 222n13; scholarship on, 6, 24, 250n23; "Bemerkungen zum französischen Film," 31; *Georg*, 3; *Ginster*, 7, 181, 190, 199; "Little Shopgirls Go to the Movies," 17, 154; "Mass and Propaganda," 59; "National Types as Hollywood Presents Them," 48, 212; "Notes on the Planned History of the German film," 145; *Ornament der Masse, Das*, 200; "street essays," 144; *Straßen in Berlin und Anderswo*, 3, 200; "Those Movies with a Message," 13, 92, 161; "Those Who Wait," 106, 107, 128, 141, 273n66; "Totalitarian Propaganda," 60, 65, 184; "Trois siècles d'art aux États-Unis," 4; See also *From Caligari to Hitler: A Psychological History of German Film*; "Hollywood's Terror Films"; *History: The Last Things before the Last*; *Theory of Film: The Redemption of Physical Reality*; Marseille Notebooks; "Mass Ornament, The"; "Propaganda and the Nazi War Film"; *Salaried Masses, The*; "Why France Liked Our Films"
Kracauerplatz, 216
Krazy Kat, 150, 167
Kris, Ernst, 12, 20, 47, 49, 213
Kristol, Irving, 36
Kuhle Wampe (dir. Dudow, 1931), 120
Kuhn, Fritz, 46, 85, 87

Labor Action, 36
Lacan, Jacques, 183
La Habanera (dir. Sierck, 1937), 72
Lang, Fritz, 21, 100–101, 106, 111, 113, 122–26, 145
language: of German propaganda, 47; Kracauer's English, 9–10, 41, 75, 145, 226n43; of *Theory of Film*, 175; universal, 171; vs. image, 121
Laocoön (Lessing), 173
Larrabee, Eric, 205
Lasswell, Harold, 47, 48, 84, 87
Last Laugh, The (dir. Murnau, 1924), 112, 144
laughter: and cinema, 28–29, 31; collective, 28; in *Dialectic of Enlightenment*, 229n10; Kracauer on, 230n12; therapeutic, 27
Lazarsfeld, Paul, 12, 47, 49, 77, 120
Leander, Zarah, 64, 72
Lebensphilosophie, 166
Lebensraum, 44, 66
Lebenswelt, 189, 191, 193, 194, 198
Leites, Nathan: *Movies: A Psychological Study*, 133
Lethen, Helmuth, 198
letzte Mann, Der (dir. Murnau, 1924), 112, 144
Levin, Thomas Y., 200–201, 260n21; *The Mass Ornament*, 3, 201
Lewis, Sinclair, 87; *It Can't Happen Here* (1935), 87
liberal humanism, 23, 158, 174; liberal humanist conception of culture, 149. See also humanism
liberalism, 12, 13, 18, 20, 22–23, 76, 87–88, 90–91, 103, 138, 150, 173; bleak, 23
Library of Congress, 47, 133, 259n9
Life aesthetics (Steichen), 159
Life of an American Fireman (dir. Porter, 1903), 206
Lost Weekend (dir. Wilder, 1945), 82
Löwenthal, Leo, 4, 13, 22, 35, 37, 84, 86–90, 116, 126, 152, 164, 188, 216; "Atomization of Man," 88, 126; "Crisis of the Individual," 126, 164, 248n53; *Prophets of Deceit*, 13, 86, 90, 116, 164
Loves of Pharaoh, The (dir. Lubitsch, 1922), 127

Lubitsch, Ernst, 114, 145; historical films, 101, 127
Lukács, Georg, 127, 166; *The Theory of the Novel*, 7

M (dir. Lang, 1931), 106, 122
Mabuse, 122–23, 139
Macdonald, Dwight, 36, 151–53, 227n50; on *Caligari and Hitler*, 134, 205; "Masscult and Midcult," 171–72; on mass culture, 156
Madame Dubarry (dir. Lubitsch, 1919), 127–28
Male Fantasies (Theweleit), 125
Mann, Thomas, 3
Marcuse, Herbert, 13, 22, 153, 216
Marseille Notebooks (Kracauer), 56, 59, 97, 146, 149, 182, 191
Marshall, John, 20, 47–48, 50, 74, 213, 223n23
Marx, Karl, 29, 167
Marxism, 14, 17, 29, 61, 110, 151
masochism, 111, 129
mass: as agent of atomization, as unrealized subject of democracy, and as motif to a critique of modernity, 127
mass communication, 49, 77, 171
mass culture, 14, 22–23, 30, 42, 130, 137, 148, 151–53, 159, 175, 182; and the New York Intellectuals, 152
masses, 60, 70, 87, 88, 121, 125–27, 130; "mass man," 113, 126, 129; "plebian" (Arendt), 129; salaried, 6, 7, 17, 60, 152, 190
mass ornament, 30, 52, 124–27, 136–38, 166; rationality of, 124
"Mass Ornament, The" (Kracauer), 6, 61, 124, 136–37, 140, 166, 169
material culture, 9, 15
Mayer, Carl, 145, 262n60
McCarey, Leo, 21, 154
McCarthy era, 16–17, 86; McCarthyism, 13–14
Mead, Margaret, 109, 120
media studies, 15, 25
mediation, 61, 99, 121, 140, 165, 167
medium-specificity, 16

Medusa, 196–97
Mekas, Jonas, 211
Menschen am Sonntag (dir. Siodmak, 1930), 144
Menzel, Gerhard, 65–66
Merton, Robert K., 120
Metropolis (dir. Lang, 1927), 101, 111, 113, 119, 121, 122–126, 130, 138; politics of, 123–25
Metz, Christian, 148, 183, 216
Mickey Mouse, 27, 230n12
middlebrow, 14, 150–52, 156, 158–59, 168, 170–72, 175
middle class, 2, 32, 60, 102, 105, 111, 115, 121, 128–29, 141, 144
Mildred Pierce (dir. Curtiz, 1945), 104
Miller, Arthur, 150
Mills, C. Wright, 106, 110
mimicry, 61
mise-en-scéne, 81–82, 100; expressionist, 103
modernism: Kracauer as theorist of, 201; literary, 14; in *Partisan Review*, 150–51, 158; political, 148
modernity, 7, 9, 129, 136–39, 147, 159, 163, 165–66; critiques of, 23, 107–8, 127–29, 129, 136
modern subject, 107, 168
montage, 52, 137; Soviet, 161
Moscow trials, 165, 266n54
mountain films, 126
movement, 30, 32, 100, 117, 142, 182, 251n26; and color, 27; and Hollywood, 33
Mülder-Bach, Inka, 191, 201
Münsterberg, Hugo, 203
Museum of Modern Art (MoMA), 3–4, 6, 12–13, 20–22, 24, 32, 47, 49, 60, 65, 109, 132–33, 145, 169, 171–76, 202–3, 209, 214. See also *Family of Man, The*; Film Library (MoMA)
music, 27, 44, 46, 52, 68, 69, 194
musicals, 100, 101
Mussolini, 85, 243n26, 247n28, 267n70
My Son John (dir. McCarey, 1952), 154
myth: and reason. *See* dialectic of enlightenment

Nachträglichkeit, 94
Naficy, Hamid, 9, 225n29
Namier, Lewis, 192
närrische Wette des Lord Aldini, Die (Lord Aldini's Foolish Bet, dir. Borgnetto, 1923), 137, 230n14
Nazi: elite, 129; ideology, 65; rule, 94; seizure of power, 41, 53; system, 77; indoctrination, 109
Nazi cinema, 18, 20–21, 44, 46, 52–58, 63–78. *See also* Nazi propaganda
Nazi Germany, 54, 57, 66, 71, 78, 139
Nazi newsreels, 36, 44, 46, 48, 62
Nazi party congress (1935), 58, 77. *See also* Nuremberg party rallies
Nazi propaganda, 18, 20–21, 44, 46, 47, 49, 40, 51*fig.*, 52–58, 60, 61, 74, 104, 132, 159, 166, 200
Nazism, 12, 14, 73, 83, 86, 90, 136
Nazi war film, 46, 50, 51*fig.*, 52–58, 60, 62, 75, 76
nation: and authoritarianism, 116–122; and cinema, 4, 22, 28, 32, 33, 48, 56, 63–64, 69, 74–76, 85, 93, 100–101, 104, 106, 130–33, 188, 212–13; decline of the nation-state, 88; German, 44; and intellectual culture, 38; and self, 61; the transnational, 43, 131, 203, 225n29
Nation (magazine), 6, 10, 26, 149
National Board of Review Magazine, 31
national cinema, 4, 32–33, 106, 130
Nielsen, Asta, 101, 216
neoliberalism, 18, 219
neophenomenology, 182
Neue Sachlichkeit, 102, 122, 260n26
Neumann, Franz, 13, 22, 60, 88, 110; *Behemoth*, 110, 253n5
New Criticism, 207, 212
New Deal, 13, 83–84, 89–90
New Leader, 36, 134, 136
New Left, 15
New Objectivity, 102, 122, 260n26
New Republic, 10, 36, 132
New School, 12, 20–21, 47, 75, 213
New Wave, 16
New Yorker, 42, 150, 156

New York Intellectuals, 11–12, 14, 19–20, 22–25, 35–38, 42–43, 84, 87, 148, 150–53, 156–58, 165, 171, 217, 219
New York Times, 57, 93, 98*fig.*, 134, 174, 216
New York University, 202
Nibelungen (dir. Lang, 1922), 111
non-anthropocentricism, 139, 168, 170, 176–77, 181–82, 185, 217
noncinematic film, 32
nonhuman, 176, 180
Noxon, Gerald, 215
nuclear war, 21, 90, 166, 171 173; threat of, 13–14, 181
nuclear family, 173
Nuremberg party rallies, 75, 77, 126

object world, 145, 177, 184–85, 191, 193
Oedipal complex, 15, 129
Offenbach, Jacques, 3, 7, 75, 181, 190, 201
Office of Strategic Services (OSS), 214, 237n28, 243n28, 253n5
Ohm Krüger (dir. Steinhoff, 1941), 72
ornament, 14, 100, 111, 123–27, 141, 188. *See also* mass ornament
Obdachlosigkeit. *See* shelterlessness
Orpheus, 182, 194, 196, 198
Orwell, George, 80, 158
Other, 199. *See also* alterity
Out of the Past (dir. Tourneur, 1947), 105
Oxford University Press, 4, 188

Pabst, G.W., 144–45, 211
Paisan (dir. Rossellini, 1946): Bazin on, 160, 267n67; Kracauer on, 154, 159–62; Warshow on, 160–62
Panofsky, Erwin, 50, 96, 99, 119, 132–33, 143, 203, 205, 206, 216; "Style and Medium in Motion Pictures," 143
paralysis, 13, 32, 57, 83, 84, 102, 108, 142, 146, 151, 164
Partisan Review, 10, 12, 14, 28, 36, 37, 38, 41, 80, 84, 94, 110, 112, 113, 134, 135*fig.*, 149–52, 157–59, 171, 187, 227n50

Patalas, Enno, 212
Pearl Harbor, 85, 227n50, 246n20
Peck, Gregory, 160
perception, 137, 145, 148, 168; alienated, 168; and consciousness, 177
Perseus, 182, 194, 196–97
phenomenology, 30, 33, 42, 139, 140, 144, 145, 146, 147, 153, 154 165, 168 167, 170, 191, 203
Phillips, William, 36, 157–58, 227n50, 266n54
photography, 22, 27, 30, 136–37, 141, 169, 171, 174, 176–77, 180–81, 188–90, 192, 215, 270n10. See also *Family of Man, The*
physical reality, 8, 14, 30, 139, 144, 146, 155, 162, 163, 167–69, 177, 181, 184, 189, 191, 198. See also *Theory of Film: The Redemption of Physical Reality*
physiology, 182–83
Plane Crazy (1928), 27
plot, 100, 101, 127, 198; of *The Cabinet of Dr. Caligari*, 113–15; of *Metropolis*, 122–23
Poland, 64, 66–72. See also *Heimkehr*
Polan, Dana, 15, 24, 105, 202, 214
political theory, 49, 134
politics, 11, 14, 16, 34, 41, 74, 78, 103, 107, 150–51, 161, 187, 219; and experience, 147, 158; and aesthetics, 17, 50, 142, 145, 148; antitotalitarian, 151; democratic, 90–91; and film, 12, 15, 20–21, 49, 55, 97, 128–30, 136–37, 142, 145–46, 162; of film theory, 14, 17, 169, 175; of Kracauer's approach to film, 75–77, 97, 128–30, 136–37, 145–46, 148–49, 169, 175, 191, 198, 217; and media, 43; and textuality, 65
Politics (magazine), 36
popular culture, 23, 150, 153, 154, 156, 160, 165
Porter, Edwin S., 206
posthumanism, 14, 18, 170, 180, 219
poststructuralism, 156
Potamkin, Harry Allan, 134

Princeton University Press, 109
propaganda, 3, 12, 18, 20–22, 44, 47–66, 68–72, 7478, 83, 90, 97, 103–4, 109–110, 116, 123, 126, 130, 132, 134, 162, 164–66, 200, 205, 208. 213–14, 237n24, 237n26
"Propaganda and the Nazi War Film" (Kracauer), 46, 50, 52, 54, 56, 60, 75–76
Proust, Marcel, 8, 178, 192, 215
psychoanalysis, 15, 57, 91, 110–11, 113, 115, 134
public opinion, 48–49, 85, 213–14
Public Opinion Quarterly, 48, 119, 133, 213
Public Opinion Research Project at Princeton, 48

Quaresima, Leonardo, 96–97, 123, 136, 252n59, 256n57

race, 86, 172
Rahv, Philip, 36, 157–58, 266n54, 267n60; "The Cult of Experience in American Writing," 158
Rancière, Jacques, 145, 262n63, 263n64
ratio, 136–37
rationality, 107, 124, 127, 136–37
rationalization, 136, 139, 166
realism, 7, 17, 18, 21, 23, 26–27, 28, 30, 32–34, 50, 52–59, 99, 102–4, 123–24, 128, 139, 144–47, 158–60, 162, 167–68, 170, 173, 177–78, 180, 191, 196–98, 225n35; cinematic, 23, 30, 56, 103, 139, 144, 147, 168, 177–78, 180, 191
reality, 4, 16–17, 26, 27, 29, 33–35, 92, 94, 99, 100, 101, 102, 124, 128, 137, 139, 141, 144–46, 153, 156, 159, 161–63, 165, 167–68, 169–70, 173, 180, 184, 187–91, 194, 215; and propaganda, 52–58, 61, 71, 72, 73, 75, 77, 104, 146. See also camera reality; physical reality
reason, 27, 52, 106 111, 114, 136–37, 163, 169, 180–81; and myth, 77, 110, 138; and terror, 78

redemption, 18, 30, 139, 146, 155, 160, 168, 189, 214. See also *Theory of Film: The Redemption of Physical Reality*
Reformation, 186–87
reification, 155, 160, 168, 198, 243n23
Renoir, Jean, 31
Rensmann, Lars, 42
Rentschler, Eric, 16–17, 73, 175
reporter films, 33
representation, 16, 66, 71, 84, 156, 189, 191, 274n13; democratic, 22, 84–85, 92, 97, 138; in Nazi propaganda, 52, 58; of politics, 18; politics of, 96, 142; and subjectivity, 18; and totalitarianism, 18, 103, 126
Richter, Hans, 203
Riefenstahl, Leni, 58–61, 64, 75, 126
RKO, 120
Rockefeller Foundation, 13, 20, 21, 47–48, 213; "Communications Group," 20, 47, 49, 214, 217; International Program, 171
Rodowick, David, 208–9
Romains, Jules, 99–100; "The Crowd at the Cinematograph," 99
Roosevelt, Franklin D., 13, 21, 85, 89; "Four Freedoms" speech, 83, 245n8, 246n20
Rosenberg, Harold, 80
Rosenbergs, 150, 156, 158
Rosenzweig, Franz, 80, 245n5
Ross, Andrew, 150
Rossellini, Roberto, 154, 160–62
Roth, Joseph, 3
Rotha, Paul, 4, 102, 174, 210
Russell, Bertrand, 171

Said, Edward, 43
salaried masses, 7, 60, 152, 154, 190
Salaried Masses, The (Die Angestellten, Kracauer), 6, 17, 60, 190
Sandburg, Carl, 178
S. A. Mann Brand (dir. Seitz, 1933), 65
Sarah Lawrence College, 149
Sarris, Andrew, 211

Schapiro, Meyer, 20; criticism of "Propaganda and the Nazi War Film," 75–78, 90–91, 103–4
Schary, Dore, 120
Schüfftan, Eugen, 10
scopophilic desire, 197
Screen, 148, 202
screen as shield, 196–97
screen theory, 7, 183
Sebald, W.G., 181, 196
Seghers, Anna, 3
semiotics, 7
Shadow of a Doubt (dir. Hitchcock, 1943), 81, 106
shelterlessness, 7–8, 89, 102
Sicherheitsdienst, 61, 242n21
Sieg im Westen (dir. Noldan, 1941), 44, 45*fig.*, 46, 54, 60, 235n7
Siepmann, Charles, 48
Sight and Sound, 215
Simmel, Georg, 4, 127, 166, 261n39
Siodmak, Robert, 3, 105–6, 144
Skeleton Dance, The (1929), 27
slapstick, 27, 30, 33, 145
Smith, Datus, 109
socialism, 37, 88, 260n17; Stalinist, 86
socialist culture, 150
socialist realism, 158
socialists, 11, 36
Social Research (journal), 75
Society of Cinematologists, 24–25, 200, 202–3, 204*fig.*, 205, 208. See also cinematology
solidarity, 42, 144, 198, 199
Sontag, Susan, 58, 259n58, 165; on interpretation, 156–57
soul, 99, 71, 101–2, 115, 180, 245n8; "at work," 117, 123; collective, 125; French, 32; middle-class German, 102, 105, 141; national, 93, 106
Soviet film, 52, 53, 151, 153, 161
Soviet Union, 66, 68, 72, 151, 159, 203
space: and film noir, 81–82; and Weimar cinema, 93, 97, 99–105, 108
spectacle, 75, 77, 186, 199, 280n39
spectator, 53–57, 63, 70, 71, 99, 104, 155, 159, 162, 166–68, 170, 182–85, 186–88, 192–93, 196–97, 273n67

spectatorship, 23, 24, 30, 155, 166, 181–83, 185, 186, 192–93, 196–97
Speier, Hans, 12, 20, 47, 49, 75, 213, 236n20
Spengler, Oswald, 93
Spiegelschrift, 64, 74
Spies (dir. Lang, 1928), 122
spiritual shelter, 106–7, 128
Stalinism, 14, 16, 87, 90, 150–51, 159
State Department, 35, 235n8
Steichen, Edward, 24, 158–59, 169–72, 174–79, 181, 185, 187. See also *Family of Man, The*
Stella Dallas (dir. Vidor, 1937), 33
Stern, Günther, 41
Stern, Seymour, 134, 136
Sterne, Laurence, 192
Straße, Die (dir. Grune, 1923), 100, 128, 144, 254n18
street films, 111
structuralism, 15, 148
"Studies in Prejudice," 13, 35, 61, 86, 115–16, 119, 121, 214. See also *Authoritarian Personality, The*
studio constructivism, 100–103, 162
Sturges, Preston, 21, 29, 174, 210, 230n12
submission, 103, 107, 110–12, 122, 129, 137, 144, 254n18
subject, 20, 22–24, 28, 52, 54, 56–58, 61–62, 65, 72, 85, 90, 101, 103, 107–8, 110–11, 119, 121, 127, 129, 148, 156–59, 164–70, 176–78, 181–85, 187–88, 192–93, 196, 199
subjective experience, 154, 158, 165
subjectivity, 18, 20–21, 24, 34, 56–58, 60–62, 78, 84, 90, 107, 158, 165, 176, 181–82, 184, 185, 192, 193, 196, 197, 198, 214; and politics, 18, 20–21, 24, 78, 84, 90, 107, 129, 158, 191, 198, 217; antitotalitarian, 14; autonomous subjectivity, 129; cinephilic, 170, 181–82, 185, 192, 197–99; critical, 7; democratic, 85, 129; exilic, 8, 192, 201; extraterritorial, 201; and film spectatorship, 24, 56–57, 170, 181–82, 184–85, 191, 197; and history, 17, 170, 180–81, 191–93, 196–98; humanist, 182, 186, 191, 217; political, 18, 87, 108; posttotalitarian/post-Holocaust, 193; weak, 185, 273n72
Suhrkamp Verlag, 200–201
surfaces, 144, 201, 262n52
"surface-level expressions" (Kracauer), 61, 140
symptomatic criticism, 28, 52, 55, 81, 91, 108, 122, 131, 139

technology, 15, 87, 123
temporality, 56, 83, 94, 194–95
Teres, Harvey, 158, 264n11
terror, 18, 23, 60–62, 64–65, 69, 72, 76, 78, 80–85, 87–91, 94, 106, 109, 112, 125, 130, 158, 162, 164, 176, 196, 198
"terror films," 20–22, 57, 60, 78, 79, 80–83, 90–91, 97, 104, 106, 175. See also "Hollywood's Terror Films"
test film, 35, 120–21, 256n46
Theorietransfer, 43
Theory of Film: The Redemption of Physical Reality, 4, 6–8, 15, 17–19, 21, 23–24, 26–27, 30–32, 34, 43, 48, 50, 55, 58, 79, 91, 99, 103, 139, 144–47, 148–49, 153, 155, 157, 159–168, 169–71, 175–77, 180–82, 186–89, 191–92, 196–97, 205, 207–212, 215–16, 268n80, 271n28 279n26. See also realism
Third Reich. See Nazi Germany
Three Caballeros, 27–29, 82–83
Thucydides, 192
Time (magazine), 134
Tin Pan Alley, 151
Toeplitz, Jerzy, 208
totalitarian communication, 47; "Totalitarian Communications Research Project," 235n8
totalitarian: dispositions, 127; politics, 78; propaganda, 41, 46, 49–50, 52, 54–55, 57–59, 61–62, 64–65, 68–72, 74, 77, 97, 164, 240n67; representations, 103; rule, 62, 103, 109, 122, 165; subjectivity, 61–62; terror, 87–89, 176

totalitarianism, 13, 18, 20, 22, 29, 48, 50, 86, 136, 164, 170, 181, 208, 213; and cinema, 82, 97, 122, 131, 134, 138.; and democracy, 75–77, 90–91, 104, 108; the Frankfurt School on, 59–60, 77; Arendt on, 23, 38, 77, 84, 89, 94–95, 112–113, 125–26, 130, 138, 165, 257n71; and Hollywood, 91, 106, 162; leftist critique of, 158; loss of experience under, 160; and mass man, 129; origins of, 13, 22, 89, 94, 112, 138, 164, 213; and popular culture, 37; and Weimar cinema, 122, 125–26, 130–31, 134. *See also* Arendt, Hannah: *The Origins of Totalitarianism*
totality, 53, 58
transparence, 157
Traverso, Enzo, 9, 232n30
Trilling, Lionel, 14, 23, 36, 37
Triumph of the Will (dir. Riefenstahl, 1935), 58–59, 61, 126, 239n58
Truman, Harry, 29, 132

Überfall (dir. Metzner, 1929), 144
Ucicky, Gustav, 63, 65–66
United Nations, 78, 133
United States Information Agency, 171
United States Office of War Information, 22
Unseld, Siegfried, 200
Ufa, 29, 101, 143
UNESCO, 48, 171, 174, 213
universalism, 150; of *Family of Man*, 171–72, 174

Valéry, Paul, 88
Vanina, (dir. Gerlach, 1922), 101
Venice film festival, 66
verlorene Sohn, Der, (dir. Trenker, 1934), 66
Vernunft, 136–37. *See also* enlightenment
Victory in the West (dir. Noldan, 1941), 44, 45*fig.*, 46, 54, 60, 235n7
Vigo, Jean, 31
Vogel, Amos, 210, 280n39

Volk, 65
Volksempfänger, 66–67
Volksgemeinschaft, 63, 65
von Harbou, Thea, 122–23
von Ranke, Leopold, 189, 193
voice-over commentary, 44, 52, 62

"Wacht am Rhein" (song), 46
wandering Jew, 194–96, 256n46
Warburg School, 119
Warner Brothers, 80
wartime communication, 13, 46, 52, 110, 213
wartime newsreels, 20, 46, 48, 53, 58, 62
Warshow, Robert, 23, 36, 38, 79, 80, 136, 148, 149–50, 152–62, 165–66, 168, 211; *The Immediate Experience*, 150, 153
Washington, D.C., 13, 47, 74, 77, 85
Wasson, Haidee, 24, 202
Weber, Max, 127; Weberian Marxism, 110; Weberian skepticism, 128
Wehrmacht, 44, 46, 68, 70
Weimar cinema, 13, 21–23, 26, 29, 32, 38, 47, 49, 82–83, 93, 96–97, 99, 101–3, 107–8, 112–13, 116, 119, 120, 122, 124, 130, 132, 134, 136, 139, 144, 146–47, 149, 162, 167, 201, 212; and democracy, 18, 103, 139, 146; history of, 77, 97, 143; and Hollywood, 22, 29, 82, 87, 104–6
Weimar Germany, 2–3, 7, 9, 13, 17, 18, 30, 33, 40, 59, 92, 93–94, 96, 99, 102–5, 107–8, 115–16, 120, 123–24, 128, 137, 140, 143–44, 153–54, 167, 175, 181, 184, 190, 192, 197, 200, 203, 212; and democracy, 18, 103, 105–6, 146; failure of, 26, 60, 105, 110, 146
Wessely, Paula, 65, 67
western, 33, 99, 100, 152, 160
white collar, 29, 232n35; See also *Salaried Masses, The*
White, E. B., 83
White, Hayden, 192
Whitehead, Alfred North, 167, 248n44
"Why France Liked Our Films" (Kracauer), 11, 19, 26, 31–34, 99, 104, 163, 174, 231n22

Why We Fight (dir. Capra, 1942–1945), 92. *See also* Army Morale films
Wiene, Robert, 95–96, 106, 113, 114–115
Wilder, Billy, 104, 106, 216
Williams, Raymond, 165
Witte, Karsten, 200
Wolfenstein, Martha: *Movies: A Psychological Study*, 133
Wolhyniendeutsche, 66, 68
World War I, 44, 85, 109, 115 129, 252n45

World War II, 13, 49, 57, 64, 68, 85, 86, 95, 162, 165, 181, 196, 208, 246n20, 266n54
World without End (dir. Rotha and Wright, 1953), 174, 186

Yorkville theater, 44, 46–47, 58, 62
young Turks, 148
youth films, 111

Zeitschrift für Sozialforschung, 3, 20, 35, 59, 76, 239n59